Spirits of Community

Spirits of Community

English Senses of Belonging and Loss, 1750–2000

K. D. M. Snell

Bloomsbury Academic
An imprint of Bloomsbury Publishing Plc

B L O O M S B U R Y
LONDON • OXFORD • NEW YORK • NEW DELHI • SYDNEY

Bloomsbury Academic
An imprint of Bloomsbury Publishing Plc

50 Bedford Square
London
WC1B 3DP
UK

1385 Broadway
New York
NY 10018
USA

www.bloomsbury.com

BLOOMSBURY and the Diana logo are trademarks of Bloomsbury Publishing Plc

First published 2016
Paperback edition first published 2017

British Library Cataloguing-in-Publication Data
A catalogue record for this book is available from the British Library.

ISBN: HB: 978-1-4742-6884-4
PB: 978-1-3500-5616-9
ePDF: 978-1-4742-6886-8
ePub: 978-1-4742-6885-1

Library of Congress Cataloging-in-Publication Data
Names: Snell, K. D. M.
Title: Spirits of community : English senses of belonging and loss, 1750-2000 / K.D.M. Snell.
Description: London : Bloomsbury Academic, an imprint of Bloomsbury Publishing Plc, 2016. | Includes bibliographical references and index.
Identifiers: LCCN 2015047333 (print) | LCCN 2015049090 (ebook) | ISBN 9781474268844 (hardback : alkaline paper) | ISBN 9781474268868 (ePDF) | ISBN 9781474268851 (ePub)
Subjects: LCSH: Community life–England–History. | Community life–England–History–Sources. | Belonging (Social psychology)–England–History. | Loss (Psychology)–Social aspects–England–History. | Social change–England–History. | England–Social conditions. | Community life in literature. | Community life–In art. | English literature–History and criticism. | Art, English–History. | BISAC: HISTORY / General. | HISTORY / Europe / Great Britain. | HISTORY / Social History.
Classification: LCC HN398.E5 S595 2016 (print) | LCC HN398.E5 (ebook) | DDC 306.0942–dc23
LC record available at http://lccn.loc.gov/2015047333

Cover design: Sharon Mah
Cover image: *The Lovers (The Dustmen)*, 1934 (oil on canvas), Spencer, Stanley (1891-1959) / Laing Art Gallery, Newcastle-upon-Tyne, UK / © Tyne & Wear Archives & Museums / Bridgeman Images

Typeset by Integra Software Services Pvt. Ltd.

To Rachael

Most history seems to carry on its back vestiges of paradise.

George Steiner, *In Bluebeard's Castle: Some Notes towards the Re-definition of Culture* (1971)

As for community … with the monasteries expired the only type that we ever had in England of such an intercourse. There is no community in England; there is an aggregation, but aggregation under circumstances which make it rather a dissociating, than a uniting, principle … It is a community of purpose that constitutes society … without that, men may be drawn into contiguity, but they remain virtually isolated … It is their condition everywhere; but in cities that condition is aggravated. A density of population implies a severer struggle for existence, and a consequent repulsion of elements brought into too close contact. In great cities men are brought together by the desire of gain. They are not in a state of co-operation, but of isolation, as to the making of fortunes; and for all the rest they are careless of neighbours. Christianity teaches us to love our neighbour as ourself; modern society acknowledges no neighbour.

Benjamin Disraeli, *Sybil, or the Two Nations* (1845)

In spite of the fact that cottagers are all on the same social level, intimacies do not thrive amongst them. If there was formerly any parochial sentiment in the village, any sense of community of interest, it has all been broken up by the exigencies of competitive wage-earning, and each family stands by itself, aloof from all the others. The interests clash … just as in trade, every man for himself is the rule with the villagers … the misfortune of one is the opportunity of another … the weakest must go to the wall. Each man is an individualist fighting for his own hand … It follows that the villagers are a prey to jealousy and suspicion … All their circumstances constrain the people to be selfish, secret about their hopes, swift to be first in the field where a chance occurs.

George Sturt, *Change in the Village* (1912)

When the world becomes too large to be controlled, social actors aim to shrink it back to their size and reach. When networks dissolve time and space, people anchor themselves in places, and recall their historic memory.

Manuel Castells, *The Information Age: Economy, Society and Culture. Vol. 2: The Power of Identity* (1997)

What is being forgotten in modernity is profound, the human-scale-ness of life, the experience of living and working in a world of social relationships that are known. There is some kind of deep transformation in what might be described as the meaning of life based on shared memories, and that meaning is eroded by a structural transformation in the life-spaces of modernity.

Paul Connerton, *How Modernity Forgets* (2009)

Contents

List of Figures

Acknowledgements

I received help from many people while writing this book, and some of them are no longer with us. I would like to thank the following for valuable advice and assistance: Derek Aldcroft, Rod Ambler, Ian Bailey, Stuart Ball, John Barrell, Anthea Bell, Martin Bell, Liz Bellamy, Ronald Blythe, Jeremy Burchardt, Jon-Paul Carr, Robert Colls, Janet Couloute, Ian Dyck, Ann Gander, Simon Gunn, Carl Hallam, Clare Hallam, Dominic Head, Andrew Hinde, Steve Hindle, David Hitchcock, Eric Hobsbawm, Elizabeth Hurren, Anna Huppert, Colin Hyde, Rachael Jones, Yukio Kaneko, Prashant Kidambi, Steve King, Jon Lawrence, Alison Light, Peter Mandler, John Martin, David Matless, Richard Moore-Colyer, Ray Pahl, Mark Rawlinson, Barry Reay, Michael Rosenthal, Ted Royle, Raphael Samuel, Samantha Shave, Brian Short, Christopher Storm-Clark, Roey Sweet, Keith Turner, Tom Williamson and Tony Wrigley. I am especially grateful to past and present colleagues at the Centre for English Local History, University of Leicester – Christopher Dyer, Alan Everitt, Harold Fox, Andrew Hopper, Richard Jones, Peter King, Charles Phythian-Adams and Kevin Schürer – and to the many students I have taught there, whose contributions to this and my earlier books have been so much appreciated. I thank the editors and publishers of the *Economic History Review*, *Family and Community History* and *Social History* for advice on earlier versions of Chapters 2, 4 and 6, respectively, and permission to publish updated research. I would like to acknowledge also with gratitude the assistance and permissions of the Fitzwilliam Gallery (Cambridge), Nicholas Penny (Director of the National Gallery, London), Lowell Libson and staff at Lowell Libson Ltd (London), the National Gallery of Canada, the Huntington Gallery (San Marino, California), the Laing Art Gallery in Newcastle upon Tyne, the British Sporting Art Trust and the National Gallery of Ireland. I am especially grateful to the very supportive editors and staff of Bloomsbury Academic – notably Ian Buck, Emily Drewe, Emma Goode and Dan Herron and my project manager Rajakumari Ganessin. It has been a pleasure working with them.

1

Introduction

'The decline of community' is a conversational staple of modernity. It is a phrase one hears regularly, in public debates, academic discussions or political arguments. It is a term that is international, for one finds it in America, Canada or Australia, in Ireland, or translated in Japan, China, Poland, Russia, Tanzania and elsewhere. Like the much debated term 'community' itself, the idea of declining community spirit is also encountered on a daily basis. Whether it is argued over as a real change of our times, or taken for granted as something that has occurred, it is often thought to underlie many modern ills. It bears upon issues of the quality of life, neighbourliness and mutual support, problems affecting the education and socialization of the young, crime and safety on the streets, welfare programmes and reforms, the responsibilities of kin and family in modern society, provision for the elderly and so much more. A huge cross-disciplinary and international literature on loneliness and modernity makes persistent references to it. Loneliness is now widely diagnosed as a modern 'epidemic' or 'plague', hugely covered in the media, seen as a salient problem of our times, strongly linked to ill health, suicide and community deficits.[1] Attitudes towards community, individualism and personal isolation characterize separate political parties and the contested role of the State, in Britain, America and elsewhere. Such ideologies are associated with national identities and related nostalgias and to a large literature exploring them.[2]

At the root of such discussion are certain historical questions: did 'community' exist hitherto; what forms did it take; has it declined in modern times; do community loss and related loneliness define modernity; what have been the personal and health consequences of any such decline; and what action needs to be taken? How do past lessons and senses of community, or its historical loss, bear upon our modern problems and debates? How have differing authors and artists in the past seen this problem, and how have they responded to the issues that it raises? These are the themes of this book. Each chapter explores ways in which representative writers or artists have depicted, responded to or overcome senses of declining community spirit. This book is my personal migration through English cultural history, with case studies since 1750, in search of historical perspective, reassurance or analogy to these modern concerns and issues.

I considered as my title the question: 'Decline of Community?' But even with an important question mark after it (which would have been lost in some references), that seemed too empirical, sociologically contentious, all-embracing, at some levels too subjective and probably too difficult to resolve. It raises huge expectations which no historian can fulfil, conclude or generalize from. And many other books, different and more sociological in nature, have equivalent titles, such as Maurice Stein's *The Eclipse of Community* or Andrew Leigh's *Disconnected: The Decline of Community and the Fraying of Social Fabric in Modern Australia*, often in the tradition epitomized by Robert Putnam's redoubtable book *Bowling Alone: The Collapse and Revival of American Community*. This represents an empirical sociological approach for which I have huge respect, often addressed here, but it is different from my own.[3]

Every chapter of this book is concerned with the meaning, change or loss of communal spirit or identity, in different periods, ways and via different sources, images or voices. These chapter subjects have been chosen for their variety, their political eclecticism, their differing appraisals of community hitherto and their interdisciplinary potential. They try to show how community was experienced by ordinary people, like the poor letter writers of Chapter 2, as well as how it was represented by highly literate participant observers, like Thomas Hardy, Adrian Bell or H. E. Bates. For this is a subject best approached with tolerance and an appreciation of wide-ranging viewpoints and differing class perspectives – from the populist sympathies of George Morland to the high Toryism of James Wentworth Day. The chapters are arranged in rough chronological order. The book moves through the terms and styles of different but relevant disciplines: mainly history, sociology, literary studies and art history. The result might jostle sensibilities which would prefer stricter historical and sequential subject matter. But such an outcome, like a musical piece varying its key, beat and volume, is inevitable in such interdisciplinary work and with intentional choice of diverse viewpoints to throw multicoloured light upon its themes.

My title *Spirits of Community* has four meanings, all of them encompassed in these chapters. First, all the authors or artists analysed here depicted community or its decline; they were themselves spirits of community, speaking for or about it, giving their own positive or negative perceptions of community. They had an intuitive feeling for something that was slipping away from them and which represented a loss of selfhood in some intangible but vital sense or spirit. Secondly, they tried to put their finger on what 'community' means or had meant: like Thomas Hardy, or Adrian Bell, or James Wentworth Day, or Anglican parish magazine editors, they spelt out what 'the spirit of community' comprised for themselves, as interrelationships, structured feeling and a sense of belonging. Thirdly, they usually described community as something partially or wholly lost, like G. K. Chesterton or Agatha Christie sensing spirits, ghosts or echoes of it, things that had gone, whether this was described nostalgically, wistfully, imaginatively (in ways that we might often question), or, as in the case of H. E. Bates with which I end this book, with a sense of qualified relief. And fourthly, those absent from community, or from 'their' community – and there are many such in these pages, such as the poor letter writers of Chapter 1, or George Morland's migrants in Chapter 3, or Hardy's Jude 'the obscure' in Chapter 5 – were *in absentia* spirits of it: essences, reminders, missing pieces, apparitions and footloose modernist elements astray from where they had belonged. All these meanings and types of historical coverage are encompassed in the title. For this book is not intended as empirical sociology, nor as historical sociology assessing past forms of human association, but rather as a cultural exodus into representations of community spirit, senses of belonging,[4] and personal feelings of loss, which have a long history before our own times.

The term 'community' itself has been subject to varying definitions.[5] It is used in sundry ways by historians and sociologists. Indeed, it has spawned a whole genre of sociological work, the 'community studies' which some believe reached their academic peak in the 1950s and 1960s, but which continued in many subsequent forms, notably in Europe, Australia and America, with increasing stress upon issues of belonging, identity and ethnicity.[6] Indeed, there seems to have been a remarkable resurgence in new and different theoretical forms of that genre from the 1980s, in some cases documenting continuity of place-based communities.[7] The great diversity and overlapping nature of modern 'communities' or networks is often stressed in current literature.[8] There are indeed many kinds of community, even assuming that one wishes to use that word. It seems to me that the word is inescapable, given that it is one of the most prominent concepts of our time. It will not go away, nor will its debates recede. They bear crucially upon too many modern issues and social problems. Even those who proscribe its use still retain it, relish arguing about it, and do not provide alternative or adequate concepts to substitute for it. In other words, this is a huge area of debate, both present-centred and historical. How can a cultural historian make a valuable contribution to it?

Accounts of the decline of 'community' today, or in recent times, are readily found, and they often communicate bitterness and senses of loss, despite earlier hardships. Here is an example, from Ronald Blythe's fine book *The View in Winter*, addressing a south Welsh mining environment, which some writers have taken to be quintessentially representative of strong or 'thick' community. This was an area, as Ronald Blythe comments, in which individuals were 'welded by hardship, rage and hope into a special society'. Even the metaphors of the following passage relate to the world of coal:

> An old miner told the writer Trevor Fishlock, 'The community spirit then was something that glowed and kept you warm like a fire. All that has gone now, of course. We used to know pretty well every person in Maerdy and now we know hardly anybody. The old community spirit has disappeared and, if you ask me, Maerdy has gone to the dogs'.[9]

As another Welsh valley dweller, the widow of an underground repairer, commented to Blythe:

> It's terrible today isn't it? Money, money, money, all the time ... I can remember the big strike. It went dark. Soup kitchens, you know, strike after strike. And they were the best days in spite of everything. People were much more sociable and kind ... You could hear laughter in the streets and on the hills as they walked. All the walking. And the laughter in the streets because the beer was stronger then. Now you don't hear a sound. It's terrible ... give me them days. We were more together then.[10]

Yet despite such modern accounts, the more I read into this subject, whether into historical, literary or sociological material, the more evident it became that our modern anxieties about weakening community are not new. The 'decline of community', a sense of it as a lost spirit, is a perennial issue and has been so for centuries. Medieval writers despaired at the desolation of communities caused by plague or forced desertion of villages. Or consider the destruction of monastic communities, with their farming estates and industrial works, as 650 monasteries were dissolved in England and Wales between 1536 and 1540. Eradicating communities through clearance was frequent in medieval and early modern England, as for example in the New Forest in Hampshire, or in many now deserted midland villages. Leicestershire, in which I write, has well over a hundred deserted medieval villages, as studied by pioneering historians like W. G. Hoskins and Maurice Beresford. These ex-community sites continue to attract widespread historical and archaeological scholarship. Early modern authors like Sir Thomas More in *Utopia* (1516) wrote about sheep which had

> become so great devourers and so wild, that they eat up and swallow down the very men themselves. They consume, destroy, and devour whole fields, houses, and cities ... [Landowners] leave no ground for tillage. They enclose all into pastures; they throw down houses; they pluck down towns, and leave nothing standing but only the church to be made a sheep-house.[11]

Such views were echoed later by Oliver Goldsmith's laments in 'The Deserted Village', published in 1770.

The poet George Crabbe, a clergyman of Leicestershire and Suffolk, considered such themes in *The Village* (1783) and *The Borough* (1810). John Clare bitterly tracked the decline of community in his lengthy poem *The Parish: a Satire*, some versions of which were too stinging to go into publication. In many other poems and autobiographical writings he lamented changes, such as enclosure, which he felt were undermining community and senses of place and belonging in his Northamptonshire village of Helpston. Like Samuel Bamford's *Early Days*, or William Cobbett's autobiographical writing, or Thomas Carter's *Memoirs of a Working Man*, or Daniel Parry-Jones's *My Own Folk*, John Clare lamented the passing of earlier days. Cobbett indeed, in his *Rural Rides* (1830), ruthlessly attacked behaviour and conduct which he thought had undermined earlier community.[12] One of the most famous and influential publications of the nineteenth century, A. W. N. Pugin's *Contrasts* (1836), explicitly set up contrasts between religiously inspired and supposedly organic communities of the mid-fifteenth century and the modern utilitarian age and architecture he was so critical of.[13] Such ideas were echoed in a host of medieval revivalist literature and art of the nineteenth century, such as Sir Walter Scott, or the Pre-Raphaelites. Hazlitt wrote of Scott as 'a mind brooding over antiquity – scorning "the present ignorant time" ... The old world is to him a crowded map; the new one a dull, hateful blank.'[14] Half a century or so after Pugin's book, as we will see in Chapter 5, Thomas Hardy represented decay of community, a sense of things falling apart, in the overall progress of his novels from *Under the Greenwood Tree* to *Jude the Obscure*. Novelists as wide ranging as George Eliot, Charles Dickens, D. H. Lawrence, Walter Machen, Jean Rhys, Richard Llewellyn, Edna O'Brien, James Kelman and Martin Amis wrote about community decline or absence, and resulting loneliness, just as novelists like William Faulkner, Thomas Wolfe, Sherwood Anderson, John Steinbeck and Carson McCullers did for America, or Knut Hamsun for Norway, or Chinua Achebe for the Ibo region of eastern Nigeria, in his book *Things Fall Apart*, a phrase that describes so much of this literature.[15]

A host of British rural writers, dealing with agrarian transformations, notably through the nineteenth and twentieth centuries, outlined such decline as they saw it.[16] One thinks for example of George Sturt in his famous book *Change in the Village*, in which he attacked enclosure as knocking the keystone out of the arch of earlier community life.[17] A large historiography discusses concepts of the medieval or early modern village community, as something lost *en route* to the twentieth century. Famine, landed clearances and emigration produced a forceful literature in the Celtic countries about communities destroyed. Many painters from George Morland (see Chapter 3) to Stanley Spencer depicted community or its loss, and, like Pugin, some of them juxtaposed in their art an imagined or hopeful community that they invited viewers to compare with the reality that they knew. Interwar articles in *The Times* expressed concern about the need to revive or strengthen community spirit.[18] Slum clearance programmes in the mid-twentieth century were often attacked for destroying urban communities. Wherever one looks in the historical and cultural evidence, communities seem to be in decline, just as they are in much historiography.[19] The thought-provoking issues of retrospective community are pervasive today – though one could debate whether they are more prominent than ever before, and whether they have more justification than hitherto. One of our leading social historians entitled a recent article: 'When we lived in communities'.[20] Countless newspaper and magazine articles have titles such as 'Our community spirit is lost'.[21] Radio programmes have titles such as 'Whatever happened to community?'[22] This is less a case of 'the world we have lost' (Peter Laslett's famous book title), as the community we have lost.

What form do these longings take? How has nostalgia varied in the past? Can one write a history of nostalgia for community? Surely, also, communities are constantly being made or remade? How rare it is to see '*new* communities' assessed as communities, rather than as stages in economic history, at least in England now or in the past. Of course, new communities have grown up in many areas, directly because of industrialization, and then after it. One thinks of communities of mining, ship-building, the textile districts, the potteries, those along canals or utopian communities.[23] Consider, for example, new communities connected with the nineteenth-century railway.[24] Or there have been the twentieth-century 'new towns' or 'garden cities', however one might wish to assess those, and the ones that will soon develop in the twenty-first century. There have been suburban commuter districts, fenland communities associated earlier with drainage and reclamation, and then with recent electronic and scientific revolutions, and so on. Community organizing, and analyses of related networks, are important sociological and political themes, more explicitly conceptualized in the social sciences than by historians.[25] And in 20–50 years' time, how will many immigrant groups of early twenty-first-century Britain view the networks and original communities by which they sustained themselves upon arrival?

One could have a lengthy discourse on how the word 'community' has been used by historians and sociologists, how this has changed and what it means here. Analysis of such usage would warrant a different book, though there are many references in the following chapters to how the term is used and how different writers and artists have conceived of it. Given such a variety of usage, it seems best to proceed with reference to how the term has been used historically. My own understanding of this flexible word allows for many ways in which writers and artists have thought about the concept, and I have left the definition wide. Even so, 'community' in most historical and traditional sociological uses is akin to the main dictionary definition: of 'the people living in one locality, or the locality in which they live'. The word refers to social relations in a place or similar spatial area, whether a village, town or urban district, or an occupational region or localized network of the kind one finds historically, such as the boot and shoe districts of Northamptonshire discussed by H. E. Bates. Those social relations may be experienced adversely or favourably; for community should not necessarily be extolled and I am not aware of any formal definitions that do that, even though much popular usage may do so. Community has often had, but does not necessarily have, an administrative dimension, involving boundaries which may be clearly demarcated or symbolic. And community usually involves a sense of belonging, for better or worse, one that can vary by social class, legal status, gender, life cycle and so on.

In most historical usage, community has not meant senses of networked, personal or virtual community. Nevertheless, we shall see ways in which such modern reapplications of the term touch upon some historical usage. There are for example concepts of the 'Anglican community' (see Chapter 4), which has had quite global connotations historically as well as pertaining to parochial units of religious administration and provision, even though many Nonconformists would query its application to them. I share some acquiescence in the idea of 'imagined communities', whether in connection with ideas about nationalism or for example in the sense of 'the agricultural community', a term used by authors like James Wentworth Day or Adrian Bell (Chapters 7 and 8), and which clearly designates an imagined community of people sharing strong interests but who cannot all know each other. Or one can think of a 'community' of coastal or water-edge East Anglian people, again who cannot all be familiar with each other, but who may (according to James Wentworth Day in Chapter 7) share certain experiences, skills, technologies, dialectal terms and the like. An imagined community of feeling, for example sharing participatory outlooks on nature, pertaining to an interlinked occupational culture, is surely valid in relation to such working experiences in a specified landscape. And in another sense we are all imagining communities if we think back, often in nostalgia, to ones we feel we have lost or have failed to attain. One could even conceive of an almost surrealist subjective history of community, involving seamless integration of separate, seemingly incongruous images and fields of nostalgia, unusual in their proportional and emotional relationships, some of them perhaps occupying one space at the same time. Furthermore, and more realistically, any process of purported memory may involve others, who are part of one's personal, virtual or networked community, a community of shared wistfulness. Perhaps that is true of some groups of historians, archaeologists or natural history writers, as for example those who recollect certain kinds of trade union solidarity or forms of close communal engagement with the natural world.

Returning then to the main issue of definition, community has historically above all been experienced in the ordering of human associations in a known space or locality, such as a village, parish, workplace or urban district. It has related to people known and conversed with at a face-to-face level, it has a spatial history with implications for present relationships, it resided in everyday knowledge and dealings and it involved a sense of belonging. This is the main sense of community discussed in this largely historical book.

This spatial dimension distinguishes historical community as understood here from a 'friendship community or network'. In my case for example, that involves relatives in Wales and parts of England, and many friends scattered widely, including academics in Europe, America and New Zealand. Most of these people do not know each other. With some of these people, mutual knowledge has derived from once living in narrowly defined spatial communities, of the kind described above. There are overlaps between these. One kind of community may thus progress into another. This may also be a generational contrast or a life-cycle change. A person may, for example, grow up in a specific place among others, whose movements elsewhere subsequently render them part of a later network and geographically diffuse 'personal community'.[26] One can conceive of many forms of personal community or more selective 'communities of affect'. But because these are ego-centred, subjective and, in most modern senses, regionally non-specific and varied – even 'private, dyadic and idiosyncratic'[27] – they are quite different from community understood in stable local terms, involving closely resident people with mutual knowledge and in an intricate mesh of localized interrelationships. Communities also interact in complex ways, and the independency of many local or personal networks today is striking compared with the past.

In a society as individualistic and mobile as ours in the West, it is deeply significant that some people wish to reapply the term 'community' to self-centred networks, for that is itself indicative of the decline of many earlier understandings of community, symptomatic of subjectivity and high individualism, and (as some would see it) an attempt to sustain meaning for an often over-valorized term that with modernity has lost much of its prior history or earlier definition.[28] This is clearly an adaption of an earlier term into different circumstances, trying to make sense of those new conditions via the terms of the past. Testimony for a longing after earlier more 'traditional communities' can be seen in the many fictional and tightly located rural or urban 'communities' with which our media is saturated – the Archers, Emmerdale, Coronation Street, EastEnders and so on – seeming substitutes for past community to which millions of listening people feel an involved sense of participation. Many analysts thus see our culture as featuring 'make-believe communities', what some sociologists or mass media experts refer to as 'pseudo-community', a term also sometimes applied to internet or online community.

Clearly, there are rival judgements about the meanings and significance of community change. As a discussion of community studies in Wales put it, the debate takes the form 'on the one hand, of anxiety about the decline of social capital and the fragmentation of face-to-face community rooted in place and, on the other, a celebration of the increasing "disembeddedness" of individuals and families and the potential that this creates for individualisation, choice, negotiation and democratic relationships'.[29] For those with optimistic interpretations of community change, this is a case of 'not nested, but networked'; and undoubtedly there are those for whom professional and/or friendship 'virtual' networks are satisfying, a result of free personal choice, perhaps a viable or preferable substitute for 'nested' community. The extension of knowledge and communication that modern technologies impart is unquestionable and rightly valued, and the supply of information has always been a crucial element of community hitherto. What is more debated is the viability, in comparative historical terms, of virtual-community forms that our technologies convey or that some assert. It is certainly the case that many *like* the loose and multiple features of virtual communities. These allow 'community' to become a fissile matter of often delocalized shared interests, though again there are historical precedents. For many people such networks can provide welcome 'community' where little of the kind would have been attainable hitherto, for example among those hitherto stigmatized.[30] Friendship networks, partially linked to current technologies, have been analysed to consider whether they supply adequate community substitution, and it is clear that replacement functions are often evident here.[31] With regard to capitalist infusion and control of the methods and tools of community today, which may be increasing – virtual community via payment and product ownership – it is certainly the case that capitalism penetrated and shaped almost all post-medieval British forms of historic community, albeit in an intensely interesting variety of changing ways. That would require a separate book to outline. One therefore needs to query the extent to which this is in general terms a 'new' development. Nevertheless, critics of virtual community and related concepts point to such issues as capitalist control of the means of communication and issues of financial or cohort exclusion, superficiality of internet use, depersonalizing effects of modern technology, pseudo-solidarities and excessive self-displays in social media, a possibly attendant eclipse of close friendships, a shallowness of modern memory and a meaning of life as residing in consumption.[32] The latter theme emerges strongly in the ending of this book, in commentary on the later work of H. E. Bates. The freedom of solitude has creative purposes,[33] but loneliness and its anxieties may cause people 'to retreat into … the sociality (or pseudo-sociality) of mass media or communication technology'.[34]

The enormous extent of modern loneliness and personal isolation demands attention and historical contextualization,[35] and I write as a past worker for the Samaritans and a member of the Campaign to End Loneliness, itself a striking example of networked charitable endeavour. We need to consider the past in comparison with the present, and in a way that is not open to charges of 'historical nostalgia', for such charges are often validations of the present or occlusions that fail to perceive the loneliness of others. Widely distributed friendship, kinship or other networks are crucial elements in the modern world, and they deserve sustained analysis. We will see some discussion of them and their antecedents (such as the globalized 'Anglican community') in historical perspective in these chapters. Yet while these may overlap with traditional localized definitions of community, they are essentially different from most historical understandings of community before modern technologies of communication and travel. Like modern media, they induce a sense of social action and community at a distance.[36] Virtual communities using the internet, or other forms of community without propinquity, and without any face-to-face visual or tactile knowledge, are even more remote. To apply the word 'community' to these seems a very considerable step from historical definitions of the term which engaged every human sense.[37]

In simple schematic terms, and I mean only that, one might loosely draw or model the evolving historical contrasts as follows:

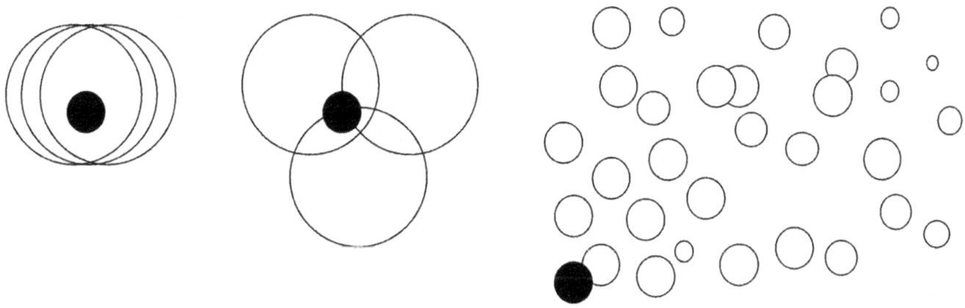

The black dot in each of the three cases refers to ego: oneself in relation to others. On the left we have the traditionally defined 'community'. Its circular domains and key themes or personnel functions overlie heavily, such that most people operate within it, and within a clearly defined geographical area or district, whether in relation to work, leisure, kinship, administration and so on, represented by such circles. There is heavy overlap of personnel. Mutual knowledge is almost complete, via interrelatedness, transitions to adulthood, shared work, visibilities of economic standing, intense gossip and so on. The development of personality structures, issues of trust and social capital, and their relation to community forms would have been much influenced by this.[38] Social divisions exist, of wealth and status – and they may indeed be multi-purposed, bitter or resentful – but they do not necessarily interfere with the complex and pervasive overlapping features of personnel. The main landowner, for example, is locally resident, even if grudgingly so, as in Thomas Hardy's *The Woodlanders*, a representation which I take to be archetypical of this kind of community. Indeed, in a small island community, anthropologically studied, the circles may exactly overlap each other.

In the middle scheme, which will still be familiar to many today, there is a central area akin to the earlier overlapping zone, in which we might place key individuals or those who seem to have a role in almost all aspects or domains of community life. But many people now spread beyond that, and in many regards functions or spheres no longer overlap. An unmooring of identities and ideas of belonging is under way, with growing disconnection from a clearly defined community sense of space. Some people commute elsewhere to work, or have dual or more senses of place, or if they work locally they do so in ways that do not interconnect with many others. Many people are not related and have no relationship to those who hitherto inhabited that community.[39] Mutual knowledge is much slighter than in the first model. The development of personalities would, arguably, vary from a more mutually overlapped or functionally encompassing community, and indeed this was commented upon by some nineteenth-century novelists.[40] Gossip here continues but is not that well-informed, effective or knowing as a form of surveillance.

Finally on the right, we find an outermost model (this is schematic and overstated) of the modern selective 'personal community', friendship network, or virtual community that is widely described now, or towards which social change appears to be progressing. It is still probably only a minority experience, despite its salience in much discussion. In it, place and overlapping functions can be slight or non-existent compared with earlier historical situations. Sensory experience of many such people (by sight, sound, touch or smell) is slight and partial, or non-existent with emails, text messaging or online community. People interconnect particularly via modern communications, leaving digital footprints subject to new forms of surveillance or leakage. They may work from home; they may have links to people at a great distance from them which are more important than many ties or individuals in their 'local community', such as neighbours, who they often do not know or wish to know. Gossip, which had earlier been a community's collective and ongoing self-portrait, is less relevant, and senses of privacy are enhanced, except for those who wish to broadcast themselves otherwise. This is largely a self-made and self-managed bespoke 'community', gliding free from place, in which people are 'networked' rather than locally 'nested', as predominantly in earlier times. One is not usually born into it, though in many regions and classes aspects of community inheritance certainly remain a feature of people's lives. One may suppose that it has implications for structures of personality historically understood and configured. It is relatively new as a prime form of social interaction, though I will later show elements of earlier relations that pre-exist it, for example affecting wide Anglican networks as revealed in parish magazines. Other precedents can readily be found, for example in eighteenth- and nineteenth-century great cities. It would be wrong to exaggerate the extent to which modern societies have reached this stage (and it seems to me that some commentators do). One can think of many rural or provincial areas where personal connectivity pertains more obviously to prior modes of community. Yet this appears to be the direction of change, and there are many whose experiences of 'community' (and even whose open advocacy) approximate to the stylized form of this third stage.

A possible metaphor to describe this emergent modern scenario, if one wishes to call it 'community', is that of a person blowing bubbles into the air on a breezy day: they float around or gradually away from you.

Hence my diagram above. People make, perpetuate or discard their own associates or friends, or connect selectively to relatives they like. Some within this 'community' seem linked as conjoint bubbles, and some may be mutually networked for varying or unknown reasons. Some are smaller than others. Some seem to refract light differently, depending on their background. Some are more volatile than others, subject to varying streams of air. And in many cases, as they get more remote, they burst. It is sometimes remarked that people live in their own little bubble, an evanescent state. If one wished to think of more personally controlling metaphors, compatible with such buoyant bubble-like imagery, then there is the idea of flying kites, and occasionally letting them go, which is perhaps more appropriate to some modern forms of friendship networks or indeed managerial styles. Other metaphors could be used: theorists speculate on the socially symbolic meanings of isolated people on railway platforms and at other 'non-places',[41] reminiscent of American paintings by Edward Hopper. Networks and human associations are persistently changing, in opportunistic and other multi-directional ways. They are becoming highly reflexive, instigated, maintained or discarded by individuals at will. As one theorist put it:

> The form of existence of the single person is not a deviant case along the path of modernity. It is the archetype of the *fully developed* labor market society. The negation of social ties that takes effect in the logic of the market begins in its most advanced stage to dissolve the prerequisites for lasting companionship … The end of this road is in all probability not harmony with equal rights, but *isolation* in courses and situations that run counter and apart from each other.[42]

Modern affiliations and networking affect identities, decision making, motivation and action. They are subject to contrasting assessments. Long-standing bonds, it is increasingly argued, are giving way to short-term connectivity: to exchanges 'until further notice', to switch-off interactions, to memory-loss 'friends', epitomized by internet use.[43] The sociologist Zygmunt Bauman in his analysis of loose and short-term relationships, 'rampant individualization' and 'quick-fix culture', has termed this 'liquid modernity'.[44] Ray Pahl referred to it more neutrally as 'our fluctuating and ever-changing personal community'.[45] These themes have been persistent for decades in countless popular songs.[46] Arguably, the nature of modern economies largely dictates these circumstances. They derive in part from senses of community deficit and lack of choice in hitherto forms of community. Many of my historical chapters show elements of that. Most commentators also stress a technology of personal community mediated via the capitalism of digital products. The history of technologies that sustain this modern situation, in relation to changing community forms, is itself a potentially fascinating subject – just as their historical counterparts might be in relation to past forms of community. Technologies are fundamental to it, such that one commentator writes: 'The various shades of loneliness are the price we pay for living in a society dominated by technology.'[47] One could of course reverse that quotation and suggest that the technologies are themselves answers to human loneliness, whether one sees the latter as a pervasive feature of the human condition or as being more attendant upon modernity and the eclipse of past communities. For technology usually arises in response to a need for it.

One reading of this emergent scenario is that perhaps we know only individuals, not community, though the intensity and effectiveness of such networks is enormously varied by person, raising many issues of egalitarianism and privilege. And there are countless persisting structural forms (e.g. a business, a university, a locale however defined) that still orientate many of these personalized networks into partial overlapped groupings. The direction of change seems widely agreed: 'thick' community (solidaristic, exclusory and conformist) gives way to 'thin' community (diverse, stressing freedom and individuality), indeed sometimes to crumbly wafer-thin community, a process of change compatible with my diagram above. The earlier forms seem to be weakening: the sense of place is usually taken to be a case in point; or one sees working from home rather than at a shared location becoming more pronounced; or freelance contractors are employed instead of regular employees. For example, the '*shinkansen* academic', travelling to different universities by Japanese bullet train, takes over from lecturers steadily employed in a stable institution; the freelance lorry driver replaces the company drivers; the often distant contractor displaces the regular farm workforce. The cultural effects of such changes increasingly render people like layered Matryoshka nesting dolls (the kind that fit within each other), in process of losing external national, cultural and community forms, opportunistically mobile, weakly inter-connective and often isolated, adopting postmodernist expedients in espousal of new eclectic, layered, self-focused or media/Web-selected identities.

It is often said that ours is increasingly an untrusting society. After all, trust needs memory, established and enduring interrelationships, habits of face-to-face sociability and respect mutually confirmed by dependable others – and cagy distrust is clearly related to personal isolation and loneliness. Trustworthiness is not notable as a feature of online community. Community in its earlier embodiments or personifications is marginal or irrelevant to many atomistic presumptions of modern thought. It often seems that only individuals are real, however anaemic that reality might be without community. Our literary awards – indicative of some readers' social recognition – go to existentialist novels about introverted loners with titles like *Atomised*.[48] Modern films have been described as *A Cinema of Loneliness*, by an author who remarks how 'passivity and aloneness … have become their central image'.[49] The godless existential idea of being condemned to be free, coupled with a growing detachment from intrinsic meanings and purposes of past community life, are widely described predicaments. We are free and alone to make of this what we will: our choices apparently make us, and they are often object-fixated, widget-wise, in this latest form of existential modernity. The *mobile* phone is the symbol of our age: the seventh sense; the need to be constantly in touch with one's personal community; the fear of loneliness; and (according to some) the expedient that helps avoid immediate conversation with those around you.

Linked in some respects to personal isolation, over the past half century we have also seen an extraordinary rise in single-person households, both in Britain and internationally, a phenomenon highly correlated with loneliness in the psychological and sociological literature.[50] Living alone is the prime explanatory variable in most quantitative analyses of subjective loneliness and, rightly or wrongly, 'solitaries' or 'singletons' have come to define or shape the modern social problem of loneliness. This invites analysis of how the scope and nature of 'solitaries' have changed through time. Prior to the early twentieth century, about 5 per cent of households were 'solitaries'. In many world cities now, over 40 per cent of 'households' are only one person, and in some (e.g. Stockholm) it is over 60 per cent.[51] In some census tracts of Manhattan and Los Angeles it is 94 per cent. The 2011 census showed that over a third of households in the UK were solitaries. The trend has been sharply upwards, especially since the 1960s. This development, on this scale, is completely unprecedented historically and is an extraordinary social transformation. It takes us beyond the known lessons of history, though it invites comparisons with past forms of community life or isolationism. It is another example of how the multi-personal component and structural links between family, household and community in their traditional senses are weakening.

This book deals with modernizing literary and artistic evidence bearing upon changing senses of community, and my discussion is not intended primarily as social-science model building, which could be developed in much more sophisticated ways. But this inescapable modern debate about the possible breadth and meanings of the term 'community', and how it has changed historically, was interestingly anticipated by Adrian Bell, the subject of Chapter 8. Displaced from Suffolk in the Second World War, he wrote about a Cumbrian settlement as follows:

> A great buzz of voices filled the air; for as the farmers' wives had nothing to do but sit and await their customers, the market was both physical rest and social club. Even as the remote farmer, mounting his fell-top, was in view of the town, so here his wife was in actual touch with the inhabitants of that great view. A certain white dot of a farmstead would stand for the face and voice and animation of a neighbour. This is true community. Without actual contact community is a sort of broadcast myth.[52]

Adrian Bell would not have contended that 'virtual communities' have a human validity commensurate with what we have often historically lost, and he would believe that this is a 'broadcast myth' of our times. Of course, there can be overlaps, affecting functions, localized political purposes, subjectivities of belonging and so on; but in general such modern forms seem experientially and analytically quite different from the face-to-face and locally situated working communities of the past.

So this is a book about spirits of community, belonging and perceptions of community loss in the English past. Yet contrary to many pessimistic accounts, these senses of loss are *not* all recent. Many of them glare out of the historical documentation long ago. There is nothing new in a nostalgic, or pragmatic, belief that community has declined. We will see extreme personal isolation in some of these historical chapters. And networks of a seemingly modern kind existed in the past too, as for example with the Anglican Church, discussed in Chapter 4. There were also historically varying definitions of 'community', of entities or collectivities that people applied that word to, as observed in the next chapter. Nor is there anything new about disappointment in community, a sense of its inadequacy or sensitivity about its failure to help people or oneself – as will be noticeable in many of these chapters. Different types and spirits of community are discussed here, with many kinds of community decline. They are covered through a variety of sources, both literary and pictorially artistic. They are variously extolled, or discussed in potentiality, or lamented as lost or in decline. In some cases, their riddance was a matter of relief and congratulation, for this is by no means always a change that elicits nostalgia. After all there was 'community' in the Gulags, in conscripted armies, in besieged cities from Stalingrad to Enugu, in the sweated garrets and worst lanes of certain textile industries, in pneumoconiosis-inducing coalmines and their accompanying settlements, or in the boot and shoe towns that H. E. Bates was so pleased to leave in Chapter 9. So much for 'industrial pastoral'. Pride in community is not part of any definition – this book does not aim to interpose that. And any valorization of a waning community can be disputed because one person's sense of community loss can be another person's 'new' community, as so often has been the case.[53] What would the London cockneys resettling in coastal Essex have thought of James Wentworth Day, as he deplored them in the 1930s and 1940s and lamented their beclouding of the former coastal communities? For a variety of reasons, relating to ageing or social substitution, one person's sense of effacement may have little in it that is tangible or widely agreed upon. It is hardly surprising that commentators fail to reach agreement in the handling of such subjective issues and varied viewpoints. In other words, 'community' as studied here is *not* necessarily a beneficial or esteemed concept. It may on the contrary be unsupportive and exploitative. The representations discussed in this book are subjective, literary and artistic historical views, some of them critical of past forms of communal identity, and they have been analysed as such.

Chapter 2 discusses one's community of legal settlement, which under settlement law governed where everyone 'belonged' and was entitled to poor relief in the past. This system lasted from long before the Settlement Act of 1662 until the mid-twentieth century, and it brought with it strong senses of local attachment and entitlement. In effect, it gave legal form and structure to 'community', in the shape of the Welsh or English parish or northern township. It is that *structure* and experiential knowledge of community as a legal right, a locality of guaranteed belonging and welfare assurance, which I wish to stress as contrasting so remarkably with the absence of equivalent structures in more recent cultural representations, such as those by H. E. Bates, with which I end this book. The chapter uses unique letters from people outlining how they legally belonged to certain communities. These are complemented by petitions to the London Refuge of the Destitute, mothers' letters to the London Foundling Hospital and further evidence from newspapers. Such sources are extremely revealing of popular mentalities, showing us much about senses of community attachment, the kinds of community that people felt they belonged to and the perceived risks and fears of losing these. What did those communities mean, and why? The sources tell us what people felt when their own communities were sometimes in danger of being lost to them, because of their migration, or because communities wanted to evade particular welfare responsibilities. I am also interested here in ideas of 'community' as 'home' and associated concepts relating to community such as neighbours, strangers, foreigners, parishioners, friends and so on. 'Communities' of friends and historical meanings of friendship are discussed here. Friendship has received much recent attention from Ray Pahl and other sociologists, interested in whether its personal networks can substitute for community in the modern world. How did such concepts affect these earlier letter writers' identities? How did hardship affect friendships and community? We are concerned here with what belonging to community and its associated ideas *meant* to people in the eighteenth and nineteenth centuries. As the chapters of this book progress, in chronological sequence, we will see shifts away from these earlier priorities and structures, towards differing values and attitudes to community, finally ending with the ostentatious individualized consumerism that H. E. Bates highlighted as supplanting earlier forms of community, and as apparently rendering the historic forms of community redundant as a social need.

The rural poor and migrants appear in pictorial form in the next chapter, which discusses how landscape painting came to depict those who were away from their home communities and appear to lack any place to associate with. Landscape painting from about 1740 to the late nineteenth century showed growing awareness of those who were community-less: the migrants, vagrants and gypsies whose mobility contrasts strikingly with mid-eighteenth-century representations of parishioners 'in their place', in hierarchical estate-like communities controlled from above. The initial discussion therefore is of a mid-eighteenth-century estate village painted by Edward Haytley, in which strong and overlooked senses of belonging and place seem to exist. However, as English landscape painting evolves, migrant and community-lacking poor begin to be seen in some of Gainsborough's paintings from the mid-eighteenth century, and this trend culminates in the indigent roadside imagery of George Morland between 1790 and his death in 1804. That imagery was then perpetuated in further painting of the nineteenth century depicting roadside poor. Imagery of such migrants was rare in the early eighteenth century, for it was an affront to patrons' ideas of parochial structure, the obligations of hierarchy, cultural associations of settlement, and commonweal care. But from the 1790s in particular such poor migrants became conspicuous in English painting, and the suggestion or criticism in many early 'realist' paintings is that a loss and displacement from community has occurred.

From the 1860s a new and hugely successful genre emerged, that of the parish magazine. Aimed at the local community, often religious in intent as well as being engaged with local life and history, this genre is a wonderful source for historical community studies. It was symptomatic of attempts to uphold particular kinds of community, focused in certain ways, and to instil in both rural and urban parishes a sense of purpose and strong community spirit. The sense of community here was local and parochial, yet it could also be partial and partisan in its religious focus, featuring rival communities. For it was often denominationally exclusive or took for granted an Anglican perspective. These sources show the church's involvement in community. And yet, as argued in Chapter 4, that perspective developed horizons well beyond a spatially constrained idea of the parish. The 'Anglican community' that it extolled was international, a long-stranded 'network community' in a Christian context, often missionary, sometimes tied by distanced funding. This was a limited-participation community of shared belief before ideas of networked global communities came to be broached via the digital advances of the later twentieth century. In other words, three concepts of community were apparent in parish magazines: parochial, denominational and internationally networked. These magazines espoused them all, in combinations and in responses to wider changes during the key period of British globalization. Just as the painter George Morland speaks to modern issues of personal isolation, so parish magazines relate in further prescient ways to other modern dimensions of the meaning of community.

The work of Thomas Hardy has often been discussed in connection with nineteenth-century rural society. His novels capture a fundamental change in community life as he saw it. The animated ideas of community found in *Under the Greenwood Tree*, his first novel, featuring the closely known affairs of the Mellstock church musicians, were utterly different from the forsaken and pessimistic accounts of community and its absences that readers undergo in his last novel, *Jude the Obscure*. Hardy described, in contrasts between these two novels, a fundamental decay of the village community, such that it is no longer worth remaining for. He showed remarkable shifts towards mobility and isolation of the individual in a city environment that lacked any earlier spirit of community that he was familiar with. Rural and urban 'communities' were also being compared by him at the end of his novelistic career, and he found both to be lamentably wanting. The pastoral themes of 'traditional' and largely self-contained community in *Under the Greenwood Tree* were supplanted by an extreme bleakness of rural prospect. Jude seeks to transcend solitude and isolation in a search for a community of knowledge, as something shared with others, beyond and superior to the perished village he has left. Yet this leads him to urban loneliness, personal breakdown, despair and the absolute solitude of death while alone in the city. In Hardy's plot the acquisition of knowledge as a form of communion with others, and the possibilities of an urban community to replace the decayed rural, have both failed. The starkness and apprehension of this transformation in community history, as represented by Britain's leading novelist of the period, is outlined and interpreted in Chapter 5.

Hardy died in 1928. In that interwar period, the English village community came to feature a new genre, that of the murder mystery and detective novel. Agatha Christie, Dorothy L. Sayers, Margery Allingham, Ngaio Marsh and many other writers saw in the English village a community in crisis, one beset by evil, such that it has become the venue for frequent murder and the need to solve such crime. What do these often critically neglected but enormously popular women novelists tell us about change and suspicion in the community, and what kinds of community were they lamenting as endangered, lost or in need of renewal? These issues are discussed in Chapter 6. What were their senses of past community life? How were the problems of community resolved in their writing? How did they respond to issues and limitations in village life during their period, and what was it about an individualized murderer besmirching the community that made this form of writing so prevalent? After all, Agatha Christie, with her accounts of the English village community in crisis, is without question the world's best-read author, with translations into over 110 languages, indeed about 6,400 separate translations, apparently selling somewhere between two billion and four billion books. Only the Bible may possibly have outsold her. Rarely has the moral order and rectitude of English 'community' come under such sustained literary scrutiny and readership. And rarely has community come to be viewed and read about with such suspicious eyes. These novelists' descriptions of unsafe change, their accounts of endangered community life and its hazards, stand in intriguing comparison with those of other authors covered in this book who raised issues of threatened community.

Those women writers were conservative in their political and social outlooks. Another conservative perspective on declining community is in Chapter 7, which considers the writer James Wentworth Day and his 'rural rides' before, during and after the Second World War. He was a very prolific and versatile East Anglian author, and a superb nature writer, who was especially concerned to document the water-edge occupational communities of the Essex coastline, the fens and the Norfolk Broads. As he saw it, ways of life and regional cultures associated with these areas were being undermined, given the expansion of London and new forms of settlement transforming the coastline, and with a centrally orchestrated second agricultural revolution destroying wetland environments. The themes of the country and the city, so strong in Hardy, are further developed here. In addition, the decline of the great estates, so obvious in his time, was leading to the disintegration of types of estate community under local elite leadership. His own responses led him into greater engagement with nature, appreciative of people-less places, finding communion with nature, in a style that was individualistic, watchful and elegiac, and which remind us of some other nature writers. Many of his conservative and anti-city views had precedents in those of William Cobbett, author of the earlier *Rural Rides* of 1822, who had been another conservative author who described community under threat in southern England in the early nineteenth century. Parallels are drawn here between the two men, showing ideological continuities and similarities and directing attention to attitudes among conservative thinkers on community and its supposed decline.

Adrian Bell, the subject of Chapter 8, was hugely popular in the mid-twentieth century and has many continuing devotees today. Leaving a disliked London to immerse himself in community and small-farm life in East Anglia, he considered how it was changing, what it meant in the past and what it offered to the modern world. His was a uniquely poetical voice for a passing rural England, a writer of beautiful and clear prose, elegiac, simple yet sophisticated in meanings. His themes continue with writers like Ronald Blythe, Richard Mabey and Robert Macfarlane. He wrote of the 'agricultural community', a wider imagined occupational community, as well as of village community which he saw fade around him from its apparently earlier heyday.[54]

In Adrian Bell we see a development that is perceptible throughout this book: of community giving way to greater familial individualism, to a narrower focus upon the private family and to a situation in which community is viewed wistfully yet is no longer needed. For community has in many ways been a casualty of rising living standards as well as of deindustrialization, population redistributions, and post-1940s planning and architecture. Its hitherto structures and mutual support, whether under parochial welfare entitlements and legalized ideas of belonging, or in working-class communities, became less necessary over the twentieth century. Family pride or breakdown, demands for privacy, the rise of living alone, envy-inducing consumerism[55] and high levels of mobility eroded it. Senses of belonging grew weaker as people left the localities of their upbringing or ancestry and commuted longer distances to work. Many now embrace family history, asking the media question 'who do you think you are', analysing their DNA, and seeking identity, purpose, belonging and perhaps a resolution of isolation in the discovery of ancestors.[56] The most individualistic societies seem to do this to the greatest extent.

The erosion of traditionally understood community reaches its most striking expression in the work of H. E. Bates, in my final chapter. 'Go with the stream, never battle against it,'[57] wrote Bates, and he moved with his times, declaring it essential that a novelist should do so. Entering into characters in the way that he did, he became a very sensitive observer of social change. His early work depicts the grim boot and shoe areas of Northamptonshire, a classic set of interlinked occupational communities, which shared many similarities with other such communities elsewhere. These contexts were extolled in some community studies after the Second World War. Yet this was an environment and local society that Bates intensely disliked, one that he was pleased to leave, even when that relocated his writing to the war in Kent or to fenland aerodromes. An intense community of fighter and bomber pilots then became his literary subject, groups of people who were temporarily formed, dissolving with peacetime, yet powerfully described in some of the finest prose of the Second World War. After the war, he continued to write about past rural life, often comically, as with the recollections of his character Uncle Silas. And with Bates's creation of the Larkin family, we reach a stage of post-1950s object consumerism and family-centred individualism that in some ways stands as an end process for 'community' as understood before online networking and/or friendship definitions. For this final scenario, so enormously popular in Bates's novels (and in their misleading television serialization), lacks community: it is ostentatious, happy-go-lucky, separated from community norms, missing any of the hitherto structures, often lonely, unsteady, somewhat vague yet lucrative in its sources of income. And its consumerism is ostentatious in Bates's novels to the point of obesity and heart attacks. 'Trade and commerce require easy-living, irreligious people,' an early sociologist wrote, as he described change to absolutely detached and universalist individualism.[58] Community is no longer needed in Bates's later short stories and novels. Through mobility, the decay of leadership, human choice and capitalistic developments, it has effectively ceased in any of the known historical forms or representations that I earlier described. With the Larkin family, and with their carefree ability to dump community in individualistic consumption of life, we have travelled a long way from the letter writers of Chapter 2 and their parishes of settlement, or the estate villages or subsequent roadside migrants of Chapter 3, or the concerned Anglican ethos of the Victorian parish magazine. We have discarded those fretful, suspicious attempts to diagnose and redress 'evil' in community of the 1920s–1950s detective-story writers and readers. And poverty, as variously displayed earlier, seems to be a thing of the past.

Some of the writers discussed here address each other, directly or indirectly. James Wentworth Day harks back to William Cobbett and indeed to countless other writers about community. The paintings of

George Morland relate to the migrant letter writers of Chapter 2, or to Thomas Hardy's itinerant stonemason, or to how the undiscerning finger of blame is pointed at 'outsiders' in some detective fiction. Earlier ideas of pastoral community are handled ironically in some interwar murder fiction, or given an elite derivation in Wentworth Day, much as they had been in Edward Haytley. Hardy's views of the church 'quire' could have come from many parish magazines, and he has clearly influenced Adrian Bell and H. E. Bates. When Adrian Bell described community behaviour such as Suffolk village-hall dances, he was resetting what Hardy had written into modern form and a different region. The sequence in *Under the Greenwood Tree* from community to more isolated family is one that presages writing in Bell and Bates. Many of these people share ideas about community as imagined in the past. Their historical imagination of community is part of what I am examining. And the themes of the country and the city run through all these chapters, variously informing ideas about community spirit.[59]

However, it is not my contention that these authors or painters form some newly discovered linkage. They are brought together here because in their own periods they all had something instructive to say about community in an historical context and its apparent decline or challenges to it. In their various ways, from village to city, and in their respective genres, terms and language, all of them knowingly expose community in crisis. They show and respond to its inadequacies, often wishing to strengthen certain kinds of community felt to be threatened. They are symptomatic of the predicaments of community and the relationships of individuals to community in their own periods. That is why they have been chosen for analysis: to illuminate those relationships and to provide an historical perspective on comparable debates and concerns in more recent times. Contrasts of this kind, and their subtle cultural nuances and historical temporalities, are hard to expound in generalized socio-economic histories put together from a great miscellany of evidence, but may be revealed with greater precision of feeling via such focused cultural analyses.

There is also an overall narrative here, about community structures, economic and social change, individualism and isolation, which in many ways is an unsettled and continuing trend. I develop elements of this expansively, aware that an evaluation of where we are now is fraught with rival optimistic or pessimistic appraisals. In other words, wishing to occupy ground that we might agree upon, a shift is outlined here from presumptive and legally encoded nested community, whether parochial and/or estate-based (the backdrops to Chapters 2 and 3), towards increasingly networked liaisons; from parochial reliance and legalized belonging under the settlement laws to individualized community-less consumption, object identification and the concerns about loneliness of recent times. This process has its manifestations, forerunners or auguries in the now historic sensitivities of commentators like George Morland, Thomas Hardy, Agatha Christie, Adrian Bell or H. E. Bates. Some of these senses of change and significance are shown here, in hopes that these emerge inevitably and clearly through the contrasts and chronologically shifting emphases of these authors and artists.

Other subjects were considered for this book, such as William Cobbett, Robert Owen, Elizabeth Gaskell, Charles Dickens, Henry Mayhew, Benjamin Brierley, George Eliot, Caradoc Evans, D. H. Lawrence, Rhys Davies, Richard Llewellyn, Gwyn Jones, Lewis Jones, Kate Roberts, Winifred Holtby, Stanley Spencer, Emyr Humphreys or Raymond Williams.[60] They expressed many ideas about community in decline, transformation or aspiration, and about human isolation, but a selection had to be made. They would not much alter the picture of change here, for they are all compatible with it. I have taken subjects that fit my main regions of researched history, from Wales across to East Anglia, from southern England to the North Midlands. This gives the book an obvious coherence, yet clearly a different selection of authors and artists could be chosen to explore these themes for Ireland, Scotland, Wales and northern England, and it would be fascinating to do that. But a historian must know his or her limitations, and it might be presumptuous for this Anglo-Welsh historian to cover authors like James Joyce or Lewis Grassic Gibbon, or historic figures like Thomas Chalmers. I am very aware that the issues in Wales, its regional and linguistic make-up, its rural and industrial experiences and the nature of its historical and cultural evidence are such as to warrant a separate book – and so the coverage here is of those regions of England which I know best historically. To judge from the literature and personal experience, the themes and arguments of this book are widely shared across Celtic countries and the English north.

My emphases are deliberate in a further regard: debate about 'declining community' has often focused upon the effects of deindustrialization, upon working-class communities and employment, upon regeneration and developing community engagement and upon new senses of place. An enormous sociological, heritage, geographical and planning literature encompasses these issues.[61] The modern predicaments of regions such as the ex-coalfields in county Durham, south Wales, the Midlands and elsewhere, the shipbuilding districts, the textile regions of Lancashire and the West Riding, and many other such areas, are undoubted. So are the effects of these changes on working-class associations and culture. I cover some of these issues and assessments for the boot and shoe manufacturing areas of Northamptonshire. Yet the consequences of post-war deindustrialization for community life are distinctive and warrant particular kinds of economic and social analysis, which they receive from others. I also wished to look at earlier depictions of community spirit and decline, indeed into periods (we often forget) in which deindustrialization was a southern English problem, affecting regions such as East Anglia, London or the south-west. It seems to me that there are deeper and longer-term changes affecting senses of community in all of England, heightened in lately deindustrializing regions, but going much wider than them – changes in structure, locality, belonging and welfare, and these and their related characterizations are my prime concerns.

A range of different classes has been encompassed, with an array of politicized opinions, from George Morland to James Wentworth Day. It is possible that some readers will favour certain chapters over others because of their ideological inclinations. Yet I have written with sympathy for all these subjects, as my empathies are far stronger than my political views. Women and gender issues feature in many of these chapters, and Chapter 6 analyses an important group of female novelists. The themes stretch across two and a half centuries. Over this long period, discussion of 'community spirit', 'community in decline', and 'internationalizing community' has been incessant to the point that it seems a leitmotif of human psychology: community as 'the imagined village',[62] as a frequently Arcadian network in the mind, plucking ideas from history about the 'spirit of community'. One might observe that apprehensions about community loss have been especially salient in connection with enclosure and agrarian change, during industrialization in the later eighteenth and early nineteenth centuries, during Scottish highland or Irish 'clearances', during nineteenth-century urban renewal, railway building and slum clearances; or the period of rural exodus from about 1850 to the later nineteenth century, during the post-1900 decades which saw most marked decline of great estates, the interwar depression, and then since the Second World War with deindustrialization, the extension of commuting, slum and housing projects, enlarged prosperity and multiculturalism. We noticed earlier that these apprehensions are highly prominent today, across public and social policy, debates about loneliness epidemics, rival assessments of the worth of online 'communities', immigration-linked 'culture clashes' and so on. As I write, the 'refugee crisis' and its inflow of peoples to the European Union witnesses further unease about the 'cultural effects of this on communities'. Not many historical periods are missing between these listed above, and in all of them there was agitated debate about community loss. The same could probably be said for most times before 1750 too.[63] Every generation seems to view community in crisis and observes pessimism about its prospects and what if anything might replace it. That is one of the main lessons of this book. This is not to deny much generational optimism. Nor is it to downplay the organizational aspirations of historic 'interest' or class-based communities, such as friendly societies, chapels, Methodist circuits, trade unions and the like, which often sought to change the ways in which people worked and lived together and to shift the meanings of 'community'. And of course periods of rapid and incessant change will always be experienced precariously. We face perturbing crises now, and they have arresting forms – for example the loneliness of many teenagers and young adults, and of community-less isolated old age with extended longevity. These are distressing problems, unforeseen side effects of other socio-demographic changes, but in a general sense they may not be as new as many theorists and practitioners think. 'Crisis of community' and the 'loss of community spirit' long predate us, whether as imagined or real predicaments.

These chapters are thus united by a shared concern: how did these artists and authors respond to the issue of declining community; what supporting principles did they reminisce about, highlight or seek to impose? How was human isolation or solitude depicted or alleviated? The letter writers of my next chapter attempted to re-establish links to 'their' community, via ideas about their legal settlements, falling back onto their rights to 'belong', showing the concepts of community and friendship that they had carried away with them. In so doing, they revealed an experiential knowledge about axiomatic formal structures of community that came to them from the early modern period, but which did not long follow them. Another view of such communities was given by Edward Haytley, in his depiction of a patriarchal and seemingly benevolent estate village. By contrast, the painter George Morland ran from 'community', angered by its elites and its debt collectors, and in unprecedented realism he showed us life 'on the road', a transient bypassing of community in risky forms of escapism and low-life solidarities. The parish magazine editors and writers sought communion, both locally and even internationally, via their vision of an 'Anglican community', a shared communion of denominational form. Like Ronald Blythe later, they were perhaps locally struck by 'the reality of public worship being multiple private worship, each voice, each closed or wide-open eye, each kneeling form contributing to the whole … It is short and beautiful this "worship", this joining in whilst staying single, and yet being a "whole"'.[64] In comparison, Thomas Hardy, with the character of Jude the obscure, sought community in the attainment of knowledge, the search for shared scholarship being an expression of Jude's efforts to overcome an increasingly desolate rural and then urban solitude. Yet this attempt to imbibe the fruits of collective consciousness induced further isolation, and Jude found instead the ultimate and complete isolation of death, the ceasing of all communions. Continuing with the theme of death, the interwar crime writers solved dire crime in community, suspiciously extracting 'evil' from it, in hopes of self-overlooked community redemption and return to a trusting harmony. James Wentworth Day brooded in conservative despair over the eclipse of waterland occupational cultures, but found his lonely solution in adventurous nature observation and an empathy with the associations of wildlife. Adrian Bell extolled occupational community, the all-sensed agrarian beauty of the time-worn and tangible, and a return to countryside locality and belonging, albeit for the isolated nuclear family. And for H. E. Bates, finishing this book in entertaining irony, familial consumerism attempted to overcome solitude, to substitute for hitherto known and repudiated community, the characters in the final phases of his writing seeking their fulfilment or refuge in an unhealthy indulgence of objects and foods from the world of high capitalism, in a formula of personal materialistic recourse increasingly exploited by psychologically adept advertisers.

Some of these writers, like Adrian Bell or James Wentworth Day, might be considered nostalgic and needlessly troubled about the senses of community, belonging and losses which they described. They will seem anti-modern and anti-technocratic. Local nested community was something that some commentators did not mourn, just like some autobiographers (indeed like H. E. Bates) who chose to escape from the often insular communities of the pre-modern village and to build new forms of community based on voluntary organization and fresh associational life. The historical phases of globalization brought new and widely travelling agendas and fashions. Anti-industrial rhetoric like that from Adrian Bell – 'the mammon of industrialism that has rotted the old forms and put nothing in their place'[65] – and his personal example of a self-documented return to community localism will certainly not appeal to some people. If Bell had his heyday it was probably during the Second World War, as so many soldiers and others considered with a new urgency what they were doing, thought apprehensively about what they had been dragged into, and pondered how they wanted to live if they survived. One historian of that era described how the spirit of comradeship fostered by mutual danger produced 'the extraordinary spectacle of the British actually speaking to each other without being introduced', a seeming expansion of the remits of community, which reminds us of the class and other barriers that had existed hitherto, which war did not remove. People were sustained as 'part of a purposive community, after perhaps spending a lifetime of social isolation. The camaraderie weakened with the ending of the great raids and disappeared entirely, abruptly, with the coming of peace but it left behind a profound and enduring sense of nostalgia.'[66]

For many, a purposive community has been hard to replicate subsequently, even if they wanted it. This is despite persistent marketing of localism as a concept and despite profitable use of modern technologies and networking. Anti-globalization sentiments are now widespread, paradoxically using the internet with great effectiveness.[67] Global warming may indeed cause our descendants to curse present-day generations, and they may sympathize with Adrian Bell when he wrote: 'Without the pole-star of a new simplicity, it seems to me, civilisation will continue by turns at deadlock or mad speed, like a machine out of control which bumps itself from one obstacle to another until it falls to pieces.'[68] Adrian Bell died in 1980, and his localist community sentiments remain controversial. Yet his thoughts about the fidelity of community, local belonging and personal fulfilment deserve respect, for like other reactions they prompt thoughtful consideration of us in time. This book aims to open up such responses to the supposed 'decline of community', to discuss what spirits of community have meant hitherto and thus to hold a wind-blown candle to the directions and associations of modern life.

2

Writing Back to Community

Home and Friends among the Poor

This chapter deals with the first part of our period, from about 1750 to 1840, and it will examine ideas about community, home, friends and belonging among the labouring poor. It uses sources that are the most authentic of their voices. These are letters or narratives regarding their poor law settlements, poor relief and related matters, which are becoming more available and appreciated.[1] Such sources allow us to address many issues. When they were written these letters really mattered, as so much depended on their outcomes. They are among the most authentic documentation for 'history from below' and historical questions of community and belonging. The concerns that they express help to place many of our modern ideas about community into historical perspective. By broadening the social base of representations in some later chapters, they allow us insights into the meanings of community among those who, in this earlier part of our period, were the majority of the population.[2]

These letters and narratives have their own formats, related to intent and administration. In some of these sources that format was quite constraining and in others more flexible. The 'authenticity' of voices from the poor also varied.[3] In most kinds of narrative there was variety of expression and purpose. As a source they stand comparison with evidence such as emigrants' letters, petitions to the London Foundling Hospital, first-person settlement examinations, letters to the poor law authorities complaining about treatment, 'briefs' or begging letters following personal hardship, or anonymous letters of protest. They remind us also of the interviews conducted by those skilled in nineteenth-century shorthand, most famously Henry Mayhew and Charles Dickens.

My focus here is on the concepts that such letters show as fundamental to the poor's existence: those of home, belonging, friends and community. These terms may have originated in elite use. 'Home' is from Old English *hām*, meaning among other things the home compounds of great men and royal estates containing residences. It was applied to one's neighbourhood from the later fourteenth century, both in relation to place and a group of people under someone's authority. 'Belonging' could mean either 'connected with' or 'being appropriate to'. These meanings influenced both socially high and low use later on.

'Friends' often meant those who were able to assist you, who were frequently in a stronger position than a supplicant. 'The term is generally applied to a friend who is in a position to help one by influencing those in power.'[4] In the eighteenth and nineteenth centuries the poorest often lacked 'friends', partly because potential 'friends' did not wish to be involved in dependent behaviour which might discredit them. However, the term 'friends' had many meanings in the eighteenth and early nineteenth centuries, as we shall see.[5]

The word 'community', from *communitas*, related in the late medieval period more to formal kinds of incorporation by charter, with restricted membership, headed by the wealthy, rather than to any people living near each other. In the eighteenth century the word was most often used in a wide sense: as in phrases such as 'the community at large', or 'the great body of the community', or 'the honour of the community', or 'the monied part of the community'. While such use often meant the whole society, it could also apply to restricted elements, such as 'the community of Wholesale Merchants in this City'. In eighteenth-century publications it infrequently meant the people of a district, although such usage was becoming more common. Raymond Williams commented that from the nineteenth century the meaning of 'community' in 'the sense of immediacy or locality was strongly developed in the context of larger and more complex industrial societies'.[6] Use of the word 'community' has evolved markedly over the past two and a half centuries, to become associated with modern debates on education, crime, health and welfare, discussion of shared values or meanings, and issues of personal identity. Modern understandings of 'community' encompass earlier handling of the word but often take on the meaning of 'neighbourhood' or a restricted spatial entity ('the parish community', 'community watch') or of culture or religion ('the Sikh community'). It can mean a community of occupations or interests, as in 'the scholarly community', or 'the farming community'. Or the term may cover people of shared consumer, sexual or recreational preferences. As we have seen, residence can be irrelevant in some modern usages of 'community', applying as they often do to 'thin' or 'invisible' networks. Examples of modern English discourse can be much extended, in some cases rendering the word completely open or utopian: 'the international community', a globalized meaning that is not as modern as some believe, as we will see in Chapter 4.[7]

Given such conceptual changes and diverse uses, it is crucial to limit terminological discussion in this chapter to the main sources 'from below' upon which it is based, relating them to the broader issues of this book. Otherwise analysis becomes nebulous and unclear in its evidence. My concern in this chapter is with the key terms of home and belonging, friends and community, among the English poor. It is important to understand the labouring poor's own vocabularies, mindsets and priorities. What or who did they feel they belonged to? How did they think about that entity, or network, or community? Did they have a clear notion of 'community' and attachment to home parish, even when far away? Or were their networks and familiarities more opportunist, loose, and in employment terms one-to-one and immediate? Faced with poverty, short-term tenures, pressure from landlords and threats of eviction from home and parish, how was it possible for the poor to conceive of 'home'? What networks of friendship or support might they depend on? How isolated, or community-dependent, were they? Such questions are persistently posed of modern and so-called 'traditional' societies in the extensive sociological literature, with its evolving generalizations about *Gemeinschaft* and *Gesellschaft*,[8] and ideas about transition from 'traditional' to modern or 'postmodern' forms of 'community'. Sources like these poor's narratives allow us to extend historical discussion, to survey people from the most populous classes during British industrialization and to consider how their notions and experiences inform important debates about community and belonging.

The strength of local attachments and belonging was very manifest among the poor in the eighteenth and nineteenth centuries. These are persistent themes in John Clare's writing. They recur constantly in cultures of local xenophobia, and they were often commented upon. The Revd Anthony Huxtable, for example, was rector of Sutton Waldron, near Shaftesbury in Dorset, a poor law guardian, farmer, and a witness before the 1847 Select Committee on Settlement and Poor Removal. He stressed the importance of the settlement laws to the poor and discussed people's local attachments in Dorset. Among the questions asked him was whether it was desirable to abolish the settlement laws, by which people became eligible for poor relief through 'belonging' to particular parishes. He felt that such repeal might broaden labourers' horizons. 'On the other hand', he said,

> the objection that presented itself to me was this, whether it would not loosen that interest which landlords now feel with regard to their parishioners, and dissolve those ties which bind persons brought up in a certain place, the

> remains perhaps of the feudal system, at all events local attachment, whether a national settlement would not tend entirely to abolish that … I think in their heart of hearts they do very much think of their parish. I had a letter the other day from a poor person who has not been in Sutton for 30 years, and it was marked with the strongest sentiment of parochial attachment. The feeling they have is, that it is their home; go where they will they have a home … I think that is owing to the parochial system, parochial attachments … There is a deep feeling about their native place, and they do feel a strong attachment to it.[9]

The Revd Huxtable stressed belonging to the parish as 'home', and such terms were used repeatedly in correspondence. This was true of the poor's letters to their 'home' parishes, or of how the poor were discussed by the officers who dealt with them, and tried to make the parishes they belonged to pay for them. 'Belonging' and 'home' were everyday administrative terms. They stemmed from the post-1662 settlement and poor laws, and their many antecedents, a legal framework structuring belonging and entitlement, and from ancillary customs, precedents, local xenophobia and folklore. I have discussed these at length elsewhere.[10] A legal settlement meant the place where one was eligible for poor relief. 'The place of settlement is the place to which a person "belongs". *To* such a place he may be removed; *from* such a place he may not be removed,' wrote E. J. Lidbetter as late as 1932 in a handbook for public assistance officers.[11] Nelson, Burn and many other earlier authorities would have accepted this statement. My aim here is to analyse key presumptions about settled belonging and community that the letters and narratives of the poor contain.

Home and belonging

We think of 'home' today in many ways: as one's country and in relation to patriotism; as a residence, the base for a family; and as property, whether rented or owned. Some people have an idea of a home town or home community, and this is buttressed by themes in popular culture and song. Occasionally some think of a 'home village', though that is perhaps not common in a country as urbanized and mobile as modern Britain. Some think of a 'home parish', but that notion may seem too implicitly religious in an Anglican sense for many people. Home in many ways is a symbol of variously understood community.[12] It is often proprietorial as a modern concept, relating to the housing of a nuclear family or single person, and the extension of home ownership in the 1980s and 1990s accentuated this.

By comparison, few among the eighteenth- or nineteenth-century poor owned their housing or home. Almost by definition they did not. Had they done so their entitlement to poor relief might have been questioned, even though owning immoveable property was one way of gaining a legal settlement. To judge from their narratives, they had two overlapping notions of 'home'. There was first the idea of 'home' as the 'homestead', usually meaning the dwelling, sometimes the place where that was, a term taken with them to British colonies, and which was domiciled there more effectively than in England. The term had slightly more connotation of a base, a place occupied, the wherewithal of an 'occupation' and a family economy in the older sense of a home/workplace than its modern equivalent. It was otherwise similar to modern understandings. It is found in some poor narratives, although it is not that widespread there.[13] In the uses of the poor, it often simply meant the base for a family 'home' that they strove not to break up. In so-called polite culture it was also sometimes linked to ideas of the 'cottage', 'cottager', and to the aesthetic of the picturesque.[14] Much cultural evidence attests to such notions of homestead, and this would include figures like Thomas Bewick, Thomas Gainsborough, William Wordsworth, Thomas Gisborne, William Cobbett, Henry Longfellow, Richard Jefferies and many others writing in the English-speaking world. And secondly, more significant here, was the idea of 'home' as one's parish or township, in the sense of the Revd Huxtable, meaning where one's legal settlement was: where one had attained or earned the status that might make one eligible for poor relief.

Both these concepts of 'home' were found in pauper letters and related narratives, and the concept of home as one's parish of legal settlement was pervasive. William King wrote back to Braintree from London in 1834: 'Perhaps Sir I May have to Coum Home and tis a Pleaseing Reflection Mixed with Humble thankfulness that I have Ever Such an Asylum My old Birth Place till then Sirs I Must Beg and Rely on your United feelings of Kindness and Help.'[15] Samuel Hearsum wrote from St Marylebone to Chelmsford in 1824, about how he might have to apply 'to Marylebone Parish to Pass me home', by way of removal, as he was in great distress.[16] Charlotte May, writing from Brighton to the overseer at Worth in 1820, complained that

> I am Still Reman in this Deplorable Stat Extremely ill unable to do anything for Myself and famyly and that Wretched husband has not been near me to bring me one farthing Since last Saturday fortnight. I [would] not have trouble you if I had the means to have brought myself and famyly home have not any Other home. Please to Send means to come home or arange some plan you think Mos Advisable.

She signed her letter 'your Unfortunate parisoner Charlotte May' and was in fear of being thought a vagrant.[17]

Another example was Davey and Susannah Rising. They wrote from Halstead to the Chelmsford overseers in 1824, saying that they were in distress, requesting money to be sent them: 'and if you most wordy Gentellmen Do not think proper to Answer our needy Request we must Be Brought home For wheare no money Can Be Earnt no Living Cannot Be had'.[18] William Webb in Ipswich wrote to Braintree saying that 'The Kellsey Peop[le] are now expecting me home … you must do as you Please aboaut sending me home.'[19] Thomas Pole wrote from Cambridge in 1808 to a Leicestershire parish, complaining that 'Everry thing is So Dear I Must Send them [his wife and child] home as my Wife is Now in the famley way a gane and I Must Be allways out in the Cuntry.'[20] Thomas and Ann Cooper in Woolwich addressed the overseer in Chelmsford in 1825, pointing out that Thomas was very ill and out of work 'and in a decline and we must come home for we have nothing here to subsist upon'. They wanted to know whether they should apply to Woolwich parish 'to be past [passed] home' with their four children, or whether their parish would send them some money to enable them to come home of their own accord.[21] Ann Hitchcock wrote from Feering (Essex) to the churchwardens and overseers of Braintree in 1823: 'Gentlemen if I am to Come Home you must let me know for I may as Well come as stop hear to be starved for my Boys cannot get no work so how am I to do But if I come home you will have to buy me Goodes for if I have to come home my Creators Will tak my goodes and chatels for money due To them.'[22] Pauper letters include countless examples of such wording. The conjunction of my home/your parish was sometimes made use of, hinting at the tensions between the words: at subtle and multiple understandings relating to rights, ownership, rates, power relations and financial consequences: 'I am fearful I shall be under the obligation of coming home to your parish.'[23] Almost every word in that statement brims over with significant meanings.

These paupers expressed a firm notion of home, equated to the legal settlement that they had variously earned and which qualified them for poor relief under the old and new poor laws. The term 'home' was so ubiquitous that one must conclude that such a parish-centred idea of 'home' as one's own settlement parish was deeply rooted in language and mentality, making it as important as any encoding or experience of social distinctions. It reflected an absolutely key concept of self and identity. Yet there were also gradations of belonging, nuances that one can see in personal languages of memory, entitlement, reminder, importunacy or threat, sometimes influenced by how they obtained their settlement.

People spoke of 'my parish', 'your parish', 'my husband's parish' and so on. These legally buttressed ideas were then coloured by senses of belonging through shared memories, reputation, family, ancestry, employment, previous residence and the like, which had no influence if they fell beyond the legal 'heads' of settlement.[24] These meanings were all affected by age and life history, varying accordingly. It was an irony of a legal system of settlement loosely fitted to life-cycle possibilities, that many people 'belonged' to a distant parish through some remote settlement-endowing event (say a yearly service in their teens), and thereafter 'belonged' there with far more *legal* right than many who resided in that parish all their lives, and yet had never managed to gain a settlement there. This irony may inform some of the tone and hesitancy of pauper letters. It must also have affected overseers' replies, which in some parishes remain more closed to us than pauper voices have been.[25] Long-term familiarity did not necessarily count for much under this system. For these poor narratives remind us that settlement law (especially between the Settlement Act of 1662 and the Poor Removal Act of 1846),[26] with its endowment of a settlement status to everybody regardless of residence, could thus disengage obligations of neighbourliness and senses of community that might flow from being neighbours. It must have muted local philanthropic incentives to provide assistance beyond formal poor law kinds. For by constructing group or individual identities among parish residents which were based on their specific legal settlements, on their understood places of belonging (i.e. many people living among us in this place are legally settled elsewhere), it must to some extent have fractured communities and shored up internal rivalries and loyalties, perhaps historically comparable to the unintended consequences of some forms of identity politics today.[27]

Clearly 'home' meant nuanced things to different people, despite its clear settlement-law meaning. There was a huge range of biographical and regional circumstances, evident in poor narratives and settlement examinations, influencing the tone of language and correspondence. There were also gendered variations. After all, men usually 'earned' their settlement, as did single women, via yearly service, apprenticeship and the like; yet married women simply took their husband's parish, which they may never even have visited, and thus sacrificed their maiden settlement or 'home'. Settlement therefore was often deeply problematical for women who upon marriage risked losing their rights in a known place where many of their relatives resided. It certainly influenced female marriage decisions about who, where and when to marry, though the demographic and social dimensions of this point have never been explored. And marriage in the wife's parish, followed by residence in the husband's parish, was customary, increasingly so in the eighteenth and early nineteenth centuries.[28] The full implications of these points for local attachment, belonging and senses of 'home' remain to be explored, inviting close gendered analysis of poor narratives.

Nor did 'home' always have associations of endearment: 'I hope you will send the above sum or I shall be under the very unpleasant necessity of coming home to Peterborough.'[29] There was no affection or nostalgia here in thinking about one's home community! The thoughts about being passed 'home' were also often phrased in wording of 'coming down', as in these examples from different letters: 'thay would sand us doun'; 'I must by som meens com doun to you'; 'my son charles soundy that was doune with you'; 'I and my famely was sant doun by them'; 'he will cum down to you'; Battersea 'will sand them doun'.[30] This common phrasing often accompanied a sense of coming 'down' from an urban to a lesser or rural place. And money sent from Rayleigh to London was written as 'to Send my monay up'.[31] 'Home' was thus a term of parish attachment, an idea of legal entitlement, a welfare security, a firm yet mutable and probably gendered concept that people carried in their minds when they left it, perhaps a place looked down upon as less urban or advantageous in other regards, as well as being a rhetorical phrase that helped to extract non-resident relief.[32] Certainly the parish 'home' was a place they could return to in hard times, or possibly obtain relief from, even when they were many miles away.

Related to this use of 'home', an explicit language of 'belonging' was also very prominent in pauper letters. Jacob Brown wrote to Great Bardfield to let them know that Laindon-cum-Basildon was 'agoon to bring me and my wife and seven children home to bardfield', even though 'i always will stand by it that i belong to the parish of landon and nother'.[33] Contested settlements like this were commonplace. They caused much worry for those among the poor who were unclear about their legal settlement and could find themselves at the centre of disputes between different parishes. Samuel Spooner wrote in 1828 from Norwich to the overseer of Braintree that 'On account of the scarcity to work I am obliged to apply to the parish to which I belong … we are in extreme distress.' Some months later he wrote again, pointing out that his allowance was insufficient, and so he had caused his family 'to be forwarded to the parish they belong'.[34] William King pointed out to the overseer in Braintree that 'we Do Not Blong to Bethnal Green' and continued: 'I Humbly Beg the Gentlemen to Remember there old Townsman.' Others wrote repeatedly about 'My Parrish', conveying the same sentiment and legal attachment.[35]

This language of 'home' and belonging was also shared by parish administrators. They used the same terms as the poor, and, while there are nuances of socially different meanings, they were clearly part of the same speech community in this respect. Of course, their attitudes to settlement and senses of 'home' were socially and parochially specific, and there was often dispute over whether someone 'belonged'. Higher social ranks had other criteria in mind as well when they considered 'belonging' in respect to themselves. Property, lineage, heraldry, intramural church burial and so on were issues and markers for those ranks, separating them from the poor. Yet with regard to the poor and their administration, there was no conflict between social ranks over what 'home' and 'belonging' legally meant. A representative of the Chelmsford parish vestry visited one pauper in London and wrote back to Chelmsford saying that 'I think 1s. pr week would prevent him from coming home.'[36] This parish language of 'home' was routinely used by overseers and parish clerks. The overseer of Falmer, for example, writing to the overseers of Worth, discussed the state of a pauper and said that 'he should go home to his Parish'.[37] The Battersea vestry clerk wrote to the churchwardens and overseers of Pangbourne (Berkshire) in the winter of 1819 about a pauper woman unable to support her family, asking 'wether you would wish us to bring them home'.[38] Home here clearly meant the home parish, the parish of settlement. Wandsworth wrote to Pangbourne, saying 'I presume you will prefer this mode of relief [non-resident relief]; to their being sent home by an order of removal, and thereby being entirely chargeable to your parish.'[39] The meaning was the same. A Mildenhall overseer wrote to Thrapston in 1829 about an elderly 'poor and industrious' couple, now 'quite incapable their work is completely done more honest and deserving people we have not in our own parish … you must make an advance in their pay or they must be sent home I think the old man may live but a very short time'.[40] In Manchester, in 1831, we find the overseer writing to Uttoxeter about John Jumps and his family: 'he belongs to your place … give us an Order to relieve them on your account or we shall be obliged to send them home to you'.[41] The use of the word 'place' here indicates the greater variation of settlement unit in northern England, where it might more commonly be a township as well as a parish.[42] The same language of 'home' appears in other areas of parish administration. For example, a minute concerning a bastardy case against Springfield parish in 1830 stated that 'they offered the W[oman] 2s a week and 20s to take her home to Berks – and so setteled'.[43] Coupled with this idea of 'home' was the language of 'belonging', ubiquitous among the poor, and also used much higher in the social scale. It was, for example, routinely mentioned by legal counsel in settlement cases, as by Mr Burnaby in Leicester in 1819: 'His son of course belongs to you and you must provide for him accordingly.'[44]

In other words, this was a pervasive language of 'home' and belonging, found across the social scale. It was used by paupers and parish administrators alike. Among the poor, regardless of their gender, it meant 'home' as one's legal settlement, safeguard, recourse and the place of presumed rights. Among ratepayers and overseers, with historical echoes from earlier concepts of ownership and ideas about property, it denoted the place bound to maintain people in need through its rates, to which another parish or township could pass unwanted burdens.

Friends

The concept of 'friends' was very frequently mentioned in pauper letters and narratives of the poor. 'Friends' today refers to a range of personally liked people who we associate with. The *Oxford English Dictionary* gives as its first meaning: 'One joined to another in mutual benevolence and intimacy. Not ordinarily applied to lovers or relatives.' Subsequent meanings encompass the latter possibilities, however: 'A kinsman or near relation. Now only in *pl.* (one's) relatives, kinsfolk, "people".' It adds that this is the only sense in the Scandinavian languages, which is interesting in relation to earlier English usage. We should note that in Scotland today, as in Ireland in the 1930s,[45] the meaning can also extend to a relative, and this was true more widely in the past. The word could also mean 'A lover or paramour, of either sex', a meaning that has been extended in modern 'girlfriend' or 'boyfriend' phraseology.

'Friends' were fundamental to family and networks. An example is the eighteenth-century political discourse of 'friends' meaning political associates. Thus one reads of 'the Friends of Lord Trentham'.[46] Or there was the related usage meaning supportive electors. 'Friends' was applied to the supporters of John Wilkes. It could apply to the associates of Clubs, or to 'friends' or members of religious societies, as with the Quakers or Society of Friends, or as with the formal 'friends' (sympathizers) of the Moravian Church.[47] Patrons of institutions like hospitals might be termed 'friends'. Another common usage was the customers of a business – for example, the widow of a tinman 'humbly hopes her Friends will continue their former Favours'.[48] The term included family in our senses today (fairly close relatives), and in the past it encompassed a wider array of connected people as well. Thus, for example, Jessy Harden in Brathay near Lake Windermere wrote in her diary about the visiting artist John Constable that he 'chose the profession of an Artist against the inclination of his friends, at least so he says, & I don't doubt him'.[49] Given well-known biographical details, 'friends' in Constable's case clearly included his parents. One can also find the master and family into which an apprentice was indentured being described as his or her 'friends'. We notice that the body of a suicide was 'sent home to her friends', and see here the use of 'home' as well.[50] Somewhat lower down the social scale, one reads about executed felons that the bodies were 'carried off by their Friends'.[51] Finally – and could one fall any lower than this sad case? – there was 'A poor Man without either Money or Friends', found dead in the winter in Tyburn Road, 'although he had cover'd himself over with Dung and loose Litter'.[52]

Modern sociologists (notably Ray Pahl) have studied 'friendship' or 'friends' in the modern sense, while being aware of earlier wider meanings.[53] However, relatives or lovers were widely called 'friends' in the eighteenth and nineteenth centuries in England and in English-speaking areas of Wales. 'Friends' in the language of the poor, as well as among the circles of poor law and charity administrators, meant a group of friends similar to our modern sense (albeit with many contextual differences), *and/or* a circle of close relatives, *and/or* a lover or seducer. These concepts were blended together in the usage of the poor and of poor law administrators. While the idea of a friend as lover, seducer or sexual client was less apparent among higher social classes, those classes used the term 'friends' in such a way when relaying the words of the poor. For example, 'Walter' in *My Secret Life*, describing his sexual behaviour in the mid-nineteenth century, and keeping close and seemingly authentic notes of female speech, depicts women having sex for money as calling their regular clients 'friends'.[54] He did not reciprocate that usage – he did not call those women *his* 'friends', although he was very enamoured of some of them. Among the poor, *all* these wider meanings of 'friends' were frequent, such that close definition of what was meant is often hard to discover. This can be both illuminating and frustrating to historians who wish to address modern debates about the meanings and function of friendship and associated networks.

Some of the key issues about friendship, which need to be set into historical perspective, are these. Their relevance to narratives of the poor will be immediately apparent. Friends are a form of informal solidarity, which some now see as increasingly supplanting earlier types of social solidarity and support, including the family in various respects. In pauper narratives, especially for the migrant poor faced with relatively low levels of social cohesion or its complete collapse, there is the issue of the respective roles of friends *vis-à-vis* relatives. Did friendship take over from the family or home community in situations of displacement or poverty? What was the *utility* of friendship, and how did that and perceptions of it vary by social class, gender, region or other factors? How were friendships affected by one's 'character', or one's repute or 'social capital' in modern terminology,[55] and how should the latter be described for the poor in this period?

Tendencies towards isolation and personal disintegration, diagnosed by some sociologists as earlier networks, communities and mutualities become weaker in modern societies, raise questions as to whether friends serve as replacements. It is increasingly argued that they can and do. Modern forms of communication, developing from and beyond letters, assist the establishment and proliferation of friendships, which are often now weakly situated geographically. Isolation and despair are very evident in many pauper narratives. And paupers were often feebly integrated into labour markets, with implications for their senses of class, connectedness, networks and income. Many narratives mention the breakdown of relations with an employer, the effort to re-establish such relations, and the problems caused by distances, whether from 'home', settlement parish, employers, 'friends' or relatives. Pauper letters themselves were a form of relatedness, but of a different kind from the personal relations most of the poor were familiar with. This raises surprisingly modern questions about their functions for those who were disembedded from their legally assumed face-to-face 'community'. That term 'disembedded' originates from Anthony Giddens. It was used by him to describe a situation of late modernity in which social activities are separated from local milieux, replaced by extended spaces and time frames: by situations of high mobility and extensive communication, which have displaced local communities of trust and mutual reliance, situations in which people have been removed from earlier immediate contexts, construct long-stranded and thin relationships, and are thus 'disembedded'. A theorist such as Giddens of course takes such a condition to pertain to more recent circumstances than those faced by the eighteenth- and nineteenth-century poor.[56]

However, the 'late modernity' of such a predicament may be questionable, especially in view of pauper letters. After all, in these letters one constantly sees assumptions and forms of behaviour that are thought by many sociologists to be 'modern' and non-traditional or even 'post-modern'. One thinks of the theme of belonging at a distance without propinquity, ideas of 'community' without constraints of place, the 'disembedding' from locality, the isolation of the individual. These were predicaments that were accentuated in some ways by industrialization, given the personal mobility that it could trigger, although they certainly pre-dated that process. They parallel in more atomized form the disconnected, often stranded 'communities' of the Quakers or the Moravians and the individual migration between them. In short, how should historians judge the quality or novelty of relatedness, whether by letter, or to 'friends', or to any apparent 'community', as shown in these poor narratives? How did the poor themselves judge this? And what is the significance of these forms of relatedness in a larger historical and sociological narrative?

Let us take examples of usage from narratives of the poor. I will initially refer to the petitions to admit children to the London Foundling Hospital in the second half of the eighteenth century. These petitions were usually made by the mothers, who needed also to show that they were 'proper objects of charity'. If accepted as such, they were balloted, and if a white ball was drawn on their behalf their child was admitted.[57] The women came from many regions in England and sometimes beyond. Some had recently arrived in London. The often poorly literate petitions tell their stories of seduction, distress, previous employment, baby's birth and related matters. They also frequently explain some details of the mother's current familial and social circumstances: whether she has relatives or 'friends' and how she is placed in respect of them.

These letters or petitions are more extensive than the quoted selections and contain vivid accounts of hardship and misfortune. However, my concern here is strictly with their language of 'friends' and relatives. Frances Dawson, for example, wrote in 1763 of how she was 'a poor Destresed young Woman drawn [?] to Grate necesety Evan to want by having a Child and the Father gone a Broad and no Friends to assist hur and that she has ben Drove to grate hardships for a Long time'. Mary Jones had been 'oblidged to leave her friends' because of her pregnancy, following the father of her baby to London. Mary Gill begged in 1770 to have her case taken into consideration, as she was 'Reduced and left void of friends Exclusive of a Friend with whom I lodge and to whom I made my case known of the hardships I have undergone even for want of all common Necessary's of life they have taken a little Compassion so as to give me a Little Assistance just to keep me from Starving'. Mary Chilman in 1770 asked the 'Dear Gentleman take Pity an releive me of my Poor Infant as I have not a Friend in the world.' She claimed that she was 'Belonging to no Parish or if I did I would not Impose on your good Charity'. Elizabeth Turpin 'laboureth … without Friends or money'. One petitioner wrote on behalf of a female infant whose mother had died, and he explained in 1770 that he and his wife 'could have no further Intelligence of any Friends belonging to Her'.[58]

Friends were people from whom one might hope for assistance. Mary Chapman was 'indebted to her Friends by the Expences which have been lately occasioned by her Laying in', while Ann Phillips in 1781 complained about the 'father being Gon and Left me and [my baby] without any Suport had it not Been for a Friend where I now am I with my Infant Had Been in Great Distress'.[59] Other women wrote in the 1770s and early 1780s of 'having no Friends to assist me in this deplorable Case', or 'being destitute of Friends', or of being 'in the deepest distress and having no friends', or of having 'not either a Friend or a penny of Money in the World', or of 'having a Child Without Eyther friends or any Person to Support me or my infant'. Some wrote of 'Friends not being able to Continue their Assistance', or of being 'in a most deplorable Condition and destitute of relief & friends', linking relief or assistance with the existence of friends, hoping for relief to those 'who are friendless & Distressed'. Susannah Alfred, 'being Sedused & not being able to provide for my Child', had 'no Friend nor Acquaintance that can be of any service to me, which has caus'd my Misfortunes to fall more heavier upon me'. In some cases, friends were a long way away, including a widower 'having the Infant [his wife] bore … his frds far off and unable to assist & Parish 200 Miles from'. Advice also seems to have been taken from friends. Jane Bowring was deserted by the father of her child and was presumed to have gone to sea 'to avoid Marrying her or keeping the Child'. She 'has no other Means of Supporting the Child which is a Boy but by a Parish or your kind Charity wou'd wish the later as she & her friends thinks they are better taken care of both in Manners and Morrals'.[60]

Concepts of shame and subsequent isolation frequently appear in these petitions, as in some other narratives of the poor. This bears upon cultures of respectability among the poor. Some women alluded to the shame that pregnancy had brought upon them, and how it had affected their connections with friends: 'As shame prevented me from applying to my friends who indeed are a great way off and might be a Means of Breaking my poor Mothers Heart if she knew of my Unhappy Situation.' Mary Smith commented in 1770 about how she would 'be expos'd to Shame amongst her Friends', while Elizabeth Skilling wrote about how she 'dare not to see my frinds which makes me Solliciate your favours'. Another woman wrote in 1771 of how 'her friends in Consequence of her Imprudent Conduct have Turned Their Backs on her and her Infant'. The importance of a woman's 'character' was often shown, and that 'character' was clearly something that affected a woman's dealings with friends as well as her employment prospects. Character seems to have related to a person's social milieu, to her or his friends and associates, as well as being a feature in a reference for employers. A 'character' was often given by employers, but the use of the term extended beyond their way of labelling servants, to general social repute, that is to a wider community meaning, and for women it often involved simple dichotomies of 'good' or 'bad' character. As this source focuses on women, it is unclear how gendered understandings of 'character' were. To a considerable extent character pertained to locality, to where a person might be known and reputed. In that sense 'character' speaks to us about the nature of 'community'. However, it does seem to have related above all to employment – that is to an important but fairly narrow tie among possible relationships. 'She can have a good Character provided she can got rid of this Burthen I will be enabled to get her living in Service as she did before having no Friends to give her any Assistance.'[61]

'Friends' were often closely linked to relatives in the letters. In 1772 Jane Brown applied 'to all my Frinds and Relations in general & to no purpose, can see no other prospect but that misery must befal me for want of even common necessaries'. Mary Browne 'was Seduced by a fair Promise of Marriage & her Seducer has now left her with a young Child & in great distress & not in any Capacity to support itt & knowns not where to find the seducer & on this Occasion her Relations & Friends will give her no Countenance'.[62] It is clear that 'friends' could also mean relatives, and some petitions seem to make that explicit. Margaret Cartwright died an hour after giving birth to twins, and she 'had no Friend or/ Relation but a Sistaer who is married to a Man that works hard for his livelihood, & not in a condition to give them any assistance'.[63] The father of Elizabeth Matlock's baby left her 'quite Destitute of all Support besides rendering me incapable of discharging what Expences my Lying inn cased which inevitably had been my ruin, had it been for … the kind Asisstance of my Brother … [who] can no longer support me in my Distress, therefore having no other Friends to Assist me in this my Miserable Situation'. The term could also mean the man who had fathered the baby in question, as was indicated by Mary Spice in 1781: 'I have had the Misfortune to be left by my Friend a most Distress'd Situation with an Infant to Support which God Knows I am not at Present Capable of Earning Bread to Eat.'[64]

Another source often mentioning friends are the narratives taken down by the secretary to the Refuge for the Destitute in London, which was established initially in Lambeth in 1804 and later moved to Shoreditch. These narratives, petitions or letters of recommendation are from the Minute Books of the Refuge. Many have been edited by Peter King and published for the period 1812–27, especially for female applicants.[65] They usually involved an interview with the potential inmate or applicant for relief. Unlike pauper letters, or many petitions to the London Foundling Hospital, they are not in the direct words of the poor but are transcribed statements close to personal narratives, having been summarized into literate and formal English, often seeming to be in the same sequence as the spoken account. Once again, there were many references to 'friends', partly because the Refuge saw the usefulness of such people after the applicant's reformation or relief. The senses of friends here were very similar to those discussed above. Some people were said to be 'completely destitute of friends'. Ann Taylor 'does not seem to have any friends & … she is destitute of every means of support'. With regard to Ann Williams, 'of the Parish of Abergavenny', it was written 'She asserts that all her friends are dead in Wales; that she has no friend, to whom she can look for assistance … that she has been a Prostitute about 2 months & does not think herself free from disease.' Diane Crowe objected to going back to Newcastle in 1812, 'on account of having no friends remaining in her native place'. We see here an attempt to make the non-existence of friends in a particular place take priority over geographical belonging and legal settlement. This was an inevitable issue under the settlement laws, especially for women who might never have been to their settlement, as they took the husband's settlement. In some cases friends were dispersed, as we would expect to find today. However, the idea of friends being concentrated in certain places prevailed, as with 'a young woman, by the name of Cherry … whose friends reside at Clapham'.[66]

It was written about Mary Pannafer in 1815 that 'She has no friends, to whom she can look for any help, the Father, mother & Brothers being buried at Shotley', in Suffolk. Here again we can see the conflation of friends with close relatives. It was said in 1815 of Susannah Yarnell that 'She has no friend, but a Brother.' Elizabeth Gilbert was brought up by her aunt and uncle. After having been 'seduced from service … she made known to her friends where she was who fetched her home [in 1820]. Her aunt says, she has been at home about six weeks, since she left her evil courses.' The same friends/relatives equation occurs in respect of a late middle-aged man named Mr Cresswell, who stated in 1819 that 'he was formerly a merchant near Manchester, was unfortunate in business & was under the Necessity of coming to London for the sake of living under the Protection of his friends (sons)'.[67]

Links between a person's character and the existence of friends, as with the admissions to the London Foundling Hospital, were often made. John Daws, aged 22 in 1821, was 'without character & friends', the one seemingly presupposing the other. Kitty Harrison in 1812 found that her adultery 'alienated her from her … friends, who would now probably have supported her'. Catherine Gilchrist has 'so grossly misconducted herself as to forfeit the protection of all her friends'. A young black woman called Sarah Holmes, said to be a native of Grenada, had 'left the West Indies & entered on board of a Ship in man's attire, on account of a disappointment in love, where she has been for many years & has lately acted as Cook & Steward. Suspecting her Sex to have been discovered at Gravesend lately, she made her escape to Chatham, where she unfolded her real character to an old Woman of Color'; and now (in 1813) she needed to 'be received into a place of retirement for a time & her character should turn out to be correct, she & her friends would provide for her'.[68]

Many of the presumptions and usages of these sources were similar to those found in pauper letters. Here is Sophia Curchin writing from Wisbech to the overseers of Thrapston in 1826:

> I do not no one friend to help me there but I hope you will be so kind as to assist me & not let me be lost as I am willing to come home if there goodness think well or have them assisting here … if I am to come home it must be in a short time or I dare not venture … I am all anxiety and more unhappy than anyone can think for at seeing so much trouble before me but I hope the Almighty will find me friends as I am sure friends at Thrapston have been kind I hope they will not forget.[69]

This shows the same language of 'home' and 'friends', a usage consistent with other poor narratives. Very occasionally, the use of 'friends' was extended to include the 'Gentlemen' or the overseer.[70] At least one pauper wrote using the word 'friend' seemingly to mean a settled resident pauper in the parish poor house: 'I suppose they [the Parish] would sooner give their friend in the House 4s6d and would not think so much about that as they do to allow me 1s6d.'[71] But this use was peevish, possibly ironic, and seems uncommon. Very rarely, one glimpses the possibility that 'friends' might refer to others from the parish, hinting at a sense of a parish-defined community of friendship, but this is uncertain and open to other meanings: 'If any Rochford friend comes this way I beg leave to say I live at Mr Hustley near Rushbrook Hall two miles off Bury.'[72] Despite strong senses of parochial attachment, it seems doubtful that the poor conceived of 'friends' strictly as fellow parishioners or as those sharing their legal settlement, and the idea of 'friends' as encompassing relatives would support that, for relatives would be scattered beyond the parish.

Of course, like any other evidence, these narrative sources have their respective and complex biases, and some of them were more or less prone to allude to the existence of friends as support networks. The evidence from the Foundling Hospital and Refuge for the Destitute has been deliberately incorporated here, partly to extend documentary range to three main sources, but also to draw attention to a feature of pauper letters. Those letters – normally letters from the poor about provision of relief from their parishes of settlement – are perhaps by their nature disinclined to mention other links or supportive possibilities. Writers stressed ties to their parish of settlement. Thus reference to 'home' as that parish, and attendant wording of parish loyalty, deference to 'the Gentlemen', and the like, tended to feature strongly. Ironically this occurred even though they were away from 'home' and thus by their actions and migration among the *least* loyal to the parish. Reference to alternative support, notably friends and/or relatives (if these were extra-parochial), was less conspicuous, although one may envisage circumstances where they would be emphasized. For example, a person requesting non-resident relief might wish to point out that the place where s/he now lived was one where s/he had friends, who might assist the writer, and that point could be used as a further argument to extract non-resident relief. 'I Certainly Can Do with Less here than I Could Do with Down in Staffordshire for I have a number of very Good friends here which would help me & had it not have been for them I should have Been very Much in want.'[73] Removing such a person from those support networks would probably increase the parochial burden, a thought that would add to other considerations about the availability of work elsewhere compared with the 'home' parish. By contrast, the existence of 'friends at home', so to speak, raised the prospect for parish overseers of making those 'friends' contribute towards a person's maintenance, even though they could only achieve that legally if the 'friend' was a spouse, parent, grandparent or child of the pauper.[74] This could be a parish vestry argument against giving non-resident relief, and most pauper letter writers would surely be aware of that. Was it wise, one might wonder, to have friends at home or to allude to them? For such reasons these sources need to be handled carefully as evidence on belonging, 'friends' and 'community'. They speak to these concepts, and they strongly assert ideas of home and belonging. They make countless allusions to friends or their absence. Yet they do this while seeking aid when vulnerable. If one wanted non-resident relief, the balance to be drawn between stressing one's legal settlement and entitlement, establishing ties of deference to 'the gentlemen', but not drawing much attention to one's home-based friends, was a delicate and subtle one, albeit one that could often be achieved by semi-literate paupers.

Conclusion

'Community' is liable to multiple meanings, and it is implied in the terms 'home', 'belonging' and 'friends'. Judging from the literature on this concept in the past, and alleged losses of it today, an extensive academic world, in a rivalry of interpretations, would expect to find it in *this* historical period, in the lives of *these* poor people. Among more eligible English historical meanings, the term 'community' could involve a spectrum of ranks in a localized society, either sharing residential space or encompassing an ensemble of people linked via shared legal settlement regardless of their residences. Or it might be thought of more narrowly as a community of ratepayers, *ipso facto* legally settled, termed 'the neighbours' in some eighteenth-century English parishes, represented by the financial policies of the overseer and vestry, who necessarily had to extend certain privileges and modes of maintenance to legally settled people. One could debate the nuances of social inclusion in any such definition. And inevitably, different sources lead one to varied emphases in historical understanding of the term.

How does the concept of community emerge through analysis of poor narratives? These sources were personal appeals to one person or a narrow clique, yet they persistently refer to ideas of belonging and incorporation. They differ from many other sources. Emigrants' letters, for example, were often read aloud in homes, pubs, chapels and even from Anglican pulpits, perhaps in a persuasive manner. Those letters from 'our emigrants' often had a communal as well as a familial spirit, expressing wide goodwill, asking questions about other people, albeit frequently seeking to persuade others to depart permanently from a community. In many other sources collective or occupational identities emerge, such that one is drawn to talk of parish, occupational or religious communities. One thinks of Luddite letters or some anonymous letters of protest,[75] even though these attack certain people. Or there were Primitive Methodist obituaries in the *Primitive Methodist Magazine*, with their mentions of people gathered in stern purpose or of conversion and devoted amity with others in the faith. Despite evidence of the excluded, disliked or stigmatized, sources indicating working-class collectivism and 'customs in common' have been extolled by E. P. Thompson and others, to point to organization and apparent unity, with confirmatory implications for a growing sense of working-class 'community' spirit during industrialization.[76]

Community is represented differently in poor narratives. The authors usually appear isolated, dependent upon a few friends – if not abandoned by their friends – having a history of disparate services with particular individuals or families, where the relationship has been almost one-to-one, much like their epistolary relationship with the parish overseer. That overseer stood like St Peter at the portals of the parish community, admitting some, blocking others, always testing eligibility. He was in some ways the arbitrator of local memory, a man who could manipulate a transactive or pooled community memory;[77] and this was a memory that also involved judgements of a moral and legal kind. It was a memory that could be in the interests of ratepayers, keen to minimize settlement-derived claims upon their rates. It could also be in the interests of the parish poor, eager to minimize competition for limited parochial goods. Yet the office of overseer was an annual one, its holder often changing; and many paupers living elsewhere, like Elizabeth Manning in Islington in 1829, worried that letters 'might be sent to the wrong person not knowing who is Overseer now'.[78] And the overseer in some cases declined to answer letters, resulting in a pauper's writing becoming ever more despairing or even angry. The sense of belonging for such people was not being recognized by their home community: they were out on a limb, discarded, unacknowledged and the tie unreciprocated. They might be cut out of local memory, discarded spirits of the parochial past, even via a cynical collective denial of their personal memory. This would be a severe shock to their sense of long-term commitments and obligations, and indeed to their entire identity, as a void yawned where they had felt they belonged.[79] Furthermore, structures of a parish community could endure, as is often the case in other small institutions, but the personnel could change markedly, such that in human terms the parish no longer seemed recognizable. Given turnover rates of 40–60 per cent every ten or so years, a parish's people might seem to change almost entirely over a few decades.[80] Upon removal under the settlement laws paupers' belonging or legal 'home' might be fought over at Quarter Sessions by two parishes both of which tried to wash their hands of them, acting through their overseers and lawyers to reject them. Parish inhabitants could come together in that process of rejection: supplying witnesses, local memory, oral testimonies, sometimes from the poor too, all marshalled to deny settlement. This is one way in which 'community' was revealed in this period, as an exclusory tight-fisted grouping, pitching itself against the external claimant, against the person who had perhaps once belonged, and who still hoped to be part of that community, but who was now hovering unwanted outside it.

In most cases the poor knew where their legal settlement was, and had notions of their 'rights' there, thus referring to their 'home' in the ways described, appealing to 'the gentlemen' or overseer. They discussed their ties to that 'home' via legal settlement, their legal entitlement – or eligibility, as overseers would normally see it. In deferential or assertive ways they were keen to remind their better-class readers of that. Away from their parish, they displayed very limited signs of absorption or fraternity elsewhere. They asked that letters to them be directed to an address which was often not their abode, almost as though their residence elsewhere was non-addressable, unestablished, but was rather a place where the letter could be collected or redirected. They often referred to problems with landlords. They made few references to any wider collective of people. A face-to-face 'community' of their own sort, whether secular or religious, was usually absent in the narratives. In some cases they had fallen into 'bad company', like the young women appealing to the London Refuge for the Destitute or the London Foundling Hospital. In other words, it was acknowledged that they were among a narrow Mollish or Twistean community of sorts, yet one that was morally suspect. There usually seemed little beyond that.

The poor in all these narratives had a strong *concept* of 'friends'; but away from home they lacked such people, and their predicament thus speaks to us about the historical functions of 'friends' in the make-up of communities. They had a notion of being absent from 'home'. There was little mention of 'neighbours' of the kind found in some parish vestry minutes,[81] nor a language of fellow 'parishioners', in the places where they found themselves.[82] Nor do the letters ever suggest solidarity among paupers or petitioners, a sense of an interlinked 'paupertariat'.[83] Mentions of clubs, friendly societies, religious groups, associations of the poor, trade societies and so on were very rare indeed, and sometimes these were only mentioned in anger or threats, probably hollow threats, in the more morally indignant letters.[84] This represents a failure of assimilation into other communities, yet an overriding and powerful sense of tied 'community at a distance', in the sense of paramount links back to their own 'home'. Departure from permanent residential relationships in one's own settlement involved an exile which, for the indigent poor, might be conditionally tolerated by parish authorities. The poor person had removed him- or herself not only from a place but also from its community and then, needing its relief, had to adopt strategies of legal assertion, or of literary deference that could amount to a language of surrender or acknowledged personal failure. In either case, their continued remote status was in question. They had to reassert their attachment, in the taken-for-granted and pervasive contemporary language of belonging and home. That might trigger non-resident poor relief, allowing them to stay away, or it might bring them back into the community.

Thus 'community', in the sense of those belonging to the parish, was reinforced and perpetuated by the legal networks created by the poor and settlement laws. Dependency and destitution re-established ties with community. It was often hard for migrant supplicants to reclaim normal membership of that community with any continuing independent status of their own, or in any other sense than through lost self-sufficiency. They needed to accept themselves as vulnerable people, currently bereft of alternative friends, neighbours and community, as belonging to a superior and often distant parish authority structure through past association with it. In these alienated cases a poverty of material standards meant rejection and a deprivation of experienced community in the place of residence: a spurned predicament 'which has brought upon me not only Shame to them that knew me, but also Poverty, Which I would gladly have hid, but Could not.'[85] The prodigal son rediscovered close kinship; the absent poor rediscovered community as an answer to indigent need. This situation forced them to backtrack to deferential attestation of earlier community, a concept that was persistently upheld by their experience of poverty, because of parochial welfare structures. The 'fear of freedom' had perhaps reasserted itself. For destitution meant re-formed allegiance to such a community, a return either in person or as part of its financial outreach capability, confirming the material value of that community. This crucial aspect of localized community as a solution to material needs will contrast with some of the community representations that I show in later chapters. For such a sense of community would later break down, or transpose to other felt or emotional meanings, with highly significant administrative, economic and cultural changes from the mid-nineteenth century eventually undercutting the parish as a supportive welfare unit dovetailed into local labour markets, and (as we shall see in my final chapter) with elevated standards of living sustaining more pervasive degrees of economic individualism, and perhaps loneliness. The 'spirit' of community was to become less material, more evanescent as a binding force or as a psychological need.

The poor, while away from their communities, appear in these narratives to be friendless yet (in modern terms) unsuccessfully individualized, vulnerable and unemployed, lonely and sometimes wandering alone.[86] They are shown in hardship and helplessness, often 'character'-less and deserted by friends, frequently shamed, sometimes disabled, often crushed by life-cycle poverty or in old age, above all as persons appealing for help.[87] As historians we may study their missives and recognize elements and feelings that connect to the community-less, isolated experiences of so many people today. There is a lineage from them to Eleanor Rigby, and, without then worrying about loneliness, countless parish officers asked, 'Where do they all come from?' Theirs was often the isolation of migrant poverty, unemployed youth, illness or old age during industrialization, whereas ours can be an isolation of youth, old age, poverty, *or* of an individualistic affluence which may proudly spurn community as something not needed. These poor people as migrants were *forced* to relate to their 'home' communities, given the lack of sympathy or help for them where they were. Yet unlike many today they always knew that they had a home community, for that was in effect what legal settlement meant. The expression of these lonely and friendless letter writers is instructive in this regard for historians of community and association. The extent of poverty and of life-cycle dependence upon the poor law was very great indeed. And all people had a settlement, which they variously earned and depended upon – for anyone could come to need it, including people much better off than those discussed here. That was fundamental to personal identities. It legally tied identity to community in ways we have subsequently lost – indeed often gratefully lost with the apparent ticket of freedom. It came to the fore of consciousness especially when people migrated. In some ways, the localized priorities and senses of community entitlement of these letter writers further qualify erstwhile stresses on commonality and shared traversing aims that once dominated historiography on the early nineteenth-century working class, as well as some sociological models of past community. These writers draw attention instead to personal isolation and the former power of the *structured legal framework of community*, focused upon the welfare-providing parish or township. As we will see, these legal frameworks or bulwarks of community characterize this but not later community history – they become absent in my chronologically later chapters. That supplies a contrast, a discontinuity within this book, but one that is historically very indicative and significant.

The evidential strength of poor narratives opens up fresh perspectives on these issues. These sources allow us to connect personal viewpoints from below with the administrative history of poor relief and settlement. With them we can analyse multiple individual perspectives and see the harrowing but different spirits of the poor emerging, as if from one of Käthe Kollwitz's haunted etchings, through the dust or muddy roads of industrializing

England's labour reallocations, as individual migrants left their community of settlement and were thrown onto their own resources. Their narratives underline how experiences of poverty and migration during the British Industrial Revolution occurred within long-established frameworks of community responsibility and ideas of belonging. Above all, these personal accounts display fundamental values and hopes of that time, ones that, despite their changing meanings, are perennial in so many ways: home, belonging, friends and community.

3

On the Road Out of Community

The Migrant Poor in Painting

The poor in community

We move in this chapter to visual representations: of the poor in community, and then outside it, on the road, absent from most structures of welfare and communal association. There are pictorial echoes here of the letter writers of Chapter 2 and foretastes of the migrant transience of characters like Jude the obscure, which we examine later. Given the pervasiveness of symbolic, imagined and visualized communities in modern analysis, it is essential to extend discussion here to artistic representations. My account starts with Edward Haytley's fine painting *The Montagu Family at Sandleford Priory* (1744), which epitomizes many of the ways in which social ranks and orders of the mid-eighteenth century were represented in oil painting. This painting is a preview of some conservative literary representations of community dealt with later in this book. It also helps to set the eighteenth-century scene for subsequent artistic changes which moved away from its reassuring harmonies.

The picture shows the poor 'in their place', firmly located in a community, as desired and probably viewed by the patron who commissioned it. Edward Montagu was a grandson of the first Earl of Sandwich. Two years earlier he had married Elizabeth, the daughter of Matthew Robinson of West Layton in Yorkshire. She later became famous as a 'feminist' 'blue stocking' and may have been the key influence in commissioning this painting.[1] Their mansion was known as the Priory, having earlier been an Augustinian Priory founded about 1200. Her husband died in 1775, aged 83. After his death she had major alterations made to the house, not visible in the painting, having it transformed by James Wyatt into the Gothic style.[2]

The painting, shown in Figure 3.1, is of a prospect in late afternoon, and in it we see the Montagu family at leisure, with Edward Montagu seated on

Figure 3.1 Edward Haytley, *The Montagu Family at Sandleford Priory* (1744).[3]

the south side of his house, near evidence of a recent game of bowls. In the near to middle distance eight haymakers can be seen, agricultural workers from the village beyond and southwards, which is the small settlement of Newtown. The viewer of this painting is situated, as if a guest, probably looking out of a first floor window of the mansion.

The picture has eschewed almost all the derivative classical referencing and design that one often finds in early to mid-eighteenth-century painters like George Lambert or Richard Wilson. The design has seemingly been influenced by Peter Paul Rubens's *A Landscape with a Shepherd and His Flock* (*c.* 1638, in the National Gallery, London),[4] with very similar alignments of watercourses and lines of view. In the design of that painting Rubens's shepherd's vantage point is akin to that of Edward Montagu, allowing us further insight into how Haytley may have seen Montagu's paternalistic role in this painting – as being like that of a shepherd over his flock. Its use of light has been influenced by Claude Lorrain's seascapes and paintings of the Roman Campagna. Yet unlike Claude's many imitators it lacks strongly buttressing or stable forms on either side, Italianate landscape features, ruins of questionably English provenance or references to classical mythology. It retains light-dark horizontal banding as a device to carry the eye into the distance but in other regards is quite different from the Claude Lorrain-inspired paintings that had been frequent hitherto. Shedding much of that genre inheritance, a painting such as this has original content and purpose which were more attuned to home-grown patron requirements. It is a variant on country house painting, and is certainly among the finest and most interesting of that genre.[5] Intricately and purposefully designed, with much topographical accuracy, it conveys subtle information about the Montagu family, their senses of gendered and social hierarchy, their almost domesticated landed management, their employees and the village community. Elite ideas about the village inhabitants are shown, which need to be seen within the context of the entire picture. The rural poor are here fitted 'in their place' or community. As such this is a striking pictorial benchmark from which to compare subsequent portrayals of migrant poor who, it will be argued, became far more visible in English painting from the mid-eighteenth century, who were separated visually from their social superiors and thus from engagement in a purportedly encompassing community life.

The Montagu family are shown relaxing. Consider their body language. The male head of the family is seated, while both women stand. His young wife through the gesture of her arms attends to him, an upturned chair behind her either indicating some carelessness, possibly linked to the game of bowls that has occurred or the promptitude with which she has risen to assist him. He appears to address a comment to her while pointing towards the dress of the other woman, who stands looking at the viewer. The lady on our left, Elizabeth's sister Sarah Robinson, holds a hand out to receive a chair from the rather unobtrusive yet well-dressed servant, who she does not look at. Her authority is undoubted. Edward Montagu is well attired, but the ladies are dressed in a way that speaks of considerable wealth.[6] Their dresses are clearly on show here and are very eye-catching. These women are conspicuous and speak to the landed status of Edward Montagu, and they call to mind the later 'blue stocking' activities of Elizabeth Montagu. The man sits; the women stand attentively yet are about to sit or have been sitting; the servant is clearly working and brings a chair with little recognition or marked colouring of him by the artist. If the women and their dresses are forms of consumption, it is also worth noting that on a stand by the man there is a telescope – another item of notable expenditure following the innovations in optical and marine instrument making of the previous seventy years. This is an instrument of inspection and control, through which an elite gentleman looks, casually crossing his legs between the billowing textures and colourful intricacies of grateful feminine dress, that seem to cast a light upon him. The telescope is a scientific device that extends his gaze, a prized possession of the male aristocrat. Its inclusion here perhaps indicates perennial male pride in gadget ownership. Yet it has male-controlled social purpose.

That telescope points directly down to the village in the distance and is perfectly aligned to peer down the main street. His viewpoint is identical to that of the shepherd in Rubens's painting, alluded to above, in that case over his flock of sheep. Proudly owned and displayed in the painting, the telescope is seemingly used to scrutinize a village and its social life in which, the painting's viewer deduces, Edward Montagu can also take pride, a community over which he exercises close yet seemingly benign control. In this small vignette of elite domestic, social and gendered power relations, with the body languages appropriate to its actors, with its subtle contrasts of gender and class, encompassing a whole community, with its display of material culture, the painter communicates essays of modern social history.

The landscape in the painting is represented as openly to be seen, stripped of the often heavy side trees or classical masonry of many early eighteenth-century paintings, for example by George Lambert. The trees are ethereal, light in appearance, summer in foliage. There is a clear sense of season here. Many of those trees and shrubs connect with the people by echoing the shapes of the female dresses, as do the piles of hay, helping to unite people and landscape into a working or leisured whole. This is an enclosed landscape, in two senses. There is no sign here of an open-field village, indeed it appears to be 'long-enclosed', in the sense that it pre-dates parliamentary enclosure. It is thus a so-called 'enclosure by agreement', which means that concentrated landownership has enabled enclosure in the absence of opposition and without the need for an Act of Parliament. Such enclosures took place most readily in, and were associated with, parishes where landownership was concentrated, that is in relatively or completely 'closed' villages.[7] Enclosure of this kind also confirms the Montagu family as long established – this is not 'new wealth' buying into country life. The enclosures in this case stretch as far as the eye can see and are enclosed in a second sense by the encircling three or four hills in the far distance. Everything within this ambit, the painting suggests, is productive, regulated, privately owned, farmed under an enclosed system, with the apparent advantages of such a system as extolled by the growing numbers of enclosure advocates in the eighteenth century. The landscape in this case is almost manicured, garden-like. All its fine details are perfectly in place; almost all the trees and shrubs are faultless in shape and disposition, and the hedges are adjusted impeccably to accommodate certain trees in the middle distance. This is a 'model' village before such a term was usually applied. However, beyond the village boundaries one sees wild waste and hills with scanty or no sign of enclosures. Within Montagu's control, under the regulation and oversight of one all-seeing eye, and as far as that technologically assisted eye can gaze, all is productive and bountiful. Beyond there is only waste and barren or poorer land.

Next, one notices two water features, between the mansion and the village. These may be re-landscaped older fisheries as once associated with the Priory, which had been founded by Geoffrey, Earl of Perche.[8] Their remnants are still discernible in modern aerial photography.[9] There are parallels again here with Rubens's painting, though these water features were real parts of Montagu's garden and estate. In a social and pictorial sense, this water separates the mansion to some extent from the village, over which it still has a good view, and from the haymakers in the left middle distance. A semi-encirclement of predominantly larch trees on the right also helps develop a sense of privacy, without disturbing the inspecting view. European larch was introduced from the Alps in about 1600. Stronger than most conifers, it was often planted on such estates as it was fast growing and used for fencing and building. Its recommended usage conforms to the needs of an enclosed village, and as such it is another indicative aspect of the painting. Just beyond the left-hand water feature is twenty or so feet of newly constructed hurdle fencing. In other words, a sense of productivity, of fish and useful timber, is combined with an aesthetic of water-designed landscape, conducing to a proper idea of social distance: the villagers are overlooked, managed, just like their landscape. They are in their place and part of a community, yet the landscape is such that they do not intrude socially on the elite who control and overlook them. They can be seen, especially via Montagu's telescope, far more readily than they can see the Montagu family, and they seem happily preoccupied with their work.

For unlike the Montagu family those villagers are almost all at work, haymaking.[10] Their grass space is productive, for hay, while the Montagu's grass space is leisured, mown closely for bowls. Women villagers work as well as men; in fact they predominate. There is as yet no problem with imagery of female agricultural workers, of the kind that would emerge later, possibly even in Gainsborough, but most markedly in the Victorian period.[11] This view of haymaking shows considerable decorum compared to some depictions, with which Haytley may have been familiar,[12] yet these haymakers are hardly exerting themselves. Their ash hay rakes are light and easily held. Their poises are studio-like, in advance of George Stubbs;[13] their dress and headwear verge towards the ostentatious by labouring standards. They are attired in a way that is intended to affirm the benevolent and generous principles of the Montagu family towards this community. These people are at a distance, yet in their place. They are mostly working but not exploited or overly disciplined, well dressed, clearly well housed in an enclosed village with impeccably thatched and well-ordered houses. They are respectable and credits to the estate, productive and harmoniously at one in a visibly hierarchical social order in which women also know their place. The internal dynamics of the Montagu family show appropriate family hierarchy, feminine and class deference, while at some remove downwards one sees villagers dressed to standard and conducting themselves in a way that in the terms of its period is also a compliment to Edward Montagu's management and benevolent control. Everyone knows their position here. There is no sign of dissent, dissatisfaction or displacement. There are no migrants passing through and no signs of conditions that might instigate out-migration or vagrancy. Surely nothing here could induce such villagers to leave this estate community and step out elsewhere in search of employment or a better deal.

The hierarchical community functions through a clear line of control, that starts with an axiomatic gendered hierarchy and deference within the leading family, and spreads downwards, and through the painting's angles of vision. The processes of patron–artist communication that have led to this result are, as usual, closed to analysis. How does a patron prescribe to an artist? We do not know what was visually suggested by whom, or how a pictorial scheme came about from artistic influences and presumptions or statements about authority and control. Nor do we know much about Edward Haytley; even his origins or dates are unknown, though he was cognizant of the very highest exemplars of prior landscape painting. However, there is no doubt that Edward Montagu has been extraordinarily well served by a highly intelligent and sensitively cooperative painter. Haytley has provided a prospect into a certain line of vision, that of the mind looking down Montagu's telescope, with no signs of dissentient social outlooks; he has added no social gibes or ambiguities of artistic delivery, such as those occasionally vented by Gainsborough,[14] and has thus been highly alert in producing this subtle and revealing commissioned painting.

Thomas Gainsborough

I have chosen just one mid-eighteenth-century landscape painting to show these values pictorially. One could have used others before 1750 to similar effect: *Wollaton Hall and Park, Nottingham* by Jan Siberechts (1697),[15]

Haytley's *The Brockman Family at Beachborough* (1744),[16] the 1738 paintings of Hartwell House gardens by Balthasar Nebot,[17] *Hawking and Haymaking* (*c.* 1720) or *Dixton Manor, Haymaking* (1710–20), the last two by unknown painters,[18] come to mind, with their depiction of order and of harmonious work orchestrated from on high. In their various ways, the poor are 'in their place' in these paintings, pictorially accommodated and part of a seemingly harmonious social order and community, unthreatening, providing an ordered picture of social ease and apparent contentment. Ragged migrant poor may be seen in some classically influenced art, for example in some of George Lambert's paintings, or in Richard Wilson's paintings of banditti,[19] influenced by Salvator Rosa, but there they are usually part of a derivative Italianate landscape that casts no unfavourable aspersion on the responsibilities of a known English estate or patron. Market traders or roadside travellers were abundant in Flemish and Dutch drawing, print-making and painting hitherto, for example in work by Wynants, Pieter Molijn or Ruisdael. The roadside poor, including vagrants or beggars, were also common, as in some of Rembrandt's remarkable and humane etchings,[20] and even gypsies were portrayed, as for example in Jacques de Gheyn's *Three Gypsies*.[21] Such figures influenced English landscape art, yet when these figures are shown *as English* in the early to mid-eighteenth century they are not usually in conspicuous poverty. Until perhaps about 1750, their English rural equivalents are very rarely shown as vagrant types. Indeed, they are often very well dressed.[22] In many cases they are shown at leisure, or at work that hardly seems toilsome,[23] and they clearly correspond to a worked and productive landscape, as in Edward Haytley's painting.

One of the first signs in England of a different rendition of what is clearly intended to be the English poor is Thomas Gainsborough's early painting *Cornard Wood* (*c.* 1746–48), sometimes called *Gainsborough's Forest* following a 1790 engraving of it.[24] This is influenced by earlier Dutch painting, notably Jacob van Ruisdael. Like some of Ruisdael's painting it appears to depict an area of forest common land and is naturalistic in its detail both of nature and the working poor. Unlike some depictions of woodlands as culturally insular,[25] the centre of the painting shows a tramp and his dog walking through the wooded landscape, trudging to the settlement in the distance, which is Great Cornard (just south-east of Sudbury) to judge from the spire,[26] and the shape of its church is replicated in the two trees on its left. These central details of the painting are shown in Figure 3.2.

The tramp has his back to us, slumped in tired walk. He has the characteristic ragged shins that William Cobbett and others later

Figure 3.2 Thomas Gainsborough, detail of *Cornard Wood* (*c*. 1746–48).

emphasized as a sign of poverty, notable in comment on early nineteenth-century Ireland or the Irish in England. The shins of the other men are carefully obscured. He is ignored by the woodland workers and the sitting woman among them who does not work. She is not yet isolated (one thinks ahead to George Morland) from protective male oversight, being amidst workers she is connected with. Her back is turned to the tramp, while a man with an axe stands by her. The tramp carries a bag tied to a stick, like many others we will see, and his dog has utility for poaching. Indeed for this reason dogs were later thought to be an uncomfortably suggestive addition to paintings of the rural poor. The hint of something amiss in rural Suffolk, that has generated this vagrant-like movement through such a wood, is unmistakable. The ragged shins were to be a feature that was repeated in some later Gainsborough paintings such as the ploughman in *Woodcutter Courting a Milkmaid* (1755),[27] and later in Constable, for example the boy on *The Leaping Horse* (1825), and other painters. In all cases, this was clearly intended as a pictorial sign of poverty, associated both with migrants and many of the non-migrant poor.

Poverty is conspicuous in some of Gainsborough's subsequent paintings, notably his *A Cottage Girl with Dog and Pitcher* (1785),[28] seen in Figure 3.3,

Figure 3.3 Thomas Gainsborough, *A Cottage Girl with Dog and Pitcher* (1785).

where the downcast look, the tired bedraggled dog, the broken pitcher, the raggedness of the girl's windblown clothing, her vulnerability to a dramatic sky and her bare feet carry unmistakable messages. In some cases Gainsborough paints the poor in a more positively dressed way, as in some of his cottage door paintings,[29] or the boy taking a break from the itinerant wagon on waste ground and doing some fishing in *Sunset: Carthorses Drinking at a Stream* (*c.* 1760), also known as *The Brook by the Way*, or most notably the foregrounded and well-dressed commoning couple in *Woodcutter Courting a Milkmaid* (1755). In these paintings the scene of leisure, access to livestock and natural resources, and semi-independence is very often symbolically overhung by a blasted oak, suggesting that this way of life will soon cease, in view of enclosure or other threats to the commons and associated community that these paintings depict. A similar use of blasted oaks is frequent in John Crome's pictures of heaths and woodland.[30] And Gainsborough's imagery of the poor is never contained on the same canvas or paper as his commissioned gentry or aristocratic pictures. These latter subjects do not appear to need or wish to see their social inferiors presented in any way, even at a distance, even in circumstances that might be indicative of mature or historic social responsibility for them. There are no village poor in *Mr and Mrs Andrews*, nor his other higher society portraits. It is very revealing that the social orders become well separated in Gainsborough, in contrast to the work of Edward Haytley and many other immediate artistic predecessors. These Gainsborough paintings are no longer about reciprocal relations between social orders in a community, about their respective positions, socially or pictorially, or about the social status accruing accordingly. Issues of communal responsibility are elided. Thus the elite are not 'tainted' in any way by imputations of failed responsibility towards the poverty-stricken or migrant poor, for those poor, whether ragged or otherwise, stand alone in what has now become a separate genre of much less saleable painting, albeit one from which Gainsborough apparently derived most satisfaction. In Gainsborough's work two distinct 'classes' of paintings have emerged, a separation of which he was well aware. One was highly profitable, although he wrote that 'I'm sick of Portraits … these fine ladies and their tea drinkings, dancings, husband-hunting, etc.' While landscapes and village subjects earned him much less, he much preferred them as 'his natural turn.'[31] The widely varied social subjects across these two genres, from the aristocracy down to the rural labourer, have become distinct, disengaged and visually unconnected with each other in his paintings. A socially connected community, however unequal, is significantly no longer the subject matter in this rural painting.

George Morland

This increasing view of poverty in Gainsborough, and accompanying signs of migrant poor, was dramatically kindled and heightened by George

Morland (1763–1804). Arduously trained by his father, Henry Robert Morland, a London artist and art dealer, George Morland was a superb draughtsman and a highly productive painter of rural themes. His short life was characterized by excessive drink, persistent debt, possible venereal disease by 1797 and reportedly an often dismissive attitude to potential patrons or clients, who had little or no control over his subject matter.[32] As one of his biographers, J. T. Nettleship, commented, he had a 'wayward hatred of polite society which became a fixed aversion in his later years'.[33] Vagrant or migrant poor were rare in Gainsborough's paintings, and are questionably migrant in his *Charity Relieving Distress* (1784),[34] or in Francis Wheatley's *Rustic Benevolence* (1791), but they became very common in Morland's work. In his personal life he is known to have often associated with migrants, gypsies, post-chaise drivers and others on the roads, indeed on occasion he joined them when escaping from his creditors. The entry in the 1812 *General Biographical Dictionary* asserts that:

> He is generally acknowledged to have spent all the time in which he did not paint, in drinking, and in the meanest dissipations, with persons the most eminent he could select for ignorance or brutality and a rabble of carters, hostlers, butchers – men, smugglers, poachers, and postilions, were constantly in his company and frequently in his pay.[35]

Fishermen and smugglers sat for him in the Isle of Wight, where one author commented rather patronizingly on 'his fondness for the society of those much beneath him'.[36] The migrant poor are a major feature in his work, especially from about 1790 onwards, when his painting largely discarded an earlier sentimentalism.[37]

Some of these images by Morland are of obvious economic migration, involving market-purpose carts, such as *Morning; or Higglers Preparing for Market* (1791), or his *The Market Cart* (n.d.), comparable to many images by W. H. Pyne, or some Gainsborough paintings and engravings representing road travel of a routine nature or of goods being moved. Sometimes, as in some of his Isle of Wight or Kentish pictures, there are suspicions or overt signs of smuggling, wrecking, poaching or other illicit activity, which he handles in a non-condemnatory way. He also painted views of army deserters, another form of migrant. Morland's poor are shown now as a class apart, as a secret people largely unknowable to the paintings' viewer, often huddled together in conversation, whether at entrances to a cave, at alehouse doors or the like. Such imagery of shared understandings seems to cast them as part of a larger entity of the labouring poor. In other cases they appear isolated and socially marginalized, seemingly destitute migrants shown as lone people or a family on the roads. An example is *The Dram* (Figure 3.4), where a migrant

Figure 3.4 George Morland, *The Dram* (n.d.).

family stop on the steps of a village inn to request drink, which is obligingly supplied, the sign of a trotting horse above the door suggesting movement. A woman with baby and young child slump tiredly on a lower step looking up expectantly as the smocked man with his back to the viewer obtains drink, watched by what is presumably their dog, while a stick and bundle lie on the ground.

This image also raises issues of religion and charity in Morland's painting. In the right distance an Anglican church is placed ironically, for in Morland's view the church offers no helpful hand to people in this predicament, and their drink-desirous migrancy takes no heed of the church's supposed moral injunctions. Indeed, in one Morland painting, which I have viewed as a mezzotint by William Ward called *The Warrener* (1806), the distant church tower is painted immediately next to a pair of bull's horns which are directed at it, suggesting the early cuckoldry and charivari insult from which, some argue, the modern 'V' sign originates, while a figure who appears to be a labourer returns to his expectant family with a pair of seemingly poached rabbits. These images differ markedly from many earlier artistic representations of the poor, when a frequent theme had been 'deserving' poor as ordained by God, and where charity towards them was a way of accessing heaven. Poverty in much early modern European and English imagery had indicated Christian forbearance, humility and *caritas*.[38] Yet with one exception involving gypsies (Figure 3.5), almost no such imagery exists in Morland's work after 1790. Discarding an earlier sentimental genre, 'deserving' and 'undeserving' categories of poor seem wholly absent, as do religious or moral criteria of presentation and judgement. There is nothing theological about Morland's images of 'the poor' and

Figure 3.5 George Morland, *Morning, or the Benevolent Sportsman* (1792).

of 'poverty' and no insistence that they are 'sinful' in their conduct. Nor are the poor caricatured or satirized, or handled in carnivalesque style, in the manner of James Gillray or some of Thomas Rowlandson's work, which included 'vagabonds'.[39] Morland's images are secular and non-judgemental views of the poor, and in his paintings the church is presented as an ironic or hostile irrelevance to the plight of those depicted and as an institution scorned by migrant poor.

In some cases the apparent titles of Morland's paintings dealing with these themes suggest that the migrants are 'gypsies', a class of people hitherto hardly treated in English painting when the settings were English, although Gainsborough had painted his *Landscape with Gypsies* in *c.* 1753–54.[40] Morland certainly mixed with gypsies and sought their company.[41] Yet it is often hard to know whether he intended a group to be 'gypsies' or not, and whether any such title can be given credence, for many were so named later by owners, dealers or galleries. Gypsies were often called 'Egyptians' at the time and in vagrancy legislation.[42] In a few Morland pictures, there are swarthy portraits of such people by roadsides or in woodland encampments with faces of such a dark hue that one must believe that a gypsy group was intended. A sitting man in Morland's *Morning, the Benevolent Sportsman* (1792) is an example of this,[43] shown in Figure 3.5. The painting and its charitable theme was unusual for Morland in that it was commissioned for Lieutenant General Sir Charles Stuart (1753–1801), who was making a moral point about benevolence and the treatment of gypsies, soon after the 1783 humane repeal of vicious Elizabethan legislation against them.[44] It is also worth noting that this 'benevolent sportsman' gives money to a group who seem to defy all notions of being 'deserving' and who even seem a little puzzled by his intervention.

Morland, along with writers like John Clare, clearly shared a view of gypsies as ejected and persecuted.[45] Yet in many other Morland paintings there are no such apparently 'Egyptian' depictions. The poor are shown wearing the same smocks, red cloaks, bonnets and hats as his rural labourers and their families, and one doubts whether the depiction is intended to be of gypsies. Many of their faces are distinctly non-'Egyptian'. The artist makes no discernible attempt to show them as gypsies, and they appear to be English migrant or vagrant poor. Among many examples of this is Figure 3.6, ambiguously entitled *Gipsy Encampment* but also known as *Travellers*, a frequently occurring title in Morland's work, as well as the pale-faced woman and child in Figure 3.7. Many such titles were given to paintings much later by engravers, dealers or owners and do not derive from the artist.

Figure 3.6 George Morland, *Gipsy Encampment*, also entitled *Travellers* (*c*. 1791).

Whether gypsy or not, these are often family groups, usually containing one to three children. In a few paintings quite an extended family, including one or more elderly persons, is indicated, as in Figure 3.6. Bundles of possessions, red cloaks, pitchers for drink, and walking sticks are frequent items. The red cloaks were standard parish poor law issue. The people are almost always waysiders, often with a fire lit, a pot over it tied under three bound sticks or placed nearby. An image of a child huddled in front of such a fire is in one of Morland's multiple-image soft-ground etchings of 1804, which also shows in the distance a much smaller outdoor image of a man and woman beside a fire.[46] In all these pictures a rather desolate air prevails. That atmosphere is reinforced by a body language that often ignores the viewer, with for example sleeping figures, or indeed a body language that can occasionally seem threatening and foreboding.

This is notable in his extraordinary painting, *Gypsies in a Wood*, or *Travellers* (Figure 3.7), where the man on the right is hulking and possibly dangerous. His broad back is turned to the observer, a fold in his smock taking on the appearance of an almost devil-like tail. He leans against an oak tree, as if to suggest allied strength. Morland is here subverting the earlier class symbolism of oak trees, for in Gainsborough and many other painters oaks had been used to indicate the longevity and axiomatic

Figure 3.7 George Morland, *Gipsies in a Wood* or *Travellers* (n.d.).

nature of elite landed power. Morland now seems to be suggesting that the standing or independence of the wayside poor, if they have any, comes from wasteland or unenclosed commons, which was not an unusual claim at the time in debates about enclosure and access to commons and wastes. Such a strongly built man, positioned by and placing his hand on this oak, appears to be a counter-statement to the presumption in eighteenth-century painting that oaks symbolize the landed elite. Morland apparently became contemptuous of the latter, both as a social class and as artistic patrons. Figure 3.7 might be interpreted as him laying down a counter-claim, on behalf of the 'landless' poor, whether through sympathetic radicalism or social conservatism in historical terms, for enclosure of wasteland was now at its peak and was depriving these people of customary landed access. The body language and the attitudes struck by the subjects are highly indicative. The other man is reclining in sleep with an overturned pitcher or jug in view, indicating both leisure and the morally suspect drinking of ale. There is no sign of sentimental treatment by the painter. There are a number of similar Morland paintings and prints to this, such as *The Wayfarers* (1784), or *Gipsies*, engraved as a mezzotint by William Ward in 1792.

Some of Morland's women are shown without male companions, in the presence of their young children, with a child pointing to a pot over the fire as if to ask if there is anything in it, as in the untitled Figure 3.8, which also

Figure 3.8 George Morland, untitled (n.d.).

shows a child seemingly lying in anguish and a baby in the wayside mother's arms. Many of the women and children in this anti-pastoral genre of his work have despairing or abjectly despondent faces. These are remarkable pictures of women's isolation, of female movement in nature and of anonymous feminine solitude in rural locations: themes which are usually addressed for a much later period in discussions of women, movement, privacy and modernity, whether in rural locations or in the city.[47] While such representations of women are often taken to be post-1900 markers of social and literary modernism, in Morland's much earlier paintings they are hardly auspicious spectacles of modernity or of women's sovereignty over themselves, for they show great female poverty and extreme vulnerability. Women's migration was commonplace at this time: as market traders or hawkers of goods, between farm or domestic services, in dairying, fish-gutting, and many other industries, upon marriage, or with their movement to the cities. Such migration often queries presumed stability of 'community'. Gainsborough's woman in *Cornard Wood* (Figure 3.2) was overlooked; whether subservient or protected she was seated among known men from a settled place, her back turned to the passing tramp. By contrast, the predicaments of Morland's women migrants often question the security of family, they query ideas of safe service and they rebuff gender-encompassing ideas of 'community'. There are indications of drink in some of these illustrations, notably *The Dram* (Figure 3.4), implying dissolute conduct; yet this is not a universal feature, and these paintings seem to eschew the moral message of a couple of Morland's earlier views of poverty, such as his *The Effects of Youthful Extravagance and Idleness*,[48] where the title suggests that blame was directed at the poor family itself.

In some of his paintings, women with a child are seemingly sexually vulnerable, with a leering male onlooker of a different class, sometimes deemed to be a 'sportsman', as in the apparently predatory and indicatively entitled *The Lucky Sportsman* (see Figure 3.9).[49] This

Figure 3.9 George Morland, *The Lucky Sportsman* (1791).

portrays a domineering armed man with a large dog questioning two women with a baby in a remote woodland area. A woman casts her eyes downwards before his stare. The bark peels off the tree. One is reminded of the worried and fearful woman in Morland's *The Door of a Village Inn*. She is standing before a mounted man on horseback with a distinctly phallic shaped, positioned and angled stick pointed at her, with a trussed bundle over his horse, one of its rear hoofs pawing the ground, while before the building, in the centre of the painting, what appears to be a female smock and a stocking are draped over a stonewall. A downcast young man tends a smoking fire with his back turned to the scene, and two sullen and silent children are in the doorway, one holding a food bowl which is stared at by the other, before a black interior.[50]

Other Morland paintings of gypsies or wayfarers repeat these suggestions, as in his *Encampment of Gipsies* (see Figure 3.10),[51] where a higher-class well dressed and hat-wearing male observer with a dog leans against a gate and looks down at three ragged women wayfarers and their equally ragged children. One central woman with a conspicuously bared

Figure 3.10 George Morland, *Encampment of Gipsies* (n.d.).

shoulder stares back at him; the angle and position of the saucepan handle has not occurred by chance, and it also points straight to the male gaze, via the eyes of a child, while a sullen man of their class sits with downcast face in the background, as though impotent to intervene.

This suggestion of sexual vulnerability was not new in English landscape art. Explicit examples include John Collet's *Landscape with a Squire and a Farm-girl* (1770),[52] William Hogarth's two paintings *Before* and *After* of 1730–31[53] and a painting by Edmund Bristow,[54] but the theme is striking in some of Morland's paintings of female migrants and wayfarers.[55] The implication seems to be that this kind of poverty, when affecting women who are outside any settled community and its oversights, made them especially prone to such predatory behaviour by higher-class males.

These paintings are 'generic' with regard to a sense of place: they have no place, no village or community and no recognizable venue of the painting. In Haytley's painting of the Montagu family we know exactly where the painting is set. In Gainsborough's *Cornard Wood* the vagrant passes through a known wood and location, towards a known place. The same is true of most such earlier depictions, leaving aside derivative Italianate settings, and of course this locational precision was highly desired by artistic patrons for reasons relating to ownership, pride and reputation. Place entails possession and responsibility, towards property and people, and of course parish officers can be named and blamed. A parish has a status, embellished in folklore for good or ill. It has a legal repute in relation to settlement and vagrancy laws. People have rights in a place and appeals can be made to Justices of the Peace. A 'community' apparently overlooks itself. But in Morland this has changed: there has been a marked decline in known locality conveyed in painting. In the very large majority of cases, whether in his farmyard, cottage or roadside scenes, let alone his winterscapes or coastal views, it is completely unclear where they are set. In a few, detective work and close biographical information can establish a probable site that, in the most general of artistic terms, has formed a basis for the painting. *The Door of a Village Inn*, for example, is probably set in Enderby in Leicestershire, given some vernacular similarities with his *View at Enderby, Leicestershire* (1792). Usually, however, his sites for migrant poor are what we might persuade a modern anthropologist such as Marc Augé to call 'non-places', referring to 'places of transience that do not hold enough significance to be regarded as "places"'.[56] And they have this significance in Morland long prior to the era of 'supermodernity' that Augé believes inaugurates them. For Augé, they take the modern form of motorways, motels and so on; in Morland they are naturalistic, roadside, anonymous and thus seemingly remote from 'community' in any known sense of eighteenth-century England. These poor are certainly in English settings, but they are out of place and community. They have no place. A few public house signs aside, significant clues about location such as country houses, readable road signs and known topographical features are almost never provided. This is deliberate, for these poor lack community, they are placeless, peripheral, homeless and roadside transients. We do not know where they are going, if anywhere. In this regard Morland differs from many other illustrators of poor migrants.[57] We do not even know what county these migrant poor may be painted in, although outside London Morland worked mainly in Kent (especially Margate), the Isle of Wight (Shanklin, Cowes, Yarmouth, Freshwater Gate) and Leicestershire (Enderby).

It is part of Morland's originality to couple empathy with placelessness in his pictures, more so than in his contemporary Thomas Bewick's comparable box woodcuts of migrants. This characteristic is part of Morland's own povertied emancipation from obligations to patrons. It separates him from the often proprietorial drawing and painting of Constable, or the very saleable views of Turner, or the artistic intent and remuneration of so many other artists. And in Morland's case this handling of wayside poverty is clearly no Rousseau or Wordsworth-derived version of romantic vagrancy,[58] with idealized or picturesque 'vagrants'. Such romanticism is seen in paintings such as James O'Connor, *A Thunderstorm: the Frightened Wagoner* (1832),[59] in which travellers' alienation from any known place adds to the terror or 'sublimity' of the scene. Morland's various paintings, entitled *Land-Storm, The Thunderstorm* or *The Approaching Storm*, show travellers in places unknowable to us and perhaps to them, but their pedestrian vulnerability and haste in the face of a storm is wholly unromanticized in mood, predicament and landscape. They are not picturesque in location. Nor in his representations of gypsies is there any trace of the romanticized 'eastern', turbaned, exotic, theatrical imagery that one sees in many other 'gypsy' depictions of this period, for example of Sir Walter Scott's Meg Merrilies.[60]

The naturalistic surrounds of these images of migrant poverty reinforce the frequent tone of despair and vulnerability. Gainsborough used blasted oaks and related symbolism to confirm the terminal nature of the unenclosed commoning life he depicted. The writing is on the wall for this form of life, he is correctly if sadly suggesting. To judge from the humane and attractive way he drew them, his sympathies often seem to be with the commoners. In some cases, rival symbolism, of for example a young birch tree, which had silver/moneyed symbolism in many European cultures, overhangs the part of the painting indicative of future directions: one of post-enclosure tenant-farmer and landlord profits and labouring wage discipline.[61] In much eighteenth-century painting, a healthy oak or beech tree symbolized longevity of landed power, durability and attachment of the landed family to the estate, as we see it used for example with the oak behind the iron seat (serving in the same way) in *Mr and Mrs Andrews*. In that case, the *nouveau riche* couple try to assert a landed connectivity that Gainsborough in their case perhaps regards with cynicism. Even so, Gainsborough does what is needed when he paints the foot of Mr Andrews on, and akin to, that tree's roots. Morland adapted and subverted this kind of tree symbolism in some of his paintings of poachers, gypsies, migrants and others involved in illicit activities. He did so largely by showing tree branches which clutched down at the painting's subjects, claw-like and tentacular, making use of the natural jagged angularity of oak branches, as though symbolizing a legal system intent on catching the nonconforming people underneath. Indeed, it is as if the tree, in this stark and wintry form, still stands for landed power, albeit power that is now capturing and punitive, rather than benevolent and socially constructive. The best example, although in this case probably not of migrant poor, is his *Ferreting* (1792), shown in Figure 3.11,[62] which was called *The Rabbit Warren* in the engraving by S. Alken.[63] (A slighter version of this artistic use of branches was seen in Figure 3.5 above.) There is no hint here that

Figure 3.11 George Morland, *Ferreting* (1792).

Morland has morally disassociated himself from this pair of men: one of them looks appealingly at the painting's viewer, both are clean-shaven, and the dog is one that was often drawn by Morland, who was notoriously fond of animals.

The same setting, with the same tree and its clutching branches, overhang his rather despondent *Gipsy Encampment* (n.d.) in the Walker Art Gallery, Liverpool,[64] accentuating a sense of desolation and isolation from any settled or supportive community. An example is shown in Figure 3.12, supposedly entitled *Gypsies*, above the glum-faced man. The bareness of the tree's branches also enhances the grim sense of season, of which Morland made more extreme use in his many countryside winterscapes. There is further irony here too. For these migrant poor under such a tree are at an opposite extreme, in their poverty, to the propertied elite pictorially associated with oak tree's hitherto. And in a very noticeable place, purposefully backlighted, one of the trees branches has been sawn off, while to the left the tree's trunk is cracked. As these trees had hitherto symbolized landed power and responsibility, then further meaning seems implicit here.

Figure 3.12 George Morland, *Gypsies* (n.d.).

To similar but even more desolate effect, there is Morland's *Rest by the Way*, or *Hillside Tramps Reposing*, of 1792 (Figure 3.13), showing a bleak landscape, with nobody else in view other than the seemingly exhausted roadside family. Here the tree or shrub just above these people is defoliated, symbolically indicative of their plight, in contrast to other greenery in the wider scene. This contributes some ambiguity of season. Unlike those in Haytley's painting, these people are removed from seasonal routines expressed in the life of a rural working community. The house in the middle distance is irrelevant to the travellers' plight, for they have not stopped by it, and that house might be virtually anywhere in marginally hilly regions of England. Furthermore, the road sign is unreadable to us. Perspective has squeezed the directional pointers to minute proportions, perhaps as if no worldly direction is possible. And that sign stands strangely on two legs, as though itself wondering which way to go. At least it is upright, which contrasts with the recumbent man, lying at such a place, dead beat, his face covered, and seemingly discarded from any community. This situation perhaps has further connotations, for it calls to mind Brewer's *Phrase and*

Figure 3.13 George Morland, *Rest by the Way* (1792), also entitled *Hillside Tramps Reposing*.

Fable wording: 'Cross-roads. All (except suicides) who were excluded from holy rites were piously buried at the foot of the cross erected on the public road.'[65] And in popular folklore at this time, the burial of the restless spirit at crossroads was deliberate, so that it does not know which way to go.

In contrast to jagged, accusatory or barren tree symbolism, there were images in which the migrant poor take hold of the trees and branches, breaking them off for firewood, usually acting illegally in such wood collecting. Morland, markedly unlike a painter such as Edward Haytley, had no hesitation in showing illegal activity among the poor, whether that be smuggling, shipwrecking, wood gathering, poaching and dealing in game, and he seems to be in sympathy with the perpetrators. One of the two children in his painting *Gathering Sticks* (1791) has a distinctly furtive look, while the other is resolute and glum. And given the clawing 'legal' symbolism of some of Morland's trees and branches, his soft-ground etching shown in Figure 3.14 has added meaning, of almost an anti-legal retaliatory nature, as the sympathetically drawn family of roadside migrants, with notably clean-shaven men, break off tree branches for their use.

Figure 3.14 George Morland, *Travellers*.

These pictures of 1790–1804 by Morland are striking in their insistence on the theme of roadside migrant poverty in a landscape of anonymity. Examples of migrant poverty could certainly be found earlier, as in Gainsborough's *Cornard Wood*, and in Dutch seventeenth-century painting or in at least three of Rembrandt's etchings. Themes of beggars and poverty call to mind Jusepe de Ribera, Georges de La Tour or Caravaggio. Yet these themes had been rare in English art, especially with regard to migrant poor. Beyond classically imitative painting, such as by Richard Wilson or George Lambert, mid-eighteenth-century rural painting had seemed more concerned to represent the poor as settled, well dressed, at a distance but respectable, part of a hierarchical working estate or parish community, often but not necessarily working, usually marshalled and shown in a way intended to reflect the patron's controlling influence and benevolence. Like the property being extolled, they appear as social assets to the patron who commissioned the painting. Such imagery would have been hung in the parlours of the well-heeled with no reluctance or embarrassment. In Gainsborough, however, one sees a bifurcation of this theme, as the social impracticality and undesirability of coexisting social strata or cross-class imagery finally asserted itself. In the work of Morland this change becomes demanding and remarkable. Poverty is represented now as frequently having a roadside location. Its signs are unmistakable and harsh. With the exception of *Morning, or the Benevolent Sportsman* (Figure 3.5), gentry are almost never shown in Morland's post-1790 paintings of migrant or excluded poor, and if representatives of a prosperous farmer class appear they often do so as male predators to isolated women or as envied pot-bellied hunters of game denied to others, as in his undated painting *A Tavern Interior with Sportsmen Refreshing*.[66]

Conclusion

I have sketched this artistic transition essentially as a chronologically evolving comparison between Haytley, Gainsborough and Morland. This change in rural artistic representation of community, or its absences, appears to bear a remarkable parallel to any historical argument that would stress a growing rural problem of English southern and midland vagrancy and itinerant poverty from the later eighteenth century. Those problems were linked to extraordinary inflation, demographic growth, growing illegitimacy, the effects of midland parliamentary enclosure both of arable land and then of wasteland, rising poor rates and seasonal or absolute increases in agrarian unemployment. They also produced increasing numbers of the poor becoming vulnerable to the settlement and vagrancy laws.[67] All of these changes posed major problems for spirits of community, whether experienced by the poor or marshalled from above. An emerging growth of class separation and a rootless loss of a sense of place or community for many among the poor are clearly signalled in the representations of rural England discussed. There are many pictorial echoes here of issues in my previous chapter. From the 1740s onwards, these changes reached an epitome in Morland's work between 1790 and 1804, accentuated by a remarkable empathy between painter and subject matter that owed much to Morland's own disassociations, predicaments and problems.[68] These images remind us that 'break-up of community', as personally experienced, and resulting social ostracism, isolation or vulnerability are not new phenomena of more recent historical periods. Morland was depicting experiences which were widespread during British industrialization and indeed Celtic agrarian trauma. The community-less individualized or familial remoteness of these images bears many resemblances to imagery and literary characterization discussed throughout the chapters of this book.

A number of themes in representations of migrant poverty predominated after the late eighteenth century. John Constable, as John Barrell has argued, tended to avoid the theme, sinking the labouring poor deep into his landscapes, although rare exceptions are the foregrounded but very shadowed wayside squatter huddled in a makeshift tent in Constable's *Dedham Vale* (1828),[69] or perhaps his earlier oil sketch of a *Man Resting in a Lane* (1809),[70] the class of that man being uncertain. Later painting of rural migrants included images of Irish famine victims. An example is Erskine Nikol, *An Ejected Family* (1853),[71] by a Scottish painter who regularly visited Ireland between 1846 and 1850, showing in this painting a family on the road because of non-payment of rent. Or one thinks of Frederick Goodall's *An Irish Eviction* (1850).[72] In Scotland and Ireland humane and sympathetic studies of migrants, 'vagrants' or roadside beggars fitted with a national narrative of dispossession and clearances, and this may be why so many individualized pictures like William Lizars, *John Cowper, an Edinburgh Beggar* (n.d.)[73] were associated with those two countries. John Singer Sargent's *The Tramp* (*c.* 1904)[74] was a rare English version of this genre, albeit painted much later. Wayside 'gypsy' groups had many illustrators, such as Frederick Walker, *The Vagrants* (1867),[75] where an ambiguity about whether the subjects are 'gypsy' or *gorgio* (the gypsy term for the non-gypsy) echoes some identification issues in Morland's work.

There were many other views of gypsies – by Philip de Loutherbourg,[76] John Phillip, Joseph Stannard,[77] Frederick Sandys, Dante Gabriel Rossetti,[78] Augustus John and others. This was a changing genre that deserves treatment in its own right. Many post-Morland 'realist' depictions come to mind of roadside poverty, of which Hubert von Herkomer's *Hard Times* (1885) is the best known.[79] A child-focused example was William Small's *The Good Samaritan* (1899),[80] depicting a doctor tending a sick wayside child. Indeed, Victorian views of childhood produced much sentimentalization of wayside poverty, including paintings such as Briton Rivière's *His Only Friend* (1871),[81] in which a barefooted ragged boy with his dog lie exhausted by a roadside milestone indicating that London is 31 miles away. Emigrant themes had become common in all four countries of the British Isles, all such pictures speaking to ideas about lost community. One thinks of Richard Redgrave's *The Emigrant's Last Sight of Home* (1858),[82] in which the about-to-leave emigrant holds his arms open towards Abinger in Surrey, a painting originally exhibited with lines from Oliver Goldsmith's poem 'The Traveller'. On the continent at this time the influential Gustave Courbet was painting scenes such as *The Charity of a Beggar at Ornans* (1868).[83] The Russian Sergei Ivanov's *Death of a Migrant Peasant* (1889), like Morland's Figure 3.13 above, is centred on a recumbent migrant on the road and 'shows the bitter consequences of failure, the collapse of all hope'.[84] After Morland's premature death, the visualization of migrant poor clearly took various forms. Many of these perpetuated the 'decline of community' realism that was pioneered by Morland after 1790 in his views of wayside poverty. Morland died in 1804. His death triggered convulsive fits in his wife who died a few days after him. Much later, 'social realism' hit the road, in the work of painters like Frederick Walker, Luke Fildes, Frank Holl or Hubert von Herkomer. These were notoriously critical of frameworks of welfare and the efficacy of belonging, and all of them were representing forsaken community by the 1860s. This social realism was instigated and defined as an innovative phenomenon in art that addressed social concerns and community deficits: one that was pessimistic or bleak, anti-romantic, critical of the establishment and a form of naturalistic realism. And yet, as with so many representations of community in the past, that later generation's 'realism' and sense of mislaid community spirit had well-founded precedents. The artistic 'social realism' that was widely seen as a new phenomenon of the 1860s and 1870s was evidently preceded by George Morland seventy or so years earlier.

4

Parochial Globalization

The Anglican Community

Parish magazines

In January 2009, the Archbishop of Canterbury, Dr Rowan Williams, publicly celebrated 150 years of parish magazines. He praised them as a 'wonderful resource', now having a combined readership of more than 1.3 million, greater than many national newspapers. Most of the Church of England's 13,000 or so parishes have a parish magazine. They are the most widely read Christian publications in the country, and many people are likely to read them without attending church. This is evidently a source that historians concerned with the meaning of 'community' need to consider.

The first edition of *The Parish Magazine*, produced by J. Erskine Clarke in January 1859, is considered the first 'proper' such publication.[1] There were earlier publications, dealing with administrative, religious or local historical issues, aimed at local inhabitants. Yet they did not normally have the regularity of appearance and practical purpose of the post-1859 genre. That genre expanded markedly, with many parish magazines starting in the 1860s, 1870s and 1880s, in all English regions from Cumberland to Cornwall, and they were successful in Ireland, Scotland and Wales as well.[2] They were stimulated by cheaper paper and printing costs, and by a marked rise in literacy after Forster's Education Act of 1870; indeed, they must have contributed to improve English and Welsh reading skills.[3] They developed even further in the early twentieth century and the inter-war period and have flourished since 1945. In 1946 Canon J. M. Swift, the Press and Information Officer of the Diocese of Chichester, in a work published by the Church Assembly, claimed that there were 11,085 parish magazines of the Church of England, with a total monthly circulation of 2,763,000.[4] Books were written on how to edit them.[5] The monthly circulation was up to 3.5 million by 1963.[6] 'For the most part', it was then written, 'these labours of love jog quietly and usefully along'.[7]

Given that parish magazines represent the idea of the parish as a community, it is perhaps surprising that they emerged when they did. After all, W. E. Tate, the Webbs and many subsequent historians thought that the period after 1834 saw 'the strangulation of the parish'.[8] The parish has frequently been discounted from then onwards. It was (the historical arguments run) sidelined by central administrations running the poor law, and increasingly coming to dominate issues such as public health, transport, education, lunacy provision and so on. The expansiveness of the Empire at that time is also without doubt, apparently turning minds towards British global rather than parochial and community issues. Religious history too has not lacked for historians who argued for processes of 'secularization' being well underway from the mid-nineteenth century,[9] with everything that implies for the role of the parish in people's lives. The parish was, after all, purportedly the most fundamental of all traditional religious units, the basis of Anglican organization, and 'secularization' was bound to undermine its salience. Parish magazines, expressing from certain viewpoints a liveliness of parish life, should have had an earlier heyday – they should, it might seem, have become a fairly moribund form of publication from the mid-nineteenth century. Why then did this parochial genre expand so markedly after 1859? What kind of local vitality did it bear witness to? What senses of 'community' did it represent, and how did editors try to impart an idea of community? Do the history and coverage of this genre tell us anything about where we are now in historically comparative terms, whether in respect of religion, localism, neighbourly obligation, leadership, local pride or community spirit? What in retrospect can historians of 'community' learn from 150 years of parish magazines?

In many ways, these magazines have been and are important expressions of community life, both in country and in town, even though they can be partial in their editors' priorities, reflecting certain local interests rather than others. They have influentially extolled an idea of 'community' even when many disputed its existence or survival. In some senses, they read like a self-justifying collective chronicle. They came towards the close of earlier oral traditions, when many saw communities fracturing, and they were a responsive form of community creation. They enhanced a sense of community among people who might not otherwise have professed it, while also being a new genre of self-publication for some parishioners. Local residents found their neighbourhood knowledge and affiliations enhanced by parish magazines; local businesses thought them useful to advertise in; and the churches saw them as beneficial for fund-raising, gospel education and the exchange of religious views. Some, like the *Heaton Review*, started as local publications but opened up in much wider ways.[10] During the Second World War exhibitions of the magazines began, helping to improve their quality and a sense of their history. In recent decades, covers and appearances have become more attractive. Parish magazines with a 'localized' inset have declined, in favour of wholly parochial publications. They are now more varied than ever, although the combining of parishes, especially in the countryside, has led to various publication mergers and wider 'parochial' remits. Further, some parish magazines now contain little religious matter and blur into the category of parish newspaper.[11]

The magazines were often sent long distances to individuals living away, maintaining long-stranded links to the community, keeping such readers in touch, allowing them to associate with features of the parish and community by communicating small endeavours and personal details. These publications thus served as cordage in forms of network communities that developed from parochial association, linking people who no longer lived in propinquity, yet who still shared a parochial interest or sense of belonging.[12] They were closely instrumental within stranded emigrant and letter-writing communities.[13] In another dimension, the internet has now further widened readership, as well as editors' senses of comparison and emulation. It has connected the magazines to wider church initiatives and has probably extended coverage of secular community events. One can now easily read about the minutiae of community life in parishes remote from one's own residence. Whatever people's individualism and senses of particular or multiple belonging, and whatever their spiritual views, they can feel involved in a 'real' community while being absent, apparently experiencing 'virtual' senses of 'community at a distance', and without responsibility or reciprocity, via such online parochial magazines. This is somewhere between understandings of 'traditional' community, and sociological meanings of 'virtual' and 'thin' communities.[14] An electronic, globalized world appears not to have diminished the attractions of parish micro-journalism. On the contrary, it seems rather to have extended its readership, almost as though one extreme required its antithesis. The novelty, or otherwise, of such a wide outreach for these community magazines will be discussed below.

In the nineteenth century, parish magazines were partly produced by the parish, the local wrapper being headed with the name of the parish or deanery, covering their own news. This was normally issued with one of the central publications of the period as an inset, which thus became 'localized', such as *Home Words* (which became the largest in circulation), *Dawn of Day*, *Church Monthly*, *The Sign* or *The Parish Magazine*.[15] The insets could be purchased at wholesale prices in whatever numbers were required, commonly between about 50 and 700, to match the output of the parish magazine. The circulation of the *Bere Regis and Winterborne Kingston Parish Magazine* in 1894, for example, was 150, but figures could be much higher. These early magazines came with the endorsement of many bishops and famed clergymen, for they were found 'most valuable as a means of uniting Church-folk, and enlisting members of the congregation in the good works of the parish'.[16] They were normally issued monthly, or at three-month intervals, and contained some illustrations. The cost was usually one penny each, rising slightly over time, and money-making seems to have been secondary to religious and social purposes. With regard to the social basis of subscriptions, the numbers printed per parish suggest wide household dissemination, and there were many accounts of them being read by labourers. The centrally published insets contained stories, often in serial form, and articles with titles such as 'Curious Church Customs', 'The Breadth of God's Commandments', 'Public Punishments of Past Days', short sermons by well-known preachers, 'Faith, Hope and Charity' by the Bishop of Lichfield and so on. *The Parish Magazine*, from which these examples come, was endorsed by the Bishop of Winchester as 'readable, varied and not without a certain dignity in the quality and bearing of its contents, a very safe and yet wide-hearted channel of the doctrines, spirit and aims of the English Church'.[17] Later such publications in the twentieth century included *Outlook*, which widened discussion to many new topics, such as child care. Reforming a genre that some felt was in the doldrums, it broached new topics; for example, 'in its film reviews [it] does not hesitate to call a lesbian a lesbian'.[18]

The parish element of the magazine in its first century of life (my main historical interest here) included a very diverse range of local material. This could encompass calendars or almanacs, Sunday school or other school business, achievements of local children, mothers' meetings, information about births, marriages and deaths, local epidemics, parish officer appointments, clerical retirements or transfers, obituaries or 'notices of parish worthies'. One often sees reports or announcements of local events such as bazaars, fetes, fairs, flower shows, jumble sales and fund-raising efforts. Or there were details of church services, lectures or sermons, concerts, coming of age celebrations for the local gentry,[19] jubilees, newly created 'harvest festivals' or thanksgivings. Programmes of events like concerts were often given. Details of postal services, carriers' services, railway or steamboat timetables were publicized. Sporting fixtures such as cricket matches were announced or reported upon. Then there were statements and accounts of local clubs and societies: friendly, benefit, clothing, burial, pig, blanket and such like. Allotments were frequently discussed. The magazine could be used to draw attention to local crimes. Comments on the weather and the state of the harvest or other agricultural activity were frequent. There were also stories of a biblical or edifying character. Wider diocesan news, and missionary work in which the parish had a hand, often featured. The magazines contained accounts of local history and earlier parish personalities, sometimes with parish register extracts, as such antiquarian interests 'set the Rector grubbing in the records of the past'.[20] Other news items relating to the parish or its external activities were published. In some instances, the magazines printed letters from an absent clergyman, most notably during wartime when the incumbent was in service elsewhere.[21] A total of 3,409 clergymen were commissioned as temporary or permanent chaplains during the First World War, many of them writing home via the parish magazine, or (if still in their parishes) using those magazines to keep in touch with those in the forces.[22] Magazine-published despatches from wars had included the Boer War, but these became very notable indeed during the First World War.[23] The magazines also published advertisements, from food dealers, undertakers, matchmakers, drink (cocoa) manufacturers, medicine makers (e.g. 'Clarke's World Famed Blood Mixture' or 'Page Woodcock's Wind Pills') and many other businesses. Guidance was also published on 'Localizing the parish magazines',[24] which assisted local editors and authors in their work and contributed to a comparative sense of how one might improve the parish element of the publication. Parish magazines could be very rural in their scope, as well as being issued by urban parishes. They were published in large numbers by both types of parishes, including many in the metropolis and major cities, making them an important source for parish and community life in all contexts.

The Church's role

These magazines were commonly edited and largely written by clergymen, although there was often local lay involvement, especially in their production. Many of them were associated with the nineteenth-century period of Anglican resurgence, which was strongly reformative, and affected the Church of England in so many administrative, architectural, liturgical and other ways. They inevitably reflect many of the nineteenth-century doctrinal changes and schisms within the Anglican Church. And they also gained from the much augmented numbers of Anglican clergy between 1841 and 1901.[25] Inevitably, they convey an Anglican sense of community and Christian purpose. Dr Rowan Williams commented that 'A good parish magazine is a wonderful resource that places the local church at the heart of the community it serves.'[26] In many ways, then, they represent 'community' as reinforced by a (shifting) social ecclesiastical ideology, attempting to define a new 'Anglicized' form of older community. Yet the late nineteenth century was a time when increasing numbers of people were envisaging (in hope, or despair) what parish 'community' might be without the Church of England. In some cases, the magazines aspired to embrace local Nonconformists. In others, one can sense the tensions and demarcations between the Anglican Church and dissenters. These publications did not often draw attention to matters pertaining to English Nonconformity, even when such chapels were present in the parish. They signal, through such occlusion, the frequent existence of rival religious communities, with the potential to fracture senses of parochial community. Indeed, they also remind us of the need for comparative study of Anglican, Catholic, Nonconformist, other religious and secularized meanings of 'community'.

The magazines highlight the parish, at a time when many denominations were based on other areas, like the Methodist circuit or district, or Catholic parish. Some religious faiths developed publications that were locally comparable to Anglican parish magazines. One thinks of Jewish Synagogue Bulletins catering for largely urban congregations. Other denominations' 'magazines', such as *The Primitive Methodist Magazine*, were aimed at larger regions or a national or international readership.[27] Many such publications were implicit rivals to the Anglican magazines, either locally, or in challenging the localness of the Anglican focus and venue. The Nonconformist challenge was at its most intense in the second half of the nineteenth century, making its views stridently known in arguments over education, burial rights, charity administration, local government reform and so on. One motive behind the founding of a parish magazine in the nineteenth century was to steal a march on this religious or even secularized opposition: to stress that the parish was still a Christian entity, in the face of alternative civil conceptions; to define the local parochial community *as Anglican* via such publication; to strengthen a 'core' of Anglican parish citizens; to evangelize and highlight the parish and its Anglican minister; and to prioritize Anglican schedules (and even church clock control) of time during transformation of timed and regularized communities. All this was in the face of alternative perspectives, loyalties and senses of time and place.[28] These issues were fundamental for local identity and rival senses of community.

Attractions or amenities promoted by the parish magazine – fetes, parties, dances, games, reading rooms, lectures and sermons, concerts, outings, medical clubs, parish guild processions and so on – were partly designed by the Church of England to hold parishioners to itself, and to make Anglican community culture seem more attractive and lively than other options. The rector of Upton Scudamore (Wiltshire) wrote about providing entertainments, saying he 'would rather see you laugh'.[29] In these regards, parish magazines would often proclaim their appeal to everyone. They were an important part of the efforts of the Church of England to perpetuate the identification of itself with the parish, in a period when that was increasingly questioned. Thus, the Croxton Kerrial (Leicestershire) magazine was 'intended for all', including 'chapel people, who do not always see clearly the church's point of view, or understand her claim as the original and ancient religion of England'.[30] The tone here may not have had the desired effect. There were also issues of clerical status and class position, alienating clergy from many parishioners. Attempts were made to address this, especially in these magazines, but one wonders how an article on 'The poverty of the clergy' was received among poorer Leicestershire villagers.[31] In addition, parish magazines frequently expounded the history of the parish from an Anglican point of view. The clergyman would often elaborate upon the history of the church – its origins, architecture, restoration, seating and bells – giving this an overarching prominence and long antecedence beyond anything else in the parish. Meetings were often advertised in the magazine at which the vicar was to deliver a paper, and these talks frequently had titles like 'Some points of interest in the history of our parish'. No doubt these augmented local senses of place and history and were welcomed by many. They are indicative too of the leisure activities and antiquarian interests of many clergy. In some cases, indeed, once the architectural and church history issues were over, the clergyman clearly ran out of things to say, and announced the end of the magazine. Many others digressed at length upon theological topics: the nature of the Trinity, the meaning of Lent, biblical parables and the lives of the Apostles. At times this can read like a printed sermon. There was in the nineteenth century a considerable appetite for theological debate, including among many poor people, and the Bible and *The Pilgrim's Progress* were staples of reading. One Kentish clergyman commented upon his early 1860s magazine that 'The working classes liked it much', more so than the farmers and gentry.[32] Yet the Anglican theological content in parish magazines may often have been unappealing or doctrinally biased, especially to inhabitants who were attracted (in relevant regions) to faiths like Welsh Calvinistic Methodism, the Primitive Methodist Church, the Bible Christians or the Salvation Army. The 'Editor's Diary' of *All the World* caught this mood well, when it remarked: 'You happened to call just when Mr Readall had just bought a copy of the parish magazine which he didn't want at all, for he would rather have Commissioner Booth-Clibborn's "Fire, Fuel, and Fanaticism."'[33] In Wales, Cornwall, many northern regions and other centres of religious Nonconformity, some magazines evolved in outlook and philosophy to cater for their readers, perhaps even under dissenting editors. Yet the most common criticism of parish magazines has always been their partial constituency, their main appeal to Anglican parishioners. That had been an initial purpose of the magazines, to bind the Anglican local community in a common sense of purpose – but then, it was often suggested, they were written 'for a closed community into which it would be presumptuous to intrude'.[34]

One of the strongest features of parish magazines was the way they documented the role of the clergy in parochial life. These publications were the published voice of the clergy, where visitation returns or diaries were their unpublished voice, and they shed much light upon the clergyman's importance. This often becomes most apparent when he left or retired, when extracts from speeches, descriptions of gifts, reminiscences and the like were published. This tradition of generosity to leaving clergy was apparent with the departure from Bream (a mining area in the Forest of Dean, Gloucestershire) of the Revd and Mrs Witherby, in 1868. After many flourishing statements showing the 'affection and esteem of all classes at Bream',

> Mr. Richard Hewlett … with a few kind and appropriate words, presented the vicar with the gold watch, for which many of the parishioners had subscribed. Mr. Witherby said, that he thanked them most heartily for their very handsome present; they could not have given me anything more useful; he had long needed a watch, and feared some of them had found Bream Church time a little uncertain, in future he hoped to be up to the time of day, for he would always carry their gift with him in his work, unless he thought he was likely to be much in a Bristol crowd …

'He knew that Foresters were not fond of strangers', but he hoped that they would welcome his successor.[35]

The Victorian clergy have often been accused of class insensitivities. Yet one notices here the clever way in which the departing vicar seems to apologize for any clerical lapses, alluding (given the gift) to issues of time; then refers to and confirms his listeners' senses of their own moral superiority over others, especially those in towns; then hints at the need for some slight change in their receptivity to outsiders. These are significant levels of interpersonal skill, and one often sees examples of this in parish magazines. For these were communities where interpersonal skills could be subtle and fine-honed: through long familiarity and personal knowledge, in the interests of everyday work in a confined area, knowing the inevitability of long-standing personal contacts. Perhaps it took such relatively close-knit communities and personal proximity to foster their development and expression. After all, the nuanced conversations in George Eliot or Thomas Hardy were written from experience of these parish communities – just as conversations in Raymond Chandler, Martin Amis or James Kelman arise from the different spoken repertoires and often loose relationships of modern urban society.[36]

The terms used in parish magazines indicate the apparent respect with which the clergy were often held – 'The Rev. gentleman intended relinquishing his charge in the village'; in this case referring to the Revd Bickmore of Husborne Crawley in Bedfordshire. Significant sums (over £40 for him) were often collected as leaving presents. 'Mr. Bickmore received loud cheers when he rose to thank his parishioners and friends for their kindness after which he spoke of his 8 years work in the parish and that during that time he had preached about 900 sermons.'[37] That is a rate of two sermons every week. No wonder he received loud cheers. Some parishes even had a 'Commemoration Day of the Death of the late Vicar of the Parish'.[38] In Bream, when the Revd H. E. Dandy left in 1896 for Kingswood near Bristol, a long eulogy followed in *The Bream Magazine* to 'their esteemed and beloved Vicar … a true friend', recounting testimonials, speeches and gifts:

> a valuable black marble timepiece and pair of vases to correspond, together with a nicely bound album, containing an illuminated address and the names of the subscribers (about 400 in number), and 15 splendid views of Bream and neighbourhood, which had been specially taken by Mr. F. F. Jones, photographer, Cinderford.[39]

The testimonial was promoted by 'a large and thoroughly representative committee, upon which were several of the leading Nonconformists of the locality'. Mr H. Cox thanked the Vicar in the name of the congregation

> for his earnest work among them, and the many valuable sermons which they had heard from him, reminding them that what they had to do was to live up to them, and carry them out in their lives: to receive the smooth stones of the Gospel from the brook, and as the stone from the sling of David sunk into the forehead of the giant Goliath, so to let them sink deeply into their heads and hearts, that they might be shown forth in their lives.[40]

The clergy were chairmen of many committees, had key roles in pastoral work, in education, the administration of justice, fund-raising, the poor law and charity management, parish sick and burial clubs, the vestry and (from 1921) the Parochial Church Council. They conducted baptisms, marriages and burials, and were instrumental in church seating, in countless festivities, musical associations and calendrical events. They were directly involved in economic life, notably through glebe farming and tithe issues. They liaised with diocesan authorities. They claimed rights in the appointment of parish officers, sometimes in assertive terms. They were often active in hunting, sports and recreations. It is apparent in some parishes that clergy were still leading 'beating the bounds' parish perambulations well into the twentieth century.[41] Whatever one's verdict on the clergy, these roles are widely shown in parish magazines, which can read as an itemization of such work and its value for the local community.[42]

There was also a strongly moral purpose underlying parish magazines. They were a medium through which clergy admonished their parishioners, making them a means of moral reform, a way to improve discipline, almost a propaganda arm for parish authorities. The vicar of Bream alluded to 'disobedience, negligence, faithlessness'.[43] The Croxton Kerrial (Leicestershire) incumbent launched into complaints about 'the filthy conversation of the wicked'. 'There is the hindrance of bad surroundings, the low tone, and conversation of men and women with whom we have to work.' What was nearly as bad, 'there is sheer laziness on Sunday morning … [which] makes the morning attendance in the vast majority of churches in England a disgrace to a Christian country'.[44] There was the (abating) problem of 'rowdiness among the young people on Good Friday',[45] or in Gosforth (Cumberland) young men hanging around the church door 'making it uncomfortable for those who have to pass through'.[46] The clergyman of St Michael's, Winterbourne (Gloucestershire), looked back upon 1879 as a bad year: 'The poor especially have had a lesson. They should be more careful, and not spend their wages as fast as they earn them. Improvidence and intemperance are the faults of too many. Rich and poor alike should learn to care for one another, and help one another.'[47] There were many comments about marriage, and the need for decorum. One finds the vicar of Studley (Warwickshire), for example, complaining that brides presented themselves for their marriage ceremony without any covering for their heads, and insisting that this be reformed. He kept a veil in the vestry, and required it to be used by any who presented themselves without a covering.[48] Many other forms of 'inappropriate' behaviour were alluded to. Having nearly finished building a new piece of churchyard wall, the Croxton Kerrial rector added ominously: 'good walls are not put up for boys to climb over', or to take short cuts over, and over graves in 'consecrated ground'.[49]

Indeed, the churchyard could be referred to in other ways in the parish magazine, notably by printing epitaphs from gravestones. These were also often used to instruct spiritually, or morally reform, parishioners. They served as a kind of local biographical history, a record of past leading families and their residences, and they helped to establish continuity. *All Saints' Headley Parish Magazine* (Hampshire) published them in 1875, and this was also a topic in twentieth-century parish magazines.[50] Memorialization was frequently referred to, discussing memorial windows to individuals, or war memorials, notably after 1918. The magazines were used to publish regulations about churchyards and burials. They debated churchyard extensions,[51] churchyard closures, the levelling of graves, memorial clearance, new cemeteries, lych gates and the impact of these upon the local community. Such an impact could be substantial, as when centrally located churchyards strong in historical and familial associations were closed, and new cemeteries were built under the Burial Acts well beyond the housing perimeters of villages. Publicity in parish magazines was also an important means to raise funds for these developments.

Church attendance was frequently referred to. Indeed, parish magazines are highly informative on issues relating to the decline of church attendance and its significance for community life. They frequently testify to a growing climate of doubt and disbelief, and it is interesting to notice that their inauguration year (1859) saw the publication of Charles Darwin's *The Origin of Species*. They give much information and clerical comment on the nature of the church services, attendances, the helpful or obstructive attitudes of employers or the beautification or attractions of the church. Having given a list of sermons to be preached by visitors during Lent, the clergyman for Heytesbury (Wiltshire) continued:

> I must earnestly invite all parishioners to make some real effort to attend these services. The attendance of female parishioners has generally been fairly satisfactory at these Lent services, but that of the male portion of them is generally lamentably scanty. What a strange and sad delusion is the idea which appears to prevail throughout England, that religion is only intended for women, and that men are concerned only with the affairs of this present life.[52]

Other clergy commented adversely about congregations. When the Bishop made his confirmation address at Bream, a devotedly listening incumbent later complained, 'The address was hardly heard in the farther corners of the Church, owing to the incessant coughing.'[53] But then, this was a mining village.

'Community'

One of the interests of parish magazines concerns the languages of 'community' and mutual respect in the past. This takes us forward in time from my discussion of such terms in Chapter 2. The articles or entries had to appeal and be understood locally. For example, the term 'neighbours' had the meaning we recognize today, or as it was used by Thomas Hardy about people associated with the Mellstock 'quire': to mean people living near to each other with certain shared community purposes.[54] But it could narrowly mean householders and ratepayers. Or it meant 'neighbouring' settlements, villages, small towns or great houses in the vicinity but not necessarily in the parish. In regions of nucleated settlement, the community was seen as the housing area, and 'neighbours' could mean nearby parishes. 'Distant neighbours' often meant places or great houses further afield. Then there was the word 'stranger', which is often found, for example, with reference to donations to the Soldiers' Institute in Warminster: 'Two subscriptions have been received … One from Mr. Haskew (a stranger).'[55] This term was frequent in local communities. Among other terms, one notices the 'better man' at competitions. The term 'parishioners' was clearly important and meaningful, although it could have religious ambiguities. Further, there was the re-application and inversion of the word 'gentleman' in the late nineteenth century, which did not override earlier usage, but which in some areas allowed it to denote men of humble working status. Thus, one finds, with regard to the thirty-first Bream Annual Flower, Fruit and Vegetable show, that two gardeners were asked to judge the competition; and the Magazine records that 'we are asked on behalf of the committee and the Society, to express their appreciative gratitude to these gentlemen, who again so kindly, and in a way to give such entire satisfaction, gave their services in this way'.[56] This terminology is socially encompassing. One sees similar regard for a social diversity of men in Bream's Volunteer Parade Service in 1896:

> in spite of a very wet day … there was a very good muster of men. The Vicar preached an appropriate sermon, reminding the congregation of the good services of the Volunteer force, at various crises of English History and of the social advantages of the Volunteer movement, serving, as it does, to unite all classes of men, and helping to bring out in them that self-respect upon which so much depends.[57]

These examples indicate a language of mutual esteem, of belonging, achievement and commonality. As a courteous language applied to people of 'low' social standing this was fairly novel, even in the relatively egalitarian 'free miner' and forester ethos of the Forest of Dean.

One preoccupation revealed in the magazines was that of school attendance. Around Warminster, competitions were held between thirteen schools to improve their attendances, and the winning school (achieving 93.3 per cent of possible attendances) held a challenge banner.[58] There were also personal medals, shields and other prizes for high attendance. The comments of school inspectors were remarked upon, the magazine being the conduit for these to be conveyed to parishioners.[59] The magazines frequently congratulated teachers, naming them and giving them wholesome community endorsement, adopting a completely positive approach that would be envied by their more modern counterparts.[60] There were also many references to Sunday schools, calling for volunteer teachers and higher attendance, or books for Sunday school libraries. 'With so much impure literature in circulation, we must all do what is possible to counteract this by providing reading which is pure and of a healthy moral tone.'[61] Local associations of Sunday schools were organized, and reported upon in parish magazines, such as the South Forest [of Dean] Sunday School Teachers' Association.[62] Many Sunday school events were recorded. In Sherington (Buckinghamshire), 'there was the Sunday School evening, with its early tea at the Rectory and the large and heavily laden Christmas Tree in the School …The Christmas Tree bore a present for each Sunday School scholar', with garments made by 'kind friends'.[63] The Sunday school anniversaries, processions and feasts were reported in much detail, as were school excursions to the seaside or other venues.

There were many collections, sales of work or events to raise money for local schools. Such local fund-raising occasions enhanced community spirit and good feeling. In Bream, for example,

> On Thursday a most amusing washing contest took place the competitors being gentlemen, and were certainly those who had not always been used to the kind of work they tried to do. Roars of laughter were caused by their efforts to win the prizes. Proceedings were enlivened by various selections of music by the Bream band on Wednesday, and the Lydney band on Thursday. [64]

In most of these cases, the magazines also published the sums of money that were raised, even if these were small. This was true of collections of many sorts: nineteenth-century parish magazines overflow with mentions of small sums of money. Modern readers can often ignore such details. Yet there is a crucial historical message here: that money – its raising and spending – was a *community-enhancing* feature, often the focus of endeavour, conviviality and reportage. This built cohesion through shared purpose, just as with the administration of church or chapel seat or pew rents designed to pay off restoration costs or chapel debts.[65] The lack of external guarantors of funding – compared with the large extraneous subsidies of recent periods – was a very prominent factor, stimulating local efforts that brought a sense of achieved community, developing pride in place and augmenting the local respect accorded to individuals who acted beneficently. This could fortify a sense of class (e.g. when a working-class religious denomination raised funds internally, or when senses of envy existed); or it could help to defuse class feeling, as when a local landowner was seen to act generously for the good of all.

Coverage of local history was a common feature of these publications, and this must have aided senses of local identity among readers. There were descriptions of how overseers and churchwardens used to operate, and how rates were assessed. Local seasonal work, 'customs' and folklore were discussed, with appeals to anyone who could shed light on them.[66] Past disputes with other parishes were addressed. An entry for Upton Scudamore (Wiltshire) in 1901 commented: 'Then we went to war with Warminster over the roads about Norridge', taking residents back to 1731, and a dispute that lasted through the 1730s and perhaps beyond.[67] Such rivalries or animosities between parishes were often linked to disputes over pauper and poor law settlement, which I discussed earlier. By the late nineteenth century one sees attempts to alleviate them. Horningsham in 1901, for example, had an entry mentioning the need for friendly meetings between parishes, which 'must do a great deal of good'.[68] Invitations to bell-ringers from other parishes to ring the church's bells were one way to encourage friendliness, and this spread in the late nineteenth century. Where once church bells had been the voice of the parish, often 'crowing' against another parish in the case of parochial sporting or legal victories, the allowing of other parishes or campanological societies to ring one's own bells was significant as an overture of appeasement or openness.

Local pride radiates from these magazines. They celebrated parochial pride and distinctiveness. After all, it has been written, 'the last thing a parish wants to do is to lose its identity'.[69] Over and again, one reads of donations to the church or endowments to the parish by parishioners who extol their local connections: the purchase of plaques, music stands or cupboards, seats, kneelers, stained glass windows and the like. Consider church kneelers: each woman made her contribution, in a fixed requested format, but with her own individual design, frequently using local symbols or motifs, showing her skills in embroidery and needlework, confirming her or her family's sense of place in church, and in local esteem and her skilled status among parish women, with a controlled theme of competition, one that was dutifully adjusted to purpose and to augmenting the beauty of the church. And such work was a supplication and dedication to God. Fine yet self-effacing in workmanship and function, such work confirmed both parochial pride and a strong sense of local belonging. I urge the reader to pause and think about the countless thousands of women who have thus made church or chapel kneelers, in their own way. For it was through humble gestures and efforts – the sorts of things that historians easily overlook – that spirits of community belonging and identity were usually manifested.

Then there was the wider pride in the church, and interest in its history, restoration and decoration:

> The Church was very tastefully decorated, the work being shared among the eldest girls in the School and Bible Class, and several 'devout women,' who gave their talents of time and skill to adorn and beautify the House of God. Flowers were kindly sent from Lydney Park, Clanna, Rockwood, Whitemead Park, Newland, and Drybrook, and from most of the gardens in the parish. Our Church never looked to greater advantage, the decorations being of a lighter character than has often been the case ... 'We love the place, O Lord, Wherein thine honour dwells.'[70]

Or one thinks of pride in the parochial achievements of children, pride in the sums or materials collected for charity, pride in the exploits of clergymen or missionaries overseas, pride in parish sporting prowess, a sense of achievement when concerts and other events passed off well, pride in church singing, pride in the church bells and their ringers, pride in flower shows or harvest festivals, and a determination to pass on diocesan or other external compliments. These sentiments were all abundant in parish magazines, seemingly more so than in their post-1945 equivalents.

Memorial statements to parishioners who had added to parish life were frequent in the magazines:

> The Preacher taking for his text I *Chron.*, xxix, 9, made allusion to the proposed memorial to Miss Alice Davies, who has been such a great benefactress to the parish, by aiding the good work of restoring the Church, building the parsonage house, and greatly aiding to the endowment of the Living. The memorial will take either the form of a stained glass window or of a new vestry, which will be built as an aisle to the present chancel, adding much to the beauty and completion of the Church.[71]

Published examples like this exist in their hundreds, proclaimed, celebrated, partly in a hope of moral emulation – biographical fragments of a life parochially esteemed and perhaps remembered in no other source.

How should one evaluate the richness, or dreariness, of nineteenth- and early twentieth-century village and small-town life? One can find it described in either way: as abundant in folklore, collective sociability, tradition and calendrical events, mutuality of work and concerted organization, proud in some cases of its leadership – or, alternatively, as impoverished, meagre in material resources, embittered, fearful, prone to sometimes vicious protest, double-faced and deferential, antagonistically class-based, squabbling, exclusionary, many of its inhabitants aspiring to leave as soon as opportunity presented itself. After 1918, there was also the despair and recrimination at military losses, and the attempts to come to terms with those. These are the interpretative polarities relating to localized 'community' that one finds, and against which one assesses problematic issues of 'community decline'. No one historical source delivers a complete picture, and parish magazines are as partial as many other kinds of evidence. However, as 'a chronicle of local doings',[72] they document an impressive array of community events: a range of activities that can eclipse the social life of many modern parishes, given the latter's high levels of individualism, occupational diversity, lengthy television watching, sometimes conspicuous consumption, car dependency, loneliness or determined privacy.

In the parishes around Warminster, for example, there were lectures on horticulture, health preservation, first aid, the origins of carol singing and many other such topics. 'Bostocks' Menagerie' visited Bere Regis in 1891, when lions, tigers, wolves, elephants, camels, monkeys and many other animals could be seen.[73] That was hardly a staple of larger village culture. Yet there were numerous descriptions in all parishes of meetings held by groups such as the Mothers' Meetings, Band of Hope, chess clubs, debating societies, Bible Classes and many more. Suppers were held for the choir or choral society. Many classes were reported upon, covering music appreciation, religious studies, history, wood carving, knitting and clothes making, domestic science, horticulture and countless other subjects. These were often linked to local societies, which appear to have been intra-parochial rather than having wider district membership.

The societies themselves conducted their own entertainments, which were often musical. Among the lively concerts offered to parishioners, one notices 'Miss Watling's Bigotphone band in bright uniform' which included plantation songs in its repertoire.[74] After a concert by the Chapmanslade Horticultural Society, a magazine commented in 1901 that 'The Committee had taken pains to exclude comic songs of the kind which are frequently received with applause, but are such a blot upon village entertainments.'[75] The playing of musical instruments seems to have been widespread. Yet one finds mounting comment to the effect that 'The music is very different from what it once was.'[76] The saga of the 'quire' in Thomas Hardy's *Under the Greenwood Tree* is visible in a number of parish magazines, as the organ (well beloved of late nineteenth-century clergymen) replaced parish gallery musicians. We will consider this in the next chapter. Hardy complained that 'The change has tended to stultify the professed aims of the clergy, its direct result being to curtail and extinguish the interests of parishioners in church doings.'[77] One senses here a fracture of community with the church, as organ replaced 'quire', and this also influenced the shape of church services. Linked to music, there were the magazines' accounts of the church bells or clock, and the issues surrounding the latter's replacement – as in Badsey in Worcestershire, featuring a new clock with 'the famous Westminster Chimes attached to strike all the quarters and the hours, for £128. The clock could be provided without the chimes for a less cost, but it would be a very pleasant variety in the life of the village to hear these beautiful chimes.'[78] The whole noise and working routines of the village were thus affected, long into the future.

Reporting of gardening societies was especially prominent, such as Bream's Cottage Gardeners' Society. *The Bream Magazine* recorded its meetings in extraordinary detail, giving the results of every competition. In 1868,

> The Fourth Annual Show was held at Colliers' Beech … and was, all things considered, better than any former one. The long drought had parched up the land, and consequently many gardens were unable to produce vegetables which were considered by their owners as worth entering for competition; hence there were only 157 articles this year against 193 last year. On the other hand the onions and potatoes were better, and the baskets and pots of flowers, and designs in grasses and flowers, more tasteful. The attendance was not so large as last year. The Lydney Volunteer Band played during the afternoon, and gave great satisfaction. At 6 o'clock the prizes, all of which were of a useful and substantial sort, – as quilts, sheets, fire-irons, tables, knives and forks, crockery, iron ware, tools, &c., many of them presents from Lady Campbell and Mrs. Noel, – were presented to the winners by Lady Campbell. The judges were the same as last year, – Mr. Collison from Clanna, and Mr. Moysey from Newland House. The following is the list of successful competitors …

And there followed a list of prizes (including those in second, third and fourth places), for twenty-two agricultural headings, including the

Ornamental Basket of Plants, Rhubarb (six sticks), Nosegay, Spring Onions (twenty-four), Collection of Medicinal Herbs, Potatoes (half peck), Best Design in Flowers, Grass &c, Parsnips and so on.[79] Few historians perusing such lists can doubt the fondness of village inhabitants for gardening, allotments,[80] and small intra-parochial competition.

Parish journalism documented the lives of women in countless ways. There were 'register'-type reports of baptisms, marriages and deaths, when the private became public – 'Many parishioners, especially the women, turn to the register first of all'[81] – reports on women's craftsmanship, education and their roles as teachers, nurses, in harvest and other agricultural work, in church decoration or in making bequests. Obituaries of women were frequent. Or there was coverage of lectures for women, on topics such as first aid or nursing. There were commonly Mothers' or Women's Unions, with anniversary festival services, Women's Clubs, Sewing Clubs, Ladies' Work Societies, Girls' Friendly Societies, shows organized by women and so on. In Kingston Deverill the rector gave a talk to the Women's Union in 1901 entitled 'Of honourable women not a few', pointing out what makes 'an honourable woman', and how one could add to their number.[82]

Over and again, the magazines bear witness to the role of sport in local communities, which could include female participation. They document novelties such as football in Bere Regis, which created much amusement among the spectators, many of whom had never seen the game played before.[83] *The Bream Magazine* reported 'a cricket match between the boys and the girls, and the ascent of Mr Mullan's fire balloons. How those balloons did go – away to Monmouthshire! and how the girls wickets went down – like ninepins!'[84] At the annual flower show in Bream, 'there was a program of rustic sports'.[85] The rising popularity of tennis and its forms of sociability in the interwar period are also very evident.

The magazines show the diffusion to parishes of new technologies affecting community entertainment and horizons. The 'gramophone', 'limelight views', magic lantern shows, 'the apparatus of dissolving views' or 'slides' became increasingly apparent. In Bere Regis in 1893, 'Mr. E. Baker, of Salisbury, gave us a fine exhibition of Cinematograph Pictures of the Coronation, of Seaside Scenes, of a Cricket and Football match, and views of Foreign Countries, diversified with musical performances on a phonograph.'[86] This technology of community took the community away from itself, allowing it to look elsewhere, yet it did so as a shared experience. Clearly, this had implications for the rural exodus which became so marked after the mid-nineteenth century. More generally, new items or developments in material culture were indicated, often with insights into their effects or significance for community life. Thus we learn of Japanese lanterns, 'violet alms bags', new altar cloths, oak eagle lecterns, new organs or harmoniums, different kinds of bicycle, village oil lamps used as street lighting, swing-boats, merry-go-rounds, red earthenware vases used in place of pickle jars, Sunday school stamps and albums. Alternatively, one has comments on the decline of other items, such as 'old English smocks'.

One is struck by the frequent mention of the role of the gentry or leading families in these parishes. In Horningsham (Wiltshire), for example, in 1900 Father Christmas came to Longleat and gave presents to 200 children and their teachers – courtesy of Lord and Lady Bath, who also provided entertainment in the form of a conjuror and gave a tea for all. 'Then cheers – real ones – for Lord and Lady Bath for their great kindness.'[87] (Notice the significance of the need to insert 'real ones'.) The same source distributed coal in the parishes of Kingston and Monkton Deverill,[88] or paid for kneelers in Horningsham church. The Duchess of Somerset arranged tea and Christmas presents for all children in Maiden Bradley (Wiltshire): 'Soon the room was filled with shouts of delight, mingled with much instrumental music, expressive of deep pleasure, if not of harmony.'[89] The Duke of Somerset contributed to the coal and clothing club of Maiden Bradley. He also presided over the West Wiltshire Working Men's Benefit Society.[90] One realizes that these magazines were often written by clergymen, who were appreciative of their patrons; yet they frequently document generosity, community spirit and leadership from above, arguably much more so than today, in a form that had major significance in the communities concerned.

It is hard to evaluate shifts in the communal life of parishes from these sources. In some regards one sees relapse, in others revival or novelties. Many villages faced demographic and economic decline in the late nineteenth century, with rural recession and the exodus from the land, and in the interwar period they suffered depression again, and the loss of men from the war. They often perceived a weakening of their community life, their magazines bearing witness to this. These publications frequently discuss falling rural population, expressing predictable concerns. Parish life was thought to be threatened by this and by the consequential change in age structures. Growing numbers of uninhabited houses were there for everyone to see. We will discuss this in later chapters on James Wentworth Day and Adrian Bell. Some magazines even had surveys of inhabited or uninhabited houses.[91] 'The result of the census shows a steady decrease of our population.' Longbridge Deverill and Crockerton (Wiltshire) had lost over 100 people in the decade after 1891, about a seventh of their population. Hill Deverill had experienced a decline from 111 to 65 people in the same period, and while there had been thirty children there under ten years of age in 1891, by 1901 there were only four.[92] It was obvious that this rural exodus had major effects upon education, church provision, clerical livelihoods, housing, and much else in community life. Such issues were often raised in parish magazines.

The *Bere Regis and Winterborne Kingston Parish Magazine* commented in 1930 about how the village social club was stagnating, the membership having fallen from fifty-six to forty. Other changes affecting senses of community included the decline in Christmas gifts or meals provided by the clergy to parishioners, as a wealthier generation of clergy died out, and as they encountered financial problems in the late nineteenth-century depression.[93] Gifts from social elites to poorer parishioners or children often diminished from the later nineteenth century, and they become less reported in parish magazines. Yet in other regards there were positive changes. One thinks of more democratic participation in village societies and governance, the effects of the parish councils and their elections after 1894 (even though their powers were very limited), new clubs such as the middle-class tennis clubs, advances in material culture or (to a lesser extent) in health care, rising disposable incomes, the extension of schooling and new venues and means of transport for holidays and outings. The male deaths of the First World War sadly contributed to far larger numbers of spinsters and widows, but they also helped the flowering of self-reliant women's associations and meetings in the interwar years.[94]

Most of the surviving parish magazines document rural parishes, and invariably they discussed agricultural work and events. Earlier prices were recounted from historical sources. The weather was compared with the past. This could include rainfall tables for a succession of years.[95] Storms and their effects on crops and gardens were recorded. Disastrous harvests and their effects were documented, as in 1931.[96] It was remarked in a tone of disappointment that tithes have fallen steadily in many villages, 'and probably will never recover', the rector seemingly writing from a personal point of view.[97] One feature that fascinated some writers was the catching of 'vermin' in the past. Aware of the harm they could do to crops, stored grain, pheasants' eggs and so on, they rarely criticized this. Upton Scudamore's entry for March 1901 dwelt at length upon the sums paid by churchwardens in the eighteenth and earlier nineteenth century for sparrows, pole cats, hedgehogs, stoats and other 'vermin'. In 1828, 251 dozen (3,012) sparrows were killed, at a total cost to the churchwardens of £4 3s. 8d. – costs that were considered too high to continue with, and so thenceforward they agreed only to pay for old hen sparrows killed.[98]

As well as noticing the hedgehog travelling furtively over the lawn, Thomas Hardy commented many times upon the dramas of neighbourhood life: the events that were as tumultuous locally as many occasions of international significance, and the importance of these to people. He would have revelled in many occurrences reported in parish magazines and realized their significance for spirits of community and local recollection. Consider just one example, which is from Bere Regis in 1892, relating to a parish church that Hardy knew well:

> There was panic in church at Evensong on Sunday 9 October when the vicar, towards the end of his sermon, had just quoted Tennyson's words 'the dead are not dead but alive'. Immediately, a 'tremendous crash was heard in the belfry, then a rumbling and a pause then another roar'. Members of the congregation, particularly those at the back, scrambled over one another in their haste to get to the door. The breaking of a 6-cwt clock weight suspension cord, which had shortly before been wound to its full height, was found to have caused the disturbance. The weight, upon hitting the floor of the ringing chamber, had rebounded with such force that it had broken out through the 2-inch thick wooden casing and finally knocked over a ladder. The incident served to recall a similar panic of some 50 years earlier, when a piece of masonry from the tower fell on the nave roof during a service. One woman is said to have hidden under the altar whilst other members of the congregation jumped out of the box pews rather than use the doors.[99]

This is material suited to a Stanley Spencer religious painting, or a Dorothy L. Sayers novel, of a community's sense of God or other presences, and an event triggering memory of an earlier one. It is permeated with superstitious augury. Such events may have been parochial, yet they were long-lasting in collective recollection and significance, and they endowed places with distinctive reputations.

Globalized parochialism

Readers might presume that parish magazines encapsulated the most narrow and circumscribed features of community life, that they were inward-looking, closed to the external world. And if this were so, a view of the parish community as insular would result, a truly 'parish pump' microcosm, 'community' as constrained spatially, requiring a narrow kind of micro-history. Yet this was far from the truth in the nineteenth century.[100] As is becoming clear, parish magazines were far from being introspectively parochial. Among wider purposes, they publicized fund-raising for distant causes. To take one example among many, Christ Church Warminster collected for the 'Waifs and Strays Society', 'to give really destitute children a start in life'. Nearly 3,000 neglected children would, it claimed, be running wild in the streets of the great towns, but for the work of this Society. 'We ought to do all we can for these poor neglected ones.'[101] In some cases, despite clerical moralizing, one finds parish magazines not wishing to dwell upon internal problems. Here is an example of such outwardly concerned writing:

> All were deeply interested in the lively 'running' Lecture which accompanied the display. The first Lecture represented 'getting up steam' amongst the tall chimneys of a smoky manufacturing town; a process which the Lecturer, we can hardly doubt, applied with success to the feelings of his hearers, whose sympathies must have been won for the furtherance of the work set before them. Dingy streets, crowded rooms, Sunday resorts of pleasure, scenes of low amusements, appeared in succession. Enough was said and seen to convince the audience of the spiritual wants of our larger towns.[102]

This is a perspective often found in the magazines: that the real social problems of the day were elsewhere, usually in the cities, but not in the village or small-town parish producing the magazine, and that the parish's assistance was needed to help solve them. This perspective confirmed an insider's view of the parish as outward looking, Christian, responsible and superior to other places.

The magazines covered many national and international features, and they are interesting as a filter through which the reception and effects of these can be viewed locally. Given the magazines' local priorities, they distil national events down to the local arena of community and family history, to what was thought significant in small localities. The 'imagined community' of the nation was thus constructed partly by parish magazines.[103] These provide a different and local perspective on historical occurrence and import, which can vary from conventional historical judgement. And numerous events, supposedly of great national consequence in grander national narratives, were utterly ignored in parish magazines, wholly eclipsed by debate about allotment provision, children's school performance or funding of the new lych gate.

Yet certain 'larger' events echo almost universally in parish magazines. For example, throughout the country, hundreds of parish magazines paid tribute to Queen Victoria when she died, often referring to the sad tolling of the parish bells. In Horningsham, all the bells were muffled except the tenor, and the effect was exceedingly 'grand and solemn, and was heightened by the furious gale which blew that day'.[104] 'Never before has such a spectacle been witnessed in the world's history as that of not only an empire in mourning, but, we may almost say, a world in tears.'[105] In Bream 'The Parish Church is draped in black, and there is but little colour observable in the Village.'[106] Many parishes solemnly sang 'O God, our help in ages past' in commemorative services, while the clergy preached on texts such as 'The souls of the righteous are in the hands of God.'

The 'parochial' outlook went well beyond 'national' concerns. We have already noticed the widening implications of changing technologies of community entertainment and their reportage. While the magazines were 'community' sources, locally written in part, they had an expansiveness of view that is often remarkable in retrospect. Repeatedly, both the parish and inset elements of these magazines documented the extremes of Empire, communicating to parishioners aspects of life in India, Africa, New Zealand, Australia, Canada and many other parts of the world. They often covered foreign wars in close detail. In many cases, there was explicit comparison with the situation in the home parish, and this must have been crucial in many decisions on whether to remain, or leave for distant countries.

One overseas region of obvious interest was the Holy Land. Parish communities seem to have been very well informed on this. For example, in Bream the 'Rev. A. W. Hands lectured on "Jerusalem" which he has personally visited. The lecture was illustrated by some clear and beautiful Magic Lantern views of the Sacred city and other places in the Holy Land, and an entertaining and graphic account given of the various scenes presented.'[107] Money was raised for local schools from such a lecture. 'The following night … Mr Hands gave a lantern lecture at the Firs Mission Room, on the "Island of Ceylon, and the work of the Church among the Natives there."' There seems to have been genuine interest in other religions, to judge from the talks given. Comment could be critical, condescending, ignorant or prejudiced – in often revealing ways – but it was internationally engaged and concerned. For example, 'After prayers and a hymn, a short address was made by the Rev. B. A. Galland, on the Rise and Progress of Mohammedanism and its tenets.'[108] Would such a talk be given by a clergyman in the Forest of Dean today? These magazines document countless talks and collections for causes or missions in foreign countries, such as the Society of the Propagation of the Gospel in Foreign Parts, which sent deputations around the parishes.[109] In Bream, 'according to custom S. Andrews Day, November 30th, is set apart for Special Intercessory Prayer in behalf of Missions; the Services on that day shall be observed and attended, as opportunities for prayer to God that He would convert the Heathen nations.'[110] Or one finds the parishioners of Kingston and Monkton Deverill (Wiltshire) setting up a working party to make garments for 'our little black children in Lebombo', who would otherwise be naked.[111]

The Revd Canon Duckworth wrote letters to his congregation at St Mark's, Hamilton Terrace, St John's Wood, London, during his visit to India as Chaplain to the Prince of Wales. These letters were initially printed in the local *St Mark's Parish Magazine.* He wrote about Bombay, discussing the Church Missionary Society, the nature of schooling and the population he found. He described the

> gaudy red and green Hindu temples, where clanging bells and squeaking fifes and deafening tom-toms announce that worship is being offered to the idols within; a Mussulman mosque, said to be the head-quarters of Mussulman fanaticism in India, the favourite resort of Wahabi bigots and pilgrims to Mecca … illuminated with exquisite taste.

One notices here criticism and praise conjoined. He complained about 'the spectacle of *idolatry* in the midst of so many tokens of vigorous material and educational progress as abound on every side in Bombay'.[112] Similarly, the Revd Luke Rivington, writing in the *Cowley St John's Parish Magazine* on Christianity in India, predicted ominously that

> when India is converted … the Church will have to bear much sorrow and disappointment. There is a difficulty in seeing the broad issues of a thing, fearfully fastened by centuries of subtle, useless, disquisition, – a tendency to fix on minute unimportant matters, a waywardness and selfishness, a wildness of credulity, an exuberance of unchastened imagination, which must, one would fear, produce a crop of heresies.

This parish magazine writing was then taken up and published elsewhere, in another magazine that seemed equally confident that India would be converted.[113]

Croxton Kerrial in Leicestershire wished 'to spread the gospel through the world' and supported the Universities Mission to Central Africa. White's 1846 *Directory* of the county confirms that this 'pleasant village is on a bold declivity of the Wold hills'; much of it belonging to the Duke of Rutland, 'who has a pleasant hunting seat' – it contained about '650 souls' and some fish ponds.[114] These souls must have been fairly excited to see, in their parish magazine, accounts of the geography of Africa and its exploration. More specifically, they read about the banks of the River Zambezi:

> lined with the densest jungle of mangroves and grasses, while creepers of a hundred kinds struggle for life among the interlacing stems. Crocodiles of all sizes, from the baby specimen which might be taken home in a bottle to the enormous bullet-proof brute as large as an eighty-one ton gun. These

> revolting animals are adjusted to their surroundings in the matter of colour in the most remarkable way: the young ones are lighter yellow, and more easily distinguished, but the full grown specimen is … like the revolting slimy tree stumps on the river bank.

Readers must have looked up from the magazines to their benign Leicestershire fish ponds with some relief. Lake Nyasa, these parishioners learnt, has 'strange people and animals along the banks', like the elephant, who 'in his native haunts … is as nimble as a kitten', and is as natural in 'the gigantic grasses and reeds of his African home as a rabbit is to Croxton Park'.[115] Many other parish magazines published descriptions of Africa, such as the account of 'Rats and elephants in central Africa' originally published in the *St. Mary Abbots (Kensington) Parish Magazine*. This comprised an account of missionary work, elephant hunting, tusks and their sales, the unfortunate practice of thieving by the people of Busoga and (Heaven forbid) the selling of women.[116]

Parish magazines were a venue for information about missionary work, 'getting together as many curios from foreign lands as possible'. They reported on displays in the parish hall, comprising photographs of missionaries, money-raising needlework, 'specimens of native work, arms and other curiosities from other parts of the world'[117] and the like. These shows often ended with a singing of 'Jesus shall reign'. A meeting in Longbridge Deverill (Wiltshire), highlighted in its magazine, featured stalls with exhibits from India, Africa, Madagascar, Melanesia, China, Japan, Canada and the West Indies. Besides these, there were 'Zulu boys, Canadian cowboys, Chinese and Japanese boys and girls in costume … [singing] their native songs in English'.[118] Money raised from this was for the Church's missions 'to the colonies and to the heathen'. Obituaries of missionaries and others dying overseas were published in the *Frome-Selwood Parish Magazine*, as for example concerning the career of the Revd Clement J. Sparks, who died in Zanzibar.[119] Foreign missions to South America were described in *St Mark's, Victoria Park, Parish Magazine*.[120] The magazines were used to cover mission work linked to anti-slavery campaigns in various parts of the world.[121] Missionaries and other overseas personnel were frequently recruited through parish magazines, drawing attention, in one example, to the need for clergy in Zanzibar and Nyasa, doctors and nurses for Magila and Zanzibar as well as for builders, carpenters, masons, schoolmasters and (not least) the urgent requirement of 'a lady for Mbweni'.[122]

Another feature of some parish magazines was the way in which the parish incorporated people from afar into its publication, as if they were extensions of the Anglican parish community. On the front page of the parish magazine of St Mark, Tunbridge Wells, mission agents in the foreign field, supported by the Church, were entered as members of the Church staff. Thus, we find 'Native Catechist at Peshawar: Azizuddin; and a Bible-woman at Lucknow, and Native Catechist in China'. This encouraged parochial readers to support them and to take a special interest 'in the locality of the work'.[123] It also must have encouraged a very outward-looking sense of the parish community. The 'loose', often international networks of today – discussed in Chapter 1 – often have no 'core' 'communities' from which they are anchored. Hence, the fluidity and individualism by which they are often now characterized. By contrast, the internationally minded nineteenth-century parish magazine was firmly anchored in localized 'nested' community, and branched out from that, while keeping its absent readers well informed of local news. Community as locality essentially remained its benchmark.

Given this idea of global outreach of the parish, of a worldwide expansiveness and sense of cosmopolitan responsibility, coupled with the Christian and more local interests of parish magazines, it is no surprise that they were emulated throughout the world. Their wider international format was often very similar to that in England, that is a parish magazine coupled with a publication like *Home Words*.[124] In such a form, they circulated in Sao Paulo, Santos, Campinas Jundiai, Sorocaba, Rio de Janeiro, Ribeirao Preto, San Francisco and many other such places.[125] St Mary's Balmain, a suburb of Sydney, had its own parish magazine, one that commented upon South Sea Missions, Melanesia, Japan, China Missions and on such topics as 'the lot of women in India', and other work by 'our fellow-Gleaners'.[126] In India, parish magazines were widely modelled on this idea. And their content echoed that of the 'home' equivalents, for example, with the successes of local Indian boys 'always published in our local parish magazine, so that they may be read by all'.[127] Such magazines were used to proselytize people nearby. For example, local Spanish ones were given to sailors in Barcelona.[128] As in England, the parish magazine was an excuse for calling at every house, taking it round, 'and thus we have a definite reason for calling at houses whose occupants do not consider themselves as members of our Church'.[129] This helped to create a spirit of community via the introductions and resulting human contact. Similar magazines were started elsewhere in Europe, as in Switzerland.[130] Further afield, in Grahamstown in South Africa, a correspondent wrote that 'I have tried to establish a little parish magazine here, by localizing the *Dawn of Day*, published by the S.P.C.K.,' but he complained of the delayed arrival of parcels containing it from England. His content was 'useful church information similar to that introduced into our English parish magazines', and his intention with such magazines was 'evangelization of the heathen'. Recent baptismal successes in this regard had been 'a Hottentot half-caste', and 'a Jew ... long convinced of the truth of Christianity'.[131]

Much more could be said on the international dimension of parish magazines, but the main points are clear. The parish magazine and the community spirit it expressed were far from being 'parochial' in their interests and sense of purpose. Primarily community based, in a traditional sense, they nevertheless reached out to parishioners who had gone overseas, connecting the parish to them, often seeing their work as an extension of Anglican work 'at home'. This made parish residents or denominational readers aware of the opportunities that the Empire offered. It also increased affection for the Empire. A sense of belonging and community identity, manifest in the many local activities that I have reported on, did not preclude these wider dimensions. On the contrary, through the publication of the parish magazines – perhaps above all else through them and what they represented – the local community extended globally, and a Christian mission overseas consolidated and gave additional moral and organizational point to the Anglican parochial concerns and idea of 'nested' 'community' at home. These differing ideas of 'community' mutually reinforced each other. This was, in other words, a globalizing doctrinal 'community', where many historians would least expect to find it, reported upon and to some degree held together by the parish magazine, having a strong sense of mission, multi-stranded, embracing others from afar who shared that mission. This is a far cry from images of local communities as 'parish-pump' based, 'parochial' in a dismissive sense, the reserve of rheumatic elderly men on a bench fretting over their prospects of staying out of the workhouse a few miles away. It helps us to understand aspects of community vitality and generative powers of the parish in the Victorian era. And it throws new light upon spirits of community during the heyday of the British Empire. No doubt it was through education in these parishes, and through the senses of endeavour, Christian mission and global opportunity propagated in their magazines, that so many people left Britain to colonize other parts of the world. This massively expanded familial networks through emigration. That emigration damaged communities at home, through the loss of key and young people, and the fact that they wanted to emigrate was significant. Yet when they arrived in far-flung places many of them remembered the values and activities engendered in their home communities and reflected in parish magazines. These 'parochial' values often transmogrified into attitudes held by imperial administrators. These are features and extensions of local and community history that should not be neglected, whatever one's interpretation and ideological views of them.

It is often thought that people in historic parish communities shared limited horizons, bearing upon their communal or denominational identities, even when we allow for internal differences by social rank. This has frequently been the view of historians, and there is much evidence to support it before the late nineteenth century. Yet when one considers the subsequent expansiveness of parochial communion that I draw attention to, and the often adventurous compass of its charitable heart, one might wonder whether such historical views are justified into the era of parish magazines. There is much debate about the effects of new technologies on personal relations and on global senses of charity or empathy. Yet whatever one's verdicts on our own international frames of concern and networks in 'post-Christian society', the evidence of this chapter suggests that we should not extol the present too strongly in relation to the past.

5

Thomas Hardy and Community

From the Village 'Quire' to Jude's Obscurity

> *The tragedy [of* Jude the Obscure*] ... is equally beautiful and terrible in its pathos. The beauty, the terror, and the truth, are all yours and yours alone. I think it would hardly be seemly to enlarge on all that I admire in your work ... but I will risk saying how thankful we should be ... for another admission into an English paradise 'under the greenwood tree'.*[1]

What does the work of Thomas Hardy suggest about change in community life? Raymond Williams commented on 'a warmth, a seriousness, an endurance in love and work that are the necessary definition of what Hardy knows and mourns as loss ... Hardy does not celebrate isolation and separation'.[2] Williams did not develop this argument, yet as a Welsh cultural-materialist literary critic he was much concerned with the theme of 'community'. Indeed, Hardy's career encompassed a key period for English rural society, one that saw massive rural out-migration and accompanying urbanization, the decline of many traditional ways of making a living in the countryside, including many rural crafts, the end of older tenures, important changes in village institutions and continuing erosion of the relative value of farm workers' earnings.[3] His novels address these and related themes, all of them bearing upon the viability and meaning of 'community'. This discussion will therefore explore Hardy's own perception of community decline, and as a prime method it will focus on two novels spanning his career as a novelist: his very early work, *Under the Greenwood Tree* (1872),[4] and his much later, and almost last,[5] major fictional work, *Jude the Obscure* (1895). The contrast between these books is very marked. The first book sees representations of rural community life as convivial, engaging and participatory, albeit threatened by certain forms of individualism. *Jude the Obscure*, on the other hand, shows us rural 'community' bleakly in decay, essentially moribund as something to escape from; and yet in the individualistic, self-seeking, 'obscure' world of the city Hardy finds nothing to replace it.

Under the Greenwood Tree

Hardy subtitled *Under the Greenwood Tree* 'A rural painting of the Dutch school'. By so doing, he invoked the idea of a settled community seen visually, as if by Hobbema or Teniers, with people framed by their natural context, and with a stress upon the ordinary and everyday features of life. He claimed that it 'is intended to be a fairly true picture, at first hand, of the personages, ways, and customs which were common among such orchestral groups in the villages of fifty or sixty years ago'.[6] This takes us back to the early nineteenth century. Hardy's own family had been intimately involved at Stinsford church in gallery musical activity, and he was an accomplished violinist. Musical melodies and rhythms influenced much of his poetry. The novel was set in the fictional 'Mellstock' parish, which was large and comprised three hamlets: a creation clearly based upon Stinsford and Lower and Upper Bockhampton. What depiction of 'community' does one find here?

The work opens on a cold and starry Christmas Eve with the meeting of the Mellstock parish choir, or 'quire', as they gather prior to their circulation around the parish. The all-male choir members address themselves as 'neighbours', a collectivizing term repeated throughout the novel.[7] 'We all know one another very well, don't we, neighbours?'[8] This term is widespread in Hardy's other writing set in the past,[9] and is often found in eighteenth- and early nineteenth-century sources like parish vestry minutes to describe parochial inhabitants. Another term frequently used in this novel (as in other documentation) is that of 'parishioners', which accompanies his frequent reference to the parish.[10] 'The parish' as a concept is very widespread in Hardy's novels and short stories. The musicians have very close mutual knowledge. Shared participatory music plays an important role in this community.[11] As gallery musicians they practise, play, socialize and even eat together in the church gallery, which would have caused disquiet among many Victorian church reformers and ecclesiologists. Their interpersonal knowledge is deep and based upon long familiarity. There are many multi-sensed signs of this in the novel. In Dick Dewey's house, his father 'did not take the trouble to turn or raise his eyes at the entry of his visitors, well knowing by their footsteps that they were the expected old comrades'.[12] The village shoemaker knows his customers' feet, and the personal histories affecting them, in great detail. Geoffrey Day's bunion, for example, and the special cordwaining expedients to accommodate this in leather, are explained by the accident received from the tread of a horse when he was a boy, 'that squashed his foot a'most to a pomace', and further details are conversationally given.[13] This is a knowable community, one in which 'the producer and the purchaser knew one another', to cite one element of Georg Simmel's influential contrast between rural and metropolitan life.[14] These villagers are sociable people, gregarious in their environment. Their sociality seemingly makes them little aware of solitude. Personal histories going back to childhoods are intimately known and talked about. 'We all then fell a-talking o' family matters ... knowen me too so many years, and I at your father's own wedding', says the innkeeper.[15] The mental limitations of a character named Leaf are 'an unimpassioned matter of parish history'.[16] People are also judged by the 'stock' they come from, with knowledge of them going back generations.[17] Allied to such personal knowledge is the fact that this is a community in which 'Advertising in any shape was scorned.' 'Trade came solely by connection based on personal respect', such that the shoemaker did not need to hang up a sign outside his workshop.[18]

However, there is a threat facing the main characters, and this forms a key theme of the novel. The choir lament the challenge to their communal existence posed by harmoniums or barrel organs: 'People don't care much about us now! I've been thinking we must be almost the last left in the country of the old string players?'[19] The new vicar aims to 'turn us out of the quire neck and crop'. 'Really, I think we useless ones had better march out of church, fiddles and all!', says one of them, with 'horrible bitterness of irony'.[20] The danger is from the new school teacher, Fancy Day, playing now as an isolated female organist: '"Perhaps she's jist come from some musical city, and sneers at our doings?" the Tranter whispered.'[21] Communal male activity is thus threatened by a young woman's individualistic musical playing. Tension between 'community' and individualism is fundamental to this novel, more so than the related theme of gender, and the Mellstock players are symbolic of the parish as a collective but challenged community.

In relation to communally produced music, and indeed to ideas of community, Hardy used the term 'quire' rather than the more conventional spelling of 'choir'. This is itself revealing. For a quire also means a bundle of sheets of paper folded together for binding into a book, especially a four-sheet bundle, folded once to make eight leaves or sixteen pages. There is also a secondary meaning for this word, which is a set of twenty-four or twenty-five sheets of paper of equal size and quality, being one-twentieth of a ream. The term thus brings together Hardy's interest in church musicianship with his literary concerns and bookish familiarities, by which he was exploring the activities of such a 'quire'. In other words, the binding together of this number of amateur musicians, in common purpose, like a literary quire, has symbolic social meaning here as well as being simply an older-fashioned and regional term for 'choir'. It serves as a symbolic statement about the binding meaning of 'community' in *Under the Greenwood Tree*, and indeed in his poems and other works that use that word.[22]

The novel also features many dialect words, even though they were edited to aid communication to more metropolitan readers. Words like mumbudgeting, a poor gawk-hammer, borus-snorus, wamble, emmet and many others like these bind the participants together communally, in a shared local world of dialectal understanding.[23] Such dialect attaches people in a locally exclusive community, and the dialectal scope in many cases may not extend far beyond the local region.[24] Habitation in such a comparatively confined space assists in preventing feelings of solitude, as compared with a sense of immensity or boundless horizon. 'Thee' and 'thou' are also in frequent use among this novel's older parishioners, and in dialectal studies these are regarded as 'pronouns of respect'.[25] The usage of 'thee' and 'thou' also acknowledges and recognizes the existence of another person within the terms of one's self-consciousness; this is an appreciation of shared mentality and (in such a context) rules out the possibility of absolute personal isolation. In terms of social hierarchy, dialect can also sometimes reveal shared values among rich and poor,[26] though its use or non-use often separates social circles, notably so in Hardy. Michael Henchard in *The Mayor of Casterbridge* wants such dialect words to be shunned by his daughter Elizabeth-Jane, for his is a class-divided community.[27] As we shall see in *Jude the Obscure*, such use of dialect significantly declines in Hardy's later writing, as Hardy and Jude break with the localized cultures of his earlier novels, and as Hardy takes up issues that are more relevant to the individualistic 'society' of a wider and more urban canvas than one signified by a 'rural painting of the Dutch school'. And the mutual recognitions and presuppositions of 'thee' and 'thou' fade away, as human isolation becomes more pronounced.

Mellstock is a community that overlooks itself closely. There are scattered farms and buildings, Hardy tells us, yet that does not prevent Dick Dewy having to disguise his feelings, and his embarrassed calling of Fancy Day's name, from some suspicious cottage windows nearby.[28] Rival courtships are a matter of common conversation and the plot of the novel evolves around them. The parishioners, complains Mrs Day, are the 'gossipest' she has ever known. '"How people will talk about one's doings!" Fancy exclaimed.'[29] As in Hardy's novel *The Well-Beloved*, courtships become known about 'with mysterious rapidity and fullness of detail'.[30] After a marriage people march round the parish in pairs, every woman with her man, or as Hardy put it, 'every man hitched up to his woman',[31] reminding us of Samuel Fildes's painting *The Village Wedding* (1883). Furthermore, the parish friendly society march at Whitsun brings many male parishioners into public visibility together, again in marching pairs, and in their best clothes.[32] At the time this novel was set, friendly societies were largely parochial in their organization, and so Hardy's use of such a society here reinforces an idea of parish community.

Within the church, which is still well attended, the gallery 'looked down upon and knew the habits of the nave to its remotest peculiarity': one person chewing tobacco, views of the reading material of certain young women, the touching of fingers by a pair of young lovers through a knot-hole between pews, the farmer's wife counting her money and reckoning her market expenses and so on.[33] In this parish, people know other people's clothes and the quality of material they are made from; and a lost meal-bag marked only with the owner's initials quickly finds its way back to her.[34]

This is a community in which some of its people 'never wasted words upon outsiders', and between some of whose workers

> ideas were seldom conveyed by any other means than nods and shakes of the head. Their long acquaintance with each other's ways, and the nature of their labours, rendered words between them almost superfluous as vehicles of thought, whilst the coincidence of their horizons, and the astonishing equality of their social views, by startling the keeper from time to time as very damaging to the theory of master and man, strictly forbade any indulgence in words as courtesies.[35]

One is reminded of a similarly worded passage at the end of *The Woodlanders*, summing up Marty South and Giles Winterborne's working alliance: 'They had planted together, and together they had felled; together they had, with the run of the years, mentally collected those remoter signs and symbols which seen in few were of runic obscurity, but all together made an alphabet.'[36] *The Woodlanders* is an account of a woodland people in decline, with their redundant alphabet of learning. It laments the decay of a rural occupational community, closely tied together in mutual understandings and familiarity, stemming from long experience of working together in the same environment. Hardy is there describing changes towards displacement, isolation and loneliness, in memory of mutual and communal activity. That dislocation and personal alienation is vividly described in the death of Giles Winterborne and in the isolation of Marty South, or in the tragic ending and despairing will of Michael Henchard in *The Mayor of Casterbridge*, or in the events that lead to the termination of Tess. This theme of lonely alienation will finally reach its greatest literary power in *Jude the Obscure*.

The communal themes of *Under the Greenwood Tree* are most prominent in the early chapters of the book, in the contextualizing descriptions of the quire and its activities. Hardy's depiction of community here is overwhelmingly that of an adult male community. Indeed, he is limited in depicting any female 'community' or women's collective cultures, though elements of such description are in *Far from the Madding Crowd, Tess of the D'Urbervilles*, and elsewhere in his disparaging accounts of women's 'gossip', or Mixen Lane, or poems like 'The Ruined Maid', even if his women are often divided by jealousies. As the story of *Under the Greenwood Tree* switches its attention increasingly to the romance of Dick Dewy and Fancy Day, the earlier emphases upon a functioning male community become less salient, though they are still present. Within this plot, the communal gives way to one-to-one courtship and the more isolated family, much as the disbanding of the gallery quire leaves the musicians then 'scattered about with their wives in different parts of the church … they all felt awkward, out of place, abashed, and inconvenienced'.[37] Fancy Day's marital choice is between men who stand differently in relation to ideas of communal activity and class. As a literary theme 'community' becomes sidelined during the novel by issues of courtship, spousal compatibility and marriage. One sees this in Hardy's subsequent novels, and this shifting emphasis from the communal to the individualistic becomes much more pronounced in *Jude the Obscure*.

Jude the Obscure: at the decayed village of Marygreen

Thomas Hardy was part of a long rural tradition of writing about community, which could take us back to Oliver Goldsmith, George Crabbe, John Clare, William Barnes, George Eliot and many others. Yet what is remarkable about the extreme anti-pastoral start of *Jude the Obscure* (1895) is the startling presumption that rural community is now dead. Indeed, this seems to follow on from themes in *Tess of the D'Urbervilles*. And so, Hardy is asking in his last great novel, what is there now? His answer is to examine individual aspirations and hopes, away from any such community of the kind explored in *Under the Greenwood Tree* (1872), *Far from the Madding Crowd* (1874), *The Return of the Native* (1879), *The Woodlanders*

(1887) and *Tess of the D'Urbervilles* (1891). Jude quickly leaves his village for a city, aspiring to personal intellectual development. There is nothing in his rural parish of Marygreen worth staying for. This will be a novel of personal aspiration, thwarted hopes, despairing sexual relations and then distressed alienation and death in a depersonalized city.

The start of the novel is indeed appallingly bleak in its description of rural life and community and is among the gloomiest accounts ever penned of such decline. It is easy to see why Swinburne looked in vain for traditional ideas of pastoral here, and hoped for such a reassuring follow-on from *Jude*, even though his hope so misjudged Hardy's direction.[38] Marygreen is stagnant, hostile, crude and brutal to children. Its ancient tracks that had been used for generations are now neglected and overgrown.[39] But it is far worse than that:

> Many of the thatched and dormered dwelling-houses had been pulled down of late years, and many trees felled on the green. Above all, the original church, hump-backed, wood-turreted, and quaintly hipped, had been taken down, and either cracked up into heaps of road-metal in the lane, or utilized as pig-sty walls, garden seats, guard-stones to fences, and rockeries in the flower-beds of the neighbourhood. In place of it a tall new building of modern Gothic design, unfamiliar to English eyes, had been erected on a new piece of ground by a certain obliterator of historic records who had run down from London and back in a day. The site whereon so long had stood the ancient temple to the Christian divinities was not even recorded on the green and level grass-plot that had immemorially been the churchyard, the obliterated graves being commemorated by eighteen penny cast-iron crosses warranted to last five years.[40]

Such displacement of stone memorials by standardized industrial products augurs poorly for Jude's subsequent and marginalized career as a stone mason. And the vane in the new Victorian gothic church has already begun to creak. 'Where is the church?' asks Sue Bridehead later in the novel, having forgotten about the new one.[41] And perhaps human life here has become more equivalent to Darwinian nature: 'Each ivy leaf overgrowing the wall of the churchless churchyard hard by, now abandoned, pecked its neighbour smartly', much like the ivy leaves in *The Woodlanders*, whose points 'scratch its underlying neighbour restlessly'.[42] In *The Woodlanders* Hardy had written about the 'trees close together, wrestling for existence, their branches disfigured with wounds resulting from their mutual rubbings and blows. It was the struggle between these neighbours that she had heard in the night'.[43] The transposed use of the word 'neighbours', by an author who had used it for convivial people in *Under the Greenwood Tree*, now suggests an ironic idea of 'community' as afflicted by fierce social

Darwinist competition, one that (for Hardy at this time) has apparently come to characterize the countryside as well as the city.

In the fields, the fresh harrow lines gave 'a meanly utilitarian air to the expanse, taking away its gradations, and depriving it of all history', eliminating associations of songs, gaiety, courtships, harvest days and rural work. Hardy is eloquent on this loss of history and local association. This leaves Jude and the rooks in 'a lonely place'. The worlds of children are usually absent in Hardy, as in his personal life. But Marygreen is also a place of violence and punishment towards a kindly child who feels that his only friends are the wheeling birds, as Jude finds to his cost when farmer Troutham repeatedly beats him with his bird clacker, swinging his slim frame round him at arm's length, 'till the field echoed with the blows'. Such violence would have been inconceivable in the more pastoral representation of community in Mellstock. As the bitter, bruised, isolated, undefended and apparently worthless Jude subsequently lies upon a heap of litter near a pig-sty, on a foggy day, he reflects that 'All around you there seemed to be something glaring, garish, rattling, and the noises and glares hit upon the little cell called our life, and shook it, and warped it.'[44]

Even when courting Arabella, talking the 'commonest local twaddle', Jude finds her house lonely and isolated, near to a 'few unhealthy fir-trees'. He is struck by the smell of piggeries and an 'oozing' stream; and his future wife has nothing in common with him. They resort to a depressing 'inn of an inferior class', where the beer is adulterated, where they look at the circular beer stains on tables and 'spittoons underfoot filled with sawdust'.[45] Older ideas of marriage have ended;[46] indeed from varied angles of view this novel expresses deep cynicism towards marriage. When they are married they take 'a lonely roadside cottage … not the sort of life he had bargained for'.[47] This village, whatever it has been, is to Hardy not a community in any sense known historically: it is a place devoid of human warmth or communal work; it is debased, decayed, de-spiritualized and socially desolate, a place in which to situate outward aspirations. For in this 'declining rural enclave', to use Terry Eagleton's term for Hardy's Dorset,[48] there is nothing worth staying for. It is a place in which 'Jude continued to wish himself out of the world',[49] a wish that he will eventually be granted. The contrasts here with the rural communities of *Under the Greenwood Tree* or of *Far from the Madding Crowd, The Woodlanders* or even of *The Return of the Native* – whatever their mounting problems and limitations – are stark and conspicuous.

The search for knowledge is an effort to surmount solitude. It is a longing for others, an attempt to share in a communal consciousness that one lacks. Jude's thirst for knowledge is as an alternative to the community he finds missing; it is a longing for communion, an attempt to rise above solitude. And so it seems natural that his individualistic, aspiring and hopeful mind turns towards the horizon – without thinking that horizons betoken desertion and detachment, let alone aloofness – towards the gleaming light spires of Christminster. Hardy later wrote that this city was 'not meant to be exclusively Oxford, but any old-fashioned University about the date of the story, 1860–1870'.[50]

In the city: the crowd and Jude's death

The plot of *Jude the Obscure* involves a rootless shifting of places that seems to deny the possibility of community. This is indicated in Hardy's sectional headings: 'At Marygreen', 'At Christminster', 'At Melchester', 'At Shaston', 'At Aldbrickham and Elsewhere' and 'At Christminster again'. This is no longer a nested community as delved into before, in *Under the Greenwood Tree*, *The Woodlanders* or *The Return of the Native*, and there is no such community in the city of Christminster. Space is disbanded in its earlier forms; people are isolated by distance, as was becoming apparent in the movements and separations of *Tess of the D'Urbervilles*, or indeed in *The Return of the Native*. There is now no unity in place. The railway is now also an important feature of such movement, removing some of the plot from place, providing a new way to experience time and place. It had earlier been glimpsed in *Tess* as the conveyor of milk to London. Simon Gatrell has even written that *Jude* is a railway novel.[51] The earlier local scenes of travel in Hardy – the man walking the dusty road, the local footpaths suitable for courtship[52] – have now largely gone. Jude, we might think, comes to live 'as-if-blinkered-and-passing-through, with no need for meaningful connection to people living locally or to the place itself'.[53] As the main characters of this novel drift away from any settled sense of place or belonging, and as they urbanize, they weaken as people, becoming ever more forlorn or desperate. This was a formula also found in Hardy's prior work, notably in *Tess of the D'Urbervilles*. In his prefaces, in his characterization or in his essay 'The Dorsetshire Labourer',[54] Hardy repeatedly emphasized the countryside and rural generational continuity as productive of individuality. This sets him apart from some urban theorists, such as Georg Simmel, for whom the apparent freedom of the city augmented individuality, albeit at the costs of suspicion, isolation, loneliness, reserve, mutual strangeness and concealed aversion to others, such that a personality as a whole may fall into neglect.[55] Hardy quoted a dictum in 1902, derived from Robert Southey, that 'Whatever strengthens local attachments strengthens both individual

& national Character.'[56] However, his urbanized characters now singularly fail to fulfil this. People in *Jude the Obscure* are isolated, alone and largely placeless, with the possible exception of donnish insiders in disunited and 'sarcophagus'-like Christminster, where there occurs the death of hopes, of children and of Jude. Knowledge and its ancillary local communities had been inclusive in Hardy's novels hitherto: one thinks of the forms of knowledge among the Egdon heath folk or the woodlanders. Yet with *Jude*, exclusion from knowledge and its community, the predicament of urban isolation and resulting loneliness are stressed by Hardy much more than in any of his preceding novels.

It is also interesting to note that the main characters in *Jude the Obscure* communicate by letter to a far greater and more personalized extent than in any previous Hardy novel. This was a feature taken to be symptomatic of a decline in face-to-face community relationships and a move away from a restricted and spatially enclosed speech community, even though it annoyed some critics who missed this significance. By comparison, Hardy had commented in *The Trumpet-Major* about the rarity of letters during the Napoleonic period, about how 'everybody in the parish had an interest in the reading of those rare documents', but also about how a letter could create misunderstanding.[57] The epigraph for *Jude the Obscure* is 'The letter killeth'. Hardy adopted this term from 2 Corinthians 3.6, where it relates to able ministration of the New Testament: 'not of the letter, but of the spirit: for the letter killeth, but the spirit giveth life'. Given the content of the novel, and of why people die within it, Hardy's complex epigraph seems to involve criticism of the failure of the highly lettered to practise biblical principles, as well as inviting adverse comparison of letters with the spirit of spatially contained communities.

In *Jude the Obscure* people pass each other on occasion, through the years, in different places, as with Arabella's appearances. Jude and Sue are 'shifting, almost nomadic'.[58] They are said to be obscure. Obscurity, it seems, is not an attribute of being well known in an obscure Dorset village. 'Whither they had gone nobody knew, chiefly because nobody cared to know.' Itinerant in living, they lack firm beliefs: 'hardly a shred of the beliefs with which he had first gone up to Christminster now remaining with him'.[59] Jude is also in effect alienated both morally and personally from his products and work as a stone mason, which Hardy draws little attention to. Indeed, he probably chose this trade for Jude because it was so itinerant in nature, and because of its ecclesiological possibilities in connection with relevant moral–religious issues of the novel. Gothic restoration (Jude's trade) is 'as dead as a fern-leaf in a lump of coal'.[60] The discussion of woodland products in *The Woodlanders*, by comparison, was an integral element of community life, just as shoemaking was in *Under the Greenwood Tree*, or shepherding in *Far from the Madding Crowd*, or the occupations of the heath in *The Return of the Native*, or the mill-work of *The Trumpet-Major*. The community-less, rootless nature of existence is now repeatedly stressed. Sue Bridehead would rather sit in the Christminster railway station than in the cathedral: '"That's the centre of the town life now. The Cathedral has had its day!" "How modern you are!"' exclaims Jude, when he hears this verdict on the university town; though he saw that 'The floating population of students and teachers … were not Christminster in a local sense at all.'[61] As Sue says to Jude: 'You are … a tragic Don Quixote … O my poor friend and comrade, you'll suffer yet!'[62] And so he does. Hardy wrote in 'The Dorsetshire Labourer', or his preface to *Far from the Madding Crowd*, about 'the recent supplanting of the class of stationary cottagers … by a population of more or less migratory labourers', and of how this has proved fatal to 'close inter-social relationships'. He predicted that this itinerant rootlessness of belief and place – replacing cathedral with railway station – was to be the unhappy pattern of the future, marking modernity and its problems.[63]

If there is a 'community' in Christminster, possibly of academics, according to Hardy it is unhelpful, censorious, condescending, fashionable, and opportunities within it are strictly limited and exclusive. Jude experiences a 'freezing negative' from it. Hardy wrote that 'the outer walls of Sarcophagus College – silent, black and windowless – threw their four centuries of gloom, bigotry and decay into the little room [Sue] occupied, shutting out the moonlight by night and the sun by day'.[64] However, his criticism was not only directed at the university: the non-academic side of the city is shown as motley and morally debased, sporting 'moral characters of various depths of shade' down to the blasphemers, gamblers, drunkards, paupers, prostitutes like 'Bower o' Bliss' and 'Freckles' and other 'animals of an inferior species'.[65] It is Jude and Sue's uncharitable rejection by a Christminster landlord that triggers the murder of their children, via Sue's despairing comments to little Father Time. Those murders occur in Christminster, capping Jude's failed hopes. This is a place where the little boy deems it a misfortune to be alive, much like Jude had done as a child in forlorn Marygreen. Jude and Sue lack and never find 'community'; but in its morally judgemental aspect community is also something *to be escaped from*, like the pair of pigeons Sue Bridehead releases.[66] For their unwed relationship needs obscurity, while in another sense Jude will die obscure – abandoned, ill and single – in the city, released in death from any faint vestiges of aspirant community that it might contain.

Hardy's anti-city views are often summed as being anti-Oxbridge, which, as seen above, is not strictly correct. In fact, they were much wider than this. Hardy spent long periods in London, for about five years as a young architect, and then between 1873 and 1912 almost every year during spring and early summer for the 'artificial gaieties' of the London season – what H. G. Wells called that 'rendezvous of political, intellectual and artistic life as the London "Season" used to be, and still to some extent is'.[67] London scenes occur in a number of his works, for example, in *The Hand of Ethelberta*, or his short story 'The Son's Veto'. And perhaps his short stories as a whole were more 'urban' than his better known novels. His most explicit and frequent discussion of London, however, occurs in his self-authored *The Life of Thomas Hardy*. It was there that his views were most forthright and uncensored, voiced in a late work (published posthumously in two volumes in 1928 and 1930), ostensibly authored by Florence Hardy but largely written and overseen by him,[68] a work that would also have no significant effect on his readerships, even in the metropolis. This was compiled from notes, letters, diaries and conversations over many years. Because of its posthumous publication and ostensible authorship, Hardy's views there on London and rural–urban comparisons did not attract the reception and publicity that arose from his later novels. His opinions of the city in *The Life of Thomas Hardy* were stronger and more condemnatory than in most of his fiction, yet they clearly expressed judgements about the city, and the possibilities of urban 'community', which extend from those in his novels.

He often leased a house in London, even falling 'into line as a London man again',[69] though unfortunately this meant having to see 'The dirty house-fronts, leaning gate-piers, rusty gates, broken bells, Doré monstrosities of womankind who showed us the rooms.'[70] In his short story 'For Conscience' Sake', he wrote of London as the sensation of standing on a pivot of the world; yet he felt that lives there were duller than in a 'despised' Dorset market town where they had enjoyed a nodding acquaintance with three-fourths of the local people.[71] 'Community' as implied here is local grown knowledge of others. Indeed, it is hard to see why Hardy spent time in London, given his remarks about it and other cities, which place him alongside a variety of other authors (as diverse as Cobbett, Ruskin, Nietzsche and James Wentworth Day as considered in Chapter 7) who had very negative responses to most cities. London is the opposite of the rural natural world: 'There are charcoal trees in the squares,' and its smoke destroys appetites.[72] He commented upon animals taken from the countryside in trucks, looking out at the green fields they were leaving for scenes of horror and slaughter in a far-off city.[73] As for the urban people, he remarked on 'that libidinousness which makes the scum of cities so noxious'.[74] He saw some Londoners as acting 'by clockwork ... like an automaton ... has a machine-made answer'.[75] He quoted a letter from Anne Procter to him in the mid-1870s: 'You are coming to live in stony-hearted London. Our great fault is that we are too much alike ... We press so closely against each other.'[76] London society gatherings were like 'beings in a somnambulistic state, making their motions mechanically'.[77] Hardy thought that residence in or near a city forced him to write in a routinized and mundane way.[78] London, he wrote, was 'that *hot-plate* of humanity, on which we first sing, then simmer, then boil, then dry away to dust and ashes!'[79] He refers to its social telegraphy and allusions, without thinking them to have any value, and even though (as we have seen in *Under the Greenwood Tree*) he had discussed their equivalents in country areas.[80] The hamlet and family people of *The Woodlanders* evinced 'shyness in showing strong emotion among each other', he thought, unlike the heated assertion of feelings by 'the people of towns'. [81] The latter were less concerned than country people to uphold long-standing relationships. Hardy wrote that Dorchester was becoming like a London suburb, because of its quickening movements, and so he feared the loss of its individuality.[82] Even so, by comparison with the city, he felt that provincialism provided the essence of individuality,[83] and his ideas of 'individuality' were posited upon his view of stronger rural personal relations and community identity.

Hardy commented at many points upon the urban crowd as a phenomenon. He was sorry, for example, to see London's uniformly dark attire replacing the 'interesting' 'speciality' of whitey-brown flecked with white clothing of Dorset rural inhabitants.[84] Such observation was typical of Hardy's comparative vision of the country and the city. The city crowd emerges as a key element at the end of *Jude the Obscure*, eclipsing and ignoring Jude as he lies dying, its noise contrasting with his aloneness and heightening his seclusion. The urban crowd in Hardy is the antithesis of rural community as he had described it in *Under the Greenwood Tree*:

> as the crowd grows denser it loses its character of an aggregate of countless units, and becomes an organic whole, a molluscous black creature having nothing in common with humanity, that takes the shape of the streets along which it has lain itself, and throws out horrid excrescences and limbs into neighbouring alleys; a creature whose voice exudes from its scaly coat, and who has an eye in every pore of its body. The balconies, stands, and railway-bridge are occupied by small detached shapes of the same tissue, but of gentler motion, as if they were the spawn of the monster in their midst.[85]

The best he could say of an urban crowd was that it may contain a small minority with sensitive souls.[86] He had thought while writing *The Dynasts* of the human race as a great network that quivers throughout when one point is touched, like a spider's web.[87] The same feeling informed his view of cities and their crowds, which connects with other urban theorizing at that time. Hardy avoided open connection with theories, wishing to evade his criticism of Fitzpiers in *The Woodlanders* that he was 'a dreamy 'ist of some sort, or too deeply steeped in some false kind of 'ism'.[88] But he was by no means alone in such thoughts about the urban crowd, given comparable thinking from writers such as Eugène Sue, Hippolyte Taine, Victor Hugo, Charles Baudelaire, Friedrich Engels, Gustave le Bon (whose *La Psychologie des Foules* appeared in 1895), Georg Simmel and many subsequent theorists of urban crowd psychology. These included Sigmund Freud, who discussed Gustave le Bon in *Group Psychology and the Analysis of the Ego*.[89] At the time of Hardy's novels, many urban painters, from William Frith to James Ensor, were depicting ominous urban crowds. Hardy was sometimes unable to sleep in London, 'partly on account of an eerie feeling which sometimes haunted him, a horror at lying down in close proximity to a monster whose body had four million heads and eight million eyes … the streets are filled with night as with a dark stagnant flood whose surface brims to the tops of the houses'.[90] 'London. Four million forlorn hopes!'[91] London, it seems, amounted to a tragedy:

> This hum of the wheel – the roar of London! What is it composed of? Hurry, speech, laughters, moans, cries of little children. The people in this tragedy laugh, sing, smoke, toss off wines, etc., make love to girls in drawing-rooms and areas; and yet are playing their parts in the tragedy just the same. Some wear jewels and feathers, some wear rags. All are caged birds; the only difference lies in the size of the cage. This too is part of the tragedy.[92]

In his short story 'The Son's Veto', he commented on how 'There are worlds within worlds in the great city',[93] a term that we shall later see Adrian Bell, another anti-Londoner, reapplying to the countryside.[94] Hardy wrote of how 'London appears not to *see itself*. Each individual is conscious of *himself*, but nobody conscious of themselves collectively … There is no consciousness here of where anything comes from or goes to – only that it is present … The fiendish precision or mechanism of town-life is what makes it so intolerable to the sick and infirm.'[95]

Georg Simmel wrote in his famous 1902 essay on 'The Metropolis and Mental Life' that 'one never feels as lonely and as deserted as in this metropolitan crush of persons',[96] a theme taken up by countless other writers. Jude sickens and dies in city isolation feebly crying for water, whispering quotations from the Book of Job – *'Let the day perish wherein I was born'* – each quotation followed by the uninterested and unhearing city crowd outside yelling 'Hurrah!'. One recalls the extreme bitterness and isolation of Michael Henchard's will at the end of *The Mayor of Casterbridge*. 'Community' in the city of Christminster is simply a mass of fashionable people amid a crowd: 'numerous dons and their wives, and undergraduates with gay female companions … Collegians of all sorts, in canoes with ladies'.[97] Jude is socially anonymous, isolated, adrift and vulnerable – 'a tragic Don Quixote' – and he has been abandoned by the two women in his life. Arabella Donn, the daughter of a pig-breeder who is repeatedly associated with pig metaphors, is indifferent to his death and absent during it, enjoying herself in the city crowd, living up to her belladonna or deadly nightshade connotations,[98] by which Hardy linked her name and character to the Christminster dons.

Jude dies obscure, without community of any sort. Death is the ultimate solitude: utter isolation, the end of all connections. Jude's efforts to gain a community after Marygreen, his attempts to share communion with others of a similar spirit via his search for knowledge – the product of combined consciousness – have come to nothing. So has his communion with women. If the pursuit of knowledge is one way of overcoming solitude and isolation, it signalled failed in his case. 'I was, perhaps, after all, a paltry victim to the spirit of mental and social restlessness, that makes so many unhappy these days … I perceive there is something wrong somewhere in our social formulas.'[99]

Conclusion

I have chosen to concentrate on two of Hardy's novels, displaying the greatest contrasts between the start and end of his novel-writing career, but the theme of the changing nature of community encompasses all his fiction and could be developed at length through his other work. This contrast, between the small intimate village community of *Under the Greenwood Tree* and the surging urban crowd at the end of *Jude the Obscure* or in *The Life of Thomas Hardy*, is in many ways a transition from *Gemeinschaft* to *Gesellschaft*.[100] We can remind ourselves that these terms, in Tönnies' theorizing, represented change from a local community of shared and often religiously based morality, neighbourhood practice, mutual endeavour, familial knowledge and memory,[101] and clear status ascriptions, to large competitive urbanized society in which each person acts according to their own personal interests, in which status is self-gained, in which divisions of labour are complex and mechanical and in which class or ethnic alliances may take precedence over local senses of belonging. Place was key in *Under the Greenwood Tree* – it is redundant and ineffectual in *Jude the Obscure*. There is a strong interest in kinship in *Under the Greenwood Tree*, but it is largely absent in *Jude the Obscure*, with the added point that cousinhood (Jude and Sue) is no basis for a lasting relationship. Religion in *Under the Greenwood Tree* is taken for granted and binding, the issue being the form of its musical accompaniment – but it is derelict, hypocritical, questioned or absent in *Jude the Obscure*. Jude is propertyless, another feature of his extra-community position, and the issues of tenure and property that had occupied Hardy in a novel like *The Woodlanders* are absent now. There is little evidence in *Jude the Obscure* (or in Hardy's other urban reflections) of a coherent 'society' and 'civilizing process'.[102] Nor does he provide any positive interpretation of some contemporary ideologies about 'collectivism' or socialism, as opposed to 'individualism'. Nothing seems gained in Hardy by individualism outside of community. Jude's failure to achieve anything by individual self-improvement appears to be Hardy's riposte to Herbert Spencer, who had put great stress upon self-improvement and self-education among artisans.[103] There are abundant senses of class in Hardy, but once a community of parishioners declines, as in Hardy's work after *Under the Greenwood Tree*, it is not replaced by any other association, such as friendly or benevolent societies, revived Anglican ideas of the parish, Nonconformist chapel membership, cooperatives, trade unions and so on. Jude the stonemason has utterly negligible fraternity or shared organization with other working men. The main protagonists in *Jude the Obscure* are 'essentially detached', to use Tönnies' wording.[104]

If there is precedent in Hardy's description of these characters as isolated in the city, we would find it from Disraeli's youthful stranger in *Sybil*, who spoke of how 'There is no community in England … Men may be drawn into contiguity, but they remain virtually isolated … In cities that condition is aggravated … In great cities men … are not in a state of co-operation, but of isolation.'[105] Hardy has added social Darwinist and urban crowd theory to Disraeli's 1845 perceptions. In massed form people comprise a heaving crowd indifferent to any suffering and lonely individual. This is an important literary moment. A usual interpretation of 'modernism' involves isolated, transitory individuals in a secularized and splintered environment derelict of community tradition. Surely we see this in *Jude the Obscure*, a free-thinking proto-modernist novel of 1895 which long predates other exponents of modernism such as Proust, Pound, Joyce, T. S. Eliot, Kafka, Virginia Woolf or William Faulkner.

Jude epitomizes the patterns of removal and alienation from small-scale rural community that are visible in many of Hardy's novels. Clym Yeobright in *The Return of the Native* is dislodged, isolated, lonely in his views, troubled by his urbanized modernity, enduring dwindling vision and seeing life now 'as a thing to be put up with'.[106] Clym mixes with people of whom Hardy says, 'In name they were parishioners, but virtually they belonged to no parish at all.'[107] People interact in *The Return of the Native*, but there is limited sign of community there. Individualistic criss-crossing of the heath, in poor visibility and ignorance of others' movements, is symptomatic of this. So, perhaps, are mummers' performances in which the actor's and audience's visions are confused by the ribboned visor disguise. This is a novel in which many characters fail to see things clearly, such as the flickering, shadowy nature of their own community. Many rural occupations, like that of the reddleman, are in decline. Most of the leading characters want to escape from Egdon Heath. Clym wishes to return, having already become an outsider by living in Paris, but he can hardly accomplish this having become 'blind' to its ways and failing to see that his idea of community no longer exists. Or there is the extreme loneliness of Michael Henchard, stressed repeatedly in *The Mayor of Casterbridge*, alongside the class-divided nature of urban life.[108] A seeming 'community' of commercial exchange in that novel is often viewed from a distance, as by women in the house overlooking the town's market. This is, as J. Hillis Miller commented, 'not so much a stable community, lasting from generation to generation, as a community in the midst of rapid and disruptive change, a community in dissolution'.[109] All its major characters come from outside, as do the farmers coming to town only for the market.[110] In *The Woodlanders*, which Hardy dated to about 1876,[111] the collapse of Little Hintock's lonely woodland community is partly through failed leadership and responsibility, epitomized by the capricious, immoral and locally ignorant estate owner Mrs Charmond, who takes no interest in the village people.[112] Her house has become 'a carcase from which the spirit had flown', with sightless shuttered windows, which contrast with the uncurtained and open windows of the rest of the community, through which individuals like Marty South can be seen working.[113] In addition to the rootlessly modern affinities of Mrs Charmond and Fitzpiers,[114] the terminated tenures, cottage destruction and the redundancy of people's local woodland skills are key themes in the decline of families, community and the 'closely-knit interdependence of the lives' in this isolated 'wood-environed community'.[115]

Or one thinks of Tess's transmigration through a variety of communities, from Talbothays to desolate countrysides like Flintcomb Ash, increasingly lacking and displaced from community, in a process that leads finally to her death. There is no community for Tess, for reasons that stem initially from her seduction, and which are compounded by Victorian sexual double standards. In terms of my discussion of community here, Tess prefigures what happens in *Jude the Obscure*. Her isolation, ostracism and thwarted aspirations (which only amount to an honest, accepting, loving marriage with Angel Clare) are a gendered variant on Jude's thwarted hopes and social rejection. Tess, with associations of John Bunyan's Pilgrim in the Valley of Humiliation, is also 'modern' in her alienation. *Jude* is thus in a direct line of continuity from Hardy's earlier novels, is a wholly logical and comprehensible development of them and is not a novel set apart from them dealing with other issues.

Indeed, Hardy's fiction, whether by intention or inadvertently, chronicles community decline and dejected individualism almost in progressive form. As L. W. Deen wrote:

> Hardy's attention is lyric and in-driving, towards the inmost emotional and suffering vulnerability of single figures isolated from one another and from the society which surrounds them … *Jude* is the logical development of a tendency towards the pathos of isolation and self-inflicted punishment clearly visible at least as early as *Return of the Native*. The action of Hardy's tragedies is almost always the doomed struggle against isolation.[116]

This is interlaced with his concerns about marriage and personal relationships, for the considerations that arise through community decay in Hardy are implicated in all his accounts of 'false' marriages, with their lack of a mutually validating community that might have ensured shared knowledge and work.[117] Failed marriage in Hardy's novels and short stories occurs through the move *out of* community, away from any community that would have endorsed knowledge of others or was based upon joint work, into apparently individualized self-seeking and related aspirations, into the 'self-indulgent vices of artificial society'.[118]

Hardy's senses of the decline of rural community – and its fictional possibilities – probably compounded the hostile reaction to *Jude the Obscure* and influenced his decision to end novel writing in favour of poetry, which most preoccupied him from the turn of the century until his death in 1928. For Hardy's poetry is a more individualistic, subjective, expressive and personal art form, one less concerned with contextualized interactions between selected people in a community than had been many nineteenth-century novels. Like his novels, his poetry remained infused with history, landscape and local incident.[119] Yet this poetry's solitary individuality and tone of memory and observation seem at one with the social modernism his novels had gradually come to express, even though that modernism (in the literary hands of others) would far traverse the poetic forms he gave it. Hardy's own trajectory through literary genres, in other words, stemmed in part from his sense of the decline of community, his responses to urbanization and his awareness of earlier rural ways of life and association coming to an end.

6

Weeding Out Village Life

Detective Fiction and Murderous Community

'I regard St Mary Mead', he said authoritatively, 'as a stagnant pool' …

'That is really not a very good simile …' said Miss Marple briskly. 'Nothing, I believe, is so full of life under the microscope as a drop of water from a stagnant pool.' [1]

It is surprising that detective fiction has been little studied by historians. After all, its publishing and sales have been phenomenal. Agatha Christie wrote over eighty detective novels, many of them with rural settings. She is the best-selling writer of books of all time. Over two billion of her books have been sold (some estimates are twice that). Only the Bible may exceed this. Her works have been translated into over 110 languages, with about 6,400 separate translations, making her the most translated novelist ever. Some other crime writers of the interwar period, such as Dorothy L. Sayers, wrote translated best-sellers, though they did not approach Christie's popularity. In other words, the detective fiction of Agatha Christie is the most common way in which the English village community has come to be known worldwide. Her fictional St Mary Mead is globally the most widely known village in writing of any form.[2] Millions of people have learnt English by reading about this village, and their presumptions about the English have been saturated with Christie's discernment. The world's best-known fictional character is probably not Hikaru Genji or Don Quixote, Heathcliff or Huckleberry Finn, Pickwick or Harry Potter – it is more likely to be an elderly spinster fond of knitting, observation and English village gossip.

One hardly needs further justification for this discussion. Yet this chapter was initially stimulated by a reading of Dorothy L. Sayers's *Five Red Herrings* (1931). The novel is set in Galloway and featured a murder among a set of artists. Five of them are 'red herrings' in the investigation. One of them, a particularly quarrelsome individual, is found dead at the bottom of a cliff, having seemingly fallen while painting. Needless to say, appearances are deceptive; his head has been bashed in and there is a murder to detect. What struck me was the intense level of *observed detail* of this novel, taken as natural in an interwar rural community. We learn who was seen catching which train, as remembered by booking clerks and the station master, about what car was seen at exactly what time, with descriptions of its driver. People running a bookstall remember strangers passing at 1.49 pm. If a car passes through, it is presumed that someone saw and recollected it. People know about others' bicycles: the make of each; that one has a rusty and twisted back mudguard and so belongs to a certain person; about the state of bicycle tyres. Gossip and common knowledge includes details of people's clothing, eating habits, daily routines and schedules. Houses are left open while people are away. The local topography is also exactly described. The novel takes intense community knowledge for granted, and the plot relies on this sharp-eyed and eavesdropping familiarity.[3]

Interwar readers of such fiction saw nothing extraordinary in this intense local knowledge. Sayers wrote: 'in a country place, where everybody knows everybody, it is impossible to keep one's movements altogether secret'.[4] The villagers are incredibly observant, with extraordinary recall. Everyone is a kind of Sherlock Holmes. This prompts a number of questions. Is there anything that we can learn from the presumptions or details of life that this detective fiction expressed about communities? What does it reveal about tensions of the times? How realistic were the novelists about communal behaviour, and how did they express ideas about community?

Detective fiction – the genre

The interwar period has been described by literary critics as 'the Golden Age' of detective fiction.[5] The genre was established earlier, by Wilkie Collins,[6] Arthur Conan Doyle, E. C. Bentley and others,[7] and these authors had considerable influence into the 1920s and 1930s. From the First World War, however, literary plots tended to become more plausible, venues more believable, while styles of writing and characterization often improved. The genre expanded markedly. Its highly selling formula was usually a game between author and reader, with rational deduction from clues. The crime was a murder. 'They say all the world loves a lover – apply that saying to murder and you have an even more infallible truth.'[8] The reader became part of the community of detection, a technique of fictional absorption by which readers would become integrated into damaged communities, in search of communal and individual redemption. Hence the choice of this subject for this book.

There was huge interest in detective fiction in the interwar period. Foremost in the genre were four female authors who frequently wrote about village communities: Dorothy L. Sayers, Agatha Christie, Margery Allingham and Ngaio Marsh. These have been termed the 'Queens of Crime' or the 'Quartet of Muses'.[9] In addition, a major figure was G. K. Chesterton, with his Father Brown stories. Conan Doyle was publishing Sherlock Holmes stories until 1927, though he is usually considered in relation to an earlier time. My interest is in how 'community' was represented by these authors. Fictional work always needs to be handled cautiously by historians.[10] Yet there is little doubt that novelists reveal much about social and community relations, valuations, opinions and prejudices, gender presumptions, speech or material culture, and this may be especially true of detective writers, given their attention to detail and issues of communal distrust. These subjects were raised extensively in this fiction. In the 1930s it was even claimed that 'The true twentieth-century chroniclers are the detective story writers.'[11] One critic wrote that 'it is perhaps as a record of social change that [Christie's] works will be most valuable to the social historian'.[12] This chapter focuses on the interwar period and these leading writers and their rural themes. The rules and presumptions of British detective fiction did not alter radically then. They did so subsequently, with the 'mean-streets' or 'hard-boiled' evolution associated with authors like Raymond Chandler.[13] Indeed, Christie's post-1945 novels were very revealing about social changes even into the 1960s, indicating attitudes and responses that she did not envisage in 1930.

The detected village

Edmund Crispin said of Christie that 'When one thinks of her, one thinks inevitably of English country life.'[14] 'In the British tradition', one critic wrote, 'the detective novelist has more often than not preferred a rural or semirural setting'.[15] The villages in these novels are imagined, through authorial experiences, yet the authors often made claims of semblance or accuracy. Christie wrote that Miss Marple's village 'is as real to me as it could be – and indeed there are several villages remarkably like it'.[16] Dorothy L. Sayers wrote of her *Five Red Herrings* that 'all the places are real'.[17] The enclosed fictional worlds of contemporary crime writing were well suited to village communities, although they could extend more widely to a Yorkshire Dale or narrowly to a country house. Conan Doyle had often chosen settings where murder occurred in wild and desolate places, well away from hamlets or villages, as on Dartmoor in *The Hound of the Baskervilles*. That writing was more like a thriller: with dangerous chases over 'the huge expanse of the moor, mottled with gnarled and craggy cairns and tors', inhabited by ravens and an escaped convict.[18] There is a community of sorts here, as people are locally known, often interrelated and dependent – but such community is shadowy, muzzled and delocalized by topography. Human connectivity is also embayed and railed in by the myth or reality of a savage hound roaming the moor.

By comparison, the interwar women writers felt no dramatic need for the 'desolate, lifeless moor'. They preferred known face-to-face communities, in which they could create and resolve a crime in the context of everyday life and an inward set of characters, where they could expound principled ideas, disrupt privacy and reassert moral authority in a relatively closed community. A village served well, as indeed did other 'closed' situations such as a long-distance train journey, a group of aeroplane passengers, the sociability of a bridge party, a Nile cruiser, a transatlantic liner, an island off Devon or a home for young offenders.[19] One could debate whether Christie was primarily a novelist of the village or a novelist of closed social milieux. Yet one can see why she was drawn to the southern English village. Murder on Dartmoor had seemed in keeping with its topography; but murder in a quiet, English nucleated village heightened the sense of moral shock because of cultural suppositions about rural as compared to urban life. Rural detective fiction was also an escape, a relaxation, conveying reassurance in detecting the villain. Given that 'Englishness' was garbed in rural dress, the detection and extraction of a murderer from village life served as a wider metaphor and symbol for nationalistic cleansing and purification.[20] Further considerations drew detective novelists to villages: change in the village and its male deaths during the Great War, the interwar rural crisis and exodus, questions about the roles of women, the dilemma of rural leadership, or the transformations of rural property holding. 'I find it very difficult to read one that is not set in rural England,' wrote W. H. Auden.[21] It is not clear whether he meant that so many were rurally set or whether he only wanted to read rural ones! Yet one can see many reasons for the attraction to novelists of fictional creations such as St Mary Mead, King's Abbot, Styles St Mary, Paggleham, Darley, Mystery Mile, Vale-of-Pen-Cuckoo or Fenchurch St Paul.

These villages were sometimes idealized or stereotyped and were often nostalgic. They were communities envisaged as potentially moral, restorable to such a homely state, and they were handled as such by quite conservative writers, at a time when the influence of the church was declining, and when rural society was seen to be in economic and social trouble or in moral decay. Dorothy L. Sayers's father was a clergyman, and the reassertion of moral authority in her novels might be interpreted as a wishful literary fulfilment of her father's moral influence in his parish. As such, the villages often serve as miniature havens or Edens, in which murder incongruously disrupts the setting. Murder is out of place and rectitude needs to be restored. There is a *puzzle* at the heart of the village community, such that it no longer seems a community: it is so suspicious. Nothing so disrupts the spirit of community as murder, by a person unknown within it. Christie's St Mary Mead is a 'quiet one-horse village'[22] and is potentially as ideal as its saintly name, despite Christie's brooding statements about evil in villages. Murderous violence is thus contrasted with Edenic rural peace: *cruor in rus*. Thus the detective, like the parish clergyman, restores the pre-murder *status quo*, the rural idyll, the sense of community and benign fair play.[23] He or she *weeds out* the evil, the nasty, the malevolent, from the flower beds where it does not belong. This weeding metaphor applied to people is frequent in Christie. In this literary genre, noticeably dominated by conservative women writers (some of them explicitly fond of gardening and well-weeded herbaceous borders), it is the role of the detective to purge the village of such *wickedness*, and return it to its apparently former nature, to its proper community self.

The village settings contain such standard features as the Old Hall, the church, the Manor, the rectory, the parish hall (by now common in villages),[24] the public house, a park and so on. They tend to be southern or midland English villages. 'Our village, King's Abbot, is, I imagine, very like any other village,' wrote Christie.[25] There are exceptions, notably in Sayers's books set in Yorkshire or Galloway, but nucleated lowland English villages are frequent settings. Village topography can be crucial to these novels, and beyond that characters traverse or get stuck in bogs, fenland drains, marshland estuaries, moorland, woodland, or whatever seems appropriate to the area. There are many contrasts between a domesticated but socially apprehensive village core, where crime now usually occurs, and the naturalistically still hazardous areas beyond. In genre terms, there were echoes here of the more dramatic contrasts in *The Hound of the Baskervilles*. Indeed, extending parallels to urban landscapes, one recalls Conan Doyle's accounts of respectable and dangerous city areas,[26] although in all interwar detective fiction the urban is seedily commercial, dissipated or dangerous.[27] Many of Thomas Hardy's anti-urban views seemed to persist. We have seen how Hardy came to show a forsaken bleakness in rural life. In this detective fiction, by the 1920s the village as a paragon of communal virtue is more comparable with the dangerous city, for the village is now murderous. In the course of murder and its detection, the internal structure of the village becomes important, with its vantage points and angles of perception. This structure is often carefully mapped out, as in Allingham's *Country Mile*, Marsh's *Overture to Death*, Christie's *The Murder at the Vicarage* or Gladys Mitchell's *The Saltmarsh Murders*.[28] The house-by-house cartography forms a grid for the plot, in a way rarely found in nineteenth-century fiction. This sense of communal place is very minute indeed, as we will find it (in Chapter 8) with Adrian Bell.

One could outline a generic cartography in the village layouts of these novels, and these divulge the hope or reality of certain kinds of community. These are still retrievably moral settings. Their structures contain the seeds of detection, of moral accomplishment spearheaded by a detective and of community recovery, an outcome that owes much to these villages' historical forms and terrain. In this sense, the historical evolution of the village, and associated aesthetic emotions, secure its resurrection, as in Stanley Spencer's contemporary and painterly search for the meanings of Cookham.[29] It seems that the minded village *is* a moral unit by virtue of its historically evolved structure. The conservative women writers wish to say this and effectively do so in the denouements of their stories. They make use of multiple viewpoints, of superadded criss-crossing individual perspectives, shaking the kaleidoscope such that events change in appearance. They use many modernist literary devices, such as stream of consciousness, or they 'do it with mirrors', even when being cynical about literary modernism.[30] These novels contain uncertain understandings, misleading impressions and countless partial perspectives, even if they resolve these eventually. Indeed, placing the present in a past framework, and representing the past in the present – as in crime fiction when murderous motives echo from a localized past – was also a 'modernist' method, notably in T. S. Eliot. There was not for these novelists a single panoptic view, with its echoes of nineteenth-century thought and workhouse control. Surveillance now comes via multiple eyes, complicating community hopes. Sundry angles of village sight inform cross-table lines of dinner-party talk, as often in Christie's work. Eventually a reassuringly fixed resolution occurs and loose ends fall into place; the jigsaw puzzle (popular in this period) still has all its pieces, just as modernist literary methods sink reassuringly back to tradition. This was not always so for Sherlock Holmes and even less so in post-1945 crime fiction. In this predestined process the morally apposite role of nucleated communities is indicated, where people overlook each other in a matrix of house and garden viewpoints, conducive to gossip, observation and detection. A stereotyped English nucleated village form produces its corollary, a predictable and reassuringly moral ending. The spirit of 'community' thankfully returns to the village.

The country house

These novels often focused on the 'country house', the authors seeing potential there as did P. G. Wodehouse, Daphne du Maurier, Noel Coward and Evelyn Waugh. In genre terms, this is sometimes said to have been relatively new. In fact, Arthur Conan Doyle's stories about Sherlock Holmes featured many rural 'cases', usually set in southern English counties, even in country houses 'all stained and streaked with damp'[31] or where 'An odour of age and decay pervaded the whole crumbling building.'[32] The interwar period was a time of severe change for country houses, with many being sold off after 1918, as we will see in the next chapter on James Wentworth Day. Many novels dwelt on this, most notably Sheila Kaye-Smith's *The End of the House of Alard* (1923). In Arthur Conan Doyle the main focus was probably the metropolis, albeit with many investigative excursions into the countryside. By the interwar years the dominant theme became the countryside, with lesser prevalence of towns.[33] In some detective novels the country house is so important as wholly to eclipse the village. Some novels hint that things go wrong and crimes occur in a country house when it becomes isolated from the village. The motives of the characters are linked to issues of inheritance, reputation, rivalry, exclusion and an inward-looking history of the family. The fiction in such cases tends to be socially exclusive. It plays on the idea of hitherto social and moral rightness being disturbed, which was well expressed by Margery Allingham: 'That house of yours across the park and this one – they were so quiet, undisturbed for centuries, it seemed that nothing terrible could happen in them.'[34]

The danger so often comes from within, and so these novels can be narrow in social reference. Intimate details of country houses also offered much to novelists whose plots and clues depended upon fine points of interiors: the placement of chairs, routines of servants, locking of rooms, creaking of particular doors, and fires in grates. This was a closely observed setting. Plans of the house were often important to the novel. Characters were drawn with reference to nice matters of arrangement, and this included some detectives, most notably the fastidious and ironically named Hercule Poirot – at five foot four inches probably as little as Miss Marple – a Belgian refugee from European turmoil, whose mannerisms made him so alert to those of others. A small detail 'out of place' was indeed of moment. It is as if the novels were responding to major social and economic change with a fussy last-ditch insistence upon the rightness of precise internal arrangements. The country house, its contents and inhabitants were natural class targets for theft and murder. Poirot himself might have exclaimed that *l'ancien ordre des choses* had rarely been so threatened. Readers with differing political views would see undermining of fastidious arrangements, ideas of moral propriety and the earlier status of country house society as promising, threatening, comic, fatuous or ironic, an augury of the decline of community. (We will see elements of this in H. E. Bates.) Agatha Christie's intelligence, seeming impartiality and skilful reliance upon conversation opened the door to many such responses.

Villagers and the poor

One rarely finds much social empathy or breadth in this fiction. Servants appear, but infrequently as developed characters, or as murderers, for the murderer needs motives, false alibis, method and personality. Servants in the 1930s were still often paid under £1 a week. Their numbers fell from 2.6 to 1.3 million between 1911 and 1921 – a large decline, though they were still numerous.[35] The 'servant problem' had long been discussed and was often mentioned in detective fiction. Indeed, servants were often seen by employers as a questionable working-class presence in households, snooping into their affairs,[36] and much criticism may stem from doubts over their presence or barely suppressed class hostilities. Suppositions deriving from class were, by this period, very strongly apparent. According to the crime writers, servants or scullery maids are apparently hard to get, often incompetent or stupid.[37] They had been 'rather simple … and frequently adenoidal, and Amy distinctly moronic'.[38] Christie in particular creates characters, including morally approved ones, who manifest distrust and low opinion of servants. 'If the opportunity arose *mine and thine* would mean nothing to her … Well, she went to Lady Ashton … and what happened? All the lace cut off her underclothes and two diamond brooches taken – and the girl departed in the middle of the night and never heard of since!'[39] Some of Margery Allingham's servants or butlers are distinctly dangerous.[40] Mr Mervyn Bunter is the main exception, a worthy assistant to Lord Peter Wimsey, deeply loyal, a man of insights; but he has no counterparts in Christie, Allingham or Marsh.

Outside the house, gardeners have a role as witnesses in *The Mysterious Affair at Styles* and are accorded slightly more respect than their nineteenth-century literary counterparts, although one sees established description in

Christie's account. A gardener, significantly named Manning, is announced by 'the clumping of hobnailed boots on the gravel'. He 'came slowly and hesitatingly through the French window, and stood as near as he could. He held his cap in his hands, twisting it very carefully round and round'. He lifts 'a finger to his forehead with a low mumble' after he's been questioned.[41] The theme of employees' incompetence and obstinacy runs through Christie's writing, even after 1945, when she could still write of a gardener that 'his best, such as it was (which was not much) was only the best according to *his* lights, and not according to those of his employer'.[42] No doubt this explained defectiveness in the herbaceous border. Into the 1960s, she referred to 'that queer way country folk have of not speaking to you direct, looking over your shoulder or round the corner, as it were, as though they saw something you didn't'.[43] Such accounts tally with some descriptions of deferential culture.[44] After all, 'Major Phillpott', says Christie, 'was God locally'.[45] Some of her other characterization is more hostile. An 'aged rustic' in *The Mysterious Affair at Styles* 'leered at me cunningly'. '"Ah, you gentlemen from the Hall – you'm a pretty lot!". And he leered more jocosely than ever.'[46] In this case, the 'aged rustic' alluded to the adulterous behaviour of a man from the Hall, and so he might have been shown as morally superior; but, presented in this way, his manner of commenting attracts no sympathy in the reader.

These detective novels contain much predictable characterization of village inhabitants, showing continuity of representations of Hodge.[47] The farm labourer was being written out of personalized existence in much earlier fiction, and he is barely more visible or credible here. Margery Allingham writes of a character named 'Anry' that he 'was afflicted with a certain moroseness which, coupled with his natural inarticulate tongue, made him something of a man of mystery in the village. He was a simple old fellow with … a slow and rather foolish smile.' Another character is 'a great sandy-haired lout', while a third is 'a great hulking cross-eyed fellow with a red moustache'. George, an 'old fellow', is a 'disgusting old cadger!' Allingham takes the term 'yokel', and from it creates a 'bokel': 'half a barmy, half a yokel'. 'They're dreadful,' says one of her characters, 'They're inveterate beggars. I hope you sent them away.' Allingham wrote with limited discernment of 'the stolid stoicism of the countrywoman who accepts birth and death, spring and winter in the same spirit'.[48] Ngaio Marsh has little to say about Dorset or other farm workers, except that they sit on back benches in the parish hall 'smelling of hair-grease and animal warmth'.[49]

Dorothy L. Sayers also shows poorer rural inhabitants in unflattering ways. She wrote in a letter about how 'I had, of course, a long connection with the Fen country of *The Nine Tailors*, since my father had two parishes in East Anglia,'[50] and she associated herself with the Isle of Ely and 'fenland' during the Second World War.[51] Her fictional Fenchurch St Paul was an architectural combination of Upwell, March and Walpole St Peter churches, and her fenland characterization was often based on local people.[52] Her accounts seem authentic when describing the problems of cross-class conversation: 'Your country-dweller is a master of pregnant silences.'[53] But unlike a sympathetic author like George Sturt, who was intent on understanding and conveyed much oral testimony, Sayers does not probe much further. Her characters are comfortable with superficial statements: 'Country people are very matter-of-fact about life and death. They live so close to reality.'[54]

In Christie, lower-class figures are rarely murderers, because they are undeveloped as characters. Yet they certainly are murderers in Sayers's novels, as in *Busman's Honeymoon* or *The Nine Tailors*. John Cawelti comments that 'in Sayers' English village evil seems to be defined more in terms of nasty, aggressive members of the lower classes trying to punch their way up the social scale'.[55] Her fenland is troubled by 'very unpleasant-looking tramps' – later versions of those we saw in Chapter 3 – who are suspected of breaking open alms boxes and otherwise vandalizing churches.[56] A farm labourer in Yorkshire leans over a gate, 'sucking a straw', makes no reply to Wimsey, but 'spat in the direction of Peter's right boot'.[57] 'You don't expect farm labourers to have nerves, do you, Lord Peter?', asks a doctor.[58] Sayers refers to Yorkshire people as 'natives … oyster-like', because they say so little, and presents them as surly, uncommunicative, rude and unimpressed by snobbish talk and irony. The 'bounders about here are all Socialists and Methodists', and some are poachers.[59] In *Busman's Honeymoon*, female villagers are backstabbing gossips. Working-class dialect in *Clouds of Witness* is rendered in Starkadder style, albeit with Yorkshire rather than Sussex words, plus a touch of Cockney for one Londoner who has moved north. These people are thus given some dialectal location, but in Sayers's work they are normally decontextualized by being removed from their homes, work or cultures and are frequently placed as dialectal or serving types into a higher social milieu.

Nor are Sayers's farmers presented empathetically. A Yorkshire farmer named Mr Grimethorpe in *Clouds of Witness* is a jealous, violent, wife-beating, boorish maniac, setting savage dogs on visitors,[60] and is eventually arrested for attempted murder when he fires a gun at Wimsey in London. That is just an aside to the main plot, gratuitously thrown in, perhaps to augment a 'Wuthering Heights' feel to the Yorkshire description. Sayers went there in 1924 'to get Lord Peter finished amid his proper surrounding – though this does not mean that I am aspiring to be the new Emily Brontë – so don't think it …', she wrote in a letter to her mother, which was largely about stockings and a 'frightfully funny' visit to the cinema with 'Aunt G'.[61] Her Yorkshire trip brought no desire to represent its farmers realistically or sympathetically. Such social stereotypes are revealing – this literary depiction shows very one-sided perspectives on untrusted community and little sense of shared community spirit.

The detectives

The detectives created by these novelists indicate much about their time and place, and genre traditions. They contrast with their forerunner, the 'masculine', logical, cold and decisive Sherlock Holmes, who had been adroit in handling the misanthropic sides of grimy Victorian London, interspersed with excursions into the iniquitous English countryside, the man whose 'rational' nature left him little time for love or women: 'I am a brain, Watson. The rest of me is a mere appendix.'[62] By 1937, however, Holmes had been 'modernised and brought up to date', according to a film reviewer in *The Times*. He 'now travels in the latest type of motor-car, and it is with sadness that we may note his genial affability when greeting a member of the fairer sex'.[63] Conan Doyle published the final Sherlock Holmes cases in 1927, so to some extent Holmes can be regarded as an interwar detective. Yet detectives had usually moved on, revealingly so, and largely in the hands of women authors. One literary critic has characterized Holmes's most famed successors as 'A foppish lord, a vain and overweight Belgian, and an elderly gentlewoman'.[64] Each is positioned in distinctive ways towards community life.

Sayers's Lord Peter Wimsey is a post-estate aristocrat in search of responsibility and a role, but often showing his social and personal inadequacies. His harrowing experiences in the First World War and his failure to come to terms with having ordered many men 'over the top' to their deaths have rendered him 'whimsical' and sometimes almost incapable of making decisions. His dreams are 'usually something to do with the War' – 'it was only the old responsibility dream'.[65] He rolls up his sleeves to show bell-ringing ability in *The Nine Tailors* and is a man of some dynamism in *Gaudy Night*; but he becomes a whimpering wreck by the end of *Busman's Honeymoon*, as he and his wife Harriet Vane await the hour of their detected murderer's execution. Shell-shocked, socially inept or rude, sometimes insensitive to Bunter – whose more lowly class organizing skills and ability to merge socially he desperately needs – dashing about with 'perilous swiftness' in an open Daimler regardless of the weather, occasionally driving it into a ditch, he is an anachronistic elite figure coming to terms with diminished responsibility, even trying to shun any responsibility at all: 'I'm never serious.'[66] His heraldic arms include '3 mice courant'; his motto is 'As my whimsy takes me'.[67] Wimsey, we are told, has 'that underlying sense of social responsibility which prevents the English landed gentry from being a total loss, spiritually speaking'.[68] He feels that he ought to pay for the church organ's new bellows.[69] His 'old responsibility dream' brings ghostly echoes of an atavistic code from the past. After the war, he cannot give an order, not even to servants – 'which made it really very miserable for him, poor lamb!' [70] His diction – the repetitive 'what' at the end of sentences, as though he needs constant affirmation – shows him to be a gulf away from the dialectal speech of many villagers. He is *au fait* with both city and countryside, 'adored by *chef* and waiters alike for his appreciation of good food', prone to express himself in affected French.[71] His chin warrants a letter of ancestral explanation to *The Times*.[72] In fact, 'there was foreign blood at the roots' of his family tree; hence the 'eccentric strain' by which Wimsey chose to smoke cigarettes in his pyjamas.[73] More irregular still, he even appears naked before a house-help – an aristocrat *sans habits* – leading to a discussion among village women of his effeminacy and supposedly class physique:

> 'Mother-naked, Mrs 'Odges, if you'll believe *me*. I declare I was that ashamed I didden know w'ere to look. And no more 'air on 'is chest than wot I 'as meself.'
>
> 'That's gentry', said Mrs Hodges ... 'Now, my Susan's first were a wunnerful 'airy man, jest like a kerridge-rug if you take my meaning.'[74]

He therefore stands as an intelligent and appropriate symbol for many among the upper classes in the interwar period: occasionally intrepid, but questionably masculine in the terms of his time, lacking a clear role, quietly suffering diminishing returns in land and the stock market, yet with lingering prestige and wealth, apparently indifferent to personal gain, disdainful of tasteless new housing built by those aspiring to elite rural status, ignoring the dereliction of land and farm buildings, flaunting pretentious learning which is often irrelevant, sidetracked into the solving of murder as a mental exercise. The police still call him 'my lord', and he can interfere in their affairs.[75] Men in his village touch their hat to him, and there appears little hatred of him because of his class.[76] He appreciates being shown 'all the proper consideration for my rank and refinement and other inferiorities', either feigning that he isn't of his class or that it is a liability. There are still deer in the park and peacocks on the terrace: 'all the story-book things'.[77] One is reminded of Laurie Lee, writing in *Cider with Rosie* that 'The Squire was our centre, a crumbling moot tree.'[78] As George Orwell commented: 'English people are extremely fond of the titled ass (cf. Lord Peter Wimsey) who always turns up trumps in the moment of emergency ... The Lord Peter Wimsey figure, the seeming idiot who drawls and wears a monocle'.[79] Yet he is a rather pointless social leftover assuming a self-appointed quasi-feudal role *vis-à-vis* crime and punishment,[80] a be-monocled residue of medieval lordship, 'looking a perfectly well-bred imbecile'.[81] He now needs the firm feminine hand of a Dorothy L. Sayers or a Harriet Vane to guide him.

Her biographers hint that Sayers created in Wimsey the man she needed, and failed to find, in her own life.[82] One clue to his attractions, beyond his need for female organizational care, was summed up in Harriet Vane's thinking about him as a symbol of 'Englishness', predictably seen in terms of English village order and hoped-for stability. Harriet

> understood now why it was that with all his masquing attitudes, all his cosmopolitan self-adaptations, all his odd spiritual reticences and escapes, he yet carried about with him that permanent atmosphere of security. He belonged to an ordered society, and this was it ... he spoke the familiar language of her childhood. In London, anybody, at any moment, might do or become anything. But in a village – no matter what village – they were all immutably themselves: parson, organist, sweep, duke's son and doctor's daughter, moving like chessmen upon their allotted squares. She was curiously excited. She thought, 'I have married England.'
>
> Her fingers tightened on his arm. England, serenely unaware of his symbolic importance, acknowledged the squeeze with a pressure of the elbow. 'Splendid!' he said, heartily.[83]

Lord Peter Wimsey bears an obvious historical relation to English rural community and is linked to understanding and changing meanings of it. He is one possible class symbol of interwar England. With his confidence problems he might be seen as a metaphor for Britain and gradual decline. The other amateur 'detective' who requires village placement is Agatha Christie's Miss Marple. She is indigenously 'rural' in a more obvious way than are many other Christie characters, such as the cosmopolitan Belgian refugee Hercule Poirot, or indeed Christie herself. Marple is an elderly spinster living in 'her old-world cottage',[84] who first appears in fiction in 1930. She says, 'I hardly ever go out of St. Mary Mead.' She is described as being 'this frail old-fashioned maiden lady', 'this typical "old maid of the village" ... [with] her quiet old-maidish ways, her amazing penetration'.[85]

She seems to have been born in the 1860s and (leaving aside film versions) in appearance she is Victorian:

> she sat erect in the big grandfather chair. Miss Marple wore a black brocade dress, very much pinched in round the waist. Mechlin lace was arranged in a cascade down the front of the bodice. She had on black lace mittens, and a black lace cap surmounted the piled-up masses of her snowy hair. She was knitting – something white and soft and fleecy. Her faded blue eyes, benignant and kindly, surveyed her nephew.[86]

Young people 'tell one that one has a Victorian mind – and that, they say, is like a *sink*.'[87] Certainly Marple is a gossip, an insider, who is polite and has endless time for others. Thus to some she seems meddlesome. Over time, we might ask, who overlooks who in the monitoring of community? 'In the art of seeing without being seen, Miss Marple had no rival.' She 'always sees everything. Gardening is as good as a smoke screen, and the habit of observing birds through powerful glasses can always be turned to account.'[88] One remembers the much more socially elite Edward Montagu viewing his village through a telescope in Chapter 3. But now it is Marple, rather than hitherto social elites, who represents the social conscience. She is the all-seeing eye in an isolated Cranford-like village that is closed in upon itself and distrustful of outsiders, though by that token this is still a village more ready for crime detection than many impersonal modern environments.

Marple herself comments that 'I don't think anything has ever happened to me … Flowers, of course, and queer messages – but that's just men, isn't it?'[89] She is what her nephew calls one of the '"superfluous women" [who] have a lot of time on their hands, and their chief interest is usually *people*. And so, you see, they get to be what one might call *experts*.'[90] The predicament of Victorian 'superfluous women' or 'the spinster problem', and then of numerous spinsters and widows after the First World War, was often remarked upon. 'Our village', wrote Christie, is 'rich in unmarried ladies'.[91] By 1921, there were 1.72 million more women than men in England and Wales. Only twenty-eight villages in England had all their men return safely from the First World War. Spinsters or widows comprised about one in twenty of the population, and 'the spinster problem' was widely discussed. Like Miss Marple, these women were coming to terms with the violence of the war and its implications for themselves. In one of her novels, Sayers runs a conversation between a woman and her doctor about 'sublimated' sexual urges, 'a thing most people suffered from', in which the woman points out that 'with two million extra women in this country it didn't seem possible, certainly, for everybody to get married'. 'My dear Miss Milsom', he replies, 'half my patients come to me because they are not married – and the other half because they are!'[92] In some interwar documentary literature one even finds notions that villages are 'preserved' for 'bright maiden ladies'.[93] The discussion of these spinsters is often unfavourable, even by women. Ngaio Marsh describes 'a museum piece, a cottage pianoforte of the nineties, with a tucked silk panel, badly torn, in front. It has a hard-bitten look. It would not be too fanciful to compare it to a spinster, dressed in dilapidated moth-eaten finery, still retaining an air of shabby gentility, but given over to some very dubious employment.'[94] In due course, a bullet from this instrument murders the novel's victim. 'There is', Marsh writes later,

> an unfortunately rather common type of church worker who is always a problem to her parish priest ... one finds this type among – dear me – among ladies who are not perhaps very young and who have no other interests ... I am sorry to say poor Miss Campanula was really an advanced – er – specimen of this type. Poor soul, she was lonely and had a difficult temperament ... she needed a doctor as well as a priest to help her.[95]

Miss Marple is a more resilient and winning version of this 'type'. It is the close village life that gives her 'unlimited opportunities of observing human nature – under the microscope as it were',[96] yet another technology of inspection. She has an acute sense of time, although in some views time has passed her by, and her clocks are always accurate to the minute.[97] She has become in effect the micro-history community inspector, of a parochial history figured in local people, whose lives are understood through gossip and intensely nosy observation. They are scrutinized as closely as the rows of knitting that Marple is so often engaged in: a line of thought that is intensely channelled and entwined by gossip. 'One has a lot of opportunities doing one's needlework round the fire.' 'Sitting here with one's knitting, one just sees the facts.'[98] The interwar period made many adverse judgements and interpretations of spinsters and their behaviour. We are usually drawn to sympathy and to gentler characterizations now, affected also by artistic licence in performances by actresses like Joan Hickson. Yet the outcomes of Miss Marple's interwoven pondering suggest comparisons with *la tricoteuse* knitting approvingly in the front row below the guillotine. For this elderly Victorian lady, albeit with distinctly non-revolutionary conservative principles, in her community but out of her time, without any apparent scruple sends interwar villagers to their judicially ordained *hangings*. It is not clear if this is a thought that the married Christie invited: but what a paradox it is that Miss Marple, almost a classic ageing spinster of her period, after the carnage of the First World War expends her time and familial loneliness in bringing community retribution in the form of death.

A gossipy community

Gossip pervades these novels. It is used to express community opinion, castigate behaviour, display ideas of neighbourliness, demarcate people by class or insider status, express gendered cultures, affirm presumptions about crime or provide information necessary for the plots.[99] It helped create a sense of verisimilitude, while also being a generic device, producing an excess of data to be analysed and verified. Ngaio Marsh, for example, makes much play with female villagers who 'adored scandal … and cloaked … passion in a mantle of conscious rectitude'.[100] The novelist who most exploits village gossip is undoubtedly Agatha Christie. It suited her subtle conversational style. She had a notion of judgemental gossip that she called 'the talk of the village', or 'village opinion', although that opinion was often divided in its verdicts, on weighty issues such as whether a 'nice girl' should act as secretary to an 'unmarried man' or whether a painter should paint 'Lettice in her bathing dress'.[101] Gossip is one of the ways in which Miss Marple gains information. Indeed, as a quintessential insider it gives Marple an advantage over marginalized and often inept policemen. Their failure to listen to insiders is usually linked by Christie to their incompetence. Poirot, like Marple, is deeply interested in village gossip. He benefits from it but does not join in. Yet it is Marple, as the archetypical village spinster, who gains most from gossip. She 'knew practically everything that went on in St Mary Mead'. She is said to be 'the worst cat in the village … And she always knows every single thing that happens.'[102] The feline analogy is frequent.

More broadly, however, the entire village is presented as all-seeing, much as it is in Dorothy L. Sayers's Galloway. Almost nothing passes unobserved. Everyone is inquisitive. 'We are not used to mysteries in St Mary Mead.' The vicar in *Murder at the Vicarage* comments on 'the detective instinct in village life. In St Mary Mead everyone knows your most intimate affairs'. People 'must eat their meals standing up by the window so as to be sure of not missing anything'.[103] Even after the Second World War, with profound village changes which were described in *The Mirror Crack'd from Side to Side*, it is said that 'You can't keep any secrets in St Mary Mead.' And even the new semi-detached houses add opportunities for knowledge and gossip: 'Thin as anything, the walls'.[104]

The gossip is said, by some of the men, to be a feminine trait: 'There's a lot of talk. Too many women in this part of the world,' says Colonel Melchett in *Murder at the Vicarage*.[105] Such emphasis is most marked in Christie and is very different from the male-dominated world of Conan Doyle. In fact, there are *male* styles and venues of gossip in other interwar detective fiction. Bunter, in *Busman's Honeymoon*, realizing the importance of such talk and the class inaccessibility of it to his master Lord Peter Wimsey, takes himself off to the village pub to listen intently. 'At the entrance of the stranger, the voices, which had been busy, fell silent, and glances, at first directed to the door, were quickly averted and screened behind lifted tankards. This was fully in accordance with etiquette.'[106] However, even in the pub there are women, conversationally engaged, in a way that contrasts with the absence of women from some descriptions of Victorian rural pub life, such as by Flora Thompson.[107] Certainly women are not marginalized in these interwar novels. The middle-class women in particular have key and often powerful roles as community influences, because of their vantage points, actions, talk and their detective skills, as with Miss Marple or Harriet Vane.

Gossip links to character and community standing and to associated motives for crime. There are also motives connected with blackmail, amidst a gossipy and reputation-based local society and country house set. By comparison with later crime genres, blackmail is a prevalent feature of this writing. Secrets have to be kept to save one's character: 'I have always been considered so – so very respectable.'[108] Yet secrets will be out, privacies must be revealed, via Poirot, Marple, Wimsey, Vane, Campion or any other detectives – there must be *no secrets* in a village community. The detection of the murder is the formal summation and triumph of community gossip, its uncovering of the final truth.

Spiritual community?

Thinking of final truths and spirits of community, the clergy in this fiction are sometimes affectionately drawn by conservative authors who might be expected to have sympathy for them – yet rather than being community leaders they are usually ineffectual, outmoded, even faddish in their tastes and hobbies, such as 'campanology', a term that Sayers popularized. Perhaps it was almost a requirement of the genre that the clergy be seen as weak, thus allowing evil to gain a foothold in a fictional village. Ngaio Marsh's clergymen are the more sympathetically described, yet they are like Walter Copeland in *Overture to Death*: gentle, ineffectual, unambitious, shabbily dressed and wearing cassocks that are 'green about the seams', trying to avoid 'unpleasantness', attractive to some middle-aged spinsters, yet 'secretly terrified of … these ladies who loomed so large in parochial affairs'. They respond to problems with feeble 'Oh, dear!' exclamations. '"I am very greatly troubled," he said. "I cannot see my way"'.[109] A view of the clergy as elderly ditherers is frequent. One of

Margery Allingham's clergymen is 'a lank old man, with a hooked nose', who has 'a look of great age', wearing a 'venerable green-black clerical coat of ancient cut', and he has 'spidery old-fashioned writing'.[110] Christie's clergy are normally like 'Dr. Pender, the elderly clergyman of the parish'; even their names suggest a venerable and prolonged existence, pending death.[111] Sayers discusses 'silver-haired vicars'.[112] Sayers was a clergyman's daughter, and her father had the livings of Bluntisham (near St Ives) from 1897 and then Christchurch (near Wisbech) from 1917. Janet Hitchman refers to the Revd Henry Sayers as 'one of God's fools if ever one existed', a statement that is hard to judge. The Revd Theodore Venables (note his name) of *The Nine Tailors* is said to be 'a life-like portrait' of Sayers's father, who restored the bells of Bluntisham church in 1910 to a ring of eight, even though he was not a bell-fancier.[113] Sayers never erected a memorial to her father, whether in Christchurch (where her parents are buried) or anywhere else, causing dismay among local inhabitants by such neglect. Her fictional representations of clergy seem consistent with the views she expressed in other non-fiction. In the opening paragraph of one of her essays on the position of women, 'The human-not-quite-human', Sayers berated the Church as having failed 'more lamentably than most, and with less excuse', to deal with the 'Woman Question'. She stressed that it is necessary 'to speak plainly, and perhaps even brutally, to the Church'.[114]

Some of the detective novels' clergy are none too moral. The vicar in Sayers's *Busman's Honeymoon* is imagined, 'under cover of a purity campaign', to accuse another man 'of corrupting the village maiden whom subconsciously he wants for himself'; or he 'may have had a morbid fancy for something else'. Sayers repeatedly describes his speech as him 'ejaculating'. Elsewhere she refers to 'this short-sighted old gentleman'.[115] A parson in *The Documents in the Case* is 'that unimaginative and completely insensitive Potts person. I cannot imagine a more dangerous influence than … a footballing parson. The harm done by men of that class is quite incalculable, and their minds are, as a rule, perfect sinks of dangerous and sublimated libidos.'[116] In Christie's *Murder at the Vicarage*, a very clerical setting, the clergyman's wife is twenty years her husband's junior, and she 'treats the village as a kind of huge joke arranged for her amusement'. She summarizes, 'My duty as a Vicaress. Tea and scandal at four-thirty'.[117] These writers were concerned with issues of evil, and with purifying the village, yet, with the exception of G. K. Chesterton's Father Brown, the authors rarely enlisted clergymen for this. It takes a detective, often an outsider, a secular agent external to the church, to reveal the truth and put things back into moral order.

This fiction suggests that the church by the 1920s is incapable of doing this, nor can it oversee behaviour so as to obviate murder in the first instance. Religion relates to the past. Murder is the current problem. These novels thus speak to an apparently secularized situation, with the church and its minister impotent and irrelevant to sustaining historical notions of morality and action. The Revd Venables in *The Nine Tailors* finally comes clanging into his own at the end of the novel, bringing organization and leadership to the flooding fenland village, though his appeal had been pretty distant hitherto, outside his group of bell-ringers. Even that bell-ringing, all *eight hours* of it, right through the night, is done with no respect to the sleepless majority of the village and might be read as a batty (and in consequence homicidal) cacophonous exercise in clerical self-advertisement. No doubt it would have been rapturously reported in *The Ringing World*.[118]

With regard to religious doctrine, the fiction says little that is complimentary. Sayers had considerable theological interests.[119] Yet she has a correspondent in *The Documents in the Case* dismissing 'the usual shifty ecclesiastical clap-trap'. A clergyman is described as

> just crossing the road now to Benediction, as he calls it. He thinks he knows all about what is right and what is wrong, but lots of people think his candles and incense wicked, and call him a papist and idolater and things like that. And yet, out of his little, cold, parish experience, he would set himself up to make silly laws for you.[120]

In another Sayers novel, the church and chapel divide is alluded to, and people seem affronted when their allegiance is misconstrued. The Church of England apparently amounts to 'a pore little bit of a sermon with no "eart in it … I'm chapel and always was, and that's the other end of the village"'.[121] Almost everything about the church, it would appear, is held in remarkably low esteem in these fictional interwar communities. One could find other sources indicating that the clergy were still figures of authority: chairing meetings, conducting valuable pastoral work and providing village leadership. Yet the fictional representations here come close to Victor Bonham-Carter's near contemporary view: 'so many country parsons are regarded with indifference and contempt'.[122]

Clued-up possessions

These fictional communities, then, are hardly much of a spiritualized world. So it seems fitting that the novels persistently refer to the socially significant material culture of the interwar period. The writers needed clues, descriptions of clothing, possessions, tools, timekeepers, furniture, means of transport and so on. They required implements of murder: paperweight-filled stockings, guns, knives, cut-throat razors, an antique sword, a hammer, a drug cabinet, a flying cactus pot, an electrified cabinet, golf clubs, a booby-trapped piano or church bells. Such artefacts are often significantly positioned within villages, with culturally understood connotations, and if they were implements of murder they had their own mystique. They place characters in time and class and help to display personalities. They indicate diverse values of the countryside and city and ways in which those could be defined and appropriated. These material and symbolic trappings of community sometimes have normal, and then contrary and murderous, functions, and so there are ironic meanings at play. Attitudes are shown through them: to a romanticized or scorned past, to the present or the future. A picture such as 'The Soul's Awakening' still adorns a wall.[123] Subtle changes in fashion are noted. Drink and its social associations are analysed: 'you're one o' them pussy-footin' slop-swallowers, and you looks it, like as if you was brought up on them gassy lemonades, all belch and no body'.[124] Dust-covered vintage port must never be shaken.[125] And let us not forget the soda siphons.

The details of interiors are often described minutely, with all their significances. Take for example this passage from Sayers's *Busman's Honeymoon*:

> The sitting room was, indeed, 'brighter' than the kitchen. Two ancient oak-settles, flanking the chimney-piece at right angles, and an old-fashioned American eight day clock on the inner wall, were all that remained of the old farm-house furniture that Harriet remembered. The flame of the kitchen candle, which Mrs Ruddle had lit, danced flickeringly over a suite of Edwardian chairs with crimson upholstery, a top-heavy sideboard, a round mahogany table with wax fruit on it, a bamboo what-not with mirrors and little shelves sprouting from it in all directions, a row of aspidistras in pots in the window-ledge, with strange hanging plants above them in wire baskets, a large radio cabinet, over which hung an unnaturally distorted cactus in a brass Benares bowl, mirrors with roses painted on the glass, a chesterfield sofa upholstered in electric blue plush, two carpets of violently coloured and mutually intolerant patterns juxtaposed to hide the black oak floor-boards … together with a few remnants of genuine old stuff and a little borrowing from the stock-in-trade of the wireless business.[126]

And after this she goes on to the other rooms and farmhouse kitchen. This era hovered between two worlds of goods: between 'the open fire and a roasting-spit' or the 'electric cooker for the days when we don't feel so period'.[127] These descriptions, with their feminine irony or insinuation, their social connotations, and their ideologically pointed inventories, bear comparison with earlier writing by Balzac, Zola or Ibsen. One also recalls William Cobbett's accounts of oaken farmhouse interiors in *Rural Rides*, or writing by Richard Jefferies, or (as we will see) by James Wentworth Day, or the details of farm inventories. One hears the loud voices of farm auctioneers, so pervasive in the 1920s and 1930s.

Material aspirations are shown, such as the nature of the marital bed: '"w'en Ruddle and me was to be wedded I says to 'im, "Brass knobs," I ses, "or nothink"'. How, asks a socially irritated Wimsey, has a lower-class woman like Mrs Ruddle come to have a clock with quarter-chimes?[128] Fine details of dress, for example of a 'lounge lizard', are analysed by a man of finer tastes.[129] In Sayers's *Hangman's Holiday*, we witness the new furniture of her time: 'aluminium chairs', 'diagrammatic furniture made of steel', alongside 'a floor of black glass', 'the tremendous illumination of electricity, reflected from a brass ceiling', 'the cubist electric fittings', a 'steel sideboard', 'modernist grates' and other emblems of modernity.[130] Agatha Christie called it 'new-fangled stuff … glass dinner table and surgical chairs made of steel and webbing … it shows the kind of chap Sandford is. Bolshie, you know – no morals.'[131] There are also countless descriptions of bicycles and motor cars, their types, engines, problems, at a time of rapid expansion of the private car and road haulage vehicles.[132] Sayers wrote of

> Motorists … grinding their way to Southend and Brighton and Margate, in the stench of each other's exhausts, one hand on the horn and one foot on the brake, their eyes starting from their orbits in the nerve-racking search for cops, corners, blind turnings, and cross-road suicides. They ride in a baffled fury, hating each other. They arrive with shattered nerves and fight for parking places. They return, blinded by the headlights of fresh arrivals, whom they hate even worse than they hate each other.[133]

Not much has changed. And inevitably 'the roadside was peppered the whole way with garages … Supplied in parts. Mass-production. Readily erected over night by any handy man'.[134]

Senses of the past

How does one manage the past, and how does one compare it to the present? 'I began by defending vermilion pillar-boxes and Victorian omnibuses, although they were ugly. I have ended by denouncing modern advertisements or American films even when they are beautiful.'[135] G. K. Chesterton, who wrote this, was born in 1874 into an epoch with a 'faintly surviving Dickensian flavour'; he became a devotee of Dickens and Victorian literature.[136] 'I never was really modern,' he wrote.[137] He was said to have known 'the English village without and within'.[138] Certainly his writing demonstrates persistent senses of the past, of rural history, and of how the present contrasted with that. It concerns things that have been, and murders or crimes that occurred *because* of a prior history, and which gain metaphorical meaning as judgements. Chesterton evoked the rural past in many ways: 'A dog-kennel and a beehive stood outside, like symbols of old English country-life'.[139] He wrote about 'the smell of something that died in the eighteenth century; the smell of dank gardens and broken urns, of wrongs that will never now be righted; of something that is none the less incurably sad because it is strangely unreal'. He describes the inner gardens of Pendragon Park. He continued: 'thinking he heard steps in front of him … [he was] inclined to conclude … that there really were other feet upon the road. He thought hazily of ghosts … he could see the image of an appropriate and local ghost … there was in the sadness more violence and secrecy … he felt as if he had got into a dream'.[140]

This is an aura often found in this literature: shivering in a past or a conscience that it cannot escape, in a present that feels like cold decline, haunted by the spirit of a community that has been – by 'the faded rose tapestry and the India carpet' and by 'this great tomb of a house with its faintly musty air and curiously archaic atmosphere'.[141] Chesterton sees the relicts of 'old landscape gardening'. He notices an old sundial standing up 'dark against the sky like the dorsal fin of a shark'.[142] In 'The Dagger with Wings' he writes that

> 'It's going to snow.'
>
> Through a low ornamental gateway of the Italianate pattern he entered a garden having something of that desolation which only belongs to the disorder of orderly things. Deep-green growths were grey with the faint powder of the frost, large weeds had fringed the fading pattern of the flower-beds as if in a ragged frame; and the house stood as if waist-high in a stunted forest of shrubs and bushes … the house itself, which had a row of columns and a classical façade … seemed now to be withering in the wind of the North Sea. Classical ornament here and there accentuated the contrast; caryatides and carved masks of comedy or tragedy looked down from corners of the building upon the grey confusion of the garden paths; but the faces seemed to be frost-bitten. The very volutes of the capitals might have curled up with the cold.[143]

Chesterton was the leader of the Distributist movement, believing that private property should be reallocated as small freeholds. In case readers should think that 'tradition' is aristocratic, linked to decaying mansions, he wrote that 'it is a great mistake to suppose that such houses stand high in chivalric traditions. Few except the poor preserve traditions. Aristocrats live not in traditions but in fashions.'[144] Indeed, some of his aristocrats came through to the present as 'an unclean spirit'; 'they had rotted in the last two centuries into mere drunkards and dandy degenerates, till there had even come a whisper of insanity'.[145]

Whatever their sanity, other aristocrats looked to the future of community as well as to its traditions. In Sayers's *Busman's Honeymoon*, Lord Peter Wimsey and his new bride, Harriet Vane, spend their honeymoon in an old country house that Harriet knew in her childhood, where a murdered man resides in the cellar, awaiting discovery. The detection will, of course, unfold a history of village rancour. In the meantime, they face a problem with their chimney and call in an ineffectual chimney-sweep. Sayers has little compunction in clearing it of the debris and soot of the past, brushing aside the ineffectual sweep and his useless Victorian methods, as one of her characters 'cleans' the chimney by firing an old duck-gun up it. We see here the metaphorical clearance of the past, the new start to village life, as the gun-blast brings down the soot of centuries:

> It exploded like the crack of doom, and it kicked … like a carthorse. Gun and gunman rolled together upon the hearth, entangled inextricably in the folds of the drape … the loosened soot of centuries came plunging in a mad cascade down the chimney: it met the floor with a soft and deadly violence and mushroomed up in a Stygian cloud, while with it rushed, in a clattering shower, masonry and mortar, jackdaws' nests and the bones of bats and owls, sticks, bricks and metal-work, with fragments of tiles and potsherds … the eruptive rumble and boom … echoed from bend to bend of the forty-foot flue.
>
> 'Oh, rapture!' cried Peter, with his lady in his arms. 'Oh, bountiful Jehovah! Oh, joy for all its former woes a thousand-fold repaid!' … the sight of Bunter, snorting and blind, and black as any Nubian Venus, struck him speechless with ecstasy …
>
> 'I knew it!' said Peter. 'Whoop! I knew it! You blasphemed the aspidistra and something awful *has* come down the chimney!'
>
> 'It's surprising the things you find in old chimneys … ornithological specimens. And two skeleton bats. And eight feet or so of ancient chain, as formerly worn by the mayors of Paggleham …'
>
> ''Ere's a bit of one o' they roasting-jacks wot they used in the old days. Look, see! That's the cross-bar and the wheel wot the chain went over, like …'
>
> 'Well,' said Peter, 'we seem to have loosened things up a bit, anyhow.'[146]

Wimsey and his bride spend their honeymoon in this old country house, loosening things up a bit, endeavouring to open it up for their future. This novel can be read as a couple's entanglement in past rural affairs and their attempt selectively to liberate themselves and move on. Detection of murder, like dramatic clearing of the chimney, is part of that community expurgation. 'We're going to stay here and exorcise the ghosts,' says Harriet Vane, and the metaphorical exorcism of Victorian and Edwardian ghosts is a preoccupation of much of this fiction, from Conan Doyle onwards.[147] Even so, they sleep in an old bed where the murdered man has slept: 'One can't escape from these things – except by living in a brand-new villa and buying one's furniture in the Tottenham Court Road.'[148]

Detecting 'evil', and village renewal

One might have thought that little in rural communities could compare in adverse description to the opium and gambling dens, 'rascally Lascars', 'garbage in the darker recesses of the underworld' and 'black roots of crime' of late Victorian London, as described by Arthur Conan Doyle. His London was akin to George Gissing's *The Nether World* and many other accounts in that dark vein. By comparison, Watson exclaims about rural Hampshire and Wiltshire: 'Good heavens! … Who would associate crime with these dear old homesteads?' One reads with surprise, therefore, Sherlock Holmes's reply:

> They always fill me with a certain horror. It is my belief, Watson, founded upon my experience, that the lowest and vilest alleys in London do not present a more dreadful record of sin than does the smiling and beautiful countryside … the reason is very obvious. The pressure of public opinion in the town can do what the law cannot accomplish. There is no lane so vile that the scream of a tortured child, or the thud of a drunkard's blow, does not beget sympathy and indignation among the neighbours, and then the whole machinery of justice is ever so close … But look at these lonely houses … filled for the most part with poor ignorant folk who know little of the law. Think of the deeds of hellish cruelty, the hidden wickedness which may go on, year in, year out, in such places, and none the wiser.[149]

Accordingly, many of Holmes's cases were set in the countryside, more than is often supposed.[150] Such rurality veiled cynicism, thwarted opportunism and insidiously concealed resolve. Agatha Christie developed this theme of rural evil. 'There is a great deal of wickedness in village life,' she wrote, and an ex-Commissioner of Scotland Yard summarizes Miss

Marple: 'St. Mary Mead is a positive hot-bed of crime and vice.'[151] 'The cosmopolitan world seems a mild and peaceful place compared with St. Mary Mead,' declares another character.[152] This question – how 'pure' are rural communities – was a much debated cultural issue. Christie used the village as a venue in which to observe 'evil' in others. Her villages have an air of threatening disquiet and danger, even among relatives and well-known people. Her puritanical views on this are not much different from those parish magazines which, as we have seen, often drew attention to 'the wickedness and indifference which abounds everywhere' in village life.[153] This is rather different from many opinions about the quality of rural communities at the time, although I have discussed adverse portrayals in Thomas Hardy. Indeed, with such an urbanized readership, as in England by this time, one wonders whether such a slant contributed to Christie's popularity.

In some other writers, the English village community is presented as a refuge from evil, where one can try (unsuccessfully) to hide away from malevolent London or American enemies. Margery Allingham's *Mystery Mile* is a good example, where evil comes from without, notably in the form of 'an immense Jew … [who] grunted like a pig'.[154] Similarly, in Allingham's *The Crime at Black Dudley* the criminal outsiders – who have taken over an old country house for their nefarious ends and (with echoes of *The Wind in the Willows*) are about to set it afire – are finally brought 'with a horrible sickening grind of smashing machinery' to a crashing automobile overturn by the bravery and horsemanship of the local Monewdon Hunt.[155] The rural has triumphed over the urban, the horse over the big torpedo-like Lanchester. In Allingham's stories, as in her documentary account of Tolleshunt D'Arcy (Essex) during the Second World War in *The Oaken Heart*,[156] the village is eventually a source for good, standing oak-like for the best of England, while coping valiantly with the disagreeable intrusions of London evacuees: 'a sudden invasion … [of which] might easily be quite as detrimental to the moral as any bombardment by enemy aeroplanes'.[157]

For Sayers, 'the reading and writing of detective stories were highly moral occupations … they should be a complete deterrence to the commission of crime'.[158] *The Nine Tailors* sees the hapless murderer tied up in the belfry and then killed by being subjected to a lengthy peal of church bells, as if God speaks and brings justice via the bells and through the bell-ringers, acting in preordained historical ways in their village campanological roles. The bells apparently stand and toll for the village's history, for its unsleeping capacity for renewal, and the riddle of the bells needs deciphering before truth can emerge. Finally, this fenland village is flooded, as though cleansed, which also drowns a partially culpable individual.[159] The village inhabitants retreat from the flood to the church, as though to an Ark – as if in a Stanley Spencer painting – and thus the village can walk morally invigorated from the church as the waters recede, and the community faces the future washed clean.

Such metaphors of renewed community spirit, often as restoration of the *status quo*, characterize much of this fiction. In a crisis period for rural life, this seems understandable. In Ngaio Marsh's *Scales of Justice* the lancing of an abscess is mentioned at various places, inviting such comparison.[160] This is a literature seeking purification and rural redemption, hoping to revive community, pointing bluntly and often inexactly to blights in village life. It does so not usually by highlighting social, political and economic faults and remedies, in the manner of much other contemporary fiction. Rather, it puritanically stresses 'evil' individual behaviour and seeks worldly salvation, implicitly contrasting 'evil' predicaments with nostalgic imagery either of a supposedly historical actuality or of an Edenic potentiality. The association of 'Englishness' with rurality is a commonplace of academic and cultural discussion. Yet a great deal of this interwar detective fiction is in effect saying, almost in the words of A. E. Coppard, that 'This is a very dirty Eden', and that 'to be far from the madding crowd is to be mad indeed'.[161] Much interwar fiction on the countryside suggests that rural life is extremely dreary and limiting: a perspective quite different from that often adopted by cultural historians of England. However, there *is* a way out, it seems, via detection of murder, that paramount crime – stability and security can then be restored. Perhaps murderers are symbols for all else that is wrong with village life, even though that shows hazy agrarian diagnosis and manifests a post-Puritan mindset. This literature, at any rate, narrows its ostensible purpose to that end. Such a murderer passes Miss Marple just as she is 'bending right over – trying to get up one of those nasty dandelions, you know'.[162] There is no doubt about the analogy in Christie's mind. The nasty dandelions (the puritanical Christie savours her weeds and words) need to be *pulled out by the roots* – the herbaceous border can then be restored to its supposed former comeliness, and the community can proclaim its approval. As Christie triumphantly holds up the dandelion, one might imagine Sir Stanley Spencer painting the acclamatory inhabitants rendering homage and gratitude.

A village 'community'?

What sort of village community is implied by this fiction? This is the crucial historical question, and my discussion has, cubist-like, come at it from various angles. Many of these fictional villages are isolated, inbred, observant, alert to the imposter and suspicious of others, especially outsiders. In Suffolk, a crime triggers talk of whether there have been 'reports of strangers in the village',[163] modern counterparts of George Morland's stragglers in woody shadows. 'In a place like this, if there're any strangers knocking about we know at once.' 'Beware of strangers,' says a fortune-teller.[164] 'Anyone as don't be born 'ere is a foreigner, ain't they?', says a 'great hulking cross-eyed fellow with a red moustache … squinting viciously'.[165] In some cases, the murder victim is an outsider, not of the village. When Roger Ackroyd is stabbed there is little sympathy for him – well, after all, he *is* from Yorkshire.[166] Mr Kettle in *Mystery Mile* is 'the village "foreigner": that is to say, he was not a Suffolk man, but had been born, so it was believed, as far away as Yarmouth, a good forty miles off.' He 'discloses' a Norfolk accent and is 'the most unpopular man in the village community'.[167] Much of this fiction distrusts 'foreigners' from further afield: Londoners, Jews, Scots, the Irish, Belgians and Americans. The untrustworthy person of questionable identity, whose character has yet to be shown, who may even be in disguise, is a recurrent figure. This theme is common in Christie's writing when it is set in more distant locations, as well as in the English village. Dislike of foreigners in her *Murder on the Orient Express* (1934) is especially notable. Such suspicion of outsiders is a continuation of fictional traditions, as in Thomas Hardy or the Brontës. In this regard, the interwar fiction reiterates supposed village perspectives that appeared much earlier in rural fiction, as well as in documentary writing.

However, the way in which some of these authors create 'a society of strangers' has less precedence. Alison Light commented on Christie's 'obsession with unstable identities, the ultimate unknowability of others'. This, Light wrote, 'puts in doubt the possibility of social exchange and meaningful community itself. It is this sense of a safe, known world thrown out of kilter which Christie's fictions share with many modernist writers.'[168] Such characters often have mixed or muddled identities, in some cases resulting from their experience of war. In some novels, people pretend to be others, almost like the early modern Martin Guerre,[169] or to be other than themselves. They often struggle to find the connections between each other: they are not of a conscious community, although it seems that they may be part of an implicit one. Yet they lack a sense of why this might be so. The 'detection' is almost a detection of 'community' itself, a revealing of obscure networks, through gossip and a jumble of intercrossing angles of vision, a 'community' that is often as yet unclear to the seeming protagonists or 'actors'.[170] And in this fiction, notably in

Christie – whose writing lends itself so obviously to drama or film – it is often the *known* and 'respectable' persons who are the murderers, in the midst of social exchange, even though authors may tease the reader with the possibility of a maundering outsider being culpable.

Indeed, in some of the novels there is little sign of an active 'village community'. This may be because of a focus on the country house or because the set of suspects is small. Or it may be because the twentieth-century community is shown as more permeable than hitherto. The fictional social range can be slight, despite an insistence on the role of gossip which implies a breadth of community, an incorporation through shared knowledge – though gossip can ostracize certain people, putting them at risk of loneliness. In some novels a wider community only appears at certain moments, as with the Monewdon Hunt in *The Crime at Black Dudley*, or one merely glimpses representative figures from it. Those, like Jeremy Burchardt, who wonder whether 'the rural community' *ever* existed might find such doubts supported by some of this fiction.[171] Others would see this as symptomatic of post-1914 social change and 'community decline'. A narrow stock of core families is often highlighted, and those 'core' families need not be upper class.[172] Allingham comments on one village that there were two main families: 'the Willsmores, lank dark people with quick beady eyes' and the Brooms, 'Sturdier, more stolid, with large and bovine faces, and every variety of fair hair'.[173] Community figureheads loom large, yet these are far from ideal, as such 'leaders' are represented as faltering and morally dubious. The clergy are largely ineffective, elderly or feeble. Even the detective 'Lord Peter' Wimsey leaves much to be desired, in an immodestly described lineage of chinly precedent.[174] Such questioning of the supposed mainstays of village life was not new in agrarian fiction: one recalls Alec d'Urberville or Mrs Charmond in Thomas Hardy. Such figures among the local wealthy have abdicated responsibility. Other such personalities appear in Conan Doyle. Irresponsible farmers and landlords abound in more focused agricultural fiction, such as that by A. G. Street.[175] Yet this questioning of village elites has rarely been so noticeable as it was in interwar detective fiction. These novels scoff at people who are performing roles that they are not ethically suited for. In fact, such figures usually comprise a troupe of *suspected murderers*, well-equipped with motives. Small wonder that community is in crisis.

I have concentrated upon certain themes in this fiction relating to rural community. This focuses and contextualizes discussion and broaches ideas that these novels are in some ways a purging or handling of fears about community malaise, so as to reinstate social and ethical steadiness derived from long-standing views of British rurality. The rural idyll *versus* evil in the village – community *versus* anti-community in the form of murder – such a dialectic is at the heart of the problems that this fiction raises. The authors require both, and their faith in one is confirmed by exploring and negating the other. Their use of murder was an attention-seeking device for community life during an uneasy period. Personalized murder is in many ways a symbol of social murder, a line of thought that occurred to many readers and reviewers concerned about village communities. Furthermore, 'evil in the village' was to some degree a metaphor for the wider state of the nation.

Many subjects central to community history were underplayed in interwar village detective fiction. One finds little on labour unrest or the Slump. Agricultural vicissitudes and politics, farm dereliction, tariff issues and rural diversification were neglected, as were new industries and their emergent new communities. Suburbanization was an incongruity glimpsed with averted eyes. The rise of fascism was of scant interest. The rural exodus was tantamount to 'the servant problem'. And despite declarations by Christie or Sayers that they wrote with 'real' villages in mind, or statements by some reviewers that this writing is of great value to historians, the results *are* fictional creations, imagined communities and stories in which murder becomes unrealistically frequent. The novels have been embroidered by nostalgic period films, displaying manners and materiality, clothing and capricious elegance, significantly altering literary characters like Miss Marple, and such films have enlarged colossal sales. Yet this genre contributes to an understanding of interwar village community and its later refashioning, and few historians would allow its interpretation to be disassociated from biography, social life and expressions of rurality. Its prime exponents were middle-class conservative women, and their attitudes are evident and worth examining. The guilt-ridden details of criminal possibility, within the fraught axes of village existence, are deeply revealing about what was then credible. Its appeal links to nationalistic connotations and to hopes about the spirit of community. Indeed, Christie was 'considered to be the most-read novelist in air-raid shelters'.[176]

Change in the village during and after the Second World War was much discussed by these authors. Allingham moved into documentary writing in *The Oaken Heart*, by then readily finding her evil in Nazi Germany. Sayers, in her story significantly named 'Striding Folly', presaged the protests of twenty-first-century mid Wales with her complaints about the electricity grid: 'like a great, ugly chess-rook swooping from an unconsidered corner, marching over the country, straddling four, six, eight parishes at a time, planting hideous pylons to mark its progress'.[177] In *Endless Night*, Christie wrote of 'the good old welfare state limping along in its half-baked way!'[178] Even more saliently and pessimistically, Christie published *The Mirror Crack'd from Side to Side*. It serves as my epilogue here, a classic in the genre of 'declining communities'. The village had seemingly been dangerously snarled up in the 1920s and 1930s. But the long-lived, black-dressed Miss Marple was having new problems of community adjustment later as well. 'One had to face the fact: St Mary Mead was *not* the place it had been. In a sense, of course, nothing was what it had been. You could blame the war (both the wars) or the younger generation, or women going out to work, or the atom bomb, or just the Government.'[179] And so Christie laments lack of community spirit, inadvertently showing us (yet again) how historically pervasive these worries are – perhaps therefore reassuring us about our self-consciously equivalent concerns today, as we migrate through cultural history in search of historical perspective, precedent or analogy. She sees new people, in tastelessly decorated houses with new plumbing, electric cookers, dishwashers, stiles replaced by iron-swing gates and tarred asphalt paths, new supermarkets – 'anathema to the elderly ladies of St Mary Mead'. There are 'the insidious snares of Hire Purchase' and other examples of 'immediate and intemperate modernization'. Much worse, there is 'The Development' and then the 'Teddy-looking boys' carrying knives. 'How different it had been in the past.'[180] Just as the interwar writing had displayed certain understandings of the Victorian and Edwardian past – nostalgic for some, albeit scorned by others of differing political beliefs like Chesterton – so this fiction continued after 1945 to offer conservative and gloomy verdicts on 'the decline of community'. 'Teddy-looking boys' … oh dear, whatever next? 'Crack'd mirrors' and 'endless night' indeed.

7

James Wentworth Day and Conservative Ideas of Community

Many people in the twentieth century were trying – however inadequately and imperfectly – to come to terms with a world which was different from, and also seemed inferior to, the preceding century of unchallenged greatness which they had experienced or which they thought they knew.[1]

I confess it. I do not like modern furniture or much of modern architecture, less or none of modern art and little of modern literature. I am, of course, an antediluvian, a reactionary, an out-of-date or, as I prefer it, a rural romanticist.[2]

In 1822 William Cobbett, the famous English writer and radical conservative, embarked upon a horse-riding tour largely of southern England. His *Rural Rides* became famous as an account of poverty-stricken communities and the political mood of rural England at that time.[3] Nearly 120 years later James Wentworth Day, another outspoken rural writer who resembled him politically in many ways, did much the same, publishing his book *Farming Adventure: A Thousand Miles through England on a Horse.*[4] He was compared at the time to William Cobbett, and it was a comparison that he relished. English agriculture had yet again been severely depressed in the interwar period. The State was felt to be neglectful of farmers and estate owners during peacetime, and yet it oppressively pursued them in war. Reform was called for, but what were the views of 'the farming community'? Wentworth Day saddled his horse in 1941 and for a thousand ridden miles, and much more by car and horsebox, he endeavoured to find out. He was accompanied by an Essex farmer named Jim Rodd. Was he a 'rubber-tyred Cobbett' for taking the car and horsebox as well, he was asked. 'Cobbett had no tarmac roads to hammer the heart out of his horses,' he replied.[5] This was probably the last period in which one could sensibly do 'rural rides' on this scale, at least in southern England.

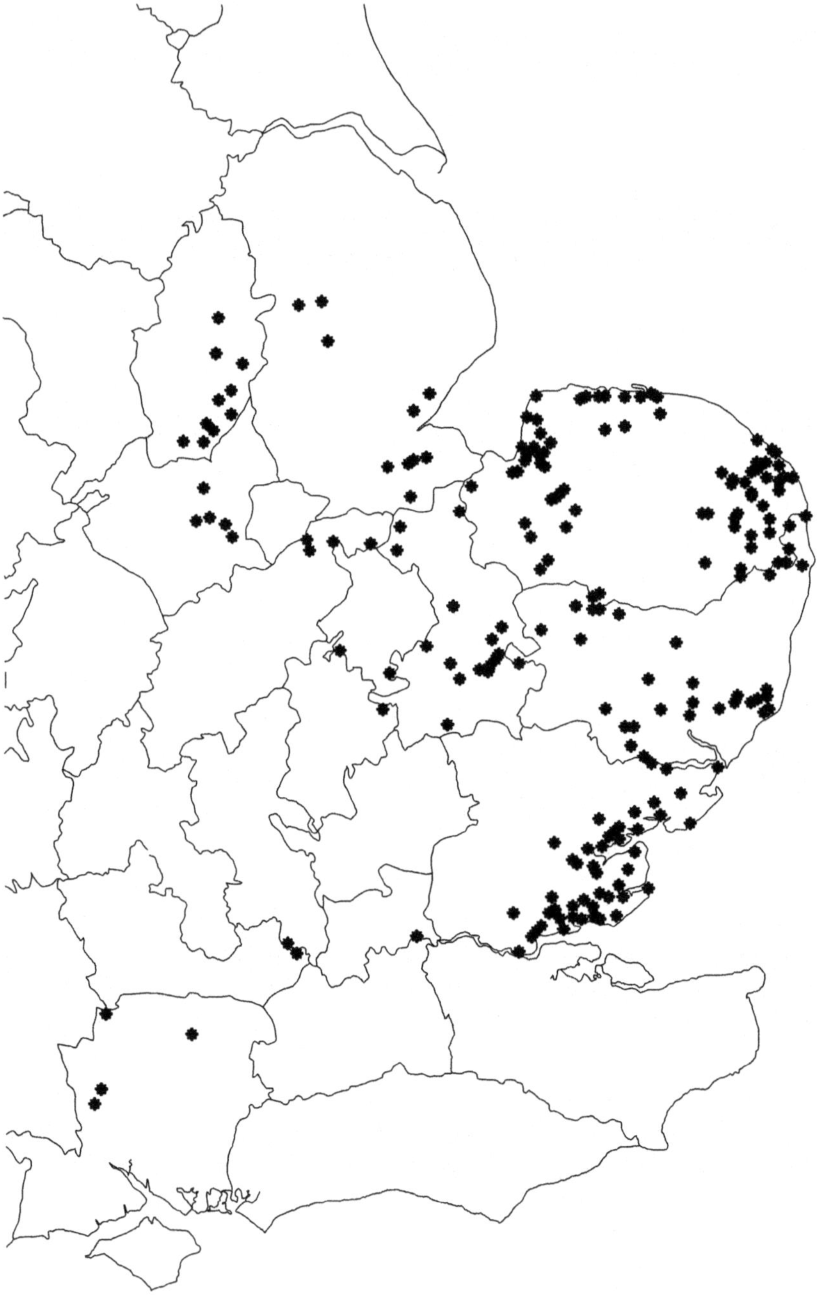

Figure 7.1 James Wentworth Day, journeys and places discussed.

Wentworth Day covered large swathes of East Anglia, but in particular he was concerned with its coastal and wetland communities that he knew best. He did subsequent rural tours with similar objectives, in all covering some 10,000 miles through Essex, Suffolk, Norfolk, Cambridgeshire, Lincolnshire, Rutland, Northamptonshire, Leicestershire and Hampshire. The places most mentioned on his rural rides and in his related farming and coastal writing are shown in Figure 7.1. His concentration on the East Anglian coastal marshlands, the Fens, the Broads and Norfolk coast is evident. Indeed, he seems in his writing to have been partly attracted to these areas because of their bird-life. Yet a major concern in a long sequence of his books and articles was to emphasize their predicaments and decline as working communities with distinctive cultures and traditions. Deeply and in some ways quixotically conservative, he was hugely aware of English history and its legacies. He was also respectful of the working-class people who made their living in wetland, marshland and coastal areas. He highlighted their disappearing livelihoods and communities in many publications. It is these that are my concern here, in studying his representations of cultural and community change in the coastal and fen areas of East Anglia.

An obituary to James Wentworth Day suggested that 'he probably wrote far too much', over forty books and countless articles.[6] (One is reminded again of William Cobbett.) Born in 1899, and dying in 1983, he was a serving and possibly under-age seaman on the First World War minesweepers. He also served in an Infantry Battalion, the Labour Corps, the London Regiment, and as a sergeant with a Prisoner of War Company doing salvage work at Bailleul and Nueve Eglise, both of which were devastated. Such service and work in clearing up battlefields, later dealing with German Prisoners of War (some of whom became long-standing friends), gave him much experience of the effects of modern war.[7] He was subsequently a war correspondent in France in the Second World War and Near East correspondent for the BBC in 1941. He was a friend and personal assistant to Lord Beaverbrook, who was described by Wentworth Day's daughter as having been 'a hard master, but he really learnt how to write then'.[8] He worked as a journalist initially for the *Cambridge Evening News* and then for a number of Fleet Street newspapers; he was the owner and editor of the *Saturday Review* and was editor at various times of the *Illustrated Sporting and Dramatic News*, of *East Anglia Life*, of *The Field* and assistant editor of *Country Life*. As her assistant, he persuaded Lady Houston to finance the aviation research that produced the Spitfire, claiming later that she was 'the lady who won the war'.[9] He was a press adviser to the Egyptian government in 1938; the crucial questioner and subsequent witness in the Harold Laski libel action against the *Daily Express* in 1946;[10] and a writer on the Queen Mother's ancestry.[11] Wentworth Day was an extremely erudite naturalist, an observant and evocative nature writer, and from 1930 the owner of Adventurers' Fen near Burwell in Cambridgeshire.[12] He was an expert wildfowler and authority on wildfowling,[13] a writer on the coastal people of Essex,[14] a nature preservationist, an outspoken critic of water and land pollution by chemicals, and a person who strongly endorsed Rachel Carson's book *Silent Spring*.[15] Indeed, his book *Poison on the Land: The War on Wildlife, and Some Remedies* (1957) covered very similar themes and significantly predated Carson's more famous work. He was twice an unsuccessful parliamentary Conservative candidate for the Hornchurch constituency in Essex. He married three times, to Helen Gardom, the writer Nerina Shute and Marion McLean (the mother of his surviving daughter Clare). His books include biographies of Sir Henry Segrave, Sir Malcolm Campbell and *King George V as a Sportsman* (1935); those on rural England, like *Farming Adventure*, *Broadland Adventure*, *Marshland Adventure*, *Harvest Adventure* and *Coastal Adventure*; books on dogs, for which he had great fondness – *The Dog in Sport* (1938) and *The Wisest Dogs in the World: Some Account of the Longshaw Sheepdog Trials Association* (1954); many publications on the modern agricultural revolution, such as *Rural Revolution* (1952) and *The New Yeomen of England* (1952); works of history and East Anglian heritage such as *A History of the Fens* (1970) and *Norwich through the Ages* (1976), and an enormous number of journalistic articles.

It is impossible here to do justice to the range and agricultural and naturalistic knowledge of such a polymath. He is especially known among twentieth-century agricultural historians for his outspoken criticism of many county War Agricultural Committees: 'Little Hitlers on the farms', as one of his chapter headings put it.[16] Yet today he is often overlooked, partly because of his very conservative, opinionated and vividly expressed views – which were often not 'politically correct' in his own lifetime, let alone now[17] – partly because of the eclecticism of his writing, and partly because earlier cultures of wildfowl shooting and trapping seem disagreeable to a modern public more concerned with nature conservation.[18] A large related literature on wildfowling and related activities going back to Gervase Markham has now been largely forgotten, as has the place of wildfowl in people's winter livelihoods and diet.[19] Many readers find it hard to take on board what David Matless has called 'his maverick conservative critique

Figure 7.2 James Wentworth Day and Mr Soapey Sponge on the Essex coast.[22]

of modern life' and (in Brian Short's words) his reputation as a 'far-right commentator', who was often disapproving about state regulation of rural affairs.[20] He also had forthright opinions about masculinity, common at the time, which call to mind some of those of Cobbett but which are out of fashion today.[21]

A sense of his stern presence can be gained from Figure 7.2, where, suitably attired for wildfowl pursuit, armed with one of his more forbidding firearms, personifying a certain brand of rural Englishness, he stares at the viewer, the image of tweed-clad steel-hardiness somewhat (and quite deliberately) compromised by the photograph's caption announcing the presence of his faithful and hugely admired dog, 'Mr Soapey Sponge'. A softer image of him as an older man is shown in Figure 7.3.

Figure 7.3 James Wentworth Day.[23]

Another wildlife writer commented that 'Jimmy Wentworth Day always reminds me of a mixture of Cobbett, Colonel Hawker, and Sir Alfred Munnings … I doubt whether anyone living today knows that [Essex] coast so well, or can write about it with such charm and veracity.'[24] He was especially a writer about water-related livelihoods and wild life, notably in the fens, the broads, and in the East Anglian coastal marshes, and arguably this is what he should be remembered for. Indeed, he was one of the most evocative and lively British nature writers of the twentieth century, and much of his nature writing is really exceptional.

My focus here will be on his conservative view of the communities and cultures in the wetland and coastal areas of East Anglia, which he saw as declining and threatened by modern life. Distinctive and 'maverick' though he undoubtedly was, his views have parallels with people like Stanley Baldwin, H. J. Massingham, W. G. Hoskins and many others.[25] His writing has unity as a conservative depiction and critique of a certain period, a representation of skill-related ebbing communities, and a nostalgic eulogy to a kind of community and social order in which well-run estates owned by historic families coexisted with a 'manly' independence among knowledgeable and respected waterland workers. Wentworth Day's views were a modern counterpart to William Cobbett, a conservative espousal of community, and an historical idealization of estates, rural yeomanry, and working-class coastal cultures and individuality.

The interwar agricultural depression

Wentworth Day's early writing took place against a prolonged backdrop of agricultural depression. Memories of this period affected his subsequent writing, as did the sense that the Conservative Party had failed agriculture, despite the rural rhetoric of leaders like Stanley Baldwin. The Corn Production Acts were repealed in August 1921 and uncontrolled prices became state policy. Food prices were falling from late 1920 to very low levels between 1930 and 1937, aggravated by the Wall Street Crash in 1929 and its consequences.[26] Farm receipts fell dramatically for grain-growing farmers, many of whom went bankrupt. From 1914 to 1938, two million acres went out of cultivation. Farm wages nationally were between about 30 and 38 shillings (an average of about 32 shillings) in 1935, and about £2 per adult man by 1938–39,[27] which was well below the £3 minimum that Wentworth Day advocated a couple of years later. One Suffolk labourer later remembered: 'It was a terrible period to be farming: everything was going down hill.'[28] Many workers left agricultural employment: in 1921 there were 996,081 agricultural workers in Great Britain – but by 1935 there were 783,600.[29] Layoffs affecting farm labour became a staple of interwar rural literature and documentary writing.[30] In 1931 only 6.1 per cent of the occupied population worked on the land, demonstrating (in wider European terms) how extraordinary the rate of British rural depopulation had been since early Victorian times. Farms were often untenanted, some became derelict, and the poor state of rural cottages was widely commented upon. Some types of farming such as dairying were more successful, given falling animal feed prices and rising urban disposable incomes. The situation was probably most adverse in East Anglia and grain-growing regions. Marketing boards (set up under the Agricultural Marketing Acts of 1931 and 1933) and other schemes helped to increase farm output in the 1930s, when British agriculture was protected through a variety of tariffs, import quotas and subsidies. The bargaining position of farmers *vis-à-vis* other sectors and the public improved somewhat after 1931, which can be seen as a turning point in British food policy.[31] The Wheat Act of 1932, for example, gave some help to cereal growers faced with very low prices, although prices fell to even lower levels in 1934–35. Mechanization was accelerating, in the form of tractors, combine harvesters, oil and petrol engines, barn machinery, threshers and especially milking machines. This was to intensify strikingly during the Second World War, which also greatly expanded the cultivated acreage. By the end of the war, British agriculture was among the most mechanized in the world.[32]

The consequences of the late nineteenth-century and interwar agricultural depressions have been much debated for rural community life. A. G. Street felt in 1939 that 'the average village had changed far more in the past twenty years than it had in the previous two hundred'.[33] The Second World War was about to alter it much further. Street noticed the effects of road transport, out-migration of the young, overseas competition, machinery, commuting to towns, all disrupting something that had hitherto been nearly 'a self-contained little community'. He thought that the changes meant 'the finish of village life as it has existed from time immemorial', with a loss of individuality and stability in rural life, as so many villages became suburb-like.[34] He accepted gains: there was improved education, housing, lighting, water, sanitation and access to arts and entertainments. Some historians, such as Paul Thompson, place the main changes earlier, believing that 'the life had drained out of southern English villages before 1914'.[35] High wartime mortality then left a sombre legacy, documented on so many village war memorials. Recent judgements on the interwar period have stressed a very mixed experience, often of depression and dereliction of community, but of some vigorously growing settlements (frequently by the sea), modern industries in rural locations, new forms of social engagement, leisure and popular culture, incomers to the countryside bringing new values, the building of village halls which accommodated dances and the latest entertainments, increased travel and widened horizons, and the like.[36] The agricultural economic vicissitudes were especially pronounced in arable areas of Essex, where there was also considerable wartime expansion of arable acreage, and the proximity of the county to London brought many social changes which Wentworth Day was not reticent about.

The Essex coast

James Wentworth Day's ashes were scattered on 'my beloved Essex Blackwater', which was entirely appropriate for a man who knew so much about it.[37] He wrote of 'those windy levels of sea-marsh and shimmering flats which are my second home',[38] after 'that wild, undrained fen which was my family heritage – a place of primeval beauty'.[39] The Essex coast is marked by irregular creeks, perhaps fifty or more in number, and their tributaries. It has been described as 'the most torn and untidy coast in England'.[40] Its marshes, 'like a gauzy and radiant fabric' when draped in mist,[41] were intersected by dykes rather than hedges, which enhanced distant visibility. Their main purpose was for summer pasture, and they were a haven for winter wildfowl. 'This is a country where men live with one foot on land and one in the sea, by plough handle and ship's tiller.'[42] It was also a coast where, in the wildfowling season, 'The wind came off the sea like a viper. It searched every crack in our oilskins, bit nose and ears, and seared necks like a whiplash.'[43] Sea banks gave some protection, from flooding, from wind, as well as to wildfowlers and to smuggling activities. Indeed, the communities of the area had thrived on the smuggling of rum, lace, Hollands gin, brandy, wine and tobacco. They hid smuggled goods in churches like those at Rochford or Bradwell, or at Hadleigh Castle, or in the many lonely marshland farmhouses. Smuggling became a widely acquiesced-in activity, even extending to the clergy.[44] Sabine Baring-Gould, who was rector of East Mersea for ten years, set his novel *Mehalah* in the Essex marshes. He wrote that 'The whole population of this region was more or less mixed up with, and interested in, this illicit trade and with defiance of the officers of the law, from the parson … to the vagabonds.'[45] Many of the area's ghost stories evolved as shields for smuggling activity.[46] This was also an area of distinctive culture, with its own dialect, nicknames, with its own terms for plants, birds and animals.[47] Its settlements often expressed intense local rivalry, as between the Essex and north Kentish coastal communities more broadly.[48] Wentworth Day wrote of how 'Each village was self-contained, bitterly jealous of the others, and just as liable to fight among themselves as against the coastguards.'[49]

Among the local livelihoods were oyster cultivation and dredging in the autumn. This inevitably aroused feuding because of the nature and temptation of oyster grounds, feuding as between Tollesbury, Burnham and Colne, with 'battles always liable to break out' between their oystermen.[50] Three to four million oysters were taken from the Colne alone every year in the 1930s, in an industry that stretched back centuries but which was big business from the early nineteenth century onwards. The Pyefleet Channel was especially noted for its oysters, as were the estuaries of the Blackwater, the Colne, the Crouch and the Roach. West Mersea's chief means of livelihood were said to be the oyster smacks. The industry was in decline by the late 1940s, however, giving way to yachting in the local economy.[51]

In addition, major local employment included boat and yacht building, for example at Wivenhoe on the Colne, and wildfowling, the latter of especial interest to Wentworth Day. Wildfowling was a flourishing enterprise in Essex, and the county had over thirty decoy-ponds along its coast from Hamford Water to Paglesham.[52] The saltings, mudflats and marshes, whether taken from the sea or uncovered at low water, were major breeding and feeding grounds for birds, though in Wentworth Day's period these wildfowl, while still numerous, were said to be 'a mere fraction of the myriads which formerly abounded'.[53] Wentworth Day often documented declining bird numbers, lamenting such decline in ways that sometimes seem at odds with his accounts of large hunting 'bags'.[54] Brent geese, for example, used to arrive 'in almost fabulous numbers',[55] and such abundance, in relatively close proximity to London markets, and in the context of low-earning rural workers, meant that wildfowling was a major way of getting a livelihood up until the mid-twentieth century, before wildlife preservation ostensibly became more of a national priority. There was both a local wildfowling community making their living from it, via decoys, punt-gunning and the like, as well as 'sporting' visitors who came to the area to shoot. The Victorian and Edwardian handbooks comment repeatedly that 'excellent shooting is to be had on the marshes round the coast, where wild ducks, geese, snipe, widgeon, teal, and other wild fowl will amply reward the sportsman'.[56] Wentworth Day had good reason to entitle one of his publications 'the coast of enchanted wings'.[57]

The marshmen

Wentworth Day thought that the Essex marshmen were quintessentially English: independent, masculine, defensive against Hitler, adventurous, Elizabethan in ideals and actions, assertive in demeanour and rich in speech and traditions. His views of them relate to the natural world and place them and their communities within it. He held marshmen and fenmen in high regard; his books are full of praise for them, and photographs of them, and he was keen to be photographed alongside them, for he was a gregarious man of journalistic skills who took much interest and pride in their company.[58] These photographs are often paradoxically reminiscent of interwar Irish folklore collecting and photography, itself a search for past community, or one is reminded of H. J. Massingham's illustrations of English craft workers, and some earlier Victorian photography of rural workers.[59] Figure 7.4 shows an example taken from *Harvest Adventure*, with Wentworth Day's original caption.[60]

Figure 7.4 'Yeoman of the sea': 'Young' George Stoker (*above*) and 'that handsome Viking, Algar Mussett' (*below*), of Mersea Island.

As in many of his books' photographs, they are shown with their tools, and their angle of view is smilingly downwards towards the photographer, who looks up at them. This fits with Wentworth Day's sincere concern to treat them with respect. His captions convey the same message: 'Ted Allen. A genius of the wild marsh'; '"Admiral" Bill Wyatt, Elizabethan philosopher of Mersea Island'; 'The late "Sooty" Mussett, a famous Essex wildfowler'; or 'The late "Gunner" Cook, a well-known professional wildfowler, also of Mersea Island'.[61] So we might laterally think: 'let us now praise famous men'.[62] One notices here that these men are *given their names* as well as his complimentary labels in Wentworth Day's publications. The comparison with H. J. Massingham and almost all other twentieth-century rural writers is irresistible, because those other writers published photographs in which the workers pictured (often close-up) were *nameless*, something of a 'type', an example of appearance or a skill being practised.[63] Middle- or upper-class people in their photographs were usually named, but not those of the lower class. Writers like Massingham, A. G. Street, J. A. Scott Watson, Robertson Scott and many others documenting rural life in this period had ample opportunity to name those people who they were showing close-up in photographs. Unlike Wentworth Day, they did not do so.

Another photograph, from his private collection and intended for publication, is shown in Figure 7.5. Again, it is carefully captioned by Wentworth Day, and I reproduce his personalized wording in the figure title. Praise for such men overflows in Wentworth Day's books. Take for example: 'George Porter and his son and the Lucases, all good fellows. I can recommend Porter personally, a most intelligent man and an excellent punt builder as well as punt gunner.'[65] Such men linked wildfowling and sea trades with occasional farming work. 'They were Wild West heroes to me in my Fenland boyhood and on my occasional visits to these coastal marshes.'[66] Some men like these receive many pages of description and commendation in Wentworth Day's writings – his tributes are lengthy, personalized, and all are highly appreciative of their skills, such as sea-wall navvying, fishing, punt-gunning or bird-decoying, though he did not favour the latter.[67] Wentworth Day was reacting against many earlier stereotypes:

> For too long too many superficially clever townspeople have impressed upon the countryman that he is dull and slow and a fool. And the countryman, who is none of these things, but remarkably wise – with an age-old, natural wisdom – incredibly cunning, and as shrewd as a magpie when it comes to judging other people, retaliates by shutting the townsman out of his life and his confidence. He lets him know just so much as does not matter and cannot be derided. The rest is silence.[68]

Figure 7.5 George Gordon, keeper on Adventurer's Fen on a turf barge at the head of Wicken Lode, Cambridgeshire.[64]

The farms and their shepherds, their marsh 'lookers', their sea-wallers, their horsemen and cowmen, ploughmen and ditchers, were on each farm 'a little community apart, interdependent, fiercely independent'.[69] Indeed, Wentworth Day's view of the Essex countryman could never have been encapsulated in the phrase 'the deferential worker', the title of a famous book on the farm labourers of that county.[70] Certainly a respect for historic owners of property ran deep in Wentworth Day, coupled with appreciation of their properties. He often wrote lyrically about elite ancestry and, by contrast, scathingly of 'the soap-boilers, brewers, nitrate magnates, political hacks, chain shopkeepers, Labour and Liberal "intellectuals," and the rest of the ridiculous train of tradesmen and opportunists whom we dress up nowadays in the ill-fitting trappings of nobility'.[71] The details of 'the old rural aristocracy' had much historical interest and rhetorical force for him. Yet he made little mention of deference, possibly because of his fenland background, and like Cobbett he would have been disconcerted by any 'non-English' grovelling or vulnerable forms of it. He wrote about one Essex marsh-keeper, John Fell, 'a natural gentleman as God made him': 'Fell has a fine Saxon disregard for all fancy titles, an immemorial native judgement of the right form of address and courtesy for man or woman. He does not raise his hat. He doffs it. "I give 'em my salute, and that's enough for any man, I reckon".'[72] This emphasis was despite Wentworth Day's enormous respect for great estates where, from some other accounts, deference and vulnerable compliance were often found. One might question some of his statements about independence on great estates. And yet, whether his depictions of the social attitudes of Essex countrymen and coastal dwellers were 'true' is not strictly my concern.[73] As in all such depictions of historic community, we are dealing here with evoked local communities of the past, ones that were often idealized, to which he gave well-articulated historical forms, and his romanticization of them sometimes came with overly bleak accounts of their collapse.

Wentworth Day commented on how 'I have known these remote fishing villages of Tollesbury and Mersea since I was a boy. I know the men who own and sail these smacks. I have trawled with them in the green seas, and hauled in the peter nets in muddy creeks.'[74] He knew the barges, smacks and other vessels they sailed in, and he commended their naval skills. He interviewed them and quoted the old barge skippers and other such men at length in his writings.[75] This was 'history from below', of a declining way of life, long before that term was invented by other historians. The Essex coastal inhabitants were virtually 'a race apart',[76] working as fishermen and fowlers, winklers and shepherds, bargemen and marsh 'lookers'. They were original and spontaneously clever in speech and dialect. Wentworth Day used their turns of phrase and words, and conveyed their dialectal speech with considerable accuracy, as for example in his amusing and evocative book *Rum Owd Boys*. Oral history abounds in Wentworth Day's writing, in accounts of past gamekeepers, decoy-men, past winters, wherry sailing, houses and the like. He was a very skilled memorizer and conversationally entertaining mimic of speech, even though he might, as one 'owd boy' remarked, tend to 'varnish a tale'. These turns of speech took many forms in his writing. Some needed translation, such as the Norfolk 'Hevving a mardle in the loke with a rare stuggy little mawther what fare to sing as pretty as a mavish' – a dialect, he wrote, too good to lose.[77] (Trans: 'Having a gossip in the lane with a good-looking young girl, whose voice is as sweet as a thrush'.) He used local naming practices, for example of birds and other features of the natural world: ox-bird (dunlin), clew or tukie (redshank), olive (oyster-catcher), reed pheasant (bearded tit), tanglepicker (turnstone), yaffle (green woodpecker), hoodie (hooded crows), butcher bird (great grey shrike) and so on. Wentworth Day related the Essex coastal people's folklore and beliefs, sometimes tracking these back centuries. He referred to the 'rough, unlettered, but nevertheless inquisitive, naturalists who abound among the fishermen and marshmen of the coast'.[78] These men were supreme individualists, sharing core family names (like Seabrook, Guiver, Goldings, Hutley, Speakman, Goodchild, Eve, Bunting and so on) which pointed to a long livelihood in the area going back generations.[79] Family lineage mattered to Wentworth Day, whether for fen labourers or marshmen or for gentry or aristocrats. 'Every man, great or humble, has the blood of men and women whose deeds and ways of life are worth resurrection. Live their lives in imagination, for a brief space, and your own is, by so much, the richer.'[80]

This was written in 1946 – yet it is the language of many genealogy-related twenty-first-century media programmes and search facilities. The ancestry of a duck decoyman, or a marsh waller, really mattered to Wentworth Day. They had a pedigree of skill and experience. Of Walter Linnett, fine puntsman and gunner, he wrote: 'the family has a long record in the annals of Essex fowling'.[81] Whether Wentworth Day was talking of fenmen (among whom he counted himself, as he had owned land in Burwell Fen and called Wicken his 'old home', his 'native parish'),[82] or writing about coastal dwellers, he saw them above all as individualists, inheriting a family tradition as such. The fenmen were the true 'aristocrats', not the 'newly-minted peers'.[83] Yet their ways of life were passing. The fen was becoming divorced from village life, 'mournful with its memories'. Like Thomas Hardy describing Egdon Heath or Marygreen, with a language of fenmen plodding homeward unearthed from Gray's *Elegy*, Wentworth Day lamented the changes. 'I, as a native fenman, mourn the uprooting of humble village ownership … I lament the passing of the turf-diggers and the eel spearers, the sedge cutters and the native "moth hunters" – village naturalists.'[84] They were a 'rough, native crew', prone to sheep stealing and non-deferential in nature, unfortunately now 'almost extinct', watermen who were similar in many ways to the coastal inhabitants of Essex.[85] He refused to condemn smugglers, decoy-pond raiders or poachers, though he wrote in 1937 about the killing of two gamekeepers that 'as a lifetime poacher … I deplore this new violence'.[86] Gangs of unemployed from the Midlands and the north were apparently moving across the countryside and sometimes attacking keepers. Leaving those gangs aside, non-violent poachers or smugglers epitomized values of anti-State individualism that he extolled, and his benign view of them was bolstered by the thought that they had a long history, going back into 'the old rough days'.[87] Indeed, Wentworth Day was not averse to joining wildfowl poachers himself, especially if it meant a rousing raid and narrow escapes on the Kentish coast.[88]

His writing contains many eulogies to such men (always men). Take for example 'Billy-Boy the Pirate Fowler of the Thames Estuary … he is a man of sterling heart and upright principles – should have been a pirate. He looks like one. For many years he lived like one. He earned his living as a pirate might have done.'

> So you may imagine him, a little short, square, leather-faced man with beady brown eyes, a rat-trap mouth, crisp short hair, and hands that would throttle a gorilla, living in a shack built of old barge-timbers right under the sea-wall on a certain lonely marsh on the Essex shore of the Thames Estuary, that part of the estuary where it is near unto open sea.

Such a man fished or shot for a living. He was a punt-gunner, a professional wildfowler. He wore gold earrings because apparently they gave him long sight and freedom from rheumatism, a freedom supported by wearing eel-skin garters beneath his knees. He salvaged. He could build boats. He had nothing to do with yachts. 'He regarded yachts merely as "pretty little owd things," and yachtsmen as "them butterfly sailors".' Unfortunately he is now 'not quite the man he was. For he has married.'[89]

The loneliness of many of these people appealed to Wentworth Day. It came with the landscape. The Essex coast was 'a lonely, sea-musical land … It is perhaps the loneliest stretch of coast between the Wash and the Lizard.'[90] *Coastal Adventure* was, he wrote, a book for those 'who love sea-marshes and the lonely fringes of the tide'. It was about those 'hermit brethren of the longshore mudflats'. Like Thoreau, he had 'a mighty love for the marsh gunners, the lonely ones', though they had kinship with the farmers and the fishermen.[91] He commented on the lonely farms, the marshes' ghostly loneliness', a loneliness indeed that assisted in activities conducted there: wildfowl shooting, decoying and smuggling. On the Broads, he was struck by the 'solitary pike-fisher, hardiest and most misanthropic of mortals', or by lonely cottages inhabited by a warrener, 'a rough, silent man' living alone, by the lonely Abbey of St Benet's on the Cowholm Marshes and the 'bleak, scanty remains of its vanished greatness'. While the women of these marshes are often 'braver to solitude than men', this loneliness, and the survival of it, was seen largely as a manly attribute by Wentworth Day, a form of true 'Englishness', part of the qualities that he counted as 'masculine'.[92] It heightened his appreciation of the coastal dweller in such regions. Much the same idea came into his thoughts about some isolated inhabitants of the fens or the Broads.

Indeed, this virtue, or affliction – situational loneliness – was so stressed by Wentworth Day that one sometimes wonders whether he is lamenting not the decline of community but the creation of new forms of community and sociability in its stead. At least one other East Anglian writer, S. L. Bensusan, wrote about how 'the community spirit has been forced upon many who did not desire to hold any intercourse with it'.[93] Certainly Wentworth Day deplored the 'veritable psoriasis of bungalows and shacks, jerrybuilt, tawdry, and dumped willy-nilly, [which] is reaching down to the shores of the upper river like a red rash … sprawling eruptions spewed out from the East End of London within the last thirty years'. They were populated by Cockneys who 'patrol the sunny waters of Burnham and similarly sheltered sea-ways, effulgent in white-topped yachting caps, brass buttons, nautical jackets, and shiny little boats, leaving usually to leeward a faint odour of the juniper berry'.[94] Canvey Island had earlier been a small village of farm labourers, fishermen and a few professional wildfowlers. It was now turning into 'a trippers' bungalow colony', 'a Cockney paradise of beer bottles and paper bags … [a] strange "village", which resembles nothing so much as a Western mining camp run up in a night by intoxicated jerry-builders … the popularity of the place is increasing enormously'. He complained about it becoming 'a nest of huts, shacks, small houses, cheap dance halls, cinemas and young men in flannels'. There would presumably have been 'community' of a sort amid such an 'architectural aura of fried-fish-and-chips', more sociability and less isolation, though far less coherence as a tightly knit occupational culture and community compared to what had been there hitherto.[95]

Fen and marsh inhabitants apparently disliked 'furriners'. Wentworth Day often reflected their views. 'We tolerated no "furriners"', such as men from Soham or Burwell.[96] The term was very widely used like this in East Anglia and indeed elsewhere.[97] Like other such xenophobic language, it expressed defence of current and often isolated communities against those seen to threaten them or to be outside their norms. One such group were the 'wandering Irish, a troublesome, murderous crew', 'for ever preening themselves and parading their wits', coming in to pick potatoes and for the corn harvest, and being scared only of the foreman's wife, 'a sharp-tongued, hard-faced woman of the marshes'.[98] Londoners were equally outsiders, apparently from a place that 'allus was a wicked owd hole'. 'Them Lunnoners fare tew be made for larfin' at.'[99] They may come to live in the marshland areas and yet be complete strangers to local people and beliefs. The countrymen seemingly shut them out of their lives and confidences.

Decline of the waterland culture

A sense of historical decline pervades Wentworth Day's writing. 'The ports that once were great and powerful are now places of rotting wharves and sleeping dogs, of gaunt and empty warehouses and ship-stores, of hulks laid up on the mud and memories that are spat into the tide by old men.'[100] As another coastal writer commented, great stakes rose from the estuaries, 'forlorn and gloomy', but no one could remember why they were planted there.[101] The waning of these traditional coastal or waterland communities and their livelihoods, in the form that Wentworth Day knew them, had apparently a number of causes. The failure of proximate great estates, with their hunting and wildfowling activities, and skilled game preservation, was something he much regretted. New landowners, shallowly rooted in the locality, had excluded local inhabitants, as in parts of the Broads. 'The result is that Barton is virtually closed for shooting and fishing to the sons and grandsons of villagers who in the past earned their living thereon by net and gun.'[102] War and related changes to the coastline were detrimental to livelihoods and traditional communities. Some estates had become 'a death-trap of mines, barbed wire, trenches, and the debris of war'.[103] German bombers offloaded their undelivered bombs onto the Essex coastline and its villages. The night skies were 'patterned with the fantastic geometry of searchlights',[104] which affected bird life and migration. Small birds of any description were shot because of wartime food scarcities.[105] Local communities' earlier relations with the natural world were greatly disturbed. Game preservation largely ended and gamekeepers joined the Forces. Military installations, airfields, defences and pollution encroached on natural habitats and nesting grounds, and destroyed oyster beds; military vehicles tore up surfaces of the land. Allied servicemen showed some local women and men a prospect of different horizons and expectations.

After the war Wentworth Day fought hard to have land returned to the farmers from whom it had been taken by the State for war purposes. As his son-in-law, Dr Carl Hallam, remembers:

> All this coastal land had been commandeered, and at the end of the war the government just weren't so keen to let go, to give it back. And of course these farmers were distraught by this – that wasn't the deal at all – and the thing I remember most about him, from that point of view, was the support he gave to those people. He became a voice for them, and he published things for them. And in the end they got their land back. You can imagine how grateful they were – thousands of acres of very productive land, that had been in their families, that had been handed over for an agreed reason, and then they weren't getting it back … You can imagine how grateful they were, when suddenly they got their family acres back. They were eternally grateful. You can go down there, and have this sense of atmosphere, of how important they thought he was, he had been to them.[106]

Even so, much changed for these coastal communities. Dengie Flats became a practice bombing range, with piles and beacons where punt-gunners had earlier sought their living. Mechanized and more chemical-based farming undermined traditional occupations and a close symbiosis between land and sea. The diminishing numbers of wildfowl because of agricultural change, marshland drainage and overzealous shooting affected many people's livelihoods. Improved transport meant that larger numbers of visitors jeopardized earlier ecological niches. Holiday camps ('the Maplin menace')[107] threatened natural habitats. Newcomers unfamiliar with the past and with local ways of getting a living were a major factor, explaining some of Wentworth Day's antipathy to Londoners. New housing and tourist towns encroached upon marshland and coast. He wrote about places like Clacton, Walton, Southend and Mersea that 'the vulgarity of the building speculators has left its ugly mark'. Such 'gimcrack' modern building seemed to be symptomatic of the 'greedy sluttish fingers of the city [which] reach out and soil it all'.[108]

It came with the supposed traits of Londoners, whom Wentworth Day felt were destroying the Essex coastal communities. London did not appeal to him, though he had worked there, wrote a book on its wildlife and praised its parks. He referred to it as 'a monstrous nightmare', 'that great unwieldy wen which now sprawls like a dish-rag beside the Thames'. One notes here Cobbett's language of 'wen'. East Anglia, he felt, could get on very well without London. He expressed much scorn for Londoners: 'the ephemeral breed from London', comprising 'butterfly yachtsmen … cockney crowds', filling local bars with Cockney voices. 'The city breeds ferret-cunning.' He attacked 'the indiscriminate shooting … with all sorts of hobbledehoys from the towns blazing away at floating bottles, harmless gulls, nesting moorhens, and even grazing cattle'.[109] Yachtsmen came ashore 'to swig beer with their blowsy women, their trousered, brassy blondes'. Or the 'swag-bellied urban golfer plods his unlovely way' (in a modern echo of Gray's *Elegy*), in what had once been a fine deer park, the sort of park 'for which democracy now has no use'.[110] These feelings against outsiders and London were quite widespread at the time. Many shared his views about 'stock-broker-infested' reaches of the Thames, which would also have endeared him to William Cobbett.[111] As one interwar speaker from across the estuary in Kent rather surprisingly declared: 'The average countryman was highly suspicious of the Londoner … In his village they threw stones at Londoners.'[112]

In the case of Wentworth Day, his views about London were coupled with a dislike of the War Agricultural Committees and an anti-centralist attitude. He loathed 'this age of bureaucratic oppression and tomfool regulation-into-starvation'. He condemned in the most forthright language Whitehall regulation of food production, incompetent bureaucrats and undertakings such as the creation of a National Park in the Norfolk Broads, which he felt would lead to such places being 'ruled, regulated, and steam-rollered out of existence'. 'Farming from Whitehall must cease', he urged.[113] These anti-State feelings permeated his writings, and he blamed such distant bureaucracy for its effects on estates, its damage to local initiatives and leadership, and the decline of local communities in the form that he knew them. 'It is far better in a rural community that such neighbourly acts should be done by neighbours, known and liked, rather than by the self-sufficient little officials of the War Agricultural Committees.'[114] Whitehall threatened to bring about the 'graveyard of that robust village individualism' which he admired.[115] The War Agricultural Committees in particular were, he felt, wasteful and ignorant. They were also evicting thousands of people from their farms and homes, disrupting local senses of belonging and lines of family ownership. Public money was being squandered by these 'petty *gauleiters*', 'these self-appointed archangels of flawless justice and unimpeachable knowledge' – 'It is rural Fascism, no less.'[116] He had little time either for the Forestry Commission, rooting 'dense, dull, Germanic blocks of closely planted conifers which will be next to useless for timber'.[117] He feared 'a slick programme of State ownership and factory-run farms',[118] and what this might do to older values of independent Englishmen and yeoman farmers. The Earls and Dukes of Bedford had drained vast fens and

> made the wilderness a plot of gold long before planners and bureaucrats were hatched from their dreary pigeonholes to tell us that no progress can be achieved without first filling in a form and then sitting back to wait interminably … When I think of the forms, officials, petrol, waste of money and time, publicity ballyhoo, and photographing of diplomaed deadheads

> which are necessary to-day before a paltry thousand acres is drained, at great cost to the taxpayer, the mind boggles at the mental state of the Ministry and its poke-noses, Army dodgers, and other indispensables, were they faced with the task of draining more than a quarter of a million acres of primeval swamp, of which notable success Thorney to-day is a permanent witness.[119]

These days of the estates were passing or past. Wentworth Day lamented the decline of great estates and the types of community they had fostered. He quoted labourers, hunt-beaters and others from the rural working class to the same effect.[120] The Victorian great estates had in fact been declining since the later nineteenth century, and Wentworth Day tended to miss the long-term economic causes of this decline. He stressed instead more immediate political causation. He regarded the change with dismay. Time and again he discussed examples of this, in all cases noting adverse effects on the rural community. Here is an example of such comment, in this case on the Sudbourne estate in Suffolk, owned hitherto by Sir Richard Wallace, then by Kenneth Clark (father of the art historian); but then came 'an eminent soap-boiler' who had made his fortune with 'Watson's Matchless Cleaner' – and apparently the estate was soon in the boiling pot:

> There is no need to follow the dreary twists of its downward fortunes. It was cut up, jobbed off, reduced to chaos and disruption, like a hundred others which have been broken by over-taxation and Government neglect of farming. The farms went down to grass and thistles. Thatch blew off the barns, and none was put back. Cottages lacked paint and mortar, and cottagers lacked work and money. Ditches choked and overflowed. Woods became rank and blind with undergrowth. Trees blew down, and there were none to saw them up. Hedges ran wild, and the villages of Sudbourne, Iken, and Butley were forlorn and down-at-heel. Their menfolk were mainly unemployed.[121]

This he felt had been the pattern 'on a thousand once well-run estates, the result of shortsighted and largely class-conscious legislation. Lloyd George, the evil genius of rural England, began it all.' 'To us, on the seaward marshes, the late Lloyd George is still the epitome of all Government greed.'[122] The decline of great estates began before Lloyd George's People's Budget of 1909, but one is not concerned here to rehearse the history of that process: through the eclipse of landed political power, rising labour and other costs, a sequence of death duties and other taxation, falling land and food prices, failure of heirs, requisitioning and the like.[123] Of interest here is Wentworth Day's insistence that estate collapse, above all other factors, was responsible for the decline of rural community as it had been known, or as he extolled it. His stress was upon human agency and policy – Lloyd George

– as triggering the decline. Such emphasis upon a blameable high-political villain was consistent with Wentworth Day's view that if only things had been left to locals and to estate owners, community would have thrived and historical continuity would have been sustained.[124] He expressed his views of the results: a lack of work, agricultural redundancy and falling investment in the land, decline of village events like flower and produce shows, poor village education, an impoverishment of deportment and clothing among village families, and an architectural dereliction that was both cause and symbol of decline.

He stared from his Essex bedroom window upon the empty desolation of a great porticoed mansion, now forlorn, and its park, gardens and home farm, which had once engaged 220 men and women of his village. All these now employed about eleven people. The owner had sold up and left, unable to pay death duties. 'The villagers are the losers', commented Wentworth Day, and he felt that this usually was the case.[125] There were many examples of this change after the First World War. Witley Court, Seaton Delaval, Bolsover, Clumber and Montacute – these and many more were mentioned by him as having become barren architectural residues. Their families had been 'part of the blood and bone of English history'.[126] Wentworth Day's praise for them was not unqualified: he hated pomposity and liked to see an 'innate modesty and open-hearted friendliness', as with the Queen Mother.[127] He was unimpressed with the building styles which were replacing their estates and great mansions: 'the ferro-concrete Mayfair flat block; the monstrous Odeons; the barrack-rows of Council cottages; the tinny tawdriness of black glass and chromium plate; and the bogus Tudoresque of the Stockbroker Period'.[128] One is reminded of Betjeman's 'various bogus Tudor bars' and his wish to blow up Slough.[129] The National Trust was an inadequate replacement of the older estates, turning a house into an exhibit only – no longer a working community and linchpin of the rural community – in Wentworth Day's view it was becoming far too big a landowner and householder.

As in much of Wentworth Day's writing in the 1930s and 1940s, the prognosis was pessimistic and these changes appeared bleak. The interwar agricultural depression, or its memories, heightened this sense of a rural England in decline, its communities depressed and younger people eager to leave the land. His suggested remedies were unlikely to occur: abolition of death duties on land, 'that most immoral of all taxes',[130] de-rating and allowances against taxation for upkeep of great houses and for allowing public access on certain viewing days. These would at least increase farmers' and cottagers' security of tenure, upgrade farmland maintenance and allow investment in farm and village properties, to general benefit. 'Community decline' for Wentworth Day meant above all the decline of landed families and their estates, which he believed was largely brought about by 'immoral' government policies.

Nevertheless, in a later book, *The New Yeomen of England*, Wentworth Day discussed a change dependent upon the break-up and sale of the great estates, documenting one of the most remarkable features of twentieth-century agricultural history: the (re)emergence of yeoman farming as the predominant form of agricultural occupancy. 'The squirearchy is disappearing.'[131] In 1911, owner-farmers occupied 11 per cent of England and Wales; by 1927 this had risen to 36 per cent; and by 1952 it was over 42 per cent.[132] Wentworth Day, while still regretting what had happened to many great estates, now showed an awareness of how rural communities could adjust and reinvigorate themselves under more fragmented ownership, with the creation of a 'new yeomanry'. William Cobbett – 'of the yeoman breed'[133] – would surely also have approved the change.

Wentworth Day's Conservatism

Conservatism, it is often said, is a habit of mind.[134] Stuart Ball's *magnum opus* on the Conservative Party between the wars outlines it as follows:

> It was a basic assumption that Conservatism 'starts from temperament rather than logic' … Conservatism 'begins as a mood and a point of view – it ends as a political system and an abiding faith'. Conservatives believed that their outlook was based upon a 'subconscious, intuitive' disposition, and was therefore different in nature from an ideology … Conservatives did not hold a single set of views; 'my party have no political bible', declared Stanley Baldwin … Nor was Conservatism defined by the working of an institution or the wisdom of a leader, for it was 'a code of principles which is above parties or personalities'. Almost all would have agreed as a starting-point that Conservatism 'exists to oppose revolutionary change'. Beyond this were principles and attitudes which were often implicit or assumed. Most Conservatives arrived at and understood these emotionally rather than intellectually, as 'a faith within himself' … Conservatism was 'a distinct way of thinking' with its own rationale, from which it derived substance and relevance: it was 'a philosophy of life and of society'.[135]

Wentworth Day certainly opposed revolutionary or violent change; indeed he accused Harold Laski of advocating precisely that. His Conservatism involved strong-willed ideas about the way a community should function, and how its estate owners and workers should be respected. He extolled 'unobtrusive efficiency and business-like paternalism'.[136] In his case this was accompanied by an overwhelmingly strong if romanticized sense of history, a view of England in the Elizabethan or medieval ages as being 'a younger, lovelier place'.[137] He clearly despaired at much of modern Britain: 'an over-populated, over-industrialised country, crawling with roads, towns, villages, railways and telegraph wires'.[138] The Victorian age contained much that he disliked, despite his views on manliness or great estates, and he often looked earlier for historical inspiration. Like other Conservatives, he accepted social differences and traditional hierarchies, thinking them natural to society. A frequent question at the time was whether there was a 'community of interest that links together all connected with the land', and if not, whether this can be created.[139] Wentworth Day undoubtedly thought that there was, being happy to toast 'The Indivisible Trinity – landowner, farmer, and labourer'.[140] Yet he also felt that this depended upon a high level of historically underpinned estate leadership and respect for skilled workers. He argued (in 1941–42) that farm labourers should have a 'decent living wage' of at least £3 weekly,[141] and preferably more, and (rather like Cobbett) he was indignant that their meat and other rations were half to a third of those for enemy prisoners of war.[142]

There was little that was authoritarian, elitist or overtly class-based in his respect for working skills and marshland activities. On the contrary, stereotypes of the rural working class are largely and surprisingly absent from his writing, as he stressed individualism and distinctiveness.[143] He thought that the influence of London was disruptive and tawdry. By contrast, he eagerly wanted to learn from marsh or fen workers and he respected their knowledge and perceptions. His books are replete with accounts of them, praise for them and photographs of them. This is Conservatism as localism, anti-centralist, paternally estate based, skill-extolling and highly participatory. It may owe something to his combination of fenland and Welsh ancestry. He relished small-scale smugglers and poachers, enjoying their activities and their anti-State attitudes. From an early age he joined them and learned from them (though he disliked drug smuggling and larger operations). He wrote the Essex coastal people's dialect and speech directly and with appreciation, shared their humour, tended perhaps to over-colour them as individuals and cultivated a sense of them as long-rooted in their areas, people to be highly esteemed as individualists, as deservedly proud as local aristocrats.

Wentworth Day's ideals of Conservatism and 'community' were also frequently infused with ideas from the natural world. For example, he liked rooks, and in his outline of the bird they take on the qualities that he ascribed to Englishmen. In the early days, apparently, the rook was 'a raider, a forager, a pirate, a cunning fellow'. (Wentworth Day was prone to extol and romanticize the Anglo-Saxons and Vikings.) But then the rook took on a different hue. 'He grew in stature as an Englishman. Mark you, he is *very* English.' He has the quality of permanence, of devotion to old things and old values, old houses and old families. The rook dwells above ancient church steeples. He caws at the top of beech avenues dating back to Charles I's time. He survived the Civil War, nesting in castle turrets – he is part of England. He is 'full of memories', of field and wood, upland plough and winter stubble, of hoar-frosted stockyards, of tide-bared mudflats. Moreover, rooks

> are very domestic, very disciplined and highly moral. When a rook marries he marries singly and not plurally. Let one bold libertine assault the wife of another rook and the whole colony will be down on him, beat him unmercifully, even possibly peck him to death. They will hold a court-martial on the matter, a gabbling parliament of talk … For the rook is a good husband. During his courtship he feeds his mistress and in marriage he provides her with bread and worms, fed from his own beak and pouch. You will not often find a rook who has more than one wife.

All this is very satisfactory. Wentworth Day married three times (to women who may not all have enjoyed smoky cabin interiors and muddy Blackwater inlets), but they weren't concurrent. He continues to describe a rookish event: when they gathered together to deal with a stork 'from some forgotten fen in Holland' – they harried him away, as if to say 'Ha! That was a foreigner – so we threw a brick at him.' 'Do you wonder that I love the rook, black but gentle, pious but piratical – the most English of all birds?' This rookish scheme of things is much more fully expounded, including discussion of the qualities of the rook's wife, who, 'like any good human wife … is the main architect of the home'. This is a rather unusual blend of Conservatism, a coastal or fenland mentality, and the natural world, each seemingly validating the other and providing a model for English community and family relations.[144]

I have drawn attention to the comparisons made at the time between Wentworth Day and William Cobbett. Wentworth Day read Cobbett while convalescing from an injury, following the thoughts of 'that robust, ranting, prejudiced old Radical as he rode from shire to shire'.[145] He was impressed by the parallels between the issues of the 1820s and those of the 1930s and 1940s. If Cobbett wrote about the vicissitudes and effects of the first 'agricultural revolution', Wentworth Day was a writer about those of 'the second agricultural revolution', as many agrarian historians use those terms. The idea for his own rural rides came from Cobbett. His *Harvest*

Adventure was advertised in *The Times* as 'The condition of rural England examined by "the modern Cobbett"'.[146] Comparisons between Cobbett and Wentworth Day are irresistible. 'Mark you', even some of Wentworth Day's literary style was from Cobbett. Today most of us tolerate Cobbett with respect and good humour, regardless of his demographic and other errors, seeing him as a populist agrarian conservative-turned radical, a yeoman ideologist espousing much from the Country Party platform of the eighteenth century, someone rooted in eighteenth-century rural popular culture. He could, as Ian Dyck pointed out, 'more readily accept innovation in politics than in culture and economic tradition'.[147] Many approve his 'Englishness'; while Wentworth Day's similar views are so close to our period that they would often be met with politically correct and scrupled misgiving.

There were the horse-riding tours, and the determination to talk to and respect ordinary people, however humble. Wentworth Day commented on 'that peculiar condescension which the middle-class "intellectuals" of that [Labour] party invariably display towards the villager'.[148] He quoted villagers' views at length with much appreciation, especially (one can wryly notice) if they matched his own. This was not necessarily a bias in reporting: after all, many studies have pointed to a higher incidence of working-class Toryism in rural areas in the mid-twentieth century.[149] He shared Cobbett's antipathy to the State, its growth (the civil service grew markedly in the 1930s), its interference, its taxation, 'tax-eaters' and fiscal incompetence. Even so, like many Conservatives, he wanted greater support for agriculture. Wentworth Day was especially scornful of the Excess Profits Tax: 'How can a farmer possibly restore fertility to his war-exhausted land under such a crushing burden of tax?'[150] Both men disliked stockjobbers and 'city parasites', especially when they moved into the countryside: 'these stock-jobbing squires', who 'strive so earnestly to ape the superficialities of the men whose ancient houses they have bought, minus most of the land and minus all the sense of responsibility, all the breeding … All desperately comic but a little pathetic.'[151] Both attacked 'the building speculators … their greedy fingers … their precious little villas'.[152]

Cobbett and Wentworth Day both used anti-Wen rhetoric and shunned Londoners, in an ongoing cultural stress upon town and country difference. In fact (and reminding us of some views in parish magazines), they were horrified by conditions in London: 'Rural Conservatism often finds it difficult to imagine the depths to which urban slumdom can fall … it must remedy this disgrace.'[153] Neither had much to say about industry, and their 'rides' took them away from it. Wentworth Day's views extolling the countryside (and individualism) remind one of Stanley Baldwin, Viscount Halifax, Eustace Percy, Churchill, Eden, Macmillan and many other Conservative politicians.[154] Baldwin wanted to create 'better, healthier, more beautiful communities than exist today', and he looked to the country for his inspiration. Cobbett and Wentworth Day praised those who stayed in one place, preferably a village, liking to see stability of people and enduring social relationships.[155] Both expressed considerable local and national xenophobia, and indeed documented it, though Wentworth Day had Welsh ancestry and respected the Welsh, leaving aside 'Lloyd George and the other class-warfare experts'.[156] 'I like the Welsh. I like their courtesy, their quick, sly charm, their bright and lucid eyes, their flowing, untrue tongue like a mountain brook after rain, their ebullient, almost foreign, gestures, and their fierce religion.'[157] Unlike many other 'fellow travellers of the right', and despite his fondness for local constancy, he liked gypsies, admired their horse fairs and country ways, and was also full of praise for George Borrow: 'that great-hearted vagabond'.[158] Nevertheless, he quoted (seemingly with approval) George Santayana's *Soliloquies in England* on the Englishman: 'He is rather glad and relieved if only natives will remain natives and strangers strangers, and at a comfortable distance from himself.'[159] Cobbett and Wentworth Day each extolled extreme individualism, and in their own persons were cantering examples of it. We 'talked of farming; of the stranglehold of bureaucrats; of the need to safeguard the future of individualism if England is to be worth living in'. The two men even made similar comparisons of landowners. Cobbett had declared Coke of Norfolk, Lord Leicester's ancestor, to be spoken of in the way in which affectionate children address a loved parent. 'That is as true to-day' remarked Wentworth Day, who was impressed with Holkham and, like Arthur Young, was always ready to praise a conscientious and efficient landlord. Cobbett, like Wentworth Day, frequently lamented a decline of earlier estate paternalism, leadership and local responsibility.[160]

Both men had some scepticism about religious life and occupation. Wentworth Day rarely mentioned religion, though he appreciated cathedral and church architecture. He was a church-goer,[161] yet he was quick to relay marsh or fen anticlerical statements.[162] 'Bishops! Rum owd pups. Allus arter your money.' The new 'grimly respectable' fen houses, he felt, looked like 'a smug crew of canting psalm-singers off to worship on Sundays and ready to swindle their neighbours on Mondays'.[163] Cobbett, by comparison, spoke of Methodists thus: 'Such a mixture of whining cant and of foppish affectation I scarcely ever heard in my life … a dish of nonsense … this bawling, canting crew … these roving fanatics'. As for the parsons, 'they were always haughty and insolent'.[164] Indeed, Cobbett wrote a whole book telling parsons how deficient and deplorable they and their bishops were.

The parallels occur even in domestic and material life and in aesthetic views. Both men had a mutual respect for enduring forms of material domestic culture. In Cobbett's case this usually involved eulogies to 'Oak clothes-chests, oak bedsteads, oak chests of drawers, and oak tables'.[165] The emphasis switched to mahogany with Wentworth Day (a more Empire-based standard), which gets many approving glances: 'a solid sort of yeoman-cum-squire appearance which argues good mahogany and old silver and roast beef', linked to other 'sound simple values which make country character'.[166] Moving on to other aspects of domestic life, Wentworth Day praised oysters for having large numbers of offspring 'with no love nonsense either',[167] reminiscent of Cobbett's anti-romantic prose approving practical wives and rosy babies. Actually, Cobbett praised 'rosy-cheeked' rural women, while Wentworth Day regretted 'apple-cheeked girls' going 'from the healthy life of the village to the pallid and flaccid joys of the town street',[168] adjectives which no doubt summed up his views about the potentiality of many urban and suburban men.

Cobbett and Wentworth Day also shared anti-intellectualism. This was despite their knowledge of history and their wide literary tastes, and their respect for improved farming techniques and some technology, although there were 'technophobic' or anti-machinery characteristics in both men.[169] Cobbett had written sensitively about 'those frivolous idiots that are turned out from Winchester and Westminster School, or from any of those dens of dunces called Colleges and Universities'.[170] His abhorrence of political philosophers like Thomas Malthus or Adam Smith is well known. Wentworth Day disapproved of 'pretentious economists from obscure universities', and indeed some of the 'slick scientific philosophies of today'. He praised science in some contexts, but many of his anti-scientific attitudes derived from repugnance of modern warfare and its technologies. Discussing grasshopper warblers, little owls, kestrels, wild duck and teal, tufted duck, or redshank 'who nest by the brown dykes', his pen suddenly turned with bitterness in comment upon 'this barbarous century'.[171] He also had an antipathy to the destruction of natural habitats and wildlife by poisons like DDT, the spread of low-grade housing and some forms of mechanistic farming.[172] He had little time for all 'the mountebank jargon beloved of the pseudo-scientist and bureaucrats'.[173] Compared to vernacular building of the past, modern farmhousing materials appalled him: 'hideous galvanized iron or that glaring and equally hideous pre-cast concrete which is now the rage among those farmers who always follow each new, so-called "scientific" fad like sheep'.[174] He didn't comment about farm asbestos, though his judgement is predictable. He valued students who had fought in the wars. Yet percipient readers might suspect him of not being entirely enthusiastic about interwar Oxbridge. He had been a reporter on the *Cambridge Evening News*. Speaking of some Cambridge students since the 1920s, he commented upon

> a few willowy-minded and willowy-bodied intellectuals who, lacking any reason for faith in themselves or their abilities – as is true of most 'intellectuals' – postured and postulated an immense superiority to the ordinary breed of their fellows ...They wrote a few bad poems. They produced a little inconsequent literature ... acted in a few shallow plays of their own callow world, and talked wordily in those little societies which are the safety-valves of universities. On the whole they were pretentious, gaseous, and disregarded. They made little mark on the world then or since ... It seemed that the breed was becoming more pansified ... They dwelt on vague Communistic possibilities ... Some of the dons were to blame. The trouble with 'intellectuals' is that they are so seldom intelligent, frequently perverts, and almost invariably conceited. I was beginning to lose a little faith in Cambridge.[175]

He much preferred the hardier Essex marshmen – even if they wore gold earrings.[176]

Conclusion

Wentworth Day could never really define himself as being part of an 'imagined community' of watermen – fen, broad or marsh. He had become an outsider despite his protestations of local knowledge, by virtue of his journalistic or editorial work. Much of his engagement with them was recreational, occasional, naturalistically aesthetic, rather than being from any such working-class community. Many of his associations were far above them in class terms, indeed right up to and including the royal family. But he derived benefit from his associations with the water-edge people – they heightened his appreciation of, and access to, the natural world. They provided subject matter for his writing and in his mind clearly gave that writing added authority. His politics appear compatible with and buttressed by some features in their popular culture. The watermen, fowlers and other marsh workers were 'very, very fond of him, they really were ... He seemed to be able to talk to anyone – and he could, he would make friends with anyone. That was a great gift. He was curious, he was interested in people.'[177] The ripostes reported in *Rum Owd*

Boys suggest a willingness to help him, tolerance, liking, appreciation of his respect for them and a friendly suspicion that he 'varnished' some of their stories. The watermen in the three main areas he discussed were apart geographically, whatever they shared in skills or experience of the natural world. Wentworth Day did not group them all into a common community, though he clearly believed that they shared many attitudes and a way of life. And his writing about them was infused with much other matter – about politics, wildlife and history – which I have tended to omit here, in a concentration upon his view of water-edge people and activities as disappearing communities. His main claim to attention today is probably as a writer about the interface between men and wildlife, which I have explored here only in relation to his theme of fading senses of community. As in varying ways with Thomas Hardy, George Morland or Adrian Bell, the communities he depicted were posited upon certain kinds of working and symbolic interactions with nature. The innovations or build-ups of people that he criticized, like the Cockneys in Clacton, or the 'bungaloid slum' and 'petrol-propelled motor-boat fiends' of the Broads, were seemingly not. He saw them as a noisy affront to nature, incompatible and a threat to it, though it seems that his own shooting fell outside such criticism.[178] His personalized observational writing about wildlife, notably birds, has not been much explored here, even though it contains his finest writing and carries an array of further meanings, about loneliness, masculinity, leisure or wildlife habits and habitats.

Wentworth Day is now often thought to have been a voice in the wilderness, albeit not a lone one. Such opinions, formed in the Edwardian era, were often held during his lifetime. He was also a populist journalist with a common touch, following many popular views in the 1930s, 1940s and 1950s. Much of what he mourned as lost or in process of being lost is terminally gone now. Ways of life have been transformed. The waterland and coastal communities, and their ways of living that he described, have largely disappeared both in fact and memory. The Essex coastline has its new materializations. The Broads are a watery assemblage of agrochemical pollution, thick green layers of toxic scum and expensive motorized yachts. The fens sink every year further below sea or old road levels, their top soils blowing away in brown clouds that are painful to the eye. Wentworth Day bitterly fought against all this, trying unsuccessfully to defend the hitherto wildness of fen, broad and marsh. 'He did love those wild damp places,' his daughter said to me.[179] It is easy to cite him in a litany of quotations that reads as a list of what is now politically incorrect. He baited his opponents in ways that invited ripostes. I do not share many of his views. But then, any historian deriding this man from a current vantage point misses many past beliefs and neglects major if romanticized senses of loss. After all, we do not scorn William Cobbett, that quintessential symbol of assertive 'Englishness', whose views were so similar to those of Wentworth Day. It is obvious that Wentworth Day was ambiguously at odds with his modernizing age. Admiring the lines of a modern yacht, he wrote that 'It seems a little odd at first, a little incomprehensible that such an age as this could produce such line, such perfect beauty in the same breath that it produces piledrivers, tanks, tugs, tanneries, gasometers, abattoirs, "planners," and other emblems of squalor, commerce, envy, and ugliness.'[180] He failed to appreciate many changes that were welcome, affecting democracy, welfare, health, women's lives, travel, workers' rights or new community development.

Yet there is much to admire in his loathing of modern warfare, his personalized eulogies to labouring men, his understanding and documentation of waterland ways of life, his condemnation of 'poison on the land', and his observant writing about wildlife. Of the imitative starling, he wrote: 'Once or twice there came the fat comfortable quack of mallard, mimicked in a sardonic low note with a chuckle at the end of it.'[181] Authors describe themselves in their descriptions of wildlife. Wentworth Day certainly did. This man was above all one of the great British wildlife writers, notably of waterland environments. Let us leave him with one of his many such descriptions, a solitary twilight watcher observing a different kind of community in the sky:

> In the winter they came, night after night, just before dusk, in tidal waves of wings. They roosted in the reed beds about the old decoy pond on our marsh. Out of the west came black banks of birds against the sunset, and the noise of their coming was like sea waves on a shingle beach. They swooped and dived against the apple-green and red of the dying sun, in magnificent evolutions that took the breath and astounded the eye. Wave after roaring wave they came, tens of thousands of whistling, twittering starlings – a Niagara of purposeful wings which rose and surged, and died away and rose again and finally, long minutes later, faded into a sleepy twitter as though a million children slept.[182]

8

Adrian Bell and the East Anglian Farming Community

It had died away – the old bluff, hospitable life of the countryside – like a summer's day. I saw it fade … from the top of my stacks as I worked, or from the window of my barn … It died slowly, like a cloudless afternoon, splendid to the last. Fewer grew the company … The country around us became lonely, thinly populated. The old community I had known on coming here ten years ago or more was now almost all gone.[1]

Fortunate the writer or artist whose parish is his universe.[2]

Adrian Bell left London for Suffolk to be a farm apprentice in 1920, a decision partly influenced by recurrent migraine, which hindered many possible careers. He lived through a period of dramatic change affecting rural communities and farming, from 1901 to 1980, and his writing vividly documents the passing of an older Victorian and Edwardian rural community. 'I saw it fade,' he wrote, in the quotation that heads this chapter, and he became a distinctive voice as he watched this. When so many others were intent on leaving the countryside for a seemingly better life in the towns or overseas, Adrian Bell turned rural, intending to become a small farmer at possibly the worst moment in modern agricultural history to make that decision. The interwar agricultural depression was about to start, and the Exchequer withdrew support for agriculture. This created in Suffolk what Ronald Blythe later described as 'a kind of beautiful, ruinous landscape of great rural poverty'.[3] A personalized sense of national betrayal was to shake the agricultural community, especially in cereal-growing East Anglia. Small farmers would be especially vulnerable. This was hardly an auspicious or well-judged start to a young man's career. It was partly for these reasons that Adrian Bell turned to writing, to augment a precarious income from farming. And after all, it seemed a time for the young: 'their elders could no longer point to the proven success of traditional procedure',[4] and they had also been responsible for the First World War. Surely a new world was immanent in the old one.

Adrian Bell had been born in 1901, in Stretford, Lancashire, the son of Robert Bell, news editor of *The Observer* (from Edinburgh and descended from small yeomen of Kirkcudbright), and his artistic wife, Fanny Hanbury. He was educated from 1915 to 1920 at Uppingham School, Rutland, an over-disciplined place that he was relieved to leave. After working briefly at *The Observer*, Bell left London for Suffolk in 1920 to become a farm apprentice to Victor Savage at Great Lodge, Hundon. In the early 1920s, he bought a small farm, Stephenson's in Stradishall, and later added to it Seabrook's Farm. His first novel, *Corduroy* (1930), was written at The Gables, Sudbury, recalling his farming apprenticeship and Hundon Great Lodge, and the second, *Silver Ley* (1931), recreated Stephenson's Farm. *The Cherry Tree* (1932) completed the trilogy. After the war and for the next three decades Bell wrote 'A Countryman's Notebook' for the *Eastern Daily Press*. He lived at many places in East Anglia, including Hundon, Stradishall, Sudbury, Weston Colville, Wissington, Redisham, Beccles, Barsham and Gillingham. In Westhall, near Beccles, he bought Brick Kiln Farm with the proceeds from *Apple Acre*. Adrian Bell died at Gillingham in 1980.[5]

Adrian Bell published over twenty-five books, including two of poetry, and is best known for the trilogy mentioned above. He wrote many other fine books, such as *Folly Field* (1933), *By-Road* (1937), *The Shepherd's Farm* (1939), *Men and the Fields* (1939), *Apple Acre* (1942), *Sunrise to Sunset* (1944), *The Budding Morrow* (1946), *The Flower and the Wheel* (1949), *The Path by the Window* (1952), *A Young Man's Fancy* (1955), *A Suffolk Harvest* (1956), *The Mill House* (1958) and *The Green Bond* (1976). His autobiography was entitled *My Own Master* (1961), and an account of his childhood was *The Balcony* (1934). In fact, much of his writing is fictionalized autobiography, 'simple and yet sophisticated books',[6] documenting his agricultural experiences, and he gained a literary reputation that matched or even exceeded H. J. Massingham, A. G. Street or C. Henry Warren. His daughter Anthea Bell wrote to me that 'since my father had a great gift for friendship his acquaintances were legion'.[7] A picture of him is in Figure 8.1. Among his friends were Edmund Blunden, who persuaded him to write,[8] Frank and Q. D. Leavis,[9] H. J. Massingham,[10] Alfred Munnings, John Nash (who illustrated some of his books), Henry Warren and Henry Williamson. One can also sense in his writing the influence of people like Richard Jefferies, Thomas Hardy, George Sturt, T. S. Eliot and Eric Gill, although he thought (in Ann Gander's words) that Hardy 'had never come close to the business end of a horse in his life'.[11] He was a member of the interwar group Kinship

Figure 8.1 Adrian Bell.

in Husbandry, but came to see that their organic ideals fell short of reality, and he did not share the right-wing views of members like Rolf Gardiner.[12] Bell was especially popular during the Second World War. By 1945 farming authors like him and A. G. Street were best sellers.[13] His books in small format could fit into a soldier's kitbag or pocket. Martin Bell wrote about how his father had

> a most extraordinary impact on readers at that time and in the cataclysmic war that followed ... His work ... had an elegiac quality. It spoke of calmer

> times and saner values. Its distinguishing feature was a sort of rooted and practical mysticism, seeing its visions and dreaming its dreams in the fields and furrows of a working Suffolk farm. [14]

One is reminded of the painter Stanley Spencer, dreaming his own dreams in Cookham.[15] Many extant letters from soldiers and prisoners of war bear testimony to their appreciation of Adrian Bell's portraits of rural England and to the cogency of his unsentimental ideas for localized and small-scale rural revival. He wrote: 'As fields are amalgamated for the huge machines of agri-business, creating savannahs, I think of the letters … from serving soldiers whose dearest wish was to subsist on a few acres of English soil after the war and live in thankfulness simply for being alive.'[16] What, Bell wondered, should the nature of friendship and community look like when the shelling and bombing had ended, and what forms of human sympathy would remain? He felt that 'Life can be extraordinarily complete, if you let it be so.'[17] To that end, Bell opted for localism, for rural community as traditionally understood. In literature he much preferred the localized observation of Gilbert White to the modernism and literary intellectualism of the 1920s. He was never ashamed to be local, or provincially East Anglian.

> As for living in narrow compass, there are worlds within worlds, and to know thoroughly the whole of a single acre of my land would have taken several lifetimes. Besides all this, the post-war world appeared to me ugly and threatening, overpopulated already with high ambitions, and would-be wresters of power. I only wanted to live in peace and earn my bread.[18]

The interwar rural depression in East Anglia overshadowed his early writing.[19] He wrote of how the wilderness began to invade neighbouring fields.[20] Many farmers scratched a living by partial cultivation of their land. Farming went down and buildings became dilapidated. Despite such conditions, there were signs of agricultural advance and adaptive change. In *By-Road* he discussed new farming methods – modern machinery, motorized transport, factory farming, new marketing and business methods, hedge removals, fruit specialization and so on – showing options for the future, and not imposing judgement. Ironically, the interwar period was a time of advance in agricultural science, technology and education. However, his own sympathies clearly lay with older styles of farming, and he had great respect for earlier rural artefacts, horse power, hand technologies and the people skilled in them, even though he knew he was describing the passing of a whole culture. The lantern was giving way to electricity, pantiles to sheet iron. Agriculture, he thought, was 'the basis of all culture.'[21] Bell and his fellow rural authors – H. J. Massingham, A. G. Street, Rolf Gardiner, Henry Williamson, W. H. Freeman, Samuel Bensusan, James

Wentworth Day and others – were probably the last generation of writers to hold that view in England. But agriculture was now highly transitional. Bell looked from his window in the late 1970s and could see only one ploughman, where the landscape in his youth had been full of horses, men and boys. Only the Black Death in the past had altered the countryside as much as modern farming.[22] Ronald Blythe knew Adrian Bell, having lived very near to him, and one thinks of his comment much later about East Anglian farming: 'what would have been a strange quietness to even our grandparents prevails'.[23] A persistent theme in Bell's farming work and land literature was an effort to link this rather empty present with the past and future in village life, to cast his eyes 'over the whole range of experience for some basis of unity, the germ of a new coherence',[24] for any possible form of community and family life within it.

Bell had a vibrant and original turn of phrase and an approachable, evocative style that could at the same time be succinct, ascetic and poetical. He wanted 'to put into words the way unrelated things came together and formed a relation'.[25] He was a particularly strong interpreter of small episodes and happenings, of moments that will never come again, fondly framing and drawing out their significance, their vitality and often their humour, bringing their details into artistic life. He revealed expansive significance in things that were small and immediate to the senses, expressing the beauty of that which is circumscribed, domestic and locally known. The shine on used tools; the movement of an earwig down the aisle during a church service, near moving boots of parson and sidesmen, as Bell in vesper gentleness prays for its safety;[26] a little spider on the hairy back of his hand; a cobweb hung with dew between post and lintel of the stable door – Adrian Bell had a way of making the everyday seem marvellous and significant. There were echoes of the romantic movement in his ability to find mystery in the ordinary, to take the amply local and discover in it a visionary world and a space of boundless possibilities. He was in a line of localists, which includes writers like Gilbert White, John Clare, Thomas Hardy or Ronald Blythe, and also in some ways an exponent of green culture before his time.[27] The poetry of farm implements, the dance of shadows and light: 'such beauty, the bright-worn, manual workaday beauty of what one used, was the light of life for me'.[28] There was a wide vista in a small physical compass. The minutiae of beauty compensated for the heavy uncouthness of husbandry: the dramatic change in colour in a tiny moth's wings as they caught the light; or the powerful Suffolk Punch hauling a loaded tumbril through heavy land. Adrian Bell's senses were acutely alive to noise, colour, dust, tools, animals and people. 'I was excited again by the dream that there was something in life which I alone knew, which I alone must tell.'[29] Wisdom came from intimately knowing a place, becoming aware of its peculiar essence and quality. Whether he was describing Suffolk or Westmorland (in *Sunrise to Sunset*),[30] his atmospheric language conveyed a vivid sense of landscape, of animal life, of the friendliness of people connected in rural work, and of how these fused to create a spirit of place and community.

When he approached Suffolk for the first time, 'The true friendliness of the scene before me lay beneath ardours of which I knew nothing.'[31] And he stressed this friendliness in his writing, partly because

> times of friendship and vivacity which are our lives (or the ornaments of our lives) stand out disproportionately to their short duration, till they seem to become the measure of our past; while the days of work, eyes to the ground, that go between, are much less easily or coherently recalled. Those are a speechless recollection; they are distilled into an emotion.[32]

Yet for Bell the physical experience of work was fundamental to provide meaning in life, to connect means with ends, and he thought that such physical familiarity was becoming lost.[33] Family farming, which he felt was rich in fundamental relationships and had a natural coherence, became central to his writing. 'My hours were long,' he wrote of his early farming life, 'but I was master of them and did not have to live as a city man, tethered to nine-thirty a.m. like a goat to a tree'.[34]

> I felt as though I could not bear life to be any the less than the aliveness I felt in me when I was first in love. I am always seeking some recognition of it also in other people ... It is only through this that I have been impelled always to try to bring something out of nothing, a poem out of my head, or a potato out of the earth, doing what I wanted to do in my own time and in my own peace, at whatever cost in money and security.[35]

Something from nothing: the phrase appears a number of times in his writing.[36] This was quite a humble man, not prone to overestimate himself, gentle in his written words, shunning ambition, blaming 'the mammon of industrialism that has rotted the old forms',[37] looking for the pole star of a new simplicity. And his attitude to work, whether to farming or to his writing about it, has much to commend it: 'If work doesn't absorb you as a child absorbed in play *don't do it*.'[38] He would cherish a morning's walk over familiar fields looking at the view, seeking the salvation of work that he found calming and clarifying. One is reminded of John Berger on his farm in the French Alps.[39] Reflective, observant and appreciative, Bell was a picker up 'of crumbs of life – shafts of sunlight, faces, words, rain-polished roads' – like a sparrow picking up crumbs.[40] 'Life offers no second chances', so he made the most of what was immediately around him.

The self-contained village community?

In open-field villages of the past, Bell thought, decision-making had been communal, embodying a sense of community and shared endeavour. He contrasted this historical interpretation with the modern village, in which administrative responsibility amounted to nothing much beyond putting a cross on a ballot paper.[41] People should be enabled to control their own affairs by their own administration. 'Today', wrote Bell, 'the whole structure of local communities is breaking up, and groping, perhaps, for a sense of a wider communal unit. Whether anything of value by the standard of human feeling can come of it … is extremely doubtful.'[42] He felt that the countryside home used to feed people, body and spirit and provide them with work and recreation like the warp and woof of a fabric – not departmentalized into work, and hobbies, and entertainment. In addition, in his youth the village shop had practically everything needed locally, beyond what villagers themselves preserved and pickled. A small community could have withstood a long siege by snow. In his early farming years the village talked about itself in such a way that it seemed to expand into a small republic.[43] Bell admired this and found much to respect in it. The nearby and proximate was understood intimately, both socially and in relation to nature. There was a closeness and cohesiveness of communities and an intimacy with their physical surroundings. Wildness and cultivation coexisted in close proximity and variety. The small and intimate could be seen and understood with boundless observation, with the small discerning eye of the writer, alive to the significance of fine detail. There were worlds within worlds.

Yet as he grew older he commented upon how this sagacity of place and shrewdness of vision changed. He noticed a new isolation and alienation between people in rural areas and their distancing from friends, how people living in a place often now had no fundamental part in that place or indeed in any place. Compared to 'the prior culture',[44] a real dispersion of mind was taking place, Bell thought, insulating people from each other in new ways, dispersing their senses elsewhere. Young people had in large numbers moved to the cities. He commented upon the lessening power of the spirit of place brought about by motor transport.[45] The spontaneous aspects of local life were decaying, leaving large numbers of lonely old people. Vividly aware of such changes, which were becoming more apparent in the 1930s, Bell wished to trace the senses of community and locality which made villages different from each other. Trying to avoid nostalgia, he wanted to document what remained of past forms of community life, of earlier forms of seeing and discerning, to judge their value and to sense where 'the budding morrow' was leading.

There was a strong sense of belonging in the Suffolk villages that he wrote about. 'How Suffolk used to suspect the "foreigner"', and that could mean someone from the next county, or even another parish.[46] Over and again, his characters comment about *how* a person belongs, or does not belong. There are many remarks in his novels such as this: 'She did not regard him as being of the village, because, though he had been born in it, his father had not.'[47] In *Silver Ley* Bell wrote about visiting the school and read the roll call, noting that there were only about half a dozen surnames in the whole parish.[48] When Mr Colville (the farmer he was apprenticed to) moved to another farm, a couple of miles away, his elderly mother lamented his departure from the parish of Benfield as though he were going to a foreign land.[49] In some cases, there had been great fixity of persons in one place. Bell knew one elderly woman who had only been off the farm four times in her life.[50] The sense of place was fundamental. Nature itself had also integrated country people in a localized sense of purpose.[51] The older men spoke of past harvests, of those they worked with, of particular crops in distinct fields. Bell commented on how central the village was to many villagers, and how villagers' views were widely shared among themselves. Village opinions were very strong, whether on matters of social life, or about the utility of certain plots of land. The dead were often in conversation, living on there. 'The village is their world: half the people they talk about are dead.'[52]

Adrian Bell often wrote about systems of exchange, commercial socializing, processes of arranging a deal, the extended, circuitous and quick-witted conversations necessary for such matters as buying a horse. Some of this lingers today. These forms of interaction went down to the smallest levels. Villagers operated forms of exchange based on intimate knowledge of each other's resources. The wherewithal of the community was annually and easily assessed. 'It is generally known, for instance, that one man's walnut-tress are laden, another man's plum-trees, another's apples. So-and-So has a surplus of potatoes, and So-and-So is going to salt a pig this autumn.'[53] Money performed a limited function within such a village, being more relevant to outside affairs, markets, seed merchants, dealing with van sellers and the like. Bell commented on how the local wheat and gleanings had hitherto been ground into flour and people ate the bread that was grown in the parish, but he noticed the mills being given up and big firms and their commercial travellers taking business from local people.[54]

Farmers did not go far unless to market or to see a horse or a cow. Yet they almost always now travelled by car, a mode of transport that Bell regretted in many ways. 'How little people walk nowadays, even in the country,' he thought.

> When you say, 'I'm going to –', naming the next village, two miles away, it is taken for granted that you are going by car. The surprise when you set out with a stick on foot is itself surprising. 'What – you are going to *walk!*' It is not only that you should have the inclination, but that you should have the time.[55]

Time, community and transport: these were interactive themes that Bell often thought about. He had become half-conscious of time, without appointments or trains to catch. Hours slowed to the drift of seasons and glided imperceptibly into one another. He observed the fundamental people of village life – the nurse, school-mistress, postman, policeman, the unobtrusive inner structure of a parish – travelling on local roads by bicycle, an emblem of quiet usefulness.[56] But a motor car has no time to have contact with anything. Speed, he thought, is in inverse ratio to true vitality in man, for he is not swift, only his machine is.[57] 'Hours, days, slip away. Driving to me was never anything but an exhausting waste of time.'[58] In driving a trap and horse, he commented on how one stops and talks to people on the way, which could incidentally also lead to farming business. However, competitors now drove cars, and so most people had to work at their pace, to their time, or fall behind. Nevertheless, Bell and his wife Marjorie opted for a pony and trap, and, beyond a concern for time, he described the different senses of space that this induced:

> Driving a pony and trap one's eyes are released from the road-hypnotism of motor travel; one gazes upon the fields and up into the trees. Gardens present themselves like Nature's shop-windows, and domestic moments through open cottage doors. The birds are not frightened from the hedges; paddocked horses look over and greet the stranger ... It is not merely the handling of reins instead of wheel; one slips into another rhythm of life altogether, as different from the mechanical as the regular jog of the trap is from the jumpy repercussions of the car on the roadway. One's radius both contracts and expands. That is to say, while the circumference of miles at one's disposal is halved, their content is more than doubled. For quiet pace is like a magnifying-glass; regions one has before passed over as familiar suddenly enlarge with innumerable new details and become a feast of contemplation ... We found we had been living in an undiscovered country ... One can only take one bite of life, whether one nibble at every land or explore thoroughly a single parish.[59]

Another Suffolk writer, George Ewart Evans, wrote that

> The car can be a great dissipater of local interest. In our first Suffolk village of Blaxhall, the only transport we had as a family was cycles, and this alone was largely responsible for helping to nurse our growing interest in the community ... we got to know the people well, lived close to them and to a great extent shared their hopes and their disappointments ... We became associated with the people of Blaxhall in a way that lasted.[60]

Bell would have agreed. Told that he would lose much time getting around by pony and trap, he asked how time could be lost when it was enjoyed. An American, he reported, said to a stranger 'from the Orient', 'Let's go by the new subway – it saves a whole minute'; to which the stranger replied: 'And what shall we then do with the minute?'[61]

The 'agricultural community'

One can sense much about Adrian Bell's understanding of community from his accounts of time, space and travel. In addition, there was his idea of 'the agricultural community', a shared endeavour of people, commercially linked, often variously related as kin, seeing themselves at auctions and other events, aware of themselves as engaged in Suffolk farming. In a sense this was an 'imagined community',[62] going well beyond the parish, for its members could never all know each other. Outsiders to this widely defined occupational community were not much discussed in Bell's early work, partly because so many people (farmers, landowners, tradesmen, craftsmen and labourers) were in effect part of it. His pride in belonging to such a community as a farmer was often evident. Take, for example, his account of the purchase of his two horses:

> I bought Darky and Dewdrop for forty-seven and forty-five guineas respectively. The auctioneer remembered my name from the things I had bought earlier in the sale. 'Mr Bell, isn't it? Yes.' It was a recognition of me as a member of the agricultural community, a farmer; no longer a youth looking at farming. Had I not received a circular that morning addressed to Mr Bell, Farmer, Benfield St George?[63]

This concept of farming community overarched localized senses of the parish or village, though parish business and related administrative matters were often mentioned. Such local spaces were endlessly varied examples of the wider farming community, expressed via farms within each village. Class is significant in Bell's writing, and he shows awareness of his own class and what that meant, yet it is a relatively weak concept. Farm people work together even though the men call the farmer 'master'. They share skills and mutual respect, assertively speak their minds and Bell prided himself on recognition or praise from workmen as well as richer farmers. Bell writes as though the labouring class were members of that farming community. There is nothing in his work to imply otherwise. The extreme labouring poverty and hardship described by earlier East Anglian writers, such as Mary Mann,[64] is largely absent in Adrian Bell, even though he wrote movingly about tramps coming into town to enter the workhouse during the Great Slump, like stragglers of a defeated army, looking into the gutters, walking stiffly as though the windows were jeering.[65] In such respects, his writing is less class conscious than some of its regional predecessors, and less so when compared to that of other contemporary rural authors like A. G. Street, whose equivalent use of the term 'farming community' implied a more elite entity: 'the farming community always had resented and always would resent any interloper from a lower social class'.[66]

The pattern of community life created its own effects in the land, manifest within a village, which were regular like the shapes of nature, caused for example by the passage of loaded carts and humans carrying goods.[67] Movements seemed to become automatic, leaving their traces, like those around a nettle patch, the ducking to avoid a sagging eave, the lifting of a door to open it. Or there were the habitual movements of people in a church, the wear on everyday places, the circuitry of the parish, the little marks that bore witness to that circuitry.[68] These had grown unplanned into beauty, which in Bell is a concept that often substitutes for ideas of practical functionality. Beauty comes from what is organic, historic, the end result of phases of trial and error, careful attempts and reconciled utilities. One is reminded of the links between art and nature in H. J. Massingham's writing. Planning, at whatever level, was often a poor substitute, for it did not grow innate and historically from within a working environment and accompanying life. This sensibility and viewpoint was part of Bell's conservatism. There is no language in Bell of the 'symbolic construction' of community, of boundaries and their meanings, nor apparent influence from wider sociological theorizing about community.[69] His thinking was too tactile, workaday, experiential and sensitively applied for that. His descriptions are direct, original, uncensored in their poetry and nothing is fitted to preconceived notions. The contrast between an academic sociology and anthropology that some think with now, and what and how Bell wrote is part of his appeal today, for his subtle intelligence was persistently probing for social and human meanings, and he did so as a deeply involved working person on a farm, in a village. Bell noticed the patterns of commonplace ritual; he saw them and their effects as things of beauty. With his eye for small detail coupled with an aptitude for generalizations, he thought about their wider significance. What interrupted these patterns, how did they change and what were such changes symptomatic of? What did they suggest about the direction of rural and local society, and the fate of the agricultural community? What potential was there for human fulfilment and happiness within current and likely shifts of society? What personal experiential losses were occurring: for Bell's poetic writing was elegiac in search of beauty; his purpose was to show it, to record his sensations of it and to disclose what framed it. A wider academic rural sociology is concerned with comparative schemes of change, with model building, with using the local to generalize from. Bell by contrast often used the localized experience of broader change to particularize from, to show how change affected the character of things that were often sensate, aesthetic, detailed and increasingly family centred.

Bell's portrayal of community did not lack appreciation of the often lively and interconnected nature of village life. He brought up three children through a succession of villages, and he was evidently very absorbed and participatory in their communities. His early account in *Corduroy* of farmer Colville (the farmer Victor Savage) and his kin networks is a fascinating portrait of how kin linked together across Suffolk villages in the early twentieth century. It involved a weekly gathering of the clan, quite a dynastic crowd of people. Three daughters had married three brothers. 'I never came to the end of the Colville family during the years I knew them.'[70] A death affected the whole village, he wrote in one of his stories, for there were so many relatives by marriage.[71] Or there were his accounts of the local forge as a meeting place second only to the inn, which recalls descriptions in George Ewart Evans. The banter of people at work, the bell-ringers perambulating the parish on Boxing Day and being invited in for drinks, the close interpersonal knowledge, the seasonal nature of sociability in an arable area, with each farmer seeing little of his friends during the harvest period – Bell's Suffolk countryside was convivial and rapidly communicative, even though comprising separated farms. 'The way news travels in the country is almost telepathic.'[72] The village of his farm apprenticeship contained the sounds of an occupational community: the rattle of chains as the horses are unhitched and led away, the voices of men, the clatter of wood as a block is kicked under a wheel, the music of steel on steel as forks are laid together.

This Suffolk farm and its social life were restorative to Bell after London's narrow sky and its apparently middle-class 'world of nervous significance': 'where the very furniture was a complex language'. He had escaped from bright electric bulbs in lotus-shaped shades, from cocktails and salted almonds in red saucers with white spots – and allied talk: 'like a workman's handkerchief – such fun' – from omelettes at their 'moments of perfection', from 'a world of hurtful probing into personality'. As he saw it, he was free from a baroque grimy-aired London arena that was 'flat and unrooted, with people gesturing and smiling as in a charade'.[73]

By comparison, Bell wrote evocatively of rural social gatherings, recording fragments of humour and expression, garnering glimpses of movement, subtle but significant gesture and sexual allure. His accounts of Suffolk agricultural shows – 'a city of pavilions pitched among the trees'[74] – or of markets, or hunt gatherings, occur frequently and in a style of writing that is interactive with community, gregarious and interested in people. Those people were themselves engrossed in work, within a mutually understanding community. Bell described the social life of markets, the forms of riposte and bargaining,[75] the accosting of farmers like Mr Colville every few yards by somebody there, the confidential remarks about bullocks – 'Tails well set up, and good wide backsides on 'em. Now, these are a nice lot' – or other more personal matters: 'A good wife is a great thing, young man, you take my word.'[76] It appeared to Bell that the cattle market and the Corn Exchange were the twin lungs of agriculture in the district and of all civilization. Yet this was not a simple world that contrasted with the human inscrutability of London. For, as evening falls,

> the flares are lit along the stalls and the flames leap fanatically and search the darkness, making the shadows of people dance upon the canvas backgrounds. They add a touch of the barbaric, for their light is the light of torches flowing with the wind. The stalls become islands of light into which people are born out of the night; in the glow their faces have the over-expressiveness of masks. Everywhere trembles the fingering of fire.[77]

This is a vibrant community, yet people seem to wear masks. Urban masks and rural masks: if the city performed nervous cocktailed charades, the rural was also complex, expressive and exuberant. With further echoes of Thomas Hardy as a fiddler of the reels, Bell also wrote about the sweaty abandon and energy of the village hop or dance, now placed amid the material culture of the interwar period.[78] Or there were his descriptions of the collective fervour of the laughing, chattering throng of the fox hunt, with bright coats and gleaming leather and steel – the 'countryside rang with the pandemonium of people hallooing'.[79] Fox hunting on Boxing

Day was also a day of duty for the gentry and entertainment for many people, a parade, a fanfare of old elegance, in which the hunting men and women were 'merely pageant players'.[80] Masks, pageants: this writing was almost a poetical non-academic anthropology, comparing the country and the city.[81]

Intrinsic to Bell's understanding of an occupational community was local tradition, an established way of doing things, speaking, conducting business, relating to others and the accompanied rituals. These united Suffolk parishes in a shared mentality, such that Bell could live in a number of villages and yet never feel that he had lost his community interest. Much of his writing documents the decline of that community with its culture of language and skill, and its segregation into smaller profiles of people who no longer shared occupational interests. This was also described in the Suffolk work of the Welsh writer George Ewart Evans. Alive to spoken language, Evans directed readers to Adrian Bell's welcome of rural speech as a revelation, as when one of the farm men directed Bell: 'You lead that mare as slowly as ever foot can fall', a terminology that Evans found in Shakespeare.[82] With the decline of such spoken and used tradition, and in the narrowing of the 'agricultural community' and its range of reference and gossipy converse, it seems that community increasingly fell in upon itself and became more restricted to the conjugal family and its narrow surrounds. Certainly the family was a growing focus in Bell's writing, from which vantage point he looked out to survey changing social and economic life. As with a writer like H. E. Bates (considered in the next chapter), this is a sequence that appears in Bell's publications: from occupational community to conjugal family existing in virtually a community-free or exonerated space.[83] It is discernible in the overall direction of his writings, and in the way their focus subtly changes over time. This was no doubt partly explainable by his own life cycle events, and partly by a real narrowing of the occupational community in Suffolk villages during his lifetime, and a sense among many better off or proud people that the human relations and mutual assistance of community were unnecessary and disposable. There is, for example, little in Bell about reciprocal borrowing of goods or exchanged labour, especially after his very earliest writing.[84] By 1956 his tone had changed from its hitherto more open community emphases, which were seemingly no longer needed or heeded: 'Thus we are as neighbourly as can be, without having to divulge one single fact about our personal affairs if we do not want to. We remain what we insular English essentially are – little islands insulated by a surf of chit-chat.'[85] One wonders if this was that different from the London he had earlier criticized.

Senses of farming and community decline

Bell commented in *The Cherry Tree* about two worn pennies with Queen Victoria fading away like a ghost on them.[86] Although he does not say so, we might think here of the spirit of past communities rubbing away in reoriented commercial exchange, accounting for so much community change in this capitalistic society. Some of the markets themselves had died, leaving empty public spaces, in which it then seemed apposite to place war memorials. For the shadows of the First World War fell everywhere: 'It was so often "Poor so-and-so" and "Poor So-and-So."'[87] The Victorian countryside with its well-populated villages was becoming redundant, though many workers remained on low pay, some living in squalid and impoverished conditions. Many cottages and farmhouses were derelict or condemned.[88] 'How desolate this once populous corner seemed to have grown,' Bell wrote of his Suffolk apprenticeship parish, and he thought that hard times caused 'the break-up of that community'.[89] The agricultural depression coupled with death duties and other forms of taxation left many older estates moribund, and their great houses were often deserted. Bell and his wife Marjorie walked to an empty manor house where the great wrought iron gates were locked. The manor looked like a blind shell. Its hedges were growing into a fortress. The old lodge-keeper was delighted to see someone. They passed over a grass-matted bridge and the old windows overlooking the area 'oppressed me with their blankness. For curtained, inhabited windows do not stare at one so hungrily – they are like eyes that signal of the life within; but when there is none, but echoing emptiness only, their look is like that of death – or madness; like the eyes of our guide that had nothing but waiting in them.'[90] The account could be replicated for many once great houses and estates in the interwar period, given their continuing decline then.

These were depressed times in many ways, 'a time unparalleled – even the old men admitted as much, which was an unheard-of concession'.[91] Farmers had often purchased their farms after the First World War, sometimes being virtually forced to do so: 'It was buy or quit', and they often bought them just before the 1921 repeal of the 1917–20 Corn Production Acts, which had guaranteed a good price for wheat and oats.[92] Many farmers suffered with adverse seasons, falling prices, large bills for dilapidations if they were tenants and labourers' defence of wages, as in the 1923 Norfolk agricultural strike.[93] Bankruptcies and indebtedness among farmers rose in 1920–23 as mortgage payments were often too high relative to income and prices of produce. Such difficulties became even more evident in 1929–33, although the rural economy recovered to some extent in 1935–39 as prices rose relative to costs. Numerous farmers adjusted to economic realities by going into dairying, vegetables or fruit, and often did well; but corn growers in Norfolk and Suffolk were among the least successful, partly because of their reluctance to lose 'caste' by diversifying into 'cow-keeping'. Many of the farmers Bell knew were swept away 'into humble corners', like a farmer Bell talked to who had failed in Wiltshire. 'It was a West Country version of our Suffolk one … Their experience and wisdom profited them nothing.'[94]

> One finds farmers who circumstances have mastered. Silent, slow-moving, numb, their yards empty, and a semi-automatic remnant of seasonal activity going on in the foul fields. The end is not far. Foreclosure: a sale. A sort of death: as real as the death of the body. A farmer, who has farmed all his life – out of a farm, what is he? Time has lost its rhythm for him: it is mere duration.[95]

Bell wrote of another farmer being 'wound up' who no longer felt that he could call anything his own:

> It dazed and rather awed him, this absolute power of the community to seize, under certain circumstances, his more private belongings. As for those goods, 'It's nothing but a lot of rubbish', said one man to another indignantly, 'a waste of time to have come all this way for' … Joe had already heard enough, and slouched off indoors. There he sat with his wife before the kitchen fire all through the sale.[96]

There was much that was melancholy in Bell's descriptions of the interwar Suffolk countryside, even though he wrote as a young man. Labour was reduced to a minimum. Fields often reverted to grass as the least labour-intensive option, overgrown hedges predominated and in many cases labourers were sacked, a few stockmen aside. Bell had a relatively small farm and was not a significant employer of labour. But of labouring men it was said that 'There's nothing to pay them with – you can't get blood out of a stone.'[97] The dole days in local towns experienced as much traffic as market days. 'They wore a look, those men, which reminded one sharply of the war. One saw it *en masse* in the faces and attitudes of soldiers about to return to the front. It was the expression of those who have nothing to live for.'[98] There were 'off-hand' farms, their houses uninhabited, or other farms that no longer had any house standing. Elderly people pointed out places where houses had stood.[99] Large trees had fallen down, and simply lay there, their timber unused for any purpose. The mills were out of action and had become private houses. The solitude of farming became ever more marked, and as winter afternoons drew towards twilight it was only the sound of animals that relieved this. 'Lonely?' – Bell began a chapter with the word, pitched as a question that many farmers asked, as he reflected on whether this was what he felt on his farm, where he was 'a half-conscious companion to myself'.[100]

Between the wars and after 1945 the agricultural shows continued, well attended and lively, displaying a progression of new technologies that Bell welcomed. There were more compact tractors, sugar beet lifters, toppers and cleaners, cabbage planters, all of them designed to conquer at last the burden of farming labour. That had so often in the past been unremitting and animal-like,[101] even if it had been more collective. Mechanization in many ways weakened traditional communal activities that had underpinned ideas of community. Bell felt that such technical development no longer tallied with the life of the countryside as he understood it. The same applied to the people. Something had been lost, or was fast declining: an older 'way of standing, a way of looking, a way of talking, that expressed a mind not smooth-shaved, and a keenness that was instinctive, which determined the outlook of the English farmer'.[102] Scientific industrialized farming – the chemical-fertilizer firms, the mechanized dairies and broiler houses, so many hedge-less and treeless fields – had come rapidly, especially during and after the war. Bell thought that it had done so at the expense of 'traditional' instincts and energies, of high-farming knowledge, hand skills and ways of relating to nature. Those earlier attitudes had imparted energies and identities. Work on a farm, he felt, is not just a thing someone does, it is what you are. 'To span the gulf between the piston and the sprouting wheat – you need a pretty powerful spark of inspired sanity to flash across that gap.'[103] As he put it in *The Budding Morrow*, 'At present we have the dynamo, but we have lost our own dynamic. The dynamic of a spiritual power which was generated for former men by church and barn, as they struggled with matter. Is it a law of our nature that when the sense of struggle is mitigated, the dynamic should degenerate?'[104]

He was keen to appreciate and use both old and new, though there is negligible religious or church content in his writing. And there is little doubt in retrospect about the vibrancy of much of the new, as advertisements and an active market for farm machinery attested. Many modernizing farmers needed to retain a deep understanding of their soils and land to apply new machinery effectively. Yet Bell was wary of modern large-scale industrial farming, and other accompanying developments such as 'gimcrack bungalows'. Like Samuel Bensusan and James Wentworth Day, he disliked the 'vulgarizing or suburbanizing' bungalows of the countryside.[105] Nor did he wish to become a complex farm switchboard operator. The engineer needed to come closer to the poet, and the poet to the engineer. Bell believed in hands-on farming, muscular exertion and tiredness, a Tolstoyan attitude to landed work in rural Suffolk, the preservation of craft and hand skills esteemed by the community. 'For labour, I feel, is the key to satisfying life, the soother of worry, preparing one also for the appreciation of food and rest.'[106] Yet he would always defiantly add the poetry to farming, searching for an imaginative and contented quality of life. The need was to take modern advances and 'make something of it that is calm and sane; happy, lovely: convert it to the service of posterity, family and home', as he felt was being achieved in Scandinavia.[107] Viewing modern engineering in an agricultural show, Bell turned with relief to the horse-shoeing competition, as a remnant of the farming past that he could appreciate, for it embodied human energies and instinct at a primary creative level. 'They are still hammering away as though life depended on it. Perhaps it does.'[108]

Civilization, he felt, was becoming a superimposed structure out of context, like bottled milk in a shop window. 'There are surviving humanities enough, thank heaven, in country places.' Yet familiarity with the intrinsic qualities of materials, which had been the secret of older craftsmen's zeal and skill, was increasingly rare, though perhaps it also extended to some scientists. Water and heat were becoming automatic, taken-for-granted. And this all connected with an idea of community as something material as well as social. There may still have been a sense of community locally, but those who experienced it appeared to be 'a world apart'; they were survivals, rare in their ability to experience primary production and the human relationships that encompass that. People had become, in so many cases, mere consumers, realizing life shallowly and transiently.[109] They had mislaid a sense of what is real. They had an aversion to looking into material creativity, and in this lay 'the unsatisfactoriness of life for the individual to-day'. The loss of direct creative skills and familiarity with natural materials, and the interaction of people with those skills,[110] was to Bell an important feature of community life that was being forfeited. 'There grows daily in the air about us a feeling that the survivors of our system will one day have to start to carve out life again in small communities.'[111] 'Carve out life' – one notices again the verb of physical action and the creativity involved.

As a man who described himself as 'a peasant at heart',[112] Bell was sadly aware of the ways in which a younger generation was moving away from the land and its earlier skills. Everywhere people were leaving, including farmers, feeling that there was no living in it any more. It is probably symptomatic that there is very little in Bell's writing about rural education or about the future of the young in the countryside.[113] Compared, for example, with Rolf Gardiner, James Wentworth Day or George Ewart Evans, he suggested almost no public programme of reform, education or renovation. He extolled a way of private living, a certain kind of engagement with the countryside, an escape from unreal pretentious urbanity and then a retreat into family. This was doubtfully political in conventional senses. May Day for him had rural and customary meaning, and he was sorry that its significance had 'dwindled' to 'class-war processions in the cities'.[114] He steered clear of the politics of men like Rolf Gardiner or Henry Williamson, and insofar as he was political this amounted to a conservative localism. After the 'vast seething sediment' of the Second World War settles, he thought with some prescience, Europe will become 'a Europe of Europeans. The English, however, are different. The longer and farther they are away, the more tenaciously they cling to the familiar hill, valley or street.'[115] The localism in Bell, while it was instinctive, appreciative and poetical, was also commended partly as a way of escaping wider conflict, deflecting patriotism away from nationalism to localism. It was not escapism for its own end. 'If we cannot learn to keep the peace in Europe, we must disperse our power into parish units.'[116] Attachment to home had permanent value in the future, and it was a shame that it had not hitherto influenced people more. 'I sometimes doubt whether the explorers should be history's heroes. If everybody had stayed at home and minded their own business, the world might have been less vexed by racial problems.'[117] Many ex-colonies of the British Empire would no doubt agree.

Unlike a much more emphatic writer like James Wentworth Day, there is negligible mention of international affairs in Bell's writing. 'Crises between nations, threats of destruction, hopes of reaching the moon' – he preferred to think of the parish's fields, ploughing, the village inn, his local place.[118] 'Perhaps I am simple, but a man with a handbarrow passing in the street is of more interest to me than a reported riot in Bombay.'[119] There was much that irritated him: form filling and bureaucracy, representatives of the Government, the will of the city being imposed upon farmers. 'Humanity evaporates on official stationery.'[120] Bell regarded rural district planning as often inimical to community, local belonging and people's senses of security in their homes and land. Community should be made from within.[121] He could resent the lack of local knowledge shown by planners. And he was disturbed by modern scientific structures on the landscape (pylons, power stations or radar installations) about which 'ordinary people' knew nothing, and over which local communities had no control.[122] He was inclined to believe that civilization, instead of increasing human contentedness, merely enlarges the possibilities of discontents.[123]

Yet little by way of a policy agenda appears in his watchful writing, either before or after the war: no remedy for the historical changes and senses of loss that he expressed, beyond an insular sense of what an individual could achieve for himself or herself. One is reminded of the tone of resignation in Thomas Hardy. One can appreciate Bell as an elegiac writer, and see what he extolled as a source of personal happiness, yet one may put down his books with little wider prescriptive sense of what they suggest in policy or communitarian terms today. There was perhaps inevitability about the changes in the countryside, determined as they were by factors like international trade and prices, technological advance, the food supply issues of the Second World War and urbanization. The East Anglian localities that Bell knew were not immune to history in any sense. They were subject to it, the state-promoted second agricultural revolution after the 1930s transforming them: ripping out their hedges, ploughing footpaths out of memory and legality, saturating the countryside with DDT and annihilating wildlife with a sickening indifference to small lives. One writer, however popular, could do little in the face of this.

The rural trades were also in decline, even that of thatching, and like many such vicissitudes Bell resigned himself to this. In his nearby small Suffolk town, the wheelwright was elderly, among the last of his trade, just as other writers described.[124] When this craftsman died, the thin procession of mourners comprised old men with dented trousers, openly flapping frock coats, whose beards rested on their chests as they walked with lowered heads, men who were near the grave themselves. One could imagine them in a Stanley Spencer painting. And as they walked, 'the sunlight flaunting in the square seemed to mock their sombre clothes … Death had thrust its spoke into the wheel of life.'[125] Nobody carried on the wheelwright's business. Earlier, two boys on bicycles had gone past the wheelwright as he was taking an iron tyre from the fire and fitting it to a wheel, with smoke and bursts of flame shooting up around the wheel, which was then watered to shrink it to size. One of the boys slowed down to watch; 'the other, bespectacled, knowing, cries, "Come *on* – that's nothing".'[126]

Adrian Bell fulfilled 'the dream that there was something in life which I alone knew, which I alone must tell': the passing of an older rural community and material way of life, through his land writing in the villages and lanes of rural Suffolk.[127] And as that life expires further into the dream world which is history, it is worth remembering the predictions of a gypsy woman to him much earlier in his career, recalled in one of his characteristic passages of pure brilliance:

> Many flaps and curtains seemed to close behind me as I entered, till the fair even grew faint, and I sat in a hot thrumming privacy with the gypsy who wore a paper flower, and red piping on her boots. She had hooded herself with a dark veil. I laid my hand, as she commanded, palm

uppermost upon the velvet-covered table, and she traced the many little lines of it, and composed on them until they became roads through a savage land, dangerously intersected, alluringly vagrant. To think that all my fortune lay in that little declivity! And there my life-line ran over the brink into nothingness, running away like water even as one tries to catch it to the lips.[128]

9

Community Individualized

From H. E. Bates's Cobbled Gloom to the Darling Buds of May

Go with the stream, never battle against it.[1]

If I claim nothing else for myself as a writer I will not deny myself versatility.[2]

Henry Bates was born in 1905 in Rushden (Northamptonshire), educated in nearby Kettering and published his first book, *The Two Sisters*, in 1926. Thereafter, he gained a wide reputation for his stories about English rural life. During the interwar years his output included *The Fallow Land* (1932), *The Poacher* (1935), *A House of Women* (1936) and *Spella Ho* (1938), which were largely set in his native Northamptonshire. He also established himself as a master of the short story or novella genre. Those stories often eschewed plots and represented episodic pictures, cross-cut through experiences, capturing fine details, significances, mood and personality in everyday life. He thought the short story 'the most fascinating of all prose forms … perfectly suited to the expression and mood of this age … of unrest, disbelief and distrust'.[3] Its appeal to him lay in the fact that it could be more concentrated, pictorial and visionary than the novel.[4] As a male writer of that time, he was remarkable in his sympathetic efforts to depict women's points of view and experiences. He moved to the village of Little Chart in Kent in 1931, converting an old granary into a home,[5] accompanied by his wife Madge Cox and in due course four children, seemingly glad to escape the boot-and-shoe towns of his home county, although he remained attached to Higham Ferrers and its surrounding countryside. *My Uncle Silas* (a collection of short stories based on his relative Joseph Betts) appeared in 1939, and he returned to this popular character in some later work.

During the Second World War, he was drafted into the RAF as a non-flying officer/author, enjoying remarkable freedom under the auspices of RAF Public Relations, his brief being to write stories on air warfare. He did this under the pseudonym of Flying Officer 'X'. His conversations and experiences with fighter pilots and Stirling bomber crews over this period produced publications such as *The Greatest People in the World, and Other Stories* (1942), *How Sleep the Brave, and Other Stories* (1943), *Fair Stood the Wind for France* (1944) and *The Stories of Flying Officer 'X'* (1952). Other stories and novels such as *The Purple Plain* (1947) and *The Jacaranda Tree* (1949) were based upon short experience in India and Burma at the end of the war, where he was sent by RAF Public Relations.[6] The wartime themes continued in later writing, as for example with his evocation of the Battle of Britain and its pilots in *A Moment in Time* (1964). Yet after the war he is best known for further writing on rural England, usually on Northamptonshire or Kent, sometimes still set back in the interwar period, such as *Love for Lydia* (1952) or *The Sleepless Moon* (1956). There were also his much more optimistic and up-beat stories featuring the Larkin family, such as *The Darling Buds of May* (1958), *A Breath of French Air* (1959), *When the Green Woods Laugh* (1960) and *Oh! To Be in England* (1963), which were largely set in Kent. Another strand of writing could be classed as nature writing, such as *Through the Woods* (1936) and *Down the River* (1937).

A highly readable three-volume autobiography was published between 1969 and 1972, shortly before his death in 1974.[7] Bibliographical work is still under way to trace all his enormous literary output, but he wrote about 126 major works, at least 323 short stories and novellas and a couple of hundred essays, articles, commentaries and introductions. He also wrote a limited amount of poetry, but confessed later that 'I never reckon I understand the mechanics of verse-making very well.'[8] Bates struggled for some years to make a living from his writing, being well aware of 'our extremely uncertain profession', as he put it to another author.[9] Yet he was immensely popular during much of his lifetime, and he was extolled by authors as diverse as D. H. Lawrence, W. Somerset Maugham, Henry Miller and Graham Greene. The latter referred to him as Britain's successor to Chekhov, and he has also frequently been compared with Turgenev and Guy de Maupassant. One reviewer in 1988 extolled 'his exuberant power of physicality, of evoking settings with delicate intensity', adding that he has 'a capacity for imaginative sympathy that is almost miraculous.'[10] Recent discussion by Dominic Head sees him as quite radical and groundbreaking, a writer in whose work 'ideas of belonging and the needs of subsistence are seen repeatedly to be at odds', which will 'give him a new currency'.[11] As Dean Baldwin commented, 'it is surprising that he is not better known or more highly regarded among academic critics or historians'.[12] Bates's work has been widely adapted into film and television serialization, especially after his death in 1974, and it is probably through such films that he is most appreciated today.[13]

He was, without doubt, one of the most significant twentieth-century English rural writers, perhaps eclipsed in some estimations only by the Powys brothers and D. H. Lawrence. Many of his plots have echoes of Hardy's novels – compare *The Feast of July* with *Tess of the d'Urbervilles* – even though he distanced himself from the allusive complexity and symbolism of Hardy's discursive prose styles: learning 'the near-fatal lesson of Hardy', and thereafter 'getting more atmosphere into ten words than Hardy ... and his kind could often get into a page'.[14] Bates prided himself on an economy of style, which is notable in his short stories. Thackeray's dictum that 'the work of fiction contains more truth in solution than the work which purports to be all true' was one that Bates agreed with and wished to put into practice.[15] He shared the focus upon individuals and their contexts found in W. Somerset Maugham. But his writing had more social and gendered breadth, more sense of community or its absences, and much more appreciation of women's feelings – one early publisher reading a manuscript thought that this author (signing as H. E. Bates) must be a woman and replied 'Dear Miss Bates'.[16] Dennis Vannatta wrote that

> Bates's contribution is distinctive because it is sociological and historical as well as literary. Like Joyce, Lawrence, Faulkner, and Hardy in an earlier time, Bates captured the heart and soul of a locale and its people. Bates's Yoknapatawpha County was the English Midlands; and his novels, novellas, and short stories of life there ... comprise a rich, colorful, living tapestry.[17]

His authorship is especially notable in covering a period of such intense change for the countryside, from 1925 till 1974.

My interest here is in his changing depictions of rural and small-town community life, from the occupational communities of farming and boot-and-shoe producing eastern Northamptonshire, through the Second World War, to his more bucolic and usually family-centred stories set in the post-war countryside. For his writing shows a fundamental shift in focus, perhaps hinted at in the titles of his autobiographies, which has wider significance: from fiction set in often struggling occupational communities that were already experiencing marked decline – being among the last literary representations they received – to tales of fighter or bomber squadron *camaraderie* and intense senses of engaged community during the war, to stories extolling a bucolic and somewhat extended family life in which 'community' as hitherto represented was largely absent and perhaps unneeded. 'Go with the stream', wrote Bates, 'never battle against it'.[18] It is time to assess this long literary career and to point out that its versatile shifts of emphasis represent changes that have wider historical significance. They are emblematic of transformed meanings, purposes and representations of community, discussed throughout this book, and as such Bates is a fitting conclusion for my main chapters.

Themes, mood and detail

One of the clearest statements of literary purpose by Bates is in an unpublished letter to his close friend Joe Braddock. He was advising Braddock about a 60,000-word manuscript which that author had given him for comment. Bates wrote that:

> I miss the essence of fiction – the creation of fictitious characters outside the author himself, their creation so that I am interested in them, believe in them & become entertained or moved by them … The novel is no place for opinions. The reader can't wait while you deliver a homily on Keats. It simply can't be done … It isn't *fictitious* enough … you write like a painter, which is as it ought to be. The colour on the page is firm and delicate. You can smell the countryside … you're a poet & shouldn't be writing novels … Any writer needs to get a quarter of million words off his chest now & then just for the sake of hearing something. If I had anything to do with your salvation as a writer I'd send you out … & make you write something about the first person you saw. I'd make you *project* yourself into the lives of outside people, & all the time write & write & write. If you're to be a writer of fiction, Joe, you must do it. It's people, people all the time, & you're the worm that must nose under their skin & eat into their minds & suck their blood & find out what they are & what they're made of. I hope this isn't preaching. It isn't meant to be. It's just my honest feelings about the whole business.[19]

His interest in people could hardly be more firmly expressed. It comes also in the final words of his 'The Writer Explains' (his introduction to *Country Tales*), where he stressed his 'passionate interest in human lives'.[20] As he commented on the work of the American writer, Katherine Anne Porter, 'This girl can create aristocrats or farm-hands at will, & so should any novelist, more or less'.[21] It is this sensitive interest in people, linked to his capture of *mood* through accompanying detail, that makes him intriguing. The meaning of detail is paramount in Bates. He even criticized his work by saying that 'in the early stories … I showed a dangerous appetite for sucking the significance out of trivialities – dangerous because it came to me so easily and naturally that it threatened to become a habit'.[22] He felt then that this limited his scope as a writer and constrained his development of literary characters.

These personal and social priorities were coupled with contrasts in sensitivity between characters, alert judgements of beauty and an ability to visualize like a painter, which have led some to comment on 'the pictorial simplicity' of his prose, on his 'prose-pictures'.[23] We have seen him comment above on how Joe Braddock wrote 'like a painter, which is as it ought to be. The colour …is firm and delicate.' So often people's judgements of others tell one more about themselves. Bates would often seem like a poet writing lyrical novels. It was rightly said in an obituary that 'he wrote with a precise felicity … [as] a prose poet'.[24] He commented in one of his letters about his *The Flying Goat* (1939) that 'It's true that there is a return to lyricism & tenderness in it.'[25] This was a man striving to escape ugliness, an intricate and subtle watercolourist of exceptional personal empathy.

Prominent among his themes are the meaning of love, the milieux in which it might flourish, what happens when it is rebuffed or never experienced, and the related issues of personal isolation and community. The contexts for much of his writing were the countryside and the boot-and-shoe towns of Northamptonshire, and the developing edges between them: the edges of the poacher,[26] the property speculator and the garage mechanic. The urban for Bates is constantly intruding upon the rural, which is often semi-rural as a result.[27] In Bates the accounts of this land and its small-town societies are needed as constraining fields and walls for the interplay of affections and the exploration of relationships. His frequent bleak imagery of this countryside reciprocates the partial or unfulfilled relationships that so often occur in his writing on the interwar years. He was then the novelist of unreciprocated affections, of love offered yet unreturned and of missed fulfilment. 'Women wilted, like flowers, from lack of attentive nourishment.'[28] Their bicycles have slow punctures.[29] His characters hope for stability and permanence, but usually fail to find it. They offer or receive the emotional security of night-time lorry drivers, caravan dwellers, drunken huntsmen[30] or itinerant salesmen. All too frequently they regard each other like indifferent or opportunistic strangers in greasy cafés. This is a land of emotionally thwarted domestic servants and ruthlessly calculative, miserly small farmers. Indeed, the two often connect.

If one were to pick a characteristic season for Bates, when he writes on interwar Northamptonshire, it would be the late autumn or winter. Many of his characters seem to fit that prospect-less and hollow season, for they are frequently hardened, insensitive, callous, romantically deprived and niggardly in what they offer others. This is markedly apparent in works like *The Sleepless Moon* – that bleak novel of shallow lower-middle-class life and marital disappointment, where the purchase of a gramophone by a man for his wife is a substitute for a sex life. Such characterization is present also in the ironically named *Dulcima*, or in many of Bates's short stories.[31] If there *is* a community out there, it seems to bring little hope or fulfilment to such people, who are so ill-suited for human warmth and affection, or whose hopes for love flounder in the meanness of their lives.

Allied to this one finds in Bates's interwar work a recurrent imagery that brings to mind the moods of some of G. K. Chesterton's writing – 'the sadness of things out of their time'[32] – of pathways to old decaying houses, dark roads, slushy mud, cold ice-skaters and winter weather. These are seasons that induce rheumatic fever or slow declines into tuberculosis. An accompanying theme, appropriately, is that of hopeful escape: from these south midland 'communities' and their squabbling boot-and-shoe towns, from 'maungy' chapel deacons and their miserable Methodism – and so to London, to the war, or further afield to the Alps, Yugoslavia, the Far East, to the Pacific Islands. Most of these were settings of other writing by him. This was Bates's own biographical trajectory, one that he relished,[33] and it is followed by many other characters within his fiction. As Bates wrote of one character who becomes a mountain climber: 'he graduated from what is sometimes called a centrist. His world enlarged.'[34] This writing of escape seems a corollary of what I discuss below.

The urban 'occupational community'

Bates was brought up in Rushden in Northamptonshire, a county strongly associated (alongside Leicestershire) with the boot-and-shoe trade. This was 'a town built around a single industry'.[35] His work probably includes the best representations in fiction of that trade and its working communities, its structures and the people associated with it. The trade was partially a 'putting-out' one, which in his lifetime combined small factory or warehouse work with the putting-out of many work processes to operatives in their own homes or ancillary domestic workshops. Small factories were often located between rows of terraced houses. Such a nineteenth-century structure survived well into the twentieth century, and its environments were an occupational community in the sense that there was closely interlinked participation in the trade. The class differences, roles of women and children, seasonal work, housing, workshops, interwar hardships and related issues were a focus for important fiction by Bates, and his writing described the nature of such an occupational community. The industry later changed radically, being liable to many closures and takeovers after 1945. There was rationalization of production and increased mechanization of all processes – many of which previously took place in home workshops, such as cutting, tacking, sewing and stitching – and changes in materials away from leather, which resulted in the loss of many footwear jobs.[36]

As Bates described it in his *Autobiography* or *The Feast of July*, this was an intimately experienced urban 'community', in which the knowledge people had about each other was seemingly almost complete.[37] His fictional accounts tend to focus upon one family, but showed its ingestion within an entire industrial system of out-work. The core meaning of community here pertained to the boot-and-shoe industry, and this industry and its networks created senses of space.[38] The environment was permeated with the smell and sounds of boot-and-shoe manufacture: the acrid greasy-sharp smoke of burning leather, the workshops with 'their rolls of kip and calf and belly-leather and the untidy mess of tins and sprigs and eyelets and brass-tacks and wax-end',[39] the smell of glue-pots, the tapping and hammering sounds of the workers – and also the significance of silence. Normally, 'In a town like Evensford everybody was rigidly governed by factory hours and the sound of factory hooters.'[40] There were the 'long columns of working-class mackintoshes floating down a street that was like a dreary black canal'.[41] But by January 'the chimneys of the little back-yard shops were mostly smokeless; there was no longer a chorus of tapping. The noise of hand-trucks running through dry streets on bare iron wheels was, except on Mondays, a skeleton echo.'[42] Unemployment brought desolation, aggravated ill health, the eating of 'bread-and-scrat', with 'Folks moonlight-flitting every night and young chaps off on tramp, workhouse to workhouse.'[43] And Bates wrote of the interwar 'demoralising blight of short-time, vain hope and utter idleness, war veterans wandering lamely from house to house pushing or carrying baskets of shoelaces, polishes, brushes, cheap underwear, buttons, dusters, safety pins'.[44]

Such a town had its respectable and disreputable ends: 'You could not go lower than Gas Street. The end of the respectable world was Gas Street.'[45] In his story 'Let's Play Soldiers', an account of childhood fighting and mimicry of soldiers at the Western Front, Bates described a slum leather factory area he called 'The Pit': 'a terrible place', with its fearsome reputation and neighbouring squabbles, and its 'little one-story hovels with sacks at their windows, the horrible squat brick prisons of outdoor privies and a few dirty flags of shirt on a washing line.'[46] The houses in these boot-and-shoe towns were connected via a network of hand trucks on iron wheels, as goods moved between factories and neighbouring houses for working. The sounds of such trucks were a characteristic of the town.

> Each house possessed a little low iron-wheeled truck …there were two constant sounds …the clack of truck-wheels running to and from the factories in the streets outside, and the hammering of shoemakers working from day-break and on into the night, by the light of little tin oil-lamps, in the dark windowed shops all along the row.[47]

Much of the town was structured around the passage of these trucks, between factories and home workshops. According to Bates, there was little to attract in these physical townscapes, with their views 'across wet granite sets, streaming on rainy days with yellow stains of horse-dung and rainbow gleams of spilled oil.'[48] These were grey smoky towns, 'benighted holes', with 'low shabby defiles.'[49] This is a description that some urban community historians may be uncomfortable with. Yet it comes from Bates's direct experience, and it is a depiction repeated for many other urban occupational communities.

It was often the role of the girls to compete for boot-and-shoe out-work, hanging around factories jostling each other in competitive hope, trying to obtain the 'uppers' to take home. 'She hated the scrubby windy little town of high asphalt causeways and yellow alley-ways where she ran like a beggar with a truck.' They even travelled long distances across country in search of such work.[50] The resulting rheumatic fever from such a lengthy walk through wintry countryside kills one character in *The Feast of July*. The shoemakers were persistently in search of employment, which they called 'occasioning', that is, work-hunting: 'touting, begging, hoping, hanging in alley-ways and about the doors of factories for whatever they would throw out to her'.[51] Family life occurred against this backdrop, within the yearly factory rhythm of activity. This pattern of industrial labour was broken mainly by the harvest, when the boot- and shoe-making families headed to the fields for a different kind of work.[52] Bates explicitly states in *The Poacher* that harvest work and gleaning 'brought together' the family, as a family work affair. While many shoemakers engaged in it, he seems not to describe it as work that united or organized a wider community in the fields.

Whenever he returned to the 'many soulless, hideous red-brick scars' of his Northamptonshire valley, Bates wrote about its culture, 'I was aware of entering some totally negative wasteland'.[53] 'Nobody had a scrap of superior feeling' in his fictional Orlingford; 'nobody in a one-eyed town like this knows Brahms from a tin of baking powder'.[54] Methodism was a main cultural form, often glimpsed in Bates's novels, and intensely disliked in his *Autobiography*.[55] The denomination infused Sunday with a repetitively tedious discipline akin to the work ethic of the factory and its outputting system. Ben Wainwright, the family head in *The Feast of July*, spends two or three hours every Saturday afternoon polishing the plain altar brass of the chapel, as 'a kind of working penance'.[56] Methodism was important in the further sense that its networks and inferences of repute could bring offers of work.

This account by Bates, distilled from representative parts of his writing, is a regional variation of occupational-community description. It is from a man who disliked what he wrote about, whose autobiographical views inform his fiction, and it covers a classic putting-out and networked occupational community. It clearly raises issues about judgement and historical assessment. In the work of some writers, such an environment is presented in the romanticized guise of what Raphael Samuel called 'industrial or urban pastoral':[57] a nostalgic hankering after a form of urban 'community' now usually lost to us, given Britain's de-industrialization. Vivid counterparts exist in descriptions of mining, ship-building, the cotton and woollen industries, hosiery, the potteries and many other industries, whether they were networked, locally scattered or highly concentrated in situation. Such occupational communities have been retrospectively subject to possibly mythic recreations by historians and novelists, who have been alternately moved by childhood memory, work processes, integrated communities, solidarity among workers or relief to have escaped.

Bates's representation lacks nostalgia and is certainly not 'urban pastoral'. According to him, this was a very dismal environment indeed. It was marked by intense competition between workers and families. The setting was sometimes dangerous and certainly precarious and depressing, dank, smell-ridden and acrid with leather burning. These Northamptonshire boot-and-shoe towns were apparently grim to every sense. In Bates's representations, they were not cooperative in their ethos. Families cast opportunistic aspersions upon each other, and they competed and struggled both for limited work and for reputations. Upon hearing of work in a certain place, the immediate thought is:

> 'Don't let Mitchy see you. Mitchy'll be off if he gits mind on it ...' The rivalry of Mitchy, always mean, that winter seemed to become sharp and desperate. Mitchell became a sinister shadow recognizable at long distances by the thin-legged run ... He pushed, too, a truck that was unlike most others: a truck of basket-work, on two low back wheels and a third still lower one, at

> the front, like a castor … paddling himself forward with one leg and then coasting with iron whistlings and clattering down the hills. It was this sound that pursued Nell as she gasped across and up the valley, desperate for work, that winter.[58]

Indeed, families struggle within themselves too, as with the three Wainwright brothers who compete, sometimes violently, for Bella, the young woman who, bedraggled and ill after having miscarried, comes by chance to their family in search of another man who she hopes to kill. Open violence is common: '"This is a rough town," the man said. "Everybody knows that. It's always been rough. You can't come into this town 'ithout somebody starts fighting. That's shoemakers all over – fighting, don't wanta let nobody else live, always fighting –."' [59]

Did Bates exaggerate the cultural barrenness of the leather towns? There were, after all, chapel-based choral societies, enthusiastically welcomed itinerant opera companies or symphony orchestras. Was his representation of urban Northamptonshire a milder version of Caradoc Evans's scathing depiction of Nonconformist culture in west Wales?[60] Whatever one's verdict, Bates had very determined ideas about how the Northamptonshire boot-and-shoe communities should be judged, and his views need to be taken seriously in retrospective assessment of Britain's urban occupational communities.

Rural isolation or occupational community?

The meaning of rural 'community' in the interwar period addresses the quality of life in the past. In some literary representations contemporary with Bates, the English village emerges with an intimately known organization and a complex interplay of personalities. One thinks, among countless examples, of the village of 'Folly Down' in T. F. Powys's *Mr Weston's Good Wine*, with levels of personal knowledge and aspersion to rival Dylan Thomas's *Under Milk Wood*.[61] 'Everything that happens is known in a village,'[62] reminding us of the interwar detective writers. In Powys's imaginative, ironic and whimsical world of simplified action, characterization and speech, people are intensely observed both by themselves and by Mr Weston, who, allegorically, is God. Houses are described, and the layout of the village is carefully assessed. To sell his 'good wine' Mr Weston needs to know his customers. He has to 'pry so deeply into all the tittle-tattle'; he needs to know all their 'hidden desires and wishes … their passions and indulgences, all their likes and dislikes, all their sorrows and joys … We have to pry as deeply as we can into their past manners and customs, and discover also in what direction their future wishes may go.' People's credit, loves, sites of seduction, drinking preferences, idiosyncrasies and views on God are talked about on the hill overlooking the village, as Mr Weston and Michael consider how they might engage villagers to live in a world of 'noble intoxication'.[63] This is highly allegorical fiction, musing on good and evil, showing feeling for subjugated women, reconstructing a village in unexpected terms, a novel that is complex in multiple meanings, with intertextual references that range from the Bible to Freud. It is far from realist or naturalistic representation, and nor is it 'modernist' in method, for complex use of allegory long precedes modernism. This novel's allegory, irony and use of literary precursors take one back to the Bible, to Chaucer, to John Bunyan in the 1670s, to Jane Austen's *Emma* (whence its title), while parodying earlier moral notions of the English village. Even so, T. F. Powys's Folly Down (based upon East Chaldon, Dorset, where he lived) is a very intimately known 1920s village indeed, opened to close scrutiny like a Stanley Spencer painting, as a community of mutually relating people.

No doubt Pop Larkin and Uncle Silas (of whom more anon) would have approved of Mr Weston's ostensible mission. And Bates wrote to Joe Braddock that 'we shall drink your health in true Silasian fashion, in mouthfuls of good wine'.[64] Yet Bates was entirely different to Powys, or more modernist writers, in his portrayal of the village and its farmsteads. While Bates could write like a prose poet, he had not 'a poet's fancy, that will at any moment create out of the imagination a new world'.[65] His pre-1958 rural writing was a form of countryside realism. While his literary influences are evident, he eschewed textual references to other authors. For him fiction expressed in cool and restrained language, using a clear graphic approach that was vivid in pictorial simplicity, picking up on casual, unsuspecting words and events, was a way of uncovering deeper truths and realities, in which 'events were implied rather than chronicled',[66] in which significance was clear and unambiguous. With this philosophy of writing, Bates was certainly trying to display social and personal truths as he sensed them, and he felt that his approach to fiction communicated most effectively, and brought him closer to subjects and readers than any documentary writer, or indeed many modernist writers.

It is thus of much interest that one does *not* find Bates presenting a closely interactive community in his rural writing – on the contrary, he repeatedly refers to 'awful country isolation', in such language or terms.[67] This was a condition that afflicted his characters regardless of their class or gender. He wrote of the house of one farm woman: 'Exposed and isolated, the wind striking at it from all quarters, it seemed to have no part with the surrounding landscape. Empty ploughed lands, in winter time, stretched away on all sides in wet steel curves.' The woman is as isolated as her house, 'fretful and almost desperate in an anxiety to establish a world beyond her own', frugally saving money as her only possible salvation. 'To her the money was like a huge and irreplaceable section of her life. It was part of herself, bone and flesh, blood and sweat. Nothing could replace it. Nothing, she knew with absolute finality, could mean so much.' She becomes almost dream-like, oblivious to the people around her. Money here is a substitute for wider human relations, as in *Silas Marner*, and when she loses it the tale ends in complete isolation.[68]

In *The Fallow Land*, Bates wrote about how 'The farm was lonely; from Sunday to Sunday hardly anyone came up the road and she looked to the child to fill that emptiness. Emptiness!'[69] The isolation of farms in novels like this was a frequent theme in interwar literature, affecting both genders. There are many examples in the wider rural genre, such as *Joseph and His Brethren*, *The Lonely Plough*, *Starvecrow Farm*, *Crag's Foot Farm* and *Joanna Godden*, and this was an isolation that lent itself to the famous characterization in *Cold Comfort Farm*.[70] It is a feature that seems strongly to downgrade the significance of 'community' in the countryside. Bruno Shadbolt, at the end of Bates's novel *Spella Ho*, 'experienced a feeling of the acutest loneliness. It seemed like the sudden concentration of years of loneliness. He was a man without friends; he had seen and known that for a long time, but now he felt it. He felt it with a sudden sharp despair that was almost terror.' Finally, we glimpse him standing alone on his terrace, 'solitary, diminutive', merging into the great house that he has fought for.[71]

At another end of the social scale, 'the man who loved squirrels' 'liked it better in the wood, alone, in the company of birds and squirrels, working away in his own time, in his own solitude'.[72] In this case, unusually in Bates's fiction, solitude is voluntary. Such solitude was also a theme in Bates's nature writing, with nature serving as a surrogate for community,[73] as indeed it was for writers such as Richard Jefferies, W. H. Hudson or Henry Williamson. Bates was interested in loners: the poacher, the solitary drinker, the night walker, the coastal cliff trekker and the gamekeeper. Most commonly, however, such solitude was enforced and unwillingly *suffered* as loneliness, often arched by 'the strange stillness of the silent land'.[74] It was frequently the insecure and unacknowledged loneliness of women. In his pre-1950s writing, Bates was perhaps unrivalled in Britain as the novelist of loneliness. This was a loneliness that bemoaned the *lack* of community, or the total failure of a supposed community to be emotionally worthwhile or meaningful to the characters described. It was a loneliness that sometimes tried to substitute other things for community – money, a great house, a woman's sons, animals, nature, travel – and yet in Bates's non-humorous writing these substitutions almost always fail. It was only with his later shift to overt humour and satire, with the Larkins from 1958, that a vacuous and personally isolating rural community found a budding standby in the large family. By then Bates had to some extent side-stepped his earlier themes of loneliness and unfulfilling community and was interpreting the all-consuming family as their historical replacement.

The countryside was, during most of Bates's writing, one of people abandoning the land and of rural industries in decline. The First World War had witnessed men taken away from agriculture, 'and gradually a strange silence and solitude settled over the fields'.[75] The interwar period continued as a time of rural exodus and depopulation, and work on the land declined throughout. 'The theme on the tip of every writer's pen was "the drift from the land" and all its consequences.'[76] This emphasis was by no means invariable in rural fiction. As we have seen, Adrian Bell in *Corduroy* enthusiastically described the opposite trajectory: 'Farming, to my mind, was … a symbol of escape … I was flying from the threat of an office job … the year was 1920.'[77] Yet just as Bates showed people departing or even emigrating without regrets from the boot-and-shoe towns, as in his story 'The Snow Line', so he also made this a theme in most of his pre-1958 rural writing. 'Then, after another look at the field, they slushed out of the gate and down the road and away, clutching scythe and bag, like two figures setting out on a pilgrimage to nowhere at all.'[78] The English countryside was frequently described as redundant, economically useless. 'The land's no good to me. I'd get shot of it to-morrow if I could,' says Jess Mortimer in *The Fallow Land*. And the woman he courts, whose struggles are the main theme of the novel, is a servant in a nearby country house which has 'a silence and odour … like … a museum. It was like death … [its rooms had] an odour of lifelessness and damp darkness.' It was a place where nobody ever called.[79] There may have been community of sorts in the boot-and-shoe towns, and Bates was surely showing a working community in his depictions there, however unpleasant and grimy he thought it was. But it seems lacking in the countryside, where his imagery was all so often of desolation and isolation. 'Country life', he wrote, 'was manifestly a form of isolation.'[80] A sense of community as a supposedly cooperative affair emerged on rare occasions, as during the funeral of Mrs Mortimer in *The Fallow Land*, when 'the house was full of mourners and strangers in black … a black crowd of people shuffled behind [the bier] and another crowd of women who dared not go into the farm stood by the gate and wept and whispered behind their handkerchiefs. The procession shuffled slowly down into the village.'[81] Even here, it is worth noting, the people are 'strangers in black', their conversation muffled into handkerchiefs, some of them not daring to go into the farm. This representation is of a stifled, hushed, emotionally stagnant and largely ineffective 'community', one that scarcely warrants that word if it carries its usual positive connotations. It is not clear what labels could replace 'community' to describe the motley, lonely cast-offs that Bates so often shows us – perhaps a dissociation, a social *disjecta membra*.

The decay of the gentry

In Bates's descriptions, a sense of rural community was not enhanced in any way by the ruling classes, or what remained of them. 'The slump was grim and stubborn; estates everywhere were breaking up,' both in Northamptonshire and Kent where Bates lived from 1931. 'It's absolutely dog eats dog.'[82] In his story 'A Girl Called Peter', Bates depicted an old rural mansion as full of dry rot and moss, uninhabited, a relic of the past.[83] An alcoholic ill-looking captain in a decaying house, flying any old flag, who cannot afford to heat his house, whose views from it are obstructed, whose old neighbours have gone and who can hardly climb a hill, stands for a decaying moribund class in 'The Flag'.[84] Or one thinks of the colonel in 'Where the Cloud Breaks': totally out of touch with the times, unable to tell what day it is.[85] In 'The Woman Who Had Imagination', a man is introduced 'in an old panama hat, a yellowish alpaca suit and a faded green bow, beaming with smiles and gestures of aristocratic idiocy'.[86] The Castle Hanwick estate, in 'The Blue Feather', is said to have 'gone to rack and ruin … you couldn't see the place for briars and nettles. Like a damn jungle everywhere.' The owner was a hideous bed-ridden woman of perverted mind, clearly insane: '"God A'mighty," he said, and I thought he gave a shiver. "There she sat. Like a white toad."' And then there was her brother Sir John Featherstone: 'Tall man, terrible thin and bent over at the top, like a parson a-prayin'. Very holler-chested, with a gruet Adam's apple like a pump handle stickin' out over one o' them high starched collars … like a blood'ound out o' sorts.' It is Bates's character Uncle Silas, the labouring man, who passes these final judgements on the upper classes. 'The place has been sold up now and they keep idiots there, or prisoners without bars.'[87] Pop Larkin offers to buy Sir George Bluff-Gore's ancestral great house, to demolish it for junk and sell on its artefacts. Sir George then had to 'go and live in a stable. They were the aristocracy, of course, these people.'[88] The landed family in *Love for Lydia* is isolated, adulterous, exploitative of poorer women, frittering their time away in dance parties by the river Nene, into which one of them falls and dies, and their significance to local people is fading fast. 'There soon won't be any people like us.' Their girls are 'coming to the end of lost races against gaiety'.[89] The burial of the last of Evensford's aristocracy is sordid, largely unattended, passing 'through a smoky December silence of factory streets to a cemetery shabby with wet chrysanthemums ... Behind the tones of the burial service came a continuous cough, hard and harsh, of factory engines, and above the flowers a smell of leather hung in the air.'[90] Lydia's physical decline caused by tuberculosis parallels the decline of the Aspen house, which she then rejects herself. Ties across class, the possibilities of new lines of social affection, were crucial for such people, for Bates believed that the erstwhile ruling classes of the countryside had little other prospect. The idea of the gentry or landed elites providing community leadership, as they had often done hitherto, was not contemplated in any of Bates's writing. Most of his characters would have found such an idea very droll.

The new rich or other rural incomers seemed unpromising. Bates depicted *nouveaux riches* as pretentious, embarrassing, crude, making jokes at the butcher's wife in 'Now Sleeps the Crimson Petal'.[91] The mind of one of Bates's resentful estate owners trawled through recent arrivals, found them wanting and revealed his own attitudes to the village:

> At heart he really detested the village ... It was nothing more than a gossip shop. And the little crust of society: the milkless wife of the retired naval fellow, commander or something; the dithering lunatic doctor, surgeon or whatever he was; and the horrible people who came to retire: dreary suburban-minded wretched people of no standing ... There was a retired schoolmaster too, a real Bolshevik, an out-and-outer; and a solicitor fellow, a counsel or something, who came at week-ends and poached such fishing as there was ... They were all divided into factions; they were all like horrible little weevils, feeding and boring away at everything with their trivial, insidious, killing gossip.[92]

As for his estate, it has been wrecked by the Second World War: 'Concrete tank bays, half ruined huts, old army kitchens and brick ovens blackened by fire, all overgrown by thick new nettles'. And now they faced 'the paltry rations of the brave new time'.[93]

Bates repeatedly attacked what he thought was the peeping, censorious, gossipy nature of small Northamptonshire village and town life, whether this was from the perspective of such a failing estate owner, or the small shopkeeper class of *The Sleepless Moon*, or from the viewpoint of 'Uncle Silas'. These embittered criticisms were especially marked in his writing set in the 1920s and 1930s, when so often he showed the damaging results of gossip. By comparison, Pop Larkin and other characters of a later era seem relatively indifferent to gossip, even to revel in it. Earlier, however, 'In a little town like Orlingford people were always over-fond of talking.'[94] The class-sneering, cold-shouldering of people, the intolerance of outsiders or of maimed soldiers from the First World War, the failure of people to relate open-mindedly and tolerantly towards each other were all targets of his writing. In *The Sleepless Moon*, one of Bates's most damningly judgemental of novels, the gossiping dressmaker of the dismal town (based upon Higham Ferrers), with her iron foot and with pins in her mouth, was symptomatic with her calculating natter and its devastating effects upon the lives of others.[95]

Uncle Silas

Bates was a novelist of greatly contrasted moods. His writing could be despairing on social conditions and relations. It could be inspirational or tragic on bomber pilots. It could also be rich in humour. 'My Uncle Silas', one of Bates's most popular characters, stands in a line of rural characterization that might include figures such as Frederick Grover (alias George Bettesworth), Lucy Bettesworth[96] and other ageing representatives of labouring life from the nineteenth-century English countryside. They are often comically represented, as initially with George Sturt's interest in Frederick Grover: 'He was something of a comic character in my eyes,' or so it was for a while, as 'I had not as yet seen in him much more than his garrulous and good-tempered quaintness … Soon, however, came hints of a life far from comic under the odd exterior,'[97] and those hints were all the more obvious in the hardships faced by his wife. There were sedate touches here of the depiction of Uncle Silas, who in Bates's writing was a character based upon Joseph Betts, husband of his grandmother's sister, a man born back in the 1840s, 'and, among other things, the biggest reprobate who ever lived'.[98]

Silas's own stories are often dubious or suspected inventions, and part of Bates's play with the reader's credibility has to do with the open question of the reliability of Silas as narrator. The reader constantly has to ask: in what sense is Silas genuine; can he be so; what do his attitudes and anecdotes stand for in social and historical terms? In the Silas stories, we see 'community' represented humorously, as an arena within which (or against which) Silas operates and enjoys himself. As in most humour, the realities underpinning it are serious, so much so that the humour is one of the few ways in which they can be handled. This is a work-based, expressive, bucolic, baudy, anti-Puritan, independent and purportedly self-made world, and like the cowslip, sloe or rosehip ingredients of Silas's wine it comes from the surrounding countryside. Silas is independently quick to make up words to depict others – such as 'maungy' (a mean, moody, miserable man) – and he describes them with facility and surety. His view of Methodism is summed up in his laconic description of a cook: 'Gal named Em Pack … Bit miserable. Chapel.'[99] There is deference, but it is cleverly exploited by Silas to ends other than heartfelt social respect; for this is a character who seems to know his betters better than they know themselves; and he is able, through his cunning, to make them endorse or behave like himself, and enjoy that, without their realizing it.[100] In 'The Foxes', Silas is reprimanded for drinking by the 'Rev. Frog-Face': 'Marning, marning! Voice like some old yoe a-lambin'. Yet when this old ewe asks Silas to catch foxes, the fox-like Silas outwits and tricks the parson into providing him with much more drink. 'Jist shows you what born fools parsons are … Adn't got twopennorth 'o split peas in 'is 'ead.'[101] It was characteristic of Bates that he could write of such social interactions from contrasting standpoints, for elsewhere Mr Fitzgerald, one of his embittered landowners, complains about 'a feeling of treachery behind the politeness, the kow-towing, the touched hat.'[102]

The characterization of the Silas stories is heightened, colourful and picaresque, and Bates argued that 'To those who find these stories too Rabelaisian, far-fetched or robust, my reply would be that, as pictures of English country life, they are in reality understated.'[103] Silas's friends, for example, have names like Tig Flawn, Tupman Jarvis, Slob Johnson, Fiddler Bollard and Ponto Pack – with their connotations of gypsy horse dealers or Cockney fairground hustlers. Silas's exploits conjoin with the subworld of gossip; they need that gossip to gain their notoriety; and their exaggeration at that level warrants Silas's own enhancement of them: Silas is literally playing a game with scandalous hearsay. Thus, he takes Queenie White – a 'maungy' man's wife – to the seaside for a fortnight: 'All the old tits wur a-twitterin' an' a-gossipin' an' a-maunderin' about it fer years. Couldn't stop talkin' about it. Loved it. Couldn't forget it. Just their drop.'[104]

These Silas stories were, at their most serious level, about the decline of earlier material forms of country life and the humour and attitudes that (Bates believed) went with them. Silas dies. His nephew later returns to his cottage.

> As I went up the lane to the house I looked for the old sign of things: smoke rising from the chimney; the old summer bird-scares, age-green hats on sticks and inside-out umbrellas and twirling shuttlecocks; scarecrows made up of old legs of Silas's pants and bell-bottomed trousers and the housekeeper's ancient hat and chemises; the ladder in the late apple trees; the bonfire filling the garden and the spinney and the fields with smoke that hung in sweet-smelling clouds under the pines and the golden cherry leaves.

> I listened for the cluck of Silas's hens and the grunting and rooting of the solitary sow he had always kept in the black sty under the elderberries at the garden end.[105]

Yet all is quiet and transformed. The garden gate and fence have been repaired and painted a sepulchral white. The lovely apple and cherry trees have been chopped down and are merely stumps. The roses have been sawn down. The garden is empty. Productive gardening has ended. The prim new owner has a white face too, 'a pasty, town white', and regards visitors as liars and tricksters. Her husband is a teetotaller. Apparently the previous owner was 'an awful old man'. The air inside is now dead, having lost its smells of old tea and earth and wine and geraniums. The stale odours of new French-polished furniture have replaced that. It had all the correctitude of a showroom in a furniture shop: 'There was something ice-cold about its parsimonious respectability.'[106] Apparently Silas's housekeeper has already visited and, in tears at what she has seen, asked for the old bath in which she used to bathe Silas. The new owner sent her away: 'I could see she was either drunk or wrong in the head.' Silas's nephew walks away thinking of 'that tart and irascible house-keeper … all broken up and stupefied, weeping her heart out for something nobody would ever understand'.[107]

The community of RAF pilots

Bates felt much frustration during the early part of the Second World War. He wrote to Joe Braddock: 'The war remains (a) a bore, (b) a bloody swindle. The budget is (a) iniquitous (b) a bloody swindle. I am confined to reviewing & a sort of melancholy contemplation of the writer I once was.'[108] In Kent he and his family were, as he reported, on the front line: 'Now blacked out, fortified & in the centre of a new theatre of potential war. So God knows if you'll ever get there [Cairo]. Anyway it doesn't matter. By August we'll all be finished, as I see it, anyway.'[109] In early September 1940 he wrote: 'News from the front line, where the battles are now terrifically fierce & planes pop down like pheasants at a local shoot … Madge saw six planes down on Sunday morning … I was fishing all the week. Ironical to sit pulling the roach out of the water while the Spitfires pulled the Jerries out of the sky.'[110] At the end of that month he was saying how

> Survival is now the important thing. London has really been knocked hard, & yet half continues to carry on with the same clumsy stoicism … For some curious reason the effect of London is emotionally a blank – you just

> stare at buildings smashed down, cross the street & go on. No emotion, no indignation. It is a new phenomenon. An awful sense of stupefaction of the conscience. I suppose its either that or go barmy.[111]

And then in late November he wrote: 'I fear dark, dark days are coming.'[112]

Yet an important role was soon found for him. Bates was drafted into RAF Public Relations as a short story writer. The aim was to show the RAF to the public not as statistics, but as real people, and Bates was given considerable artistic freedom for this purpose. As he put it, the proposition was that 'figures ... mean nothing, but that a pilot with a pint of beer in his hand and a popsie in bed can illuminate the troubled business of war in a way that will bring war and its participants vividly, excitedly, even painfully alive'.[113] Bates seems to have discovered in the RAF a spirit of community and shared purpose that took him by surprise and eclipsed anything he had known hitherto. This was the comradeship of small groups of men on a fenland or other aerodrome. Bates was based at Oakington in Cambridgeshire, and later at Tangmere near Chichester. In one sense, it was odd to have found a sense of community at these places: for the RAF comprised a bewildering array of nationalities and men, from all parts of the Empire, brought together for a relatively short period. In some cases, this was for a very brief period indeed as so many in Bomber Command were killed or taken prisoner: 'there were some deeply dark days on that often fog-shrouded fenland that winter'.[114] For much of Bates's experience at Oakington the airmen comprised the crews and support teams of Stirling bombers, and later he was with Hurricane squadrons. The crews had come from all over the world: Holland, France, Poland, New Zealand, Australia, Canada, Africa, the West Indies, Lithuania, Indo-China, Tahiti, Switzerland, the USA and Czechoslovakia as well as the countries of the British Isles.[115] All of them 'belong to us'.[116] 'What we were doing was a new experience in the world. Until our time no one had ever been on fire in the air. Until our time there had never been so many people to hear of such things and then to forget them again.'[117]

United in their endeavour, they formed a community of the air, with their own language and mutual understandings, their own stress and shared risks, their mutual 'great trust and admiration and affection'.[118] They had their own ideas of honour and sacrifice, their own 'very personal' or shared hatreds of an enemy who had, in many cases, killed their families or taken over their countries.[119] In Bates's cameos of aerial warfare these veterans of young age spoke 'the odd, boyish, sometimes silly service language that came out of their exclusive world, for nobody else to understand. Behind this language, you could take refuge from the fear and reality of the business'. 'Wizard: the word had grown crusts on it.'[120] They talked of their Mae Wests, the vis, airscrews, cough-drops, popsies, tough tits or pieces of cake. They carried their rabbit feet and other mascots.[121] They felt like the young pilot from Kalgoorlie, 'that he had something damnable and cruel and hideous to wipe out from his conception of what was a decent life on earth. Every time he went up something was vindicated.'[122] And behind such a man lurked the colonial communities backing the war effort, who in his case had initially tried to keep the war a secret from him, and who then, upon his return to western Australia, comprised 'the largest gathering of folks anyone had ever seen on the farm … everyone from thirty miles around and one or two people from fifty miles away … At night they sang hymns and old songs in the drawing-room round the piano, and they slept in round beds on the floor.'[123]

These men looked down upon the rural farms and inhabitants whose problems Bates had hitherto described, and, whatever Bates's earlier verdicts, the airmen seem to have seen these communities as looking up at them. One pilot described by Bates came from Somerset, from a family home 'bound to earth, lighted by that cheap paraffin lamp which they carried from room to room'. His parents had been killed by a loose bomb landing on their farm.

> He roared over fields and woods and roads and over the little dusty blue towns and over remote farms where he could even see the hens feeding and scuttling in the dark winter grass. He came so low once that for a second or so he saw people in the fields. For an instant he saw a man and woman working. They raised flat, astonished faces to look at the great 'plane overhead … They might have been old or young, he could not tell; they lifted their heads and in a second were cut off by the speed of the 'plane. But in this second, as he saw them transfixed on the earth below him and before the speed of the 'plane cut them off forever, he remembered his own people. He remembered them as they lived, simple and sacrificing, living only for him, and he saw them alive again, the same simple people, the same humble, faithful, eternal people, giving always and giving everything: the greatest people in the world.[124]

This was a new language for Bates, far removed from his idiom hitherto, one of domestic patriotism that may seem sentimental today, but it conveyed wartime emotions and had great appeal. Its pictorial imagery – the flat astonished faces raised upwards amid the farmyard hens – might have come from a painting by Stanley Spencer, another commissioned wartime artist. Yet Bates was in awe at the sense of purpose of these squadrons. This was new to a writer who had hitherto seen little that was valid in community life. It brought to his writing an awareness and appreciation of community as shared endeavour. Whether the squadron was in preparation, in action, or its men in a dinghy after being shot down, or tramping through occupied France after crash landing, or spirited away by death, Bates dwelt on how they cooperated and shared memories and danger. Even little details mattered, for Bates never missed meanings of detail. 'From setting our watches together we got a sense of unity.'[125] Franklin, the Wellington bomber pilot in *Fair Stood the Wind for France*, 'felt keenly … their interdependence, profound and clear and inexpressibly tense, and the trust he had in them.'[126] As Bates later wrote in his most violent novel, set in India after Partition, 'It was exactly as he remembered it once with a squadron of fighter pilots: all the physical heartiness, underlined by fear of death, all the jolly exultation in little things, above the ache in the bone.'[127] And as the war progressed, and successes occurred more regularly, he wrote of how

> It was one of those periods in a station when the unity and life of a good squadron becomes too strong to become a local thing, compressed within itself, meaning something only to a few people. It breaks out, and spreading, warm and energetic and fluid, becomes a large thing, meaning something to many people … The squadron was good and proud and knew itself … They had found each other … all of us felt it there … a squadron which is at the crest of things.[128]

Yet this feeling was short-lived, this mettlesome community scattered to the winds. 'And finally it was time to say good-bye … the sergeant pilots fondled the busts of each other's Mae Wests and said heavy farewells.'[129] A year later, Bates returned to the pub that the squadron had frequented, and the landlord no longer recognized him. '"Fancy me forgettin". He looked up at me with eyes large and tender with regret. We shook hands. "But you know, sir, they come an' go. That's the truth. They come and go."'[130] The community of the squadron had dispersed globally from its small fenland base. In such a society, so mobilized, whether for peacetime or war production, 'community' was potentially intense yet in fact fleeting and changeable, easily forgotten, as temporary as people sheltering in a subway, or waiting on a platform. The 'community' of such a squadron was an accentuated metaphor for much wider modern experience.

The Larkins: a consuming family replaces community

The decline of a needed working relation with land, with resources stored for different jobs, of property that is *productive* rather than a statement of taste – these are themes in Bates's writing. One recalls another Silas, Silas Marner, using the resources around him in his home-based weaving.[131] Bates's Uncle Silas makes the most of what he stores near him, and we have seen how any humour in Bates's writing disappears when he shows how Silas's cottage lost its fruitful meaning and immediate productivity, when taken over by new owners. As Adrian Bell wrote, describing slightly earlier utilitarian attitudes towards gardens: 'They always speak of "farming" a garden in Suffolk.'[132] These concerns over changing material life were shared by other writers on the mid-twentieth-century countryside, such as H. J. Massingham.[133] It is no surprise then, that in Bates's depictions of rural life after the Second World War, most notably in the stories about the Larkin family, he dwelt so lovingly upon the beauty of clutter or 'rubbish', the accoutrements of farmsteads, the litter of household surroundings, whether as relics of the past or as items of utility to families. The charm of discarded clutter, whether useful or not, was a thread that connected the Larkins to Silas. So were the hedonistic drink and sex-fond proclivities of people determined to extract as much pleasure as possible from life. '"Mek the most on it while you can, boy," [Silas] said, "Mek the most on it while you can,"'[134] an injunction that the Larkins would certainly have endorsed.

Yet the emphases of Bates's stories set in the post-war Kentish countryside were in most respects remarkably different from the themes he had handled hitherto. Some critics thought that Bates, into this period, had 'nothing new to say', or even (in the words of Angus Wilson) that he had 'sold out', but such judgements seem to me inappropriate.[135] The Larkin stories and novels are remarkably prescient and adapted to the changed circumstances of 1950s and 1960s England and are intensely interesting as a result. The post-war period depressed him. 'I had supposed', Bates wrote, 'that the aftermath of war would find expression, after the long dark tragic years, in light and joy. It never occurred to me, even remotely, that it might well express itself in a sourness even darker.'[136] But he subsequently developed a stream of 'comic' writing that should also be read as a cutting satire on social trends in consumption and community-less familial individualism. He wrote of his earlier novels – mentioning *The Fallow Land*, *The Poacher* and *A House of Women* – that these were 'in a sense, historical novels, portions of a world that has vanished … the Second World War revolutionized the countryside as nothing, not even railways, had done before'.[137] The changes in Bates's writing were now, yet again, a manifestation of his stated 'own philosophy: to go with the stream, never to battle against it'.[138] However one judges that politically,[139] it seems to be the key to what made him so reflective of the different eras in which he wrote, and thus so versatile as an author. The Larkin stories are materially effusive, glorying in abundance and ways to consume it, a stark contrast to the H. E. Bates who had hitherto been a writer exploring hardship, poverty and the unfulfilled material and emotional hopes of women. The Larkin stories are also divorced from any sense of occupational community, either agricultural or industrial, and their focus is overwhelmingly upon one large unmarried family and its pleasurable activities, outings and consuming tastes. Bates had seen a functioning, if problematic, occupational community in the interwar years, one that was without much substance as families competed for niggardly resources. His writing in the post-war decades suggests that any such 'community' was supplanted by the highly consuming family,[140] a 'greedy' body bypassing alternative social institutions. The boot-and-shoe milieux had social norms, sanctions, domestic expectations and mutual knowledge, a shared experience of the trade. These had affected employment, religion, courtship and much else. In those respects they had functioned as communities, whatever their inadequacies, internal rivalries and senses of dreary disappointment. By comparison, the world of the Larkins is overwhelmingly family-centred, gypsy-like in its economic heterogeneity, individualistic, sexually gratified, socially foot-loose and quite unfastened in its extra-familial social ties. There is here a marked weakening of external controls over the family. Bates had again moved with the times. Indeed, his representation prefigures the 'adaptive family' of more recent decades: extemporaneous, often unmarried, unrestrained by normative rules; accustomed to 'flexible', part-time, non-gendered working environments; and substituting an ostentatiously indebted consumer culture for earlier social and religious codes.

'The Larkins' secret is in fact that they live as many of us would like to live if only we had the guts and nerve to flout the conventions.'[141] There was something of himself in Pop Larkin, Bates wrote: 'a passionate Englishman, a profound love of the nature, of the sounds and sights of the countryside, of colour, flowers and things sensual; a hatred of pomp, pretension and humbug; a lover of children and family life; an occasional breaker of rules, a flouter of convention.'[142] Some have written of the Larkin family as escapist whimsy, of their television serialization as a 'mood of escapist abandon.'[143] The popularity of that serialization by Yorkshire Television, produced by Bates's son Richard, was extraordinary: the audience grew to over twenty million people; yet whether that was associative or escapist is debatable.[144] Within the longer span of Bates's *writing* a description of 'escapism' seems misplaced. The Larkins are not *escaping* from anything, beyond the sentiments of proscriptive community. On the contrary, they are engaging more fully with everything that has become available around them, and having the nerve to do so fully, even while the reader wonders in surprise about the means of livelihood that enable them to do so. This family – and it is the all-consuming *family* that is now the overwhelming emphasis, not community or a hope for it – can be read on two planes. On the one hand, there is their enjoyment of an enviable life, but also, Bates wrote, they are 'a reflection on the revolution that had overtaken post-war England', a revolution that was especially marked in the countryside. Standards of living had increased dramatically.

> In the early thirties not a single farm worker in my village had a car, many not even a bicycle; today many have two cars, many a cottage inhabited by a family displays four, five, even six cars; few village shops sold anything but mouse-trap cheese, fat bacon, candles, paraffin, tart oranges and boiled sweets; today every one has its deep freeze dispensing scampi, smoked salmon, spaghetti Bolognese and exotics of every kind ... Ma and Pop unashamedly enjoyed their love and champagne and Primrose her seduction by flesh and poetry in the fields.[145]

Bates's community-based writing set before 1939 had depicted material culture and living conditions in many grim ways. Some features of this have been seen in his writing on the boot-and-shoe towns and surrounding outputting villages. In 'An Aspidistra in Babylon', set in 1921, he wrote of the 'stuffy little boarding-house, the smell of frying fish and bacon ... curtains of green chenille, antimacassars, and brass pots of aspidistra'.[146] Like George Orwell, his interwar writing often dwelt upon threadbare upholstery and dusty geraniums, the intractability of the gas mantle, the struggle to afford a new dress, the humdrum interiors of lower-middle-class life and the frustrations of women. One is truly in a different world with the Larkins of the late 1950s; indeed, one is constantly astonished by abundance and an eagerness to consume it. The village post office has become much more fully stocked, including with foreign items. 'Vast sums' are paid out as child allowances, at least that is what it seems to a Miss Pilchester.[147] Rural folk want the new commodities and complain when they are absent. Children are admonished: 'Now bleedin' be quiet or else ... If you don't shut your gob you won't have no scampi.'[148] And the Larkins are at an even higher plane than this, with their tin trunks stuffed with money, and their items of conspicuous consumption like the Rolls Royce and champagne. They eat 'massive breakfasts' submerged under seas of tomato ketchup. Huge quantities of ice cream, icy buns, chocolate biscuits, fish and chips and the like are fattened upon. And their glass and chromium cocktail cabinet is 'shaped like an elaborate glass and silver ship ... Spanish galleon ... "Cost us a hundred and eighty ... with the extra sets of goblets. The brandy lot ... And the silver bits for hot punch and all that."'[149] 'Perfick'. Ma Larkin quivers like a colossal jelly – every time one breast goes into the bra the other comes out – and Bates is also close to predicting obesity being plumped forward as a major issue thirty years later. A visiting road planner contemplates with astonishment their 'lavish living, the vintage port, the expensive burgundy, the expensive taste combined with ghastly taste, the flamboyance and the vulgarity'.[150] Small wonder then that Pop Larkin spends the duration of Bates's interestingly entitled novel *A Little of What You Fancy* petulantly and parsimoniously recovering from a copulation-induced heart attack, in hopes that he can then resume extravagant consumption of drink, food and sex where he left off.[151] These hopes are, happily, fulfilled on the final page.[152] This title, A *Little of What You Fancy*, is both an English understatement, given the consumption involved, as well as alluding to Marie Lloyd's music hall song of pre-1922 days. The original song title's ending 'does you good' – whatever its meanings for Marie Lloyd and her audiences – has now come to be omitted by Bates. One is left smiling at his quietly shrewd omission. Within the English literary traditions of pastoral, all this is a rather new, prodigal and prophetic development.

John Betjeman wrote in a 1958 review of Bates's emerging Larkin fiction that 'I cannot help feeling that tragedy and disaster lie below its surface.'[153] The dialectic between comedy and tragedy was obvious, and one says that without the inevitable later macro-economic reflections about a hugely indebted society. This happy abundance, for all the larking merriment and heart disease it causes the Larkin family – and for all its stress upon the individualistic unwed family as the consuming and living unit – seems to accompany a vacuum in senses of community. It induces levels of personal isolation that supply Bates with at least some continuities from his earlier writing. Varied discourses of comedy, ironic pastoral, personal alienation from community and social critique are all apparent. Loneliness remains a feature in Bates's characterization, especially for some of his women. Miss Pilchester's 'only really conscious impression was being alone. The village street was utterly deserted. The whole place was like something stricken, itself dead, with not a soul in sight.'[154] The pub landlord contemplates women drinking: 'That was largely the trouble with women in the country [he thinks]. Frustrated and lonely, they got at it in secret and then didn't know when to stop.'[155] The Larkin family have a social circle of only about six people, a few of whom live in London.[156] Convention, whatever that is, can now be ignored and flouted as a sign of one's individualism. Community norms seem absent. Nobody has the time to organize anything.[157] When the Larkins have a party, half of their 'guests' – 'odd acquaintances' – are uninvited or unknown.[158] Nevertheless, familial secrets are largely protected: the visiting tax inspector gives up in despair when trying to find out about the Larkins' income.[159] If there is any 'community' here at all, and one doubts that, it is neither a village community in any previously known or imagined form, nor an occupational community of the kind whose limitations were exposed by Bates in novels like *The Feast of July*. In any case, such 'community' concepts have become virtually meaningless by now.

Many in the village are treated opportunistically or with contempt. 'The gentry', Pop Larkin thinks, are 'really half-dopes'. Contrary to some of their historically wistful penchants, Larkin 'couldn't for the life of him' think of any worthwhile aspects of social or architectural life 'other than material' ones. He is eager to demolish their old mansions, to '"Pull the flippin' thing down". Pop gave one of his piercing, jolly shouts of laughter ... "Lot o' good scrap there."'[160] The trashing of local memory was a common theme then and subsequently.[161] Pop Larkin epitomizes this. There are rural incomers, 'a new kind of country gent', who had

> invaded the countryside ... with one avowed intention: namely that of shooting pheasants ... all too frequently [they] shot each other as well ... This new passion for having a place in the country had brought so many mugs out of hiding that even Pop, sometimes, thought it wasn't quite fair. It was daylight robbery. It was cruel to take their money.[162]

The place is littered with 'stockbroker chaps who played at farming'.[163] 'You made it in the city and lost it on the land. The countryside had never been so full of ragged-trousered brokers – what he called the Piccadilly farmers – pouring their money down the furrows'.[164] Other 'foreigners' 'used the country as a mere convenience'. A physics professor, in Miss Pilchester's view, 'did not belong. His cottage was a mere weekend bolt-hole for escape from London and the exhausting routine of teaching physics to long-haired and unwashed students.'[165] 'He buzzed in and out of the countryside as and when it suited him, a nuisance, impermanent, contributing nothing. Such people didn't ... belong to the countryside. They were nothing more than fleeting parasites ... looked on ... with both suspicion and contempt'.[166] There is nothing new in some of these attitudes (we earlier considered William Cobbett and James Wentworth Day on London stockbrokers), nor in such village scorn of outsiders.[167] Yet around the Larkins there is a greater than ever abundance of such people, and a signal failure of them to cohere into any kind of known community.

The Larkin philosophy is unperturbed and well adapted to all this: one manipulates such people to make money, to consume more, and if one has heart attacks 'the National Elf lark' sorts things out for you. H. E. Bates had once again moved adeptly with the times, into the era of 'You've never had it so good.' He was now breaking in a striking way from many of his earlier preoccupations. It is remarkable that he did so at that time. Always adapting his fiction to social history, as early as 1958 he was dealing with social, economic and public health themes that were to be increasingly salient for the next fifty and more years. Community hardly exists. Nor does a pretence of it. It's the individualistic family that matters, and its consumption. Well, Ma Larkin thinks, as her husband lies stricken in bed upstairs after his heart attack, they

> had three television sets, including the new colour one, a Rolls-Royce, a Jaguar, and an estate car just for running about in, a washing machine, a washing-up machine and a spin drier, a deep freeze that was too big to go into the kitchen and had consequently to stand in one of the out-houses, three ponies for the children to ride, a heated swimming pool, the new French bar, a private cinema ...with nice plush seats and a fridge so that everybody could have ice creams ...a nice boat and a nice boat-house to put it in, and above all plenty to eat and drink. You couldn't say they lacked for very much.[168]

'Ma couldn't grumble'. Maybe Pop Larkin would continue to say: 'Perfick'.

So much for social comment. Perhaps this was Bates's resurgent Methodist upbringing and earlier experiences, still affecting his self-discipline and social judgement. A strong part of him had rebelled against that background: criticizing a lugubrious and interfering Methodism; writing in depressing terms about the boot-and-shoe communities and the interwar farming communities; or, much more humorously, cooking up personalities like Uncle Silas or Pop and Ma Larkin. These anti-conventionalist retorts to his past assist his versatility of theme and characterization. And in rejecting his own past he shared much with a post-1950s society casting aside its own communal history spirits and senses of domestic thrift.

We have come a long way from the concerns about 'nested' community, and legal 'belonging' to parishes, of the poor letter writers during early industrialization, from the idealized, in-your-place, estate village of patriarchal Edward Montagu or from the displacement from settled community of George Morland's roadside migrants, as discussed earlier in this book. It has been stressed in those earlier chapters that extreme isolation, displacement, loneliness and a failure of community to support people are nothing new – we have been there before, in intense and despairing forms, though perhaps on a lesser scale. Following Hardy's Jude, we have travelled through a variety of troubled, lost or 'obscure' communities, to a highly affluent situation where community is apparently no longer needed. In such a reified reality, amid a 'fantasy world of desirable products',[169] the meaning of life has apparently come to reside increasingly in motorized cavalcades of consumption. The crowded cathedral-like shopping centres, with their car pollution and asthmatic children, have replaced Sunday's chapels, churches and much of the older fervent worlds of the parish magazine. Uncle Silas and Pop Larkin are not on record as reading religiously motivated parochial magazines, though their views of the clergy were well demonstrated and perpetuated those of the interwar crime writers. Bates could hardly miss the growing secularization that was such a feature of his lifetime. Unlike the crime writers, the Larkins did not worry about the mortifying sin of murder in the village, and the subsequent need for community regeneration. In literary creation at least, the closely latticed and moralizing nature of much community life hitherto had enhanced motives, suspicions and possibilities of crime. The modern themes of consumption, psychologically adept advertising, secularization and shallowness of 'community' have been hugely expanded upon since Bates wrote. The Larkins are a social warning, a striking augury of their times: of individualism, abandonment of community, obsessive consumption and related health issues. It is hardly surprising that they were so popular, especially when the last aspect was ignored in their television serialization. They are the world we have gained.

Yet they were also for Bates a relieved cheery endorsement of later abundant life, a token of his liberation from the bleak boot-and-shoe communities of his youth. This shines through in a personally illuminating letter from him: ambiguous, both depressed and joyful, yet largely positive. So let him endearingly sign off my account of him. Here he is writing to his old friends Joe and Muriel Braddock,[170] a few years before his death in 1974:

> I'm glad the Larkins amused you. That, of course, is what they are for & I am glad to note, in the few reviews I have so far seen, that this thought is echoed – i.e. that people are getting just a bit tired of all the dreary codswollop that has made the 60s so depressing. Anyway it cheers me to know that Ma & Pop have acted like restorative medicine to many, many people ...
>
> England looks so wonderful at the moment. One could almost weep at what I call 'the green sweetness of life'.
>
> Love to you all
>
> H. E.

10

Conclusion

This book has highlighted the essential contrasts between the earlier structures of community and belonging, and the free-wheeling personal networking and consuming individualism of today. It has shown how different our modern society is to the expectations and axiomatic structures of the parish or poor law ideas of local settlement, of legalized belonging and community entitlement, of the eighteenth and nineteenth centuries. Belonging and senses of community in any period are a personally varied state of mind, complex in diversity, senses of focus or merging of options. Yet in many earlier periods, we have noticed, this is a state of mind that ties in much more closely with administrative structures shaping 'community' and with localized spatial identities. A break-up of those earlier community *structures* of belonging has been a theme of this book: of templates of parochialism, in which identities were highly localized and mediated through legal concepts of welfare and attained settlement, in which people had rights in localities where they belonged and in which a multitude of differing local communities were entrenched and culturally constructed with these in mind. This was a common pattern across all of England and Wales, established in law and custom, even though there was variety in the forms it took. These systems of belonging, exemplifications and bases of community have radically altered over time. The 'spirit' of community has become less rooted in local material conditions, less framed by structures of need and legal entitlement, less religious at least in administratively Anglican or Nonconformist Christian senses, more evanescent, transcendent and choosy as a necessary force or as a mental requirement.

For many now, 'community' is not needed, or has become understood simply as 'people who share certain interests' – as one of my younger students defined it to me recently. The modern networking 'community' is voluntary, needing to be maintained, being flexibly abandoned or opportunistically adapted according to changing circumstances. It allows free-floating choices and attachments, and positions people very differently and spatially in relation to others compared with the past. It isolates people from many of the earlier faded structures and obligations that were once highly important and security endowing. In its sometimes failed forms, in its individualized kite-flying with loose attachments, it can be a recipe for loneliness, not least among those who do not use or relish its methods of connectivity. It is sustained by new selective, overwhelmingly capitalist and as yet still partially incorporating technologies. These traverse or displace many earlier features or cohesions of community, such as localized welfare systems, ideas about 'home' and 'friends', much of the religious spirit and ethics of local community, or locally shared occupational identities and class-based solidarities.

One of the lessons of this book has been the extent to which people in the past diagnosed or depicted problems of 'declining community', or 'crises of community', and we have seen many such examples here. In some cases, the tone of these has been lamenting, in others glad. There is nothing new in our concern with this issue in recent decades, and while one does not wish to minimize current social problems nor the creditable efforts to deal with them, we have certainly been here before, in very many ways. Even so, there is a transition disclosed in this book, over the past few centuries. One can describe the historical changes in different ways, just as one can use different metaphors. I have shown some of the processes involved in the contrasts between these chapters, which give culturally expressive and documentary form to phases of this. The legalized structures of our earliest period were widely acquiesced in: they drew rich and poor together in broadly shared structural understandings of what the parish community was. Wealthy and poor had a common terminology of belonging, 'friends' and community in these respects. This was the case even though 'community' could also extend beyond the parish in many ways, and even though parochial communities certainly rarely meant social unity in any avoidance of distinction and inequality. It has been stressed here how often past 'community' involved internal conflict and dissentient opinion. Of course such communities frequently entailed this, within and between them, precisely because the personalities and tensions in them were so often unavoidable. This is obvious in sources such as John Clare's *The Parish: A Satire*, the Revd John Skinner's Somerset diary, M. K. Ashby's *Joseph Ashby of Tysoe*, in industrial novels from Mrs Gaskell to D. H. Lawrence or in the Welsh writing of Caradoc Evans.[1] That conflict may not often have been class based in its earlier forms, for class overrides and traverses locality in most estimates or theory, and these people had strongly localized attachments and prerogatives.[2] It may often have featured relatively mild discord, based on envy or rivalry, via the excitable slurs of gossip: consider for example Dylan Thomas's *Under Milk Wood*. But whatever its forms, I have stressed throughout that 'community' – especially when it is understood structurally and administratively – does not exclude conflict, and in anti-nostalgic ways it needs to be understood as often involving that. It may be that in their more idealized or wishful forms, some of the earlier community styles and principles approximated to the landscape painting produced by Edward Haytley in 1744, as discussed in Chapter 3. This had been a style of community as expectantly all-seen from above, patriarchal in both gendered and socially hierarchical meanings of that word, a localized prospect, with people 'in their place' both socially and by appropriate distance geographically or spatially, apparently content with their coordinated rank in social life. Yet while such 'estate villages' in the standards of their time often enjoyed preferential welfare and employment systems, there are reasons not to be nostalgic about this, not least because such community representation was always partial in view. The date of Haytley's painting (1744) also reminds us of the Vagrancy Act of that year, with its litany of potential vagrant classifications and offences. There is no doubt that such sanguine communal depictions had their darker sides not shown for view – the roadside vagrants with scarred backs, the spurned 'Egyptian' or gypsy, the humiliated single mother, white-sheeted and undertaking penance in church. What did 'community spirit' mean to such people?

Some earlier ideas about community, depicted in my opening chapters, persisted in later ideas propagated in parish magazines. However, they did so in forms that lacked many of their earlier binding and obligatory economic coordinates, and in which elite guidance was often more clerical, following the Anglican revival of the mid-nineteenth century. They were now community orientated in differing, partial, religiously motivated and sometimes exclusionary ways. The parish was losing its coherence as an economic reality, one in which 'community' had been bound together via parochial and (until 1868) church rates, through mainly localized labour markets, and with 'ethical' ideas about community cohering because of settlement law and welfare needs and methods.

The break-up of the earlier structures has been seen here in various depictions, from George Morland's peripatetic roadside migrants, an embarrassment to contemporary art patrons, or the increasingly obscure Jude, as he leaves the demoralized village for the impersonalized town, or the frequent anti-Nonconformity of the Anglican parish magazine, or the class-based suspicions and finger pointing of the crime-infatuated interwar detective writers and readers. These all show representational stages in the dissolving of earlier models of community. So do the hoped-for insistence upon an East Anglian 'agricultural community' in the writings of Adrian Bell, like Thomas Hardy sceptical about alternative urban styles of living. Or there were the waning water-edge occupational and estate communities described by James Wentworth Day. These writers were aware that much of their writing occurred in periods of national abdication of support to agriculture, and people collectively engaged in it. They were all strongly conscious of ideas of community slipping away from localized economic footings. So were many writers on occupational communities, notably during the last century of British de-industrialization – and many forms of voluntary association and so-called thick (or close, cohesive) community have fallen away too, often because an industrial base perished with international competition. That is a narrative we are all familiar with, whatever our region, generation or political experience. One thinks of the marching faces of Maerdy Colliery in the Rhondda valley, remembered now as solemn spirits from the past. Yet when that pit closed in 1990, only seventeen out of 300 workers there wished to remain in the industry and transfer to other collieries. Further, in termination of this book, we have seen the intensely disliked occupational boot-and-shoe communities of H. E. Bates's youth, before he brought us, with some amused but affectionate irony, to the individualized, opportunistic, consumer-fixated world of the 1960s and beyond, presaging many of the problems facing us today of living beyond apparent economic means, and of indulgence-related ill-health.

As the subjects of this book make clear, these changes in senses of community go well beyond a working-class or industrial narrative. One could write such a book as an analysis of industrial community and its questions of cohesion – extending my discussion of H. E. Bates – but of course the changes analysed here go much wider and affect many more. The broader transition in community representation has evidently been a widespread one of material conditions, for the ending of earlier structures and spirits of community has been related in complex ways to economic prosperity: from the pauperism or hungry letter writers of the late eighteenth or early nineteenth centuries, to the superabundant clued materialism of the crime writers, and then to the food consumption and obesity exemplars – remediable by 'the National Elf lark' – of H. E. Bates's Larkin family. Sources of security have indeed shifted from the local arena to national rights and benefits, via a succession of legislation, from 'parish state' to the welfare state. The individualized problems of today, whether in the form of Eleanor Rigby or of more affluent loneliness – with the social science and psychology that came with modernity as first-aid explication of isolation and individualism – are often related to absent local structures, to senses of loss in hitherto socially and legally constructed community, also affecting many forms of working- and middle-class organization. For now we often lack communities of mutual reliance, and we seek to establish some such in a perplexing personalized diversity of local or international ways. Our many commentators reassure us that modern friendship networks, or communication technologies, or welfare states, are adequate or better substitutes for previous communities and associations, endowing us with freedoms that our ancestors often lacked and (could they envisage them) might have aspired to gain. Past spirits of community have ceased to be needed for economic if not social reasons, and the trans-local nature of modern individualism and technologies releases the potential of colossal creativity, unprecedented market penetration and internationally communicated reflection. Yet one can think of many modern attempts to offer community forms and language to disclose or make up for what has historically been left behind. And in some respects, perhaps, this book is one of them.

Notes

Chapter 1

1 Mental Health Foundation, *The Lonely Society?* (London, 2010); T. Dumm, *Loneliness as a Way of Life* (2008, Cambridge, Mass., 2010); R. Weiss, *Loneliness: The Experience of Social and Emotional Loneliness* (Cambridge, Mass., 1973); C. Killeen, 'Loneliness: an epidemic in modern society', *Journal of Advanced Nursing*, 28 (1998); J. T. Cacioppo and W. Patrick, *Loneliness: Human Nature and the Need for Social Connection* (New York, 2008); A. S. Franklin, 'On loneliness', *Geografiska Annaler. Series B, Human Geography*, 91 (2009); I. Kar-Purkayastha, 'An epidemic of loneliness', *Lancet*, 376 (2010). Loneliness in the medical and psychological literature is associated with increased incidence of heart attack, strokes, cancers, bulimia nervosa, drug abuse, alcoholism, unhealthy diets, less exercise, sleep deprivation, depression, anxiety and premature death.

2 The literature on British national identity, rurality and nostalgic loss is voluminous and relevant to ideas about community spirit. See e.g. R. Williams, *The Country and the City* (London, 1973); M. J. Wiener, *English Culture and the Decline of the Industrial Spirit, 1850–1980* (Cambridge, 1981); P. Wright, *On Living in an Old Country: The National Past in Contemporary Britain* (1985, Oxford, 2009); R. Colls and P. Dodd (eds), *Englishness: Politics and Culture, 1880–1920* (London, 1986); P. Mandler, 'Against "Englishness": English culture and the limits to rural nostalgia, 1850–1940', *Transactions of the Royal Historical Society*, 7 (1997); D. Matless, *Landscape and Englishness* (London, 1998); R. Colls, *The Identity of England* (Oxford, 2002); R. Colls, '"When we lived in communities": working-class culture and its critics', in R. Colls and R. Rodger (eds), *Cities of Ideas: Civil Society and Urban Governance in Britain, 1800–2000* (Aldershot, 2004); P. Mandler, *The English National Character: The History of an Idea from Edmund Burke to Tony Blair* (New Haven, Conn., 2006). On English individualism and community see A. Macfarlane, *The Culture of Capitalism* (Oxford, 1987).

3 M. R. Stein, *The Eclipse of Community: An Interpretation of American Studies* (Princeton, 1960); A. Leigh, *Disconnected: The Decline of Community and the Fraying of Social Fabric in Modern Australia* (Sydney, 2010); R. Putnam, *Bowling Alone: The Collapse and Revival of American Community* (New York, 2001).

4 I do not wish to repeat past publications, and so the theme of local belonging, often important in these pages, is not expanded upon in the detail which it received in

my *Parish and Belonging: Community, Identity and Welfare in England and Wales, 1700–1950* (Cambridge, 2006).

5 G. A. Hillery, 'Definitions of community: areas of agreement', *Rural Sociology*, 2 (1955); A. Macfarlane, *Reconstructing Historical Communities* (Cambridge, 1977), ch. 1 (and for criticism of community studies); A. Macfarlane, 'History, anthropology and the study of communities', *Social History*, 2 (1977); C. J. Calhoun, 'History, anthropology and the study of communities: some problems with Macfarlane's proposal', *Social History*, 3 (1978); C. J. Calhoun, 'Community: towards a variable conceptualization for comparative research', *Social History*, 5 (1980); T. Bender, *Community and Social Change in America* (1978, Baltimore, 1982), esp. chs 1–2; A. Mason, *Community, Solidarity and Belonging: Levels of Community and Their Normative Significance* (Cambridge, 2000), ch. 1; B. Alleyne, 'An idea of community and its discontents: towards a more reflexive sense of belonging in multicultural Britain', *Ethnic and Racial Studies*, 25 (2002).

6 The literature is extensive, but see R. Frankenberg, *Communities in Britain: Social Life in Town and Country* (1966, Harmondsworth, 1970); G. Crow and G. Allan, *Community Life: An Introduction to Local Social Relations* (Hemel Hempstead, 1994); C. Bell and H. Newby, *Community Studies: An Introduction to the Sociology of the Local Community* (London, 1971); E. Davies and A. D. Rees (eds), *Welsh Community Studies* (Cardiff, 1960); and G. Lewis, 'Welsh rural community studies: retrospect and prospect', *Cambria*, 13 (1986), providing a welcome defence of the genre. Influential subsequent discussion includes M. Strathern, *Kinship at the Core: An Anthropology of Elmdon, a Village in North-West Essex in the Nineteen-Sixties* (Cambridge, 1981); A. P. Cohen (ed.), *Belonging: Identity and Social Organisation in British Rural Cultures* (Manchester, 1982); A. P. Cohen (ed.), *Symbolising Boundaries: Identity and Diversity in British Cultures* (Manchester, 1986); V. Amit (ed.), *Realizing Community: Concepts, Social Relationships and Sentiments* (London, 2002); V. Amit and N. Rapport, *The Trouble with Community: Anthropological Reflections on Movement, Identity and Collectivity* (London, 2002).

7 G. Crow, 'Community studies: fifty years of theorization', *Sociological Research Online*, 7 (2002).

8 For example, J. Rutherford (ed.), *Identity: Community, Culture, Difference* (London, 1990).

9 R. Blythe, *The View in Winter* (1979, Harmondsworth, 1981), p. 200.

10 Ibid., pp. 211–13.

11 T. More, *Utopia and a Dialogue of Comfort* (1516, London, 1951), p. 26.

12 J. Clare, *The Parish: A Satire* (1820, London, 1986); E. Robinson (ed.), *John Clare's Autobiographical Writings* (Oxford, 1986); S. Bamford, *Early Days* (London, 1841), on the family economies, folklore and ethos of an earlier Lancashire handloom-weaving community and attacking the growth of classes; T. Carter, *Continuation of*

the Memoirs of a Working Man (London, 1850), pp. 27, 239, stressing his 'growing dislike and dread of change', his sense of increasingly standing alone 'like a withered tree in the midst of a desolate and dreary wilderness'; D. Parry-Jones, *My Own Folk* (Llandysul, 1972), on earlier Carmarthenshire communities. Autobiographical statements praising past communities as compared with the present abound throughout Cobbett's writing, but see W. Cobbett, *The Autobiography of William Cobbett: the Progress of a Plough-Boy to a Seat in Parliament* (1933, London, 1967); G. D. H. Cole (ed.), *The Life and Adventures of Peter Porcupine* (1796, London, 1927); I. Dyck, *William Cobbett and Rural Popular Culture* (Cambridge, 1992); A. Nicolson, *Arcadia: The Dream of Perfection in Renaissance England* (London, 2008), ch. 12.

13 A. W. N. Pugin, *Contrasts* (1836, Leicester, 1969).

14 W. Hazlitt, *The Spirit of the Age, or, Contemporary Portraits* (1825, London, 1969), p. 96.

15 C. Achebe, *Things Fall Apart* (1958, London, 2006). The title is from W. B. Yeats' poem 'The Second Coming'.

16 G. Cavaliero, *The Rural Tradition in the English Novel, 1900–1939* (London, 1977), with chapters on 'The land of lost content' and 'Romantic landscapes'.

17 G. Bourne [Sturt], *Change in the Village* (1912, Harmondsworth, 1984).

18 For example, 'Village community councils', *The Times*, 11 Aug. 1925, p. 9.

19 Examples include W. G. Hoskins, *The Midland Peasant: The Economic and Social History of a Leicestershire Village* (London, 1957); B. J. Davey, *Ashwell, 1830–1914: The Decline of a Village Community* (Leicester, 1980).

20 Colls, 'When we lived in communities'.

21 H. Dixon, 'Our community spirit is lost', *Daily Telegraph*, 21 Dec. 2013, p. 4.

22 'Whatever happened to community?', BBC Radio 4 (9 Dec. 2013).

23 D. Hardy, *Utopian England: Community Experiments, 1900–1945* (London, 2000).

24 R. Gant, 'Railway villages in south west Monmouthshire, 1850–1965: a community perspective', *Local Population Studies*, 90 (2013); K. Hudson, 'The early days of the railway community in Swindon', *Transport History*, 1 (1968); G. Revill, '"Railway Derby": occupational community, paternalism and corporate culture, 1850–90', *Urban History*, 28 (2001); D. K. Drummond, *Crewe: Railway Town, Company and People, 1840–1914* (Aldershot, 1995).

25 D. Walls, *Community Organizing: Fanning the Flame of Democracy* (Cambridge, 2015).

26 On this concept, see R. Pahl, *On Friendship* (Cambridge, 2000), p. 17.

27 A summary of this view in L. Jamieson and R. Simpson, *Living Alone: Globalization, Identity and Belonging* (Basingstoke, 2013), p. 155.

28 For example, in a poll of 2,000 people by the Holocaust Memorial Trust, 64 per cent of British people said that they rarely or never socialized with people from their area. 'Most Britons hardly know their neighbours', *Daily Telegraph*, 25 Jan. 2013, p. 9.

29 N. Charles and C. A. Davies, 'Studying the particular, illuminating the general: community studies and community in Wales', *Sociological Review*, 53 (2005), p. 672.

30 For valuable pre-internet discussion, see E. Goffman, *Stigma: Notes on the Management of Spoiled Identity* (1963, Harmondsworth, 1990).

31 Pahl, *On Friendship*; L. Spencer and R. E. Pahl, *Re-thinking Friendship: Hidden Solidarities Today* (Princeton, 2006).

32 See e.g. R. Stivers, *Shades of Loneliness: Pathologies of a Technological Society* (Lanham, Md., 2004); G. Lovink, *Networks without a Cause: A Critique of Social Media* (Cambridge, 2011); P. Connerton, *How Modernity Forgets* (Cambridge, 2009); or more positively N. K. Baym, *Personal Connections in the Digital Age* (Cambridge, 2010); V. Miller, *Understanding Digital Culture* (London, 2011).

33 A. Storr, *Solitude* (1988, Harmondsworth, 1988).

34 C. R. Long and J. R. Averill, 'Solitude; an exploration of the benefits of being alone', *Journal for the Theory of Social Behaviour*, 33 (2003), p. 40.

35 British and North American studies show that 30–50 per cent of those surveyed feel lonely; 10–25 per cent report severe loneliness. See e.g. C. R. Victor and A. Bowling, 'A longitudinal analysis of loneliness among older people in Great Britain', *Journal of Psychology: Interdisciplinary and Applied*, 146 (2012); A. Rokach, 'Alienation and domestic abuse: how abused women cope with loneliness', *Social Indicators Research*, 78 (2006); A. Rokach and H. Brock, 'Loneliness: a multidimensional experience', *Psychology: A Journal of Human Behaviour*, 34 (1997); K. D. M. Snell, 'Agendas for the historical study of loneliness and lone living', *The Open Psychology Journal*, 8 (2015). The statistics may be worsening. The Mental Health Foundation (J. Griffin), *The Lonely Society?* (London, 2010), p. 12, found that only 22 per cent of people surveyed never felt lonely, and 42 per cent have felt depressed through loneliness. Loneliness especially afflicts very young adults and the elderly.

36 M. Wark, *Telesthesia: Communication, Culture and Class* (Cambridge, 2012).

37 On virtual or 'online communities', see e.g. H. Rheingold, *The Virtual Community: Homesteading on the Electronic Frontier* (1993, London, 2000); J. Preece, *Online Communities: Designing Usability, Supporting Sociability* (Chichester, 2000).

38 N. Elias, *The Society of Individuals* (New York, 2001); H. O'Connor and J. Goodwin, 'Revisiting Norbert Elias's sociology of community: learning from the Leicester re-studies', *The Sociological Review*, 60 (2012), pp. 482–4, on the relation of personality structures to shifts in the structure of human relations.

39 This theme is developed in K. D. M. Snell, 'Churchyard closures, rural cemeteries and the village community in Leicestershire and Rutland, 1800–2010', *Journal of Ecclesiastical History*, 63: 4 (2012).

40 T. Hardy, 1912 preface to *Far from the Madding Crowd* (1874, London, 1971), p. vi.

41 M. Augé, *Non-Places: Introduction to an Anthropology of Supermodernity* (1995, London, 2000). See also Chapter 5, on the significance and symbolism of the railway in Thomas Hardy's novel accounts.

42 U. Beck, *Risk Society: Towards a New Modernity* (1986, London, 2007), p. 123 (his italics).

43 Z. Bauman, *Liquid Love: On the Frailty of Human Bonds* (Cambridge, 2003); Z. Bauman, *Community: Seeking Safety in an Insecure World* (2001, Cambridge, 2007); or the discussion and many references in Franklin, 'On loneliness'.

44 Bauman, *Liquid Love*, pp. vii–xi, 7, 13, 66.

45 Pahl, *On Friendship*, p. 167.

46 For example, B. Dylan, 'It's all over now, Baby Blue'.

47 Stivers, *Shades of Loneliness*, p. 6.

48 M. Houellebecq, *Atomised* (1998, London, 2000).

49 R. Kolker, *A Cinema of Loneliness* (1980, Oxford, 2011), p. 10.

50 M. Hughes and W. R. Gove, 'Living alone, social integration, and mental health', *American Journal of Sociology*, 87 (1981); D. Perlman and L. A. Peplau, 'Loneliness research: a survey of empirical findings', in L. A. Peplau and S. Goldston (eds), *Preventing the Harmful Consequences of Severe and Persistent Loneliness* (Washington, 1984), p. 34; M. J. Essex and S. Nam, 'Marital status and loneliness among older women; the differential importance of close family and friends', *Journal of Marriage and Family*, 49 (1987), p. 95; S. Stack, 'Marriage, family and loneliness: a cross-national study', *Sociological Perspectives*, 41 (1998); H. Brock and A. Rokach, 'Coping with loneliness', *Journal of Psychology*, 132 (1998); Victor and Bowling, 'A longitudinal analysis of loneliness among older people in Great Britain', pp. 323, 327.

51 E. Klinenberg, 'One's a crowd', *The New York Times, Sunday Review*, 4 Feb. 2012; E. Klinenberg, *Going Solo: The Extraordinary Rise and Surprising Appeal of Living Alone* (2012, New York, 2013), pp. 147, 208, 213–22 on Sweden. His book only covers urban areas, and interprets this development more favourably than other commentators, though he is aware of the many adverse consequences.

52 A. Bell, *Sunrise to Sunset* (London, 1944), p. 75.

53 Innovation in community structure (e.g. Silicon Valley) is discussed in K. Giuffre, *Communities and Networks: Using Social Network Analysis to Rethink Urban and Community Studies* (Cambridge, 2013).

54 On agricultural 'occupational community', see H. Newby, *Country Life: A Social History of Rural England* (London, 1987), pp. 76–103, 220–2. Many villages were becoming more of an 'occupational community' during the nineteenth and early twentieth centuries, because of rural deindustrialization and thus a situation in which their 'whole existence was intimately bound up with the fortunes of a single industry – farming'. This was to change again after *c.* 1945, given transport developments, commuters and occupational diversification, when 'the "locals", faced with an invasion of "their" community by outsiders, tended to retreat in upon themselves, forming a community within a community' (ibid., pp. 77, 222).

55 R. Hoggart, *The Uses of Literacy* (London, 1957), covers the then new consumerism affecting senses of working-class community.
56 For fascinating recent discussion, see G. Redmonds, T. King and D. Hey, *Surnames, DNA, and Family History* (Oxford, 2011).
57 H. E. Bates, *An Autobiography* (London, 2006), p. 514.
58 F. Tönnies, *Gemeinschaft und Gesellschaft* (Leipzig, 1887), trans. as *Community and Society* (Cambridge, 2001), pp. 260–1.
59 R. Williams, *The Country and the City* (1973, London, 1985).
60 For further regional options, many of whom wrote directly about 'community', see K. D. M. Snell, *The Bibliography of Regional Fiction in Britain and Ireland, 1800–2000* (Aldershot, 2002).
61 For example, R. Turner, *Coal was Our Life: An Essay on Life in a Yorkshire Pit Town* (Sheffield, 2000); B. Dicks, *Heritage, Place and Community* (Cardiff, 2000); K. Bennett, H. Beynon and R. Hudson, *Coalfields Regeneration: Dealing with the Consequences of Industrial Decline* (Bristol, 2000); M. Neary, *Faith in the Coalfields: Community Regeneration or Managing Decline?* (London, 2002).
62 G. Boyes, *The Imagined Village: Culture, Ideology and the English Folk Revival* (Manchester, 1993); and one thinks of the early twenty-first-century folk band The Imagined Village, with its international influences.
63 C. Phythian-Adams, *Desolation of a City: Coventry and the Urban Crisis of the Late Middle Ages* (Cambridge, 1979); C. Dyer, 'The English medieval village community and its decline', *Journal of British Studies*, 33 (1994); R. Hutton, *The Rise and Fall of Merry England: The Ritual Year, 1400–1700* (1994, Oxford, 1996); E. Duffy, *The Voices of Morebath: Reformation and Rebellion in an English Village* (2001, London, 2003).
64 R. Blythe, *A Year at Bottengoms Farm* (2006, Norwich, 2007), p. 60.
65 A. Bell, *Apple Acre* (1942, London, 1943), p. 42.
66 E. R. Chamberlain, *Life in Wartime Britain* (London, 1972), pp. 52–3; M. Donnelly, *Britain in the Second World War* (London, 1999), p. 33.
67 See especially M. Castells, *The Information Age: Economy, Society and Culture. Vol. 2: The Power of Identity* (1997, Oxford, 2007).
68 A. Bell, *The Cherry Tree* (1932, London, 1949), p. 42.

Chapter 2

1 T. Sokoll (ed.), *Essex Pauper Letters, 1731–1837* (Oxford, 2001); P. Sharpe, '"The bowels of compation": a labouring family and the law, *c.* 1790–1834', in T. Hitchcock, P. King and P. Sharpe (eds), *Chronicling Poverty: The Voices and Strategies of the English Poor, 1640–1840* (Basingstoke, 1997); J. S. Taylor, 'Voices

in the crowd: the Kirkby Lonsdale letters, 1809–36', in Hitchcock, King and Sharpe (eds), *Chronicling Poverty*; T. Sokoll, 'Old age in poverty: the record of Essex pauper letters, 1780–1834', in Hitchcock, King and Sharpe (eds), *Chronicling Poverty*; G. C. Smith, '"The poor in blindnes": letters from Mildenhall, Wiltshire, 1835–6', in Hitchcock, King and Sharpe (eds), *Chronicling Poverty*; A. Tomkins, 'Self presentation in pauper letters and the case of Ellen Parker, 1818–1827', *Women's History Notebooks*, 6 (1999); S. King, 'Friendship, kinship and belonging in the letters of urban paupers, 1800–1840', *Historical Social Research*, 33 (2008). Pauper letters are used in T. Hitchcock, *Down and Out in Eighteenth-Century London* (London, 2004); there may be over 10,000 of these letters in existence: S. King, 'Pauper letters as a source', *Family and Community History*, 10 (2007), p. 167.

2 The poor were about 70–90 per cent of the English population in the late eighteenth and early nineteenth century. 'Pauper' means those needing poor relief, who were between 5 and 50 per cent of a parish population at any one time. Higher proportions of the poor needed relief at some point in their lives. On terminology, see J. R. Poynter, *Society and Pauperism: English Ideas on Poor Relief, 1795–1834* (London, 1969); G. Himmelfarb, *The Idea of Poverty: England in the Early Industrial Age* (London, 1984), ch. 3.

3 A few letters raise issues of 'authorship', see Sokoll (ed.), *Essex Pauper Letters*, pp. 568, 570, 591, 593; N. Pilbeam and I. Nelson (eds), *Poor Law Records of mid Sussex, 1601–1835* (Lewes, 2000), p. 382.

4 E. C. Brewer, *Brewer's Dictionary of Phrase and Fable* (1870, London, 1986), pp. 454–5.

5 A. Macfarlane, *The Family Life of Ralph Josselin, a Seventeenth-Century Clergyman: An Essay in Historical Anthropology* (Cambridge, 1970); D. O'Hara, *Courtship and Constraint: Rethinking the Making of Marriage in Tudor England* (Manchester, 2000); N. Tadmor, *Family and Friends in Eighteenth-Century England: Household, Kinship, and Patronage* (Cambridge, 2001), ch. 5.

6 R. Williams, *Keywords: A Vocabulary of Culture and Society* (Glasgow, 1976), p. 65.

7 Expansive usage is not new: e.g. 'the great community of the world', in 'Proceedings and intelligence', *Missionary Register*, 1 June 1828. On wide modern usage of 'community', see R. Putnam, *Bowling Alone: The Collapse and Revival of American Community* (New York, 2000), pp. 273–4; Z. Bauman, *Community: Seeking Safety in an Insecure World* (Cambridge, 2001); G. Delanty, *Community* (London, 2003); G. Day, *Community and Everyday Life* (Abingdon, 2006). DNA patterning and surname-sharing extends debates into new historical fields and conceptions of community and identity. G. Redmonds, T. King and D. Hey, *Surnames, DNA, and Family History* (Oxford, 2011).

8 F. Tönnies, *Gemeinschaft und Gesellschaft* (Leipzig, 1887), trans. as *Community and Society* (Cambridge, 2001).

9 *Sixth Report from the Select Committee on Settlement* (P.P. XI, 1847), pp. 151–2, 159.

10 K. D. M. Snell, *Parish and Belonging: Community, Identity and Welfare in England and Wales, 1700–1950* (Cambridge, 2006), esp. chs 2–3; J. S. Taylor, 'The impact of pauper settlement, 1691–1834', *Past and Present*, 73 (1976); and J. S. Taylor, *Poverty, Migration, and Settlement in the Industrial Revolution: Sojourners' Narratives* (Palo Alto, Calif., 1989). The latest discussion, strongly linking settlement law and practice with the right to relief, is L. Charlesworth, *Welfare's Forgotten Past: A Socio-legal History of the Poor Law* (London, 2009).

11 E. J. Lidbetter, *Settlement and Removal* (London, 1932), p. 39 (his italics).

12 On modern home community, see N. Rapport and A. Davison (eds), *Migrants of Identity: Perceptions of 'Home' in a World of Movement* (Oxford, 1998).

13 S. King, T. Nutt and A. Tomkins (eds), *Narratives of the Poor in Eighteenth-Century Britain. Volume 1: Voices of the Poor: Poor Law Depositions and Letters* (London, 2006), pp. 263, 266, 268.

14 J. Barrell, *The Spirit of Despotism: Invasions of Privacy in the 1790s* (Oxford, 2006), ch. 5.

15 Sokoll (ed.), *Essex Pauper Letters*, p. 149. In all quotations, syntax, spelling, capitalization and parentheses are as in the originals.

16 Ibid., p. 178.

17 Pilbeam and Nelson (eds), *Poor Law Records of mid Sussex*, p. 379.

18 Sokoll (ed.), *Essex Pauper Letters*, pp. 179–80.

19 Ibid., p. 117 (1829).

20 Record Office for Leicestershire, Leicester and Rutland (ROLLR), 17D 64/F/224.

21 Sokoll (ed.), *Essex Pauper Letters*, p. 214.

22 Ibid., p. 101.

23 King, Nutt and Tomkins (eds), *Narratives of the Poor*, p. 84 (Elizabeth King, writing from Ely to Thrapston, 1825).

24 The legal heads of poor law settlement – the ways one came to 'belong' to a parish or township and thus to be eligible there for poor relief – were birth for an illegitimate person; marriage for a woman, who thereby lost her maiden settlement and now belonged to her husband's settlement; serving a public annual office in the parish; payment of parish rates; renting property with a combined annual value of £10 or more; by yearly service for a full year while unmarried (this 'head' was abolished in 1834); serving a legal indentured apprenticeship and residing in the parish for 40 days during one's term; owning estate in the parish; and, if none of these applied, one took one's paternal settlement. Snell, *Parish and Belonging*, ch. 3.

25 Many parishes have surviving overseer correspondence; e.g. Market Harborough (Leics.), ROLLR, DE1587/155–156, 164–170 (1702–1829). On overseers' letters in north-west England, see S. King, '"It is impossible for our vestry to judge his case into perfection from here": managing the distance dimensions of poor relief', 1800–40, *Rural History*, 16 (2005).

26 9 & 10 Vic. c. 66 (1846), which introduced the concept of poor law 'irremovability' after five years residence or for a year after widowhood.
27 A. Sen, *Identity and Violence: The Illusion of Destiny* (New York, 2006).
28 Snell, *Parish and Belonging*, pp. 184–6.
29 King, Nutt and Tomkins (eds), *Narratives of the Poor*, p. 71 (1833).
30 Ibid., p. 28 (1829); p. 30 (1830); p. 24 (1829); p. 14 (1824); p. 20 (1827).
31 Sokoll (ed.), *Essex Pauper Letters*, p. 576 (1833).
32 On non-resident relief, see J. S. Taylor, 'A different kind of Speenhamland: nonresident relief in the Industrial Revolution', *Journal of British Studies*, 30 (1991); S. King, *Poverty and Welfare in England, 1700–1850: A Regional Perspective* (Manchester, 2000), pp. 186–8, 238–9; King, 'It is impossible'; Snell, *Parish and Belonging*, ch. 3.
33 Sokoll (ed.), *Essex Pauper Letters*, p. 100 (n.d.).
34 Ibid., pp. 105, 110.
35 Ibid., pp. 112, 116 (1828–29).
36 Sokoll (ed.), *Essex Pauper Letters*, pp. 178–9 (1824).
37 Pilbeam and Nelson (eds), *Poor law Records*, p. 380 (1826).
38 King, Nutt and Tomkins (eds), *Narratives of the Poor*, pp. 10–11.
39 Ibid., p. 14 (1824).
40 Ibid., p. 116.
41 Ibid., p. 239.
42 In referring to 'parish' in connection with settlement I use the term to mean 'parish or township'. (In northern poor law practice, the township was often the poor law/settlement unit rather than the wider parish, and this was also true of some southern, midland and Welsh places.)
43 King, Nutt and Tomkins (eds), *Narratives of the Poor*, p. 162.
44 ROLLR, 17 D 64/F/231 (21 May 1819).
45 R. Pahl, *On Friendship* (Cambridge, 2000), pp. 34–5, where he also notes this previous elision of 'friend' and relative for England.
46 'To the Worthy Electors of Westminster', *London Evening Post*, 14 Dec. 1749; L. Namier, *The Structure of Politics at the Accession of George III* (London, 1929).
47 J. C. S. Mason, *The Moravian Church and the Missionary Awakening in England, 1760–1800* (London, 2001), p. 199.
48 'The Business of the late Mr. William Richards', *London Evening Post*, 10 Nov. 1748; 'John Stanley, Apothecary', *Dublin Mercury*, 1 Aug. 1769.
49 Jessy Harden, unpub. diary, 9 Sept. 1806, cited in J. L. Fraser, *John Constable, 1776–1837* (Newton Abbot, 1976), p. 41.
50 'Articles of intelligence from the daily papers of yesterday', *Gazetteer and London Daily Advertiser*, 27 Dec. 1760.
51 'London', *General Evening Post*, 27 Oct. 1748.

52 *Daily Gazetteer*, 1 Jan. 1740.

53 Pahl, *On Friendship*; R. E. Pahl and D. J. Pevalin, 'Between family and friends: a longitudinal study of friendship choice', *British Journal of Sociology*, 56 (2005); L. Spencer and R. E. Pahl, *Re-thinking Friendship: Hidden Solidarities Today* (Princeton, 2006); R. Pahl, 'Friendship, trust and mutuality', in J. Haworth and G. Hart (eds), *Well-Being: Individual, Community and Social Perspectives* (Basingstoke, 2007); A. Bray, *The Friend* (2003, Chicago, 2007); and, for such issues in a black urban community in mid-western America, C. B. Stack, *All Our Kin* (1974, New York, 1997).

54 Walter, *My Secret Life* (1972, London, 1984), pp. 271, 283, 285, 286, 289, 335.

55 On 'social capital' see J. Field, *Social Capital* (London, 2003); P. Bourdieu, *Outline of a Theory of Practice* (1972, Cambridge, 1977).

56 A. Giddens, *The Consequences of Modernity* (Cambridge, 1990); A. Giddens, *Modernity and Self-Identity: Self and Society in the Late Modern Age* (Cambridge, 1991). On a closely related theme, making many relevant generalizations, e.g. about vagrant morality as characteristic of the present, see U. Beck and E. Beck-Gernsheim, *Individualization: Institutionalized Individualism and Its Social and Political Consequences* (2001, London, 2002).

57 The petitions are in the archive of the Thomas Coram Foundation, London Metropolitan Archive. I use here A. Levene (ed.), *Narratives of the Poor in Eighteenth-Century Britain. Volume 3: Institutional Responses: The London Foundling Hospital* (London, 2006), pp. 171–365.

58 Ibid., pp. 179–80, 200, 203, 206–7.

59 Ibid., pp. 280, 297–8.

60 Ibid., pp. 208, 222, 224, 226, 238, 244, 247, 252, 259. 269, 291, 295, 309.

61 Ibid., pp. 214–16, 228–9, 266.

62 Ibid., pp. 198, 242.

63 Ibid., p. 327 (1792). The use of 'friends' to describe relatives was common in emigrants' letters, e.g. Sarah Varley wrote from Cincinnati to her brother and sister, addressing them 'Dear Friends'. Sarah Varley to Thomas Varley, in Tadcaster, 23 Jan. 1843. Letter in the possession of Keith Turner (Oadby, Leics.), whose collection of emigrants' letters has many mentions of 'friends' in this and other senses.

64 Levene (ed.), *Narratives of the Poor*, pp. 204, 318.

65 P. King (ed.), *Narratives of the Poor in Eighteenth-Century Britain. Volume 4: Institutional Responses: The Refuge for the Destitute* (London, 2006), pp. 67–438.

66 Ibid., pp. 81, 87–8, 93, 128–9 (dated 1812–14).

67 Ibid., pp. 153–4, 236, 321.

68 Ibid., pp. 79, 110–11, 211, 258.

69 King, Nutt and Tomkins (eds), *Narratives of the Poor*, p. 97.

70 Sokoll (ed.), *Essex Pauper Letters*, p. 557 (n.d.), p. 418: 'you, who have been my friend'; in the same sentence he calls the overseer 'Sir' (1822).

71 Ibid., p. 209 (Arthur Tabrum writing from London to the vestry clerk, Chelmsford, 1825).

72 Ibid., p. 588 (Mary Craske writing from Rushbrooke (Suffolk) to Joseph Wise in Rochford, 1809).

73 King, Nutt and Tomkins (eds), *Narratives of the Poor*, p. 226 (John Sayer writing from Oxford to the overseer of Colwich, Staffs., 1810).

74 43 Eliz. c. 2 (1601) laid down what were considered to be normal obligations of kinship. This phraseology of kin obligation was long enduring; e.g. the 1927 Poor Law Act, s. 41.

75 Issues of personal or collective motivation in such sources are raised in M. Reed and R. Wells (eds), *Class, Conflict and Protest in the English Countryside, 1700–1880* (London, 1990).

76 E. P. Thompson, *The Making of the English Working Class* (1963, Harmondsworth, 1975); E. P. Thompson, *Customs in Common* (1991, London 1993).

77 On 'transactive memory', G. Smith, 'Beyond individual/collective memory: women's transactive memories of food, family and conflict', *Oral History*, 35 (2007).

78 Sokoll (ed.), *Essex Pauper Letters*, p. 595.

79 Compare the account of an 'ethical community' in Bauman, *Community*, pp. 72, 98–9, and his analysis of identity stories.

80 P. Laslett, *Family Life and Illicit Love in Earlier Generations* (Cambridge, 1977), ch. 2.

81 ROLLR, DE 2555/24 (Houghton on the Hill, 27 Mar. 1744): 'Whereas the Majority of the Neighbours have met together at the Church to do the Busyness of the Parish, namely …' etc. The term 'neighbours' is widely used here. It is also on mid-eighteenth-century gravestones in this Leicestershire parish. 'Neighbours' implied self-sufficient residency in a place, in contrast to pauper status or itinerancy. It did not necessarily mean equals.

82 A rare reference to 'the parishans' is in Sokoll (ed.), *Essex Pauper Letters*, p. 555; in King, Nutt and Tomkins (eds), *Narratives of the Poor*, p. 597, a man in Chelmsford in 1830 seems to understand the term 'Perisioners' to mean ratepayers or their officers.

83 The term 'paupertariat' was used (and rightly dismissed) by D. Englander, 'From the abyss: pauper petitions and correspondence in Victorian London', *London Journal*, 25 (2000), p. 80.

84 For example, Samuel Parker from Kidderminster writing to the overseers of Uttoxeter, in King, Nutt and Tomkins (eds), *Narratives of the Poor*, pp. 265–71 (1833–34).

85 Levene (ed.), *Narratives of the Poor*, p. 267 (petition of Elizabeth Edwards to the London Foundling Hospital, 1772).

86 Among references to walking and its problems, see King, Nutt and Tomkins (eds), *Narratives of the Poor*, pp. 30, 119–20, 122, 222, 226, 231, 243, 262–3, 267; and for the tramping system see ibid., p. 93 (1826).

87 It is significant that one nineteenth-century slang meaning of 'to go home' was 'to die' and 'gone home' meant 'to be dead'. E. Partridge, *The Penguin Dictionary of Historical Slang* (1937, Harmondsworth, 1980), p. 452.

Chapter 3

1 For further discussion of this painting, using the Montagu archives, see S. Hindle, 'Representing rural society: Labor, leisure, and the landscape in an eighteenth-century conversation piece', *Critical Inquiry*, 41 (2015). On Elizabeth Montagu, see H. Guest, *Small Change: Women, Learning, Patriotism, 1750–1810* (Chicago, 2000). Haytley painted another picture of Elizabeth Montagu: *Elizabeth Montagu Standing in a Wooded Landscape* (*c*. 1750) (British Sporting Art Trust).

2 'Sandleford', *VCH: a History of the County of Berkshire*, vol. 4 (London, 1924), pp. 84–7.

3 Private collection (image by kind courtesy of Lowell Libson Ltd), reproduced in colour in M. Rosenthal, *British Landscape Painting* (Oxford, 1982), p. 41.

4 Rubens's painting is reproduced in K. Bazarov, *Landscape Painting* (London, 1981), p. 45.

5 J. Harris, *The Artist and the Country House: from the Fifteenth Century to the Present Day* (London, 1995).

6 On such consumption, see N. McKendrick, J. Brewer and J. H. Plumb (eds), *The Birth of a Consumer Society: The Commercialization of Eighteenth-Century England* (London, 1982); J. Brewer and R. Porter (eds), *Consumption and the World of Goods* (London, 1997); M. Berg and H. Clifford (eds), *Consumers and Luxury: Consumer Culture in Europe, 1650–1850* (Manchester, 1999); M. Berg and E. Eger (eds), *Luxury in the Eighteenth Century: Debates, Desires and Delectable Goods* (Basingstoke, 2002).

7 Early and pre-parliamentary enclosure was often associated with concentrated landownership; while late parliamentary enclosure was linked with fragmented landownership. See M. Turner, *English Parliamentary Enclosure* (Folkestone, 1980); M. Turner, *Enclosures in Britain, 1750–1830* (London, 1984). On 'open' and 'closed' villages, see D. Mills, *Lord and Peasant in Nineteenth-Century Britain* (London, 1980); B. A. Holderness, '"Open" and "close" parishes in England in the eighteenth and nineteenth centuries', *Agricultural History Review*, 20 (1972); S. Banks, 'Nineteenth-century scandal or twentieth-century model? A new look at "open" and "close" parishes', *Economic History Review*, 41 (1988); C. Rawding, 'Society and place in nineteenth-century north Lincolnshire', *Rural History*, 3 (1992); D. Spencer, 'Reformulating the "closed" parish thesis: associations, interests, and interaction', *Journal of Historical Geography*, 26 (2000).

8 J. M. Wilson, *The Imperial Gazetteer of England and Wales* (Edinburgh, 1874), vol. 5, p. 753, in its entry for Sandleford Priory, refers to fisheries.

9 http://www.bing.com/maps, search for Sandleford Priory and Newtown. The alignment of the village is as shown by Edward Haytley. Appropriately, Sandleford Priory is now St Gabriel's School for Girls.

10 One figure, in the middle of the painting, is seemingly asleep, despite Montagu's telescope directed towards him. I would interpret this as a comic painterly touch and an allusion to gently indulgent forms of control and oversight. A more complex interpretation is developed in Hindle, 'Representing rural society'.

11 K. Sayer, *Women of the Fields: Representations of Rural Women in the Nineteenth Century* (Manchester, 1995); R. E. Pahl, *Divisions of Labour* (Oxford, 1984); K. D. M. Snell, *Annals of the Labouring Poor: Social Change and Agrarian England, 1660–1900* (Cambridge, 1985), ch. 1; P. Sharpe (ed.), *Women's Work: The English Experience, 1650–1914* (London, 1998); N. Verdon, *Rural Women Workers in Nineteenth-Century England* (Woodbridge, 2002); P. Lane et al. (eds), *Women, Work and Wages in England, 1600–1850* (Woodbridge, 2004).

12 Compare Hogarth and Lambert's *Scene in a Hay-field at Rickmersworth*, with its 'female sobbing … some disaster having recently befallen her', J. Nichols and G. Steevens, *The Genuine Works of William Hogarth* (London, 1817), vol. 3, p. 101; J. Barrell, 'Sportive labour: the farmworker in eighteenth-century poetry and painting', in B. Short (ed.), *The English Rural Community: Image and Analysis* (Cambridge, 1992), pp. 105–6; and the ribaldry associated with haymaking in 'The Merry Hay-Makers', in V. de Sola Pinto and A. E. Rodway (eds), *The Common Muse: An Anthology of Popular British Ballad Poetry, 15th–20th Century* (1957, Harmondsworth, 1965), pp. 323–4.

13 George Stubbs, *Haymakers* (1785), Tate Gallery. London.

14 Compare the ambiguities of Gainsborough's famous *Mr and Mrs Andrews* (*c.* 1750), in the National Gallery, a work apparently delivering on patron requirements (oak tree and wrought iron seat suggesting landed stability, the hunting rights, agricultural improvement, church presence, etc.), but which is also a sexual and social satire on a *nouveau riche* recently married couple. Note the fertility symbols of the sheaf of wheat and the shell on the bench, the seed-drilling evidence, the goat-testicle shapes of the powder and shot bags (which had sexual connotations then), the exact rendition of a penis in the appropriately positioned fold of Mr Andrews's coat (compare the dog, and note the truncated branch above Mrs Andrews), female sexual symbolism by the tree's root, the gormless and sly looks respectively of Mr and Mrs Andrews. A shot pheasant was apparently to be painted in her lap (J. Hayes, *Gainsborough* (New York, 1975), p. 203). A shot bird, and in such a position, had sexual meaning then. Significantly, the painting was unfinished; perhaps this young couple were not as gullible as Gainsborough

thought. Modern commentators often seem occluded to these sides of eighteenth-century popular culture. Gainsborough – signing himself 'Yours up to the hilt' to some women – was certainly 'a man about town' in his conduct (A. Graham-Dixon, *A History of British Art* (Berkeley, 1999), p. 111). This painting, unlike the slightly earlier one by Haytley, significantly excludes any village poor, although the effects of their labour are everywhere in a painting much concerned with private ownership.

15 Yale Center for British Art, Paul Mellon Collection. Space is limited here to reproduce all the pictures referred to, but an internet search will produce the image required.

16 National Gallery Victoria, Australia.

17 Museum Resource Centre, Buckinghamshire County Council.

18 Both are reproduced in Rosenthal, *British Landscape Painting*, p. 29. For other examples see Harris, *Artist and the Country House*.

19 *Landscape with Banditti Round a Tent* (1752), or his *Landscape with Banditti: The Murder* (1752), both in the National Museum of Wales (Cardiff), reproduced in D. H. Solkin, *Richard Wilson: The Landscape of Reaction* (London, 1983), pp. 179–80.

20 K. G. Boon, *Rembrandt: The Complete Etchings* (London, 1977), print numbers 211, 233, and see also 20, 33, 44, 62, 97, 98, 99.

21 Art Institute of Chicago.

22 For example, Balthasar Nebot, *The Gardens at Hartwell House, Buckinghamshire, with Two Bastions and Men Scything* (1738), in M. Rosenthal, *British Landscape Painting* (Oxford, 1982), p. 39; Thomas Gainsborough, *The Road from Market* (1767–68), in ibid., p. 70. I exclude urban depictions here, notably the moralizing and satiric imagery of Hogarth.

23 See J. Barrell, *The Dark Side of the Landscape: The Rural Poor in English Painting, 1730–1840* (Cambridge, 1980) on representations of work and leisure among the rural labouring poor.

24 The National Gallery, London. For further discussion of this painting, see M. Rosenthal, *The Art of Thomas Gainsborough: 'A Little Business for the Eye'* (New Haven and London, 1999), pp. 191–6; M. Cormack, *The Paintings of Thomas Gainsborough* (Cambridge, 1991), p. 38.

25 Compare T. Hardy, *The Woodlanders* (1887, Harmondsworth, 1981).

26 The Sudbury churches have towers; only St Andrew, Great Cornard, has a spire.

27 Collection of the Marquess of Tavistock.

28 Courtesy of the National Gallery of Ireland, Dublin.

29 J. Barrell, *The Spirit of Despotism: Invasions of Privacy in the 1790s* (Oxford, 2006), ch. 5.

30 John Crome, *The Blasted Oak* (watercolour, *c.* 1808), in Norwich Castle Museum and Art Gallery. On commoners, see J. M. Neeson, *Commoners: Common Right, Enclosure and Social Change in England, 1700–1820* (Cambridge, 1993).

31 O. Millar, *Thomas Gainsborough* (London, 1949), pp. 9–10.

32 Barrell, *Dark Side of the Landscape*, pp. 89–130; W. Collins, *Memoirs of a Painter being a Genuine Biographical Sketch of that Celebrated Original and Eccentric Genius, the late Mr. George Morland* (1805); G. Dawe, *The Life of George Morland* (London, 1807); R. Richardson, *George Morland, Painter, London (1763–1804)* (London, 1895); J. T. Nettleship, *George Morland and the Evolution from Him of Some Later Painters* (London, 1898); M. Hardie, 'George Morland: the man and the painter', *The Connoisseur* (July 1904), pp. 156–63; G. C. Williamson, *George Morland: His Life and Works* (London, 1904); D. H. Wilson, *George Morland* (London, 1907); W. Gilbey and E. D. Cuming, *George Morland: His Life and Works* (London, 1907); Arts Council of Great Britain, *George Morland: An Exhibition of Paintings and Drawings* (London, 1954). Some doubts about a stress on lowly association and radicalized depiction are in A. Wyburn-Powell, 'George Morland (1763–1804): beyond Barrell: re-examining textual and visual sources', *The British Art Journal*, 7 (2006). It seems to me that Morland's painting becomes increasingly different in social attitude from *c.* 1790 compared to his earlier more sentimental work.

33 Nettleship, *George Morland*, p. 10, and p. 16 for his dislike of the 'whims' of patrons; Gilbey and Cuming, *George Morland*, pp. 2, 13, 45, 187–9; Richardson, *George Morland*, p. 55.

34 E. Langmuir, *Imagining Childhood: Themes in the Imagery of Childhood* (London, 2006), pp. 12–13.

35 A. Chalmers, 'Morland, George', *The General Biographical Dictionary: Containing an Historical and Critical Account of the Lives and Writings of the Most Eminent Persons in Every Nation, Particularly the British and Irish* (London, 1812), vol. 22, p. 410.

36 H. Garle, *A Driving Tour in the Isle of Wight, with Various Legends and Anecdotes; also a Short Account of George Morland and His Connection with the Island* (Newport, Isle of Wight, 1905), p. 144.

37 An earlier work (being engraved by 1789 by his brother-in-law William Ward) showed *The Effects of Youthful Extravagance and Idleness*: a cracked bare plate, smashed window, broken plaster ceiling, a woman mending ragged clothing, a mood of despondency, a starving dog, inadequate heat, etc. From 1790 Morland turned more to rural themes, and his views of poverty were then largely set out of doors, on roadside verges or in woodland clearings.

38 T. Nichols, *The Art of Poverty: Irony and Ideal in Sixteenth-Century Beggar Imagery* (Manchester, 2007), and (as editor) *Others and Outcasts in Early Modern Europe: Picturing the Social Margins* (Aldershot, 2007).

39 'Vagabonds' (n.d.), shown in Phillips Auctioneers, *Watercolours, Drawings and Original Illustrations* (London, 2001), p. 4.

40 Tate Gallery, London.

41 Nettleship, *George Morland*, pp. 18, 24, 31, 33, 35. Morland's views of 'gypsies' bear resemblances to those of W. H. Pyne, though Pyne's gypsies seem more practical in their accoutrements; see Pyne's *Rustic Vignettes for Artists and Craftsmen: All 641 Early Nineteenth-Century Illustrations from Ackermann's Edition of the 'Microcosm'* (New York, 1977), plates 28 and 29. Pyne worked on his *Microcosm* between 1802 and 1807. See also George Beaumont's *Woodland Scene with Gipsies* (Ashmolean Museum, Oxford), possibly first shown in 1800, although in this case the gypsies are very recessive in the landscape; L. Herrmann, 'Sir George Beaumont: disciple of Sir Joshua Reynolds', in Leicester Museum and Art Gallery, *Sir George Beaumont of Coleorton, Leicestershire* (Leicester, n.d.), p. 7. Predictably enough, Morland (despite doing much work in Leicestershire) was not among Beaumont's artistic and poetic associates, although Beaumont's painting shows resemblances to Morland's *Gipsy Encampment* (1791), reproduced in Gilbey and Cuming, *George Morland*, opposite p. 124.

42 17 Geo. II, c. 5, s. 2. Under this 'All persons pretending to be gypsies, or wandering in the habit or form of *Egyptians*', were deemed rogues and vagabonds. The quotation (his italics) is from the discussion of 'Egyptians' in R. Burn, *The Justice of the Peace, and Parish Officer*, vol. V (London, 1814), pp. 582–4.

43 The Fitzwilliam Museum, Cambridge.

44 By 23 Geo. III, c. 51, which repealed 5 Eliz. c. 20, 'to the honour of our national humanity', Burn added, *Justice of the Peace*, vol. V, p. 584, thinking back for example to executions of gypsies under 5 Eliz. c. 20 in Suffolk a few years before the Restoration. In Yorkshire in May 1596, 106 adult gypsies were condemned to death, though many were reprieved during the executions because of the screaming of their children. K. Bercovici, *The Story of the Gypsies* (1929, London, 1930), pp. 229–30. In England, they were last hanged (for being gypsies) in the 1650s in Bury St Edmunds. A. M. Fraser, *The Gypsies* (Oxford, 1992), pp. 132–5.

45 On Clare and gypsies, 'the so-called sooty crew', see J. Bate, *John Clare: A Biography* (London, 2003), pp. 53–5, 93–9.

46 Published London, 2 Jan. 1804, by John P. Thompson of Gt. Newport Street (possession of K. D. M. Snell).

47 W. Parkins, *Mobility and Modernity in Women's Novels, 1850s–1930s: Women Moving Dangerously* (Basingstoke, 2009); S. Walton, '"Going out, going alone": modern subjectivities in rural Scotland, 1900–21', in G. Goodman and C. Mathieson (eds), *Gender and Space in Rural Britain, 1840–1920* (London, 2014).

48 The date of the painting is unclear, but there is a mezzotint by William Ward in 1789. There are revealing and presumably self-reflexive comparisons here to Morland's *The Artist in His Studio with His Man Gibbs* (n.d.), Castle Museum, Nottingham, an image of artistic penury reproduced in Barrell, *Dark Side of the Landscape*, p. 96.

49 Courtesy of the Huntington Art Collections, San Marino, California.

50 A detail of this troubled and suggestive image of farmer dominance and lower-class female vulnerability is the cover for Barrell's *Dark Side of the Landscape*.

51 The Fitzwilliam Museum, Cambridge.

52 Reproduced in Solkin, *Richard Wilson*, p. 132.

53 *Before* (Fitzwilliam Museum, Cambridge) is reproduced in Rosenthal, *British Landscape Painting*, p. 36. The sexual mockery in *Mr and Mrs Andrews* by Gainsborough is briefly outlined in my note 14 above.

54 See Bristow's painting of a labourer molesting a farm woman in an unnamed painting at Deene Park, Northamptonshire (no date, n. 185).

55 The theme is apparent in his other work: for example, the seduction scene in *The Country Stable* (1792) (another version is called *The Carrier's Stable*); or *The Barn Door*; or the two women being grabbed by or repulsing hunters in *Mid-day at the Bell Inn* (n.d., a pen and Indian ink drawing); or in *Virtue in Danger* as engraved by J. Fittler; or in the handling of a woman by two men in *The Departure, Winter* (1792) (National Trust, Upton House); and in one of his multi-imaged soft-ground etchings of 1792 a woman is rebutting male advances, her face showing extreme distaste, in an image akin to a scene in *A Carrier's Stable* (1793), a mezzotint by William Ward from a Morland painting.

56 'Marc Augé', http://en.wikipedia.org/wiki/Marc_Aug%C3%A9 (19 Sept. 2011); see his *Non-Places: Introduction to an Anthropology of Supermodernity* (1995, London, 2000).

57 For example, 'M. T.', *The Hospital of St Petronilla at Bury*, an engraving published on 1 January 1781 by Richard Godfrey (possession of K. D. M. Snell), where the migrant man with stick, backpack and dog is shown passing in front of the named hospital (which was at Southgate Street in Bury St Edmunds), and he is positioned under two signs indicating directions for London and Ipswich.

58 C. Langan, *Romantic Vagrancy: Wordsworth and the Simulation of Freedom* (Cambridge, 1995).

59 National Gallery of Ireland, Dublin.

60 Compare the illustrations discussed in P. Garside, 'Picturesque figure and landscape: Meg Merrilies and the gypsies', in S. Copley (ed.), *The Politics of the Picturesque: Literature, Landscape and Aesthetics since 1770* (Cambridge, 1994). D. E. Nord, *Gypsies and the British Imagination, 1807–1930* (New York, 2006), p. 170, comments that almost every British writer on gypsy life 'associated Gypsies with nostalgia for a pastoral, preindustrial, or lost world and, concomitantly, with the Edenic origins of a vanished England'. By comparison, there is no trace of this in Morland's pictures of them. On stereotypes of the British gypsy, see J. Okely, *The Traveller-Gypsies* (Cambridge, 1983), pp. 1–37; D. Mayall, *Gypsy-Travellers in Nineteenth-century Society* (Cambridge, 1988); and more widely in Europe, J.-P.

Clébert, *The Gypsies* (1961, Harmondsworth, 1967); I. Fonseca, *Bury Me Standing: The Gypsies and Their Journey* (London, 1995).

61 Consider the contrasts in his *Woodcutter Courting a Milkmaid* (1755) between the trees overhanging the common land (on the right) and the enclosed parts of the scene (on the left). See Snell, *Annals of the Labouring Poor*, p. 172, on this painting.

62 Courtesy of the British Sporting Art Trust. Another version of this painting lacks the clutching branches and is reproduced in Williamson, *George Morland*, between pp. 72–3.

63 A similar painting is *Rabbiting* (1792), Tate Gallery, London.

64 Reproduced in Reading Museum and Art Gallery, *George Morland, 1763–1804: Paintings, Drawings and Engravings* (Reading, n.d.), catalogue n. 15.

65 E. C. Brewer, *The Dictionary of Phrase and Fable* (1870, Leicester, n.d., 1894 facsimile), p. 310.

66 Faustus Gallery London, reproduced in Barrell, *Dark Side of the Landscape*, p. 126.

67 For discussion of these themes, see Snell, *Annals of the Labouring Poor.* Leicestershire, where Morland arguably did his best work, was one of the counties most affected by parliamentary enclosure, with 47 per cent of the county thus enclosed.

68 The empathy in Morland for these migrant poor is much more evident than in his associate Thomas Rowlandson; for example the latter's pen-and-ink drawing *Vagabonds*, where satiric purpose is obvious.

69 John Constable, *Dedham Vale* (1826), in the National Gallery of Scotland, Edinburgh. I have already alluded to the raggedness of the canal boy on Constable's *The Leaping Horse* (1825), and canal or river-focused art is of course another genre relating to mobility, not covered here.

70 Reproduced in A. Bermingham, *Landscape and Ideology: The English Rustic Tradition, 1740–1860* (1986, London, 1987), p. 121.

71 National Gallery of Ireland, Dublin.

72 Leicester Museum and Art Gallery.

73 Fitzwilliam Museum, Cambridge.

74 Brooklyn Museum, New York.

75 Tate Gallery, London.

76 *The Evening Coach, London from Greenwich* (1805), Yale Center for British Art, Paul Mellon Collection.

77 *Two Studies of a Gypsy Encampment* (1830), in Norwich Castle Museum.

78 *Portrait of Aggie Manetti (a Gypsy Girl)* (1862), in Birmingham Museum and Art Gallery.

79 Manchester City Art Gallery.

80 Leicester Museum and Art Gallery.

81 Manchester City Art Gallery.

82 Tate Gallery, London.

83 The Burrell Collection, Glasgow. On this and some other imagery of gypsies (by Dante Gabriel Rossetti and the Expressionist painter Otto Müller), see S. Dearing, 'Painting the other within: gypsies according to the Bohemian artist in the nineteenth and early twentieth centuries', *Romani Studies*, 20 (2010); see also G. Doy, *Picturing the Self: Changing Views of the Subject in Visual Culture* (New York, 2005), pp. 176–8.

84 D. Jackson, *The Wanderers and Critical Realism in Nineteenth-Century Russian Painting* (2006, Manchester, 2011), p. 47, and see p. 14.

Chapter 4

1 J. Erskine Clarke was the vicar of St Michael's, Derby. For examples of his *The Parish Magazine*, see *John Johnson Collection: Prospectuses of Journals*, 40 (33, 64, 65), Bodleian Library, University of Oxford. See also P. Croft, *The Parish Magazine Inset* (Blandford Forum, 1993); P. Croft, *A Victorian Church Newspaper* (Blandford Forum, *c.* 1993); O. Chadwick, *The Victorian Church: Part II* (1970, London, 1972), pp. 426–7.

2 Many places in Wales had parish magazines, e.g. Beaumaris, Mold, Bangor, Denbigh, Llandudno, Conwy, Ynyscynhaiarn, Abermaw, Aberdare, Llanrwst or Ruabon. See *North Wales Chronicle*, 14 Aug. 1875; 29 July 1876; 21 Jan. 1882; 23 Feb. 1884; 19 July 1884; 22 Dec. 1888; 10 Dec. 1892; 18 May 1895; *Baner ac Amserau Cymru*, 27 Dec. 1875; and *Y Genedl Cymreig*, 16 Mar. 1892; 14 Dec. 1887.

3 This role has been missed by historians. Even D. Vincent, *Literacy and Popular Culture: England, 1750–1914* (Cambridge, 1989), does not mention parish magazines. Welsh reading skills were improved by the magazines, as there was limited literature in Welsh dealing with rural and countryside issues. G. H. Jenkins (ed.), *The Welsh Language and its Social Domains, 1801–1911: A Social History of the Welsh Language* (Cardiff, 2000).

4 'Ecclesiastical news. Advice on editing parish magazines', *The Times*, 18 Nov. 1946, p. 9, on Swift's work; C. R. Forder, *The Parish Priest at Work: An Introduction to Systematic Pastoralia* (London, 1959), p. 216; G. Rowles, *The Technique of the Church Magazine* (London, 1955); Croft, *Parish Magazine Inset.*

5 Canon J. M. Swift, *Editing a Parish Magazine* (London, 1946), and his *The Parish Magazine* (London, 1939).

6 'Zephyr of change blows among parish magazines', *The Times*, 20 Feb. 1963, p. 8.

7 'Parish magazines', *The Times*, 4 Apr. 1962, p. 13. The idea of them as 'labours of love' appealed to readers: 'Parish magazines', *The Times*, 22 Feb. 1963, p. 13.

8 W. E. Tate, *The Parish Chest* (Cambridge, 1960), p. 22, citing the Webbs. These issues are discussed in K. D. M. Snell, *Parish and Belonging: Community, Identity and Welfare in England and Wales, 1700–1950* (Cambridge, 2006).

9 E. R. Wickham, *Church and People in an Industrial City* (1957, London, 1969); D. Martin, *A General Theory of Secularization* (Oxford, 1978); A. D. Gilbert, *The Making of Post-Christian Britain: A History of the Secularization of Modern Society* (London, 1980). Recent historiography has placed less stress on urbanism and industrialization as conducing to 'secularization', pointing to non-urban factors in religious decline, and pushing discussion of waning religious belief and attendance into the twentieth century. J. Cox, *The English Churches in a Secular Society: Lambeth, 1870–1930* (Oxford, 1982); H. McLeod, *Religion and Society in England, 1850–1914* (Basingstoke, 1996); S. J. D. Green, *Religion in the Age of Decline: Organisation and Experience in Industrial Yorkshire, 1870–1920* (Cambridge, 1996). Compatibility of urbanism with high religious observance is clear in K. D. M. Snell, *Church and Chapel in the North Midlands: Religious Observance in the Nineteenth Century* (Leicester, 1991); K. D. M. Snell and P. S. Ell, *Rival Jerusalems: The Geography of Victorian Religion* (Cambridge, 2000), ch. 12. This later decline ties in with arguments for continued vitality and administrative importance of urban and rural parishes after 1834. On the remarkable growth of new urban parishes in the nineteenth century, see Snell, *Parish and Belonging*, ch. 7.

10 D. Russell, 'The *Heaton Review*, 1927–1934: culture, class and a sense of place in inter-war Yorkshire', *Twentieth Century British History*, 17 (2006). Initially a parish magazine of a Bradford suburb, this remained 'proud of local achievement and [was] anxious to see "national" life as something experienced close to home' (p. 323).

11 On related Anglican literature, see L. Billington, 'The religious periodical and newspaper press, 1770–1870', in M. Harris and A. Lee (eds), *The Press in English Society from the Seventeenth to Nineteenth Centuries* (Cranbury, N.J., 1986); A. J. Lee, *The Origins of the Popular Press in England, 1855–1914* (London, 1976); Croft, *Victorian Church Newspaper*.

12 For 'network communities' in Christian contexts, see R. Lewis and A. Talbot-Ponsonby (eds), *The People, the Land and the Church* (Hereford, 1987), pp. 26–9.

13 D. A. Gerber, *Authors of Their Lives: The Personal Correspondence of British Immigrants to North America in the Nineteenth Century* (New York, 2006).

14 G. Delanty, *Community* (London, 2003), pp. 169–75; G. Day, *Community and Everyday Life* (London, 2006), pp. 24, 227–30.

15 The best discussion of the insets is Croft, *Parish Magazine Inset*. See *The Mission Field* (1 Jan. 1868), p. 19; *Church Missionary Gleaner* (1 June 1866), p. 72, for advertisements outlining typical contents of parish magazines. Diocesan leaflets were also sometimes inserted and may indicate increasing consciousness of diocesan identity. A Scottish parish magazine was the illustrated *Life and Work: A Parish Magazine*, a monthly that (at 106,000 copies in 1900) had the largest circulation of such magazines there. *John Johnson Collection: Prospectuses of Journals*, 33 (33), Bodleian Library, University of Oxford.

16 'The Parish Magazine', *John Johnson Collection: Prospectuses of Journals*, 13 (33), Bodleian Library, University of Oxford. Some clergy must have started magazines to impress their archdeacon or bishop.

17 *The Parish Magazine* (1893), in the *John Johnson Collection: Prospectuses of Journals*, 40 (65), Bodleian Library, University of Oxford.

18 'Zephyr of change', p. 8. For mid-twentieth-century criticism of parish magazines – 'this unhappy little parish paper' – see Forder, *Parish Priest at Work*, pp. 215, 363.

19 One Derbyshire parish magazine recently 'celebrated' the *centenary* of the 'coming of age' of the 8th Lord Vernon in 1909, wishing 'to mark and celebrate this occasion in a variety of ways'. *Sudbury Sketch*, 61 (May and June 2009), p. 10.

20 'Upton Scudamore', *The Parish Magazine, Warminster* (Jan. 1901), p. 8; 'The old parchment register', or 'The vestry book', *Bream Magazine* (Dec. 1900); 'Historical scraps', *Bream Magazine* (Jan. 1901); *Illustrated London News* (18 Apr. 1896), p. 499, citing St Martin's-in-the-Fields parish magazine; R. W. Ambler, *Churches, Chapels and the Parish Communities of Lincolnshire, 1660–1900* (Lincoln, 2000), pp. 207–8. Parish magazines for All Saints Headley (Hampshire), Appleby Magna (Leicestershire), Badsey (Worcestershire), Bere Regis (Dorset), Bream (Gloucestershire, Forest of Dean), Husbands Crawley (Bedfordshire) and Warminster (Wiltshire, and its nearby parishes) are available online at http://www.parisharchive.co.uk/publications_magazines.htm. I used these versions, alongside *Appleby Magna Parish Magazine*, Record Office for Leicestershire, Leicester and Rutland (ROLLR), DE 5566. Other magazines are as referenced.

21 An example was the *St. Barnabas Parish Magazine*, publishing letters from the Revd Samuel Green, an army chaplain, to his Norwich parishioners. S. J. McLaren (ed.), *Somewhere in Flanders: A Norfolk Padre in the Great War* (Dereham, 2005).

22 R. Lee, *Rural Society and the Anglican Clergy, 1815–1914: Encountering and Managing the Poor* (Woodbridge, 2006), pp. 190–1.

23 See letters from soldiers in parish magazines in K. Grieves (ed.), *Sussex in the First World War* (Lewes, 2004); P. Wright, *Nailsea, 1916–1923: The Great War and Its Aftermath through the Pages of Christ Church Parish Magazine* (Nailsea, 2003).

24 J. Erskine Clarke, *Hints on Localizing the Parish Magazine* (London, *c.* 1866).

25 There were 14,613 clergy in 1841 (England and Wales), rising to 25,363 by 1901. A. Haig, *The Victorian Clergy* (London, 1984), p. 3. Comparative issues arise, and figures from different sources vary slightly (e.g. over whether chaplaincies are included), but there seem to have been 15,488 full-time paid clergy in 1961, 13,920 in 1992, 9,764 in 2005 and 8,135 in 2010, a number still falling. Archbishops' Commission on Rural Areas (ACORA), *Faith in the Countryside* (Worthing, 1990), pp. 138–9; R. Gledhill, 'Vicar shortage may leave Church little more than a sect', *The Times*, 30 Sept. 2011, p. 17; http://www.vexen.co.uk/UK/religion.html#Ministers (1 June 2015).

26 M. Beckford, 'Archbishop of Canterbury, Dr Rowan Williams, celebrates 150 years of parish magazines', *Daily Telegraph*, 13 Jan. 2009, http://www.telegraph.co.uk/news/religion/4228972/Archbishop-of-Canterbury-Dr-Rowan-Williams-celebrates-150-years-of-parish-magazines.html (1 June 2015).

27 Some Nonconformists imitated or prefigured the localized Anglican parish magazine. 'Ecclesiastical notes', *North Wales Chronicle*, 21 Aug. 1897; Croft, *Parish Magazine Inset*, p. 24.

28 For discussion of time in relation to community, see P. Glennie and N. Thrift, *Shaping the Day: A History of Timekeeping in England and Wales, 1300–1800* (Oxford, 2009). Nonconformist denominations were often absent from English parish magazines, but became more noticeable in recent decades. For example, *Bream Magazine* (Sept. 1976) welcomed the new Methodist minister and children from a Methodist Sunday school.

29 'Upton Scudamore', *The Parish Magazine, Warminster* (Jan. 1901), p. 8.

30 *Croxton Kerrial Parish Magazine* (Jan. 1899), p. 1. ROLLR, DE 3136/18/1.

31 *Croxton Kerrial Parish Magazine* (Sept. 1901), ROLLR, DE 3136/18/27.

32 N. Yates, R. Hume and P. Hastings, *Religion and Society in Kent, 1640–1914* (Woodbridge, 1994), p. 88. On the reverse view of working-class attitudes to the Anglican church, see Society for the Liberation of Religion from State Patronage and Control, *The Country Clergy and the Country Poor* (London, *c.* 1886), and the sources it cites (Joseph Arch, Dr Jessop, Canon Girdlestone, Mr Bright and the Reverends C. W. Stubbs and W. Bury).

33 'Editor's Diary', *All the World* (1 June 1894), p. 476. The reference is to Arthur Booth-Clibborn, the ex-Quaker and Salvation Army leader (1855–1939), who married Catherine ('Katie') Booth. He referred to himself as 'Commissioner of the Salvation Army for France and Switzerland'.

34 'Zephyr of change', p. 8.

35 *Bream Magazine* (Dec. 1868). In the next issue of this magazine one reads: 'we sail in the old ship as ever, in every way sea worthy; but our old Captain is gone – we have a new one, and he is on his way to join us and take command. We cannot forget how well the ship and ship's company worked of old; not one of us, but looks forward with some anxiety to the future. Still, we remember this, our late captain took care to leave his ship in good order; his next-in-command sticks to her like his second self; she can hardly founder in this condition; and our last orders were, to give the stranger a chance.' This metaphor of the parish as a sailing ship, encountering strangers, relates well to senses of international mission which I discuss later.

36 A critical view of 'loose relationships', 'frantic, frivolous interaction', 'quick fix culture' coupled with a decline of social skills in modern society is in Z. Bauman, *Liquid Love: On the Frailty of Human Bonds* (Cambridge, 2003), pp. xi–xii, 7, 35–6, 63–6.

37 *Husborne Crawley Parish Magazine* (Jan. and Mar. issues, 1900). Praise for the clergy upon their leaving might not have quite the meaning given in the text earlier.

As one recent member of the clergy said to me: 'They always talk well of you when you go. The phrase is "Dead cats over the wall" … meaning that they were pretty useless and you're pleased they're gone.'

38 *Bream Magazine* (Oct. and Nov. 1888). The late vicar, the Revd J. F. Gosling, had died six years earlier.

39 *Bream Magazine* (Aug. 1896).

40 Ibid.

41 *All Saints' Headley Parish Magazine* (Jun. 1919 and May 1936); *St Matthew's Parish Magazine, Ipswich* (Jun. 1878), republished in *The Ipswich Journal* (1 June 1878). Indeed, some clergy-led perambulations continue into the twenty-first century: one in Holcot (Northamptonshire) is known locally as the 'Olcot 'obble'. (Information from Richard Moore-Colyer.)

42 Another recent stress on the diligence of the clergy is E. Royle, 'The parish community through the vicarage window: nineteenth-century clergy visitation returns', *Family & Community History*, 12 (2009).

43 *Bream Magazine* (Jan. 1869).

44 *Croxton Kerrial Parish Magazine* (Jan. 1899), ROLLR, DE 3136/18/1; ibid. (Apr. 1899), DE 3136/18/4, on 'wickedness and indifference'.

45 *Croxton Kerrial Parish Magazine* (May 1899), ROLLR, DE 3136/18/5.

46 *The Parish Magazine, Gosforth* (Nov. 1890), cited in W. M. Williams, *The Sociology of an English Village: Gosforth* (London, 1964), pp. 181–4, with many other clerical complaints in this magazine, for example, about church vandalism, or support for the General Strike. On gangs of youths insulting church-goers, see J. Obelkevich, *Religion and Rural Society: South Lindsey, 1825–1875* (Oxford, 1976), p. 81.

47 *The Parish Post, St Michael's, Winterbourne* (Feb. 1879), www.frenchaymuseumarchives.co.uk/Archives/Parish_Records/Frenchay/Parish_Mags/1879.rtf (1 June 2015).

48 *Studley Parish Magazine* (Oct. 1905), http://dspace.dial.pipex.com/town/square/fk26/localpast/97sp/stud.htm (29 May 2009).

49 *Croxton Kerrial Parish Magazine* (July 1900), ROLLR, DE 3136/18/14.

50 *All Saints' Headley Parish Magazine* (Jan. and Feb. issues, 1875); 'Historical scraps', *Bream Magazine* (Mar. 1901).

51 *All Saints' Headley Parish Magazine* (Dec. 1907 and Aug. 1909). On community history, churchyard extensions and new village cemeteries, see K. D. M. Snell, 'Churchyard closures, rural cemeteries and the village community in Leicestershire and Rutland, 1800–2010', *Journal of Ecclesiastical History*, 63 (2012).

52 'Heytesbury', *The Parish Magazine, Warminster* (Mar. 1901), p. 2.

53 *Bream Magazine* (May 1868).

54 T. Hardy, *Under the Greenwood Tree* (1872, Harmondsworth, 1985), pp. 50, 57, 41, 103, 104, 155, and see my Chapter 5.

55 'Christ Church, Warminster', *The Parish Magazine, Warminster* (Mar. 1901), p. 2.

56 *Bream Magazine* (Aug. 1896). In many other parish magazines, 'gentleman' continued in more traditional usage, coupled with signs of strong social stratification. For example, *The Parish Magazine, Gosforth*, which began in 1887 – see Williams, *Sociology of an English Village*, p. 117.

57 *Bream Magazine* (Oct. 1896).

58 'The Rev. R. Powley's School Challenge Banner', *The Parish Magazine, Warminster* (Feb. 1901), p. 1.

59 'Corsley', *The Parish Magazine, Warminster* (Feb. 1901), p. 3; *Bream Magazine* (Aug. 1888).

60 For one of many examples, 'Longbridge Deverill, Crockerton and Hill Deverill', *The Parish Magazine, Warminster* (Feb. 1901), p. 5.

61 'Christ Church, Warminster', *The Parish Magazine, Warminster* (Feb. 1901), p. 2.

62 *Bream Magazine* (July 1888).

63 *The Parish Magazine, Sherington* (Feb. 1912), http://www.mkheritage.co.uk/shhs/parishmag.htm (11 Nov. 2014).

64 *Bream Magazine* (Aug. 1896).

65 On the community and financial roles of church and chapel fund-raising, bazaars and the like, see Green, *Religion in the Age of Decline*, pp. 165–76; and on the community significance of church and chapel seating and pew rents, see Snell and Ell, *Rival Jerusalems*, ch. 10.

66 This citing of historical sources continues in parish magazines; e.g. *Newtown Linford Magazine* (Dec. 2008/Jan. 2009), where poignant historical detail about a dairy maid scalding herself is prefaced by notice of events held in the church, notably 'Brass Band Concert to launch opening of New Toilets', featuring the Ratby Co-operative Band. 'Tickets on the door at £6'.

67 'Upton Scudamore', *The Parish Magazine, Warminster* (Feb. 1901), p. 8.

68 'Horningsham', *The Parish Magazine, Warminster* (Mar. 1901), p. 3.

69 'Parish magazines', *The Times* (22 Feb. 1963), p. 13.

70 *Bream Magazine* (Aug. 1867).

71 *Bream Magazine* (Aug. 1888).

72 *Bream Magazine* (Jan. 1869).

73 *Bere Regis and Winterborne Kingston Parish Magazine* (1891).

74 'Imber', *The Parish Magazine, Warminster* (Feb. 1901), p. 5.

75 'Corsley', *The Parish Magazine, Warminster* (Mar. 1901), p. 7.

76 Warminster (Minster and S. John's), *The Parish Magazine, Warminster* (May 1901), p. 1.

77 Hardy, *Under the Greenwood Tree*, author's preface, 1896, p. 33.

78 *Badsey (with Aldington) and Wickhamford Parochial Magazine* (Sept. 1902).

79 *Bream Magazine* (Sept. 1868).

80 J. Burchardt, *The Allotment Movement in England, 1793–1873* (London, 2002) is the authoritative study.

81 Swift, *The Parish Magazine*, p. 29.
82 'Kingston Deverill', *The Parish Magazine, Warminster* (May 1901), p. 5.
83 *Bere Regis and Winterborne Kingston Parish Magazine* (1887).
84 *Bream Magazine* (Sept. 1897).
85 Ibid.
86 *Bere Regis and Winterborne Kingston Parish Magazine* (1903).
87 'Horningsham', *The Parish Magazine, Warminster* (Jan. 1901), p. 4.
88 'Kingston Deverill', *The Parish Magazine, Warminster* (Jan. 1901), p. 6.
89 'Maiden Bradley', *The Parish Magazine, Warminster* (Jan. 1901), p. 6.
90 'Maiden Bradley', *The Parish Magazine, Warminster* (May 1901), p. 6.
91 *All Saints' Headley Parish Magazine* (May 1901, June 1905, July 1919). On rural out-migration, see P. A. Graham, *The Rural Exodus* (London, 1892); J. Saville, *Rural Depopulation in England and Wales, 1851–1951* (London, 1957); K. J. Cooper, *Exodus from Cardiganshire: Rural-Urban Migration in Victorian Britain* (Cardiff, 2011).
92 'Longbridge Deverill, Crockerton and Hill Deverill', *The Parish Magazine, Warminster* (May 1901), p. 6.
93 *Bream Magazine* (Dec. 1900). On reforms needed in the Anglican Church in the nineteenth century, see P. Virgin, *The Church in an Age of Negligence: Ecclesiastical Structure and Problems of Church Reform, 1700–1840* (Cambridge, 1989); and on clergy predicaments in the late nineteenth century, see Chadwick, *The Victorian Church: Part II*; Yates, Hume and Hastings, *Religion and Society in Kent, 1640–1914*, pp. 53–90; Green, *Religion in the Age of Decline*; Ambler, *Churches, Chapels and the Parish Communities of Lincolnshire*.
94 V. Nicholson, *Singled Out: How Two Million Women Survived without Men after the First World War* (2007, London, 2008).
95 'Upton Scudamore', *The Parish Magazine, Warminster* (Feb. 1901), p. 8.
96 *All Saints' Headley Parish Magazine* (Sept. 1931).
97 Warminster (Minster and S. John's), *The Parish Magazine, Warminster* (Jun. 1901), p. 1.
98 'Upton Scudamore', *The Parish Magazine, Warminster* (Mar. 1901), p. 7. See also D. Anderson, '"Noyfull fowles and vermin": parish payments for killing wildlife in Wiltshire, 1533–1863', *Wiltshire Archaeological and Natural History Magazine*, 98 (2005); and especially T. Williamson, *An Environmental History of Wildlife in England, 1650–1950* (London, 2014).
99 *Bere Regis and Winterborne Kingston Parish Magazine* (1892).
100 In the twentieth century, too, there was often insistence that the magazines should not 'become purely parochial in outlook'. For example, E. J. Hay Hicks, 'The religious press. Value of parish magazines', *The Times*, 2 Oct. 1954, p. 7.
101 'Christchurch, Warminster', *The Parish Magazine, Warminster* (Mar. 1901), p. 2.

102 *Bream Magazine* (Aug. 1888).

103 For the concept of 'imagined community' see B. Anderson, *Imagined Communities: Reflections on the Origin and Spread of Nationalism* (1991, London, 2006).

104 'Horningsham', *The Parish Magazine, Warminster* (Feb. 1901), p. 4.

105 'Longbridge Deverill, Crockerton and Hill Deverill', *The Parish Magazine, Warminster* (Feb. 1901), p. 4.

106 *Bream Magazine* (Feb. 1901).

107 *Bream Magazine* (Mar. 1894).

108 *Bream Magazine* (Dec. 1867).

109 *Bream Magazine* (Oct. 1876).

110 *Bream Magazine* (Nov. 1876).

111 'Kingston Deverill', *The Parish Magazine, Warminster* (Jan. 1901), p. 5.

112 'The Prince's Chaplain at Bombay', *Church Missionary Gleaner* (1 July 1876), p. 73 (his italics).

113 'Notes of the week', *The Friend of India and Statesman* (16 May 1879), p. 430.

114 W. White, *History, Gazetteer, and Directory of Leicestershire, and the Small County of Rutland* (Sheffield, 1846), p. 231.

115 *Croxton Kerrial Parish Magazine* (Mar. 1899), ROLLR, DE 3136/18/3.

116 'Rats and elephants in central Africa', *St. Mary Abbots (Kensington) Parish Magazine* (Oct. 1896), reprinted in *The Journal of the Manchester Geographical Society* (1 Jan. 1896), p. 74.

117 'Corsley', *The Parish Magazine, Warminster* (May 1901), p. 3.

118 'Longbridge Deverill, Crockerton and Hill Deverill', *The Parish Magazine, Warminster* (May 1901), p. 5.

119 Reprinted as 'The Rev. Clement J. Sparks', *Central Africa* (1 Nov. 1889), p. 165.

120 The extract from the parish magazine was reprinted in *The South African Missionary Magazine* (1 Mar. 1889), p. 69.

121 'Lectures for the British and Foreign Anti-Slavery Society', *The Anti-Slavery Reporter* (1 Sept. 1893), p. 290, from the parish magazine for St Mary's West Kensington.

122 These recruitment efforts from a parish magazine were reported upon in 'Home jottings', *Central Africa* (1 June 1896), p. 106.

123 'A true missionary', *The Illustrated Missionary News* (1 July 1894), p. 106.

124 'Red letter notes from the mission field' were regularly published in *Home Words for Heart and Hearth*, for example, by the Revd R. Wood-Samuel, or 'By our own correspondents', ibid. (1911), pp. 1, 25, 49, 73, 97, 145, 169, 193, 217, 241, 265, bound with the *Barwell & Stapleton Parish Monthly Magazine* (1911) (author's copy).

125 'Brazil', *The South American Missionary Magazine* (1 Jan. 1896), p. 14; *North Wales Chronicle* (13 Oct. 1900). I use the original sources' spellings.

126 'Gleaners Union for prayer and work', *Church Missionary Gleaner* (1 Aug. 1892), p. 126.

127 'Our scholars', *The Coral Missionary Magazine* (1 Apr. 1885), p. 49.

128 'Barcelona', *The Greater Britain Messenger* (1 Apr. 1882), p. 63.

129 'The Bilbao Chaplaincy', *The Greater Britain Messenger: Colonial and Continental Church Society* (1 Feb. 1893), p. 48.

130 'Reviews and notices', *The Alpine Journal* (1 Feb. 1889), p. 255.

131 'Grahamstown', *The Mission Field* (1 Sept. 1879), p. 389.

Chapter 5

1 A. C. Swinburne, Letter to Thomas Hardy (n.d., *c.* 1896), in F. M. Hardy, *The Life of Thomas Hardy, 1840–1928* (New York, 1965), pp. 270–1.

2 R. Williams, *The Country and the City* (1973, London, 1985), p. 213, see also p. 210.

3 On these issues in Dorset, see B. Kerr, *Bound to the Soil: A Social History of Dorset, 1750–1918* (London, 1968); M. Williams, *Thomas Hardy and Rural England* (London, 1972); J. H. Bettey, *Rural Life in Wessex, 1500–1900* (Gloucester, 1987); J. H. Bettey, *Man and the Land: 150 Years of Dorset Farming, 1846–1996* (Dorchester, 1996); K. D. M. Snell, *Annals of the Labouring Poor: Social Change and Agrarian England, 1660–1900* (Cambridge, 1985), ch. 8. On Dorset migration, see P. J. Perry, 'Working-class isolation and mobility in rural Dorset, 1837–1936: a study of marriage distances', *Trans. of British Geographers*, 46 (1969); K. D. M. Snell, *Parish and Belonging: Community, Identity and Welfare in England and Wales, 1700–1950* (Cambridge, 2006), ch. 4.

4 The writing of this novel probably dates from 1867. See R. L. Purdy, *Thomas Hardy: A Bibliographical Study* (1954, London, 1979), p. 7.

5 *The Well-Beloved* was published in 1897, but was written ten years earlier.

6 T. Hardy, *Under the Greenwood Tree* (1872, Harmondsworth, 1985), p. 33, preface of 1896. A similar claim for the historical truthfulness of this account of church musicians (and the shoe-making shop in which much conversation occurs) is in F. M. Hardy, *The Life of Thomas Hardy, 1840–1928* (London, 1965), pp. 92, 394, and see pp. 8–12, 125, 248, 318, 376. (This work, ostensibly by his second wife, was written by Thomas Hardy.) See also his General Preface to the Wessex Edition of 1912, reprinted in T. Hardy, *The Woodlanders* (1887, Harmondsworth, 1985), p. 443, where he claims that he wrote 'in order to preserve for my own satisfaction a fairly true record of a vanishing life'. The church quire is also the subject of his poem 'The Dead Quire', in J. Gibson (ed.), *Thomas Hardy: The Complete Poems* (1976, Basingstoke, 2001), pp. 255–9.

7 Hardy, *Under the Greenwood Tree*, pp. 41, 50, 54, 57, 103, 104, 155, 192, 217.

8 Ibid., p. 104.

9 Hardy, *The Trumpet-Major* (1880, Harmondsworth, 1987), pp. 82, 118, 207, 383; Hardy, *Woodlanders*, pp. 234, 235, 434; or see his short stories 'A few crusted characters: the superstitious man's story', in *Selected Short Stories* (Ware, 1996), pp. 151, 152; 'Enter a dragoon', in *A Changed Man, The Waiting Supper and Other Tales* (1893, London, 1913), p. 158.

10 Hardy, *Under the Greenwood Tree*, pp. 111, 128.

11 On music and Thomas Hardy, see M. Asquith, *Thomas Hardy, Metaphysics and Music* (London, 2005; C. M. Jackson-Houlston, 'Thomas Hardy's use of traditional song', *Nineteenth-Century Literature*, 43 (1989); E. Sherman, 'Music in Thomas Hardy's life and work', *The Musical Quarterly*, 26 (1940); T. Armstrong, 'Hardy, history, and recorded music', in T. Dolin and P. Widdowson (eds), *Thomas Hardy and Contemporary Literary Studies* (Basingstoke, 2004).

12 Hardy, *Under the Greenwood Tree*, p. 44.

13 Ibid., p. 52.

14 G. Simmel, 'The metropolis and mental life (1903)', in G. Bridge and S. Watson (eds), *The Blackwell City Reader* (Oxford, 2002), p. 12.

15 Hardy, *Under the Greenwood Tree*, p. 155.

16 Ibid., p. 105.

17 Ibid., p. 118.

18 Ibid., pp. 98–9.

19 Ibid., p. 58. On these themes, and their symbolic importance for community and parish life, see also Hardy, 'A few crusted characters', in his *Selected Short Stories*, pp. 160–1. For such musical changes, affecting Nonconformist chapels as well as Anglican churches, see V. Gammon, '"Babylonian performances": the rise and suppression of popular church music in England, 1660–1870', in E. Yeo and S. Yeo (eds), *Popular Culture and Class Conflict, 1590–1914* (Brighton, 1981); R. Slack, *Lands and Lead-miners: A History of Brassington, in Derbyshire* (Chesterfield, 1991), pp. 170–1.

20 Hardy, *Under the Greenwood Tree*, pp. 73, 100.

21 Ibid., p. 61, and see Author's Preface, p. 33, on the 'isolated organist', with implications for depleted and disinterested church congregations.

22 Ibid., p. 235, n. 2.

23 Ibid., pp. 99, 100, 102, 188, 190. See Hardy's account of the value of understanding dialect, in '"Hodge" as I know him: a talk with Mr Thomas Hardy', *Pall Mall Gazette*, 54 (2 Jan. 1892), an interview reprinted in M. Ray (ed.), *Thomas Hardy Remembered* (Aldershot, 2007), pp. 7–8.

24 W. W. Skeat, *English Dialects from the Eighth Century to the Present Day* (Cambridge, 1911), pp. 106–12; M. F. Wakelin, *English Dialects: An Introduction* (1972, London, 1981), pp. 84–108. With an aim to study dialect localism, the English Dialect Society was coincidentally founded the year after the publication of *Under the Greenwood Tree*.

25 Hardy, *Under the Greenwood Tree*, p. 221; Wakelin, *English Dialects*, p. 112.

26 P. Joyce, *Visions of the People: Industrial England and the Question of Class, 1848–1914* (Cambridge, 1991), p. 299.

27 T. Hardy, *The Mayor of Casterbridge*, p. 148. 'The higher a person's position on the social scale, the less his speech is regionally marked'. A. Hughes and P. Trudgill, *English Accents and Dialects* (London, 1979), pp. 10–11.

28 Hardy, *Under the Greenwood Tree*, pp. 91–2.

29 Ibid., pp. 128, 211.

30 T. Hardy, *The Well-Beloved* (1897, London, 1914), p. 333.

31 Hardy, *Under the Greenwood Tree*, pp. 216–17.

32 Ibid., pp. 138, 217; see also J. S. Udal, *Dorsetshire Folk-Lore* (1922, Exeter, 1989), pp. 58–62; S. Morley (ed.), *Oxfordshire Friendly Societies, 1750–1918* (Chipping Norton, 2011).

33 Hardy, *Under the Greenwood Tree*, p. 70.

34 Ibid., pp. 163, 172.

35 Ibid., p. 123.

36 Hardy, *Woodlanders*, p. 399.

37 Hardy, *Under the Greenwood Tree*, p. 195.

38 See note 1.

39 T. Hardy, *Jude the Obscure* (1895, London, 1974), pp. 30, 39. 'Marygreen' was based on Fawley in Berkshire. Hardy took Jude's surname from the place, and his orphaned grandmother spent the first thirteen years of her life there, leaving it without regrets.

40 Ibid., pp. 30–1.

41 Ibid., pp. 144, 388.

42 Ibid., p. 144; Hardy, *Woodlanders*, p. 131.

43 Hardy, *Woodlanders*, p. 378. The symbolism of trees in Hardy, especially in this novel where they denote a social Darwinist interpretation of fractiously competitive 'community', develops themes of tree symbolism that I discuss for Gainsborough and Morland in Chapter 3.

44 Hardy, *Jude the Obscure*, pp. 33–5, 37–8.

45 Ibid., pp. 64–6.

46 Ibid., pp. 387, 417.

47 Ibid., pp. 79, 80.

48 T. Eagleton, *Criticism and Ideology: A Study in Marxist Literary Theory* (1976, London, 1982), p. 131.

49 Hardy, *Jude the Obscure*, p. 50.

50 Hardy, *Life of Thomas Hardy*, p. 433.

51 S. Gatrell, 'Wessex', in D. Kramer (ed.), *The Cambridge Companion to Thomas Hardy* (1999, Cambridge, 2005), p. 29.

52 See especially Hardy, *The Trumpet-Major*, containing much about footpaths and parishes linked by them; or his 'The romantic adventures of a milkmaid', in *A Changed Man, The Waiting Supper and Other Tales* (1893, London, 1913), p. 324.
53 I adapt this quote from L. Jamieson and R. Simpson, *Living Alone: Globalization, Identity and Belonging* (Basingstoke, 2013), p. 20.
54 For example, Hardy's 1912 preface to *Far from the Madding Crowd*; T. Hardy, 'The Dorsetshire labourer', *Longman's Magazine* (July 1883), reprinted in J. Moynahan (ed.), *The Portable Thomas Hardy* (London, 1977).
55 Simmel, 'The metropolis', pp. 15, 16, 18.
56 Cited in M. Millgate, *Thomas Hardy: A Biography* (New York, 1982), p. 422.
57 Hardy, *The Trumpet-Major*, pp. 150, 158, 236–7.
58 Hardy, *Jude the Obscure*, p. 328.
59 Ibid., pp. 328–9.
60 Ibid., p. 104.
61 Ibid., pp. 153, 137. The philosopher Bernard Williams, then Provost of King's College Cambridge, once said to me that Oxbridge more resembles a railway station platform than a settled community.
62 Ibid., p. 226.
63 See his lengthy letter to Rider Haggard, in Hardy, *Life of Thomas Hardy*, pp. 312–14; his 'The Dorsetshire labourer'; his preface to *Far from the Madding Crowd* (1874, London, 1971), pp. v–vi; T. Hardy, *Tess of the D'Urbervilles* (1891, London, 1970), pp. 394–6; T. Dolin, 'The contemporary, the all: Liberal politics and the origins of Wessex', in Dolin and Widdowson, *Thomas Hardy and Contemporary Literary Studies*; Snell, *Parish and Belonging*, pp. 198–201, on the very marked decline of hitherto high levels of parochial endogamy in rural Dorset after *c.* 1885.
64 Hardy, *Jude the Obscure*, p. 352. When Ruskin College was founded, one idea was to name it the College of Jude the Obscure.
65 Ibid., pp. 44, 139–42, 170.
66 Ibid., pp. 326–7.
67 Hardy, *Life of Thomas Hardy*, p. 245; H. G. Wells, *The Work, Wealth and Happiness of Mankind* (London, 1932), p. 474.
68 A recent edition of this *Life* presents Thomas Hardy as joint author with Florence Hardy: *The Life of Thomas Hardy, 1840–1928* (London, 2007).
69 Hardy, *Life of Thomas Hardy*, p. 121.
70 Ibid., p. 234.
71 T. Hardy, 'For conscience' sake', in *Selected Short Stories*, p. 45.
72 Hardy, *Life of Thomas Hardy*, p. 225; Hardy, 'The romantic adventures of a milkmaid', p. 315.
73 Hardy, *Life of Thomas Hardy*, p. 434.
74 Ibid., p. 165.

75 Ibid., p. 140.
76 Ibid., p. 101.
77 Ibid., p. 184.
78 Ibid., p. 149.
79 Ibid., pp. 246–7 (his italics).
80 Ibid., p. 208.
81 Hardy, *Woodlanders*, p. 86.
82 Hardy, *Life of Thomas Hardy*, p. 353.
83 Ibid., p. 147. This engages with contemporary debate: e.g. J. Hannay, 'Provincialism', *Cornhill Magazine*, 11 (June 1865), pp. 673–5 : 'Provincialism is the residuum which remains after the course of events has drawn the ablest men away', and he is scornful about 'provincial' wit, literature and politics; see also N. Page, 'Art and aesthetics', in D. Kramer (ed.), *The Cambridge Companion to Thomas Hardy* (1999, Cambridge, 2005), p. 51. Rousseau had earlier argued that the small town held 'more original spirits, more inventive industry, more really new things … because the people are less imitative … each draws more from himself'. Cited in R. Sennett, *The Fall of Public Man* (1974, London, 2002), p. 121.
84 R. Worth, 'Clothing the landscape: change and the rural vision in the work of Thomas Hardy (1840–1928)', *Rural History*, 24 (2013), p. 207.
85 Hardy, *Life of Thomas Hardy*, p. 131.
86 Ibid., p. 185.
87 Ibid., p. 177.
88 Hardy, *Woodlanders*, p. 149.
89 S. Freud, *Group Psychology and the Analysis of the Ego* (1922, London, 1959), in which see pp. 6–18 on Gustave le Bon.
90 Hardy, *Life of Thomas Hardy*, p. 137, and see p. 226 on their 'kiln-dried features'. On early twentieth-century fear of urban crowds, see J. Bourke, *Fear: A Cultural History* (2005, London, 2006), pp. 70–1.
91 Hardy, *Life of Thomas Hardy*, p. 218.
92 Ibid., p. 171.
93 Hardy, 'The son's veto', in *Selected Short Stories*, p. 23.
94 See Chapter 8.
95 Hardy, *Life of Thomas Hardy*, pp. 206–7 (his italics).
96 Simmel, 'The metropolis', p. 16.
97 Hardy, *Jude the Obscure*, pp. 423, 426.
98 Deadly nightshade (*Atropa belladonna*): the genus name *Atropa* derives from *Atropos*, one of the three Fates in Greek mythology; *bella donna* means beautiful woman in Italian; the plant was used to dilate eyes by women to enhance attractiveness (cf. Arabella Donn's false hair); it was used by witches in folklore, and for poisoned arrows in the past; and deadly nightshade has Victorian connotations of ladies of the night. Hardy would have been well aware of all this.

99 Hardy, *Jude the Obscure*, pp. 345–6.

100 F. Tönnies, *Gemeinschaft und Gesellschaft* (Leipzig, 1887), trans. as *Community and Society* (1887, Cambridge, 2001).

101 Ibid., p. 22.

102 N. Elias, *The Civilising Process: Sociogenetic and Psychogenetic Investigations* (Oxford, 2000).

103 H. Spencer, *Essays on Education and Kindred Subjects* (1861, London, 1976).

104 Tönnies, *Gemeinschaft und Gesellschaft*, trans. as *Community and Society*, p. 52.

105 Benjamin Disraeli, *Sybil, or the Two Nations* (1845, Harmondsworth, 1984), pp. 94–5. The quotation is given more fully at the start of my book.

106 Hardy, *Return of the Native*, p. 225; and see J. Hillis Miller, 'Individual and community in *The Return of the Native*: a reappraisal', in K. Wilson (ed.), *Thomas Hardy Reappraised* (Toronto, 2006).

107 Hardy, *Return of the Native*, p. 177.

108 Hardy, *Mayor of Casterbridge*, pp. 63–8, 88, 90, 103, 139.

109 J. Hillis Miller, 'Speech acts, decisions, and community in *The Mayor of Casterbridge*', in Dolin and Widdowson, *Thomas Hardy and Contemporary Literary Studies*, pp. 46–7, 52.

110 Hardy, *Mayor of Casterbridge*, p. 195.

111 The plot may date back to 1874–75. M. Millgate, *Thomas Hardy: His Career as a Novelist* (London, 1971), p. 250.

112 Hardy, *Woodlanders*, pp. 80, 87, 249–50.

113 Ibid., pp. 45–8, 163, 217.

114 Compare Wells, *The Work, Wealth and Happiness of Mankind*, p. 474: The rich now 'follow their own devices as they were never disposed to do so before. In other words, their solidarity is disappearing. They are free and individualized beyond all precedent.'

115 Hardy, *Woodlanders*, p. 44.

116 L. W. Deen, 'Heroism and pathos in *The Return of the Native*', in R. P. Draper (ed.), *Thomas Hardy: The Tragic Novels* (1975, London, 1985), p. 130.

117 Snell, *Annals of the Labouring Poor*, ch. 8.

118 T. Hardy, 'On the western circuit', in *The Distracted Preacher and Other Tales* (Harmondsworth, 1979), p. 261.

119 M. Schmidt, *Reading Modern Poetry* (London, 1989), p. 61.

Chapter 6

1 A. Christie, *The Murder at the Vicarage* (1930, London, 2005), p. 248.

2 Bethlehem has a population of about 30,000 and is clearly a town rather than a village.

3 D. L. Sayers, *Five Red Herrings* (1931, London, 1982), pp. 30–3, 41–2, 46, 52, 63, 68, 80–3, 88–9, 97–9, 100–1, 123.

4 Ibid., p. 63.

5 H. Haycraft, *Murder for Pleasure: The Life and Times of the Detective Story* (1951, New York, 1974), p. 158; E. Mandel, *Delightful Murder: A Social History of the Crime Story* (London, 1984), p. 22; J. Symonds, *Bloody Murder: From the Detective Story to the Crime Novel: A History* (London, 1972); W. L. Chernaik, M. Swales and R. Vilain (eds), *The Art of Detective Fiction* (London, 2000); M. Priestman (ed.), *The Cambridge Companion to Crime Fiction* (Cambridge, 2003); S. Rowland, *From Agatha Christie to Ruth Rendell: British Women Writers in Detective and Crime Fiction* (Houndmills, 2001).

6 W. Collins, *The Moonstone* (1868, Harmondsworth, 1995), is sometimes taken as the first detective novel in English, although crime writing brings to mind Edgar Allan Poe and Dickens among others. On Victorian detective fiction, see L. Frank, *Victorian Detective Fiction and the Nature of Evidence: The Scientific Investigations of Poe, Dickens and Doyle* (2003, Basingstoke, 2009), esp. chs 5–7 on Conan Doyle.

7 E. C. Bentley, *Trent's Last Case* (London, 1913).

8 Christie, *Murder at the Vicarage*, p. 249.

9 M. Shaw and S. Vanacker, *Reflecting on Miss Marple* (London, 1991), p. 27.

10 Among discussions, see P. J. Keating, *The Haunted Study: A Social History of the English Novel, 1875–1914* (London, 1989); K. D. M. Snell (ed.), *The Regional Novel in Britain and Ireland, 1800–1990* (1998, Cambridge, 2008), pp. 1–53.

11 'New detective novels: chronicles of crime', *The Times*, 8 June 1937, p. 22. Janet Hitchman commented on Dorothy L. Sayers' novels that it is surprising 'how much social history there is … packed into them'. D. L. Sayers, *Striding Folly* (1972, Sevenoaks, 1987), p. 20.

12 E. F. Bargainnier, *The Gentle Art of Murder: The Detective Fiction of Agatha Christie* (Madison, 1980), p. 35.

13 R. Chandler, 'The simple art of murder', in *The Second Chandler Omnibus* (London, 1962); N. Pearson and M. Singer (eds), *Detective Fiction in a Postcolonial and Transnational World* (Abingdon, 2009).

14 E. Crispin, 'The mistress of simplicity. A conversation with H. R. F. Keating', in H. R. F. Keating (ed.), *Agatha Christie: First Lady of Crime* (London, 1977), p. 42.

15 D. Porter, *The Pursuit of Crime: Art and Ideology in Detective Fiction* (London, 1981), p. 190.

16 Quoted in Shaw and Vanacker, *Reflecting*, p. 1.

17 B. Reynolds (ed.), *The Letters of Dorothy L. Sayers: 1899–1936: The Making of a Detective Novelist* (London, 1995), pp. 309–10.

18 A. Conan Doyle, *The Hound of the Baskervilles* (1902, London, 2007), pp. 33, 67–8, 70, 82–3, 85, 197–8. Wild landscapes exist in some of G. K. Chesterton's

writing, e.g. 'The honour of Israel Gow', in *The Innocence of Father Brown* (1911, Harmondsworth, 1962); but they are much rarer in interwar fiction.

19 Respectively, A. Christie, *Murder on the Orient Express* (London, 1934); A. Christie, *Death in the Clouds* (London, 1935); A. Christie, *Cards on the Table* (London, 1936); A. Christie, *Death on the Nile* (London, 1937); A. Christie, 'The Million Dollar Bond Robbery', in *Poirot Investigates* (1924, New York, 2000); A. Christie, *Ten Little Niggers* (London, 1939); A. Christie, *They Do It with Mirrors* (1952, London, 1980).

20 On 'Englishness' and its rural conception see M. J. Wiener, *English Culture and the Decline of the Industrial Spirit, 1850–1980* (Cambridge, 1981); R. Colls and P. Dodd (eds), *Englishness: Politics and Culture, 1880–1920* (London, 1986), esp. A. Howkins, 'The discovery of rural England'; S. Featherstone, 'The Nation as pastoral in British literature of the Second World War', *Journal of European Studies*, 16 (1986); A. Light, *Forever England: Femininity, Literature and Conservatism between the Wars* (London, 1991); P. Mandler, 'Against "Englishness": English culture and the limits to rural nostalgia, 1850–1940', *Trans. Royal Historical Society*, 7 (1997); D. Matless, *Landscape and Englishness* (London, 1998); R. Colls, *The Identity of England* (Oxford, 2002); G. Boyes, *The Imagined Village: Culture, Ideology and the English Folk Revival* (Manchester, 1993); K. Grieves (ed.), *Sussex in the First World War* (Lewes, 2004), ch. 10.

21 W. H. Auden, 'The guilty vicarage', in R. Winks (ed.), *Detective Fiction: A Collection of Critical Essays* (Englewood Cliffs, N. J., 1988), p. 15.

22 Christie, *Murder at the Vicarage*, p. 111.

23 On 'rural idyll' myths, see J. Burchardt, *Paradise Lost: Rural Idyll and Social Change since 1800* (London, 2002).

24 K. Grieves, 'Common meeting places and the brightening of rural life: local debates on village halls in Sussex after the First World War', *Rural History*, 10 (1999); J. Burchardt, 'Reconstructing the rural community: village halls and the National Council of Social Service, 1919 to 1939', *Rural History*, 10 (1999); J. Burchardt, '"A New Rural Civilization": village halls, community and citizenship in the 1920s', in P. Brassley, J. Burchardt and L. Thompson (eds), *The English Countryside between the Wars: Regeneration or Decline?* (Woodbridge, 2006).

25 A. Christie, *The Murder of Roger Ackroyd* (1926, London, 2002), p. 7.

26 A. Conan Doyle, 'The man with the twisted lip', in *The Adventures of Sherlock Holmes* (1891, Harmondsworth, 1987), or his *The Sign of Four* (1890, London, 2001).

27 For example, D. L. Sayers, *Murder Must Advertise* (1933, London, 1986).

28 G. Mitchell, *The Saltmarsh Murders* (1932, London, 2009), p. 244.

29 Stanley Spencer's paintings of Cookham or Burghclere deal with village resurrection and re-engagement in community life. Spencer shared with detective

writers an intense eye for local detail. His idea of heaven was to 'spend all my time lolling on window-sills'. M. Collis, *Stanley Spencer: A Biography* (London, 1962), pp. 203–4.

30 Christie, *Murder at the Vicarage*, p. 247: 'He is supposed to be a brilliant novelist … His poems have no capital letters in them, which is, I believe, the essence of modernity.'

31 A. Conan Doyle, 'The adventure of The Copper Beeches', in *Adventures of Sherlock Holmes* (1891, London, 1987), p. 279.

32 A. Conan Doyle, 'The adventure of the Sussex vampire', in *The Case-Book of Sherlock Holmes* (1927, Harmondsworth, 1965), p. 106. Wilkie Collins' *The Moonstone* was also largely set in a country house.

33 Urban examples were Sayers, *Murder Must Advertise*, set in London; her *The Unpleasantness at the Bellona Club* (1921, London, 1970), set in London and Paris; or her *Gaudy Night* (1935, London, 1955), set in Oxford.

34 Allingham, *Mystery Mile* (1929, London, 2004), p. 65.

35 P. Deane and W. A. Cole, *British Economic Growth, 1688–1959* (1962, Cambridge, 1969), p. 143.

36 See e.g. W. Foley, *A Child in the Forest* (1974, London, 1978), pp. 184–9, 192.

37 A. Christie, 'The herb of death', in *The Thirteen Problems* (1932, London, 2005), pp. 188–91; Christie, *Murder at the Vicarage*, p. 118; A. Christie, 'The affair at the bungalow', in *Thirteen Problems*, p. 222.

38 A. Christie, *The Mirror Crack'd from Side to Side* (Glasgow, 1962), p. 12.

39 Christie, 'A Christmas tragedy', in *Thirteen Problems*, p. 170; Christie, 'The affair at the bungalow', p. 224; Sayers, *Unpleasantness*, p. 129: 'Look what a boom there has been lately in criminal butlers and thefts by perfect servants.'

40 For example, the butler in M. Allingham, *The Crime at Black Dudley* (1929, London, 1950).

41 A. Christie, *The Mysterious Affair at Styles* (1920, London, 1994), pp. 67–9.

42 Christie, *Mirror Crack'd*, p. 7.

43 A. Christie, *Endless Night* (1967, London, 2007), p. 11.

44 H. Newby, *The Deferential Worker* (1977, Harmondsworth, 1979); K. D. M. Snell, 'Deferential bitterness: the social outlook of the rural proletariat in eighteenth- and nineteenth- century England and Wales', in M. Bush (ed.), *Social Orders and Social Classes in Europe since 1500* (London, 1992).

45 Christie, *Endless Night*, p. 13.

46 Christie, *Mysterious Affair at Styles*, p. 86.

47 K. D. M. Snell, *Annals of the Labouring Poor: Social Change and Agrarian England, 1660–1900* (Cambridge, 1985), pp. 5–14, 381–91; A. Howkins, 'The discovery of rural England', in Colls and Dodd (eds), *Englishness*; A. Howkins, 'From Hodge to Lob: reconstructing the English farm labourer, 1870–1914', in M. Chase and I.

Dyck (eds), *Living and Learning* (Aldershot, 1996); M. Freeman, 'The agricultural labourer and the Hodge stereotype, *c.* 1850–1914', *Agricultural History Review*, 49 (2001).

48 Allingham, *Mystery Mile*, pp. 46–7, 68, 96–7, 186.

49 N. Marsh, *Overture to Death* (1939, London, 2001), p. 86.

50 Reynolds, *Letters*, p. 409 (letter of 13 Dec. 1936).

51 D. L. Sayers, 'Aerial reconnaissance', *Fortnightly*, 160 (1943), p. 270; or her poem 'The English War', in B. Gardner (ed.), *The Terrible Rain: The War Poets, 1939–45* (London, 1966), p. 45.

52 J. Hitchman, *Such a Strange Lady: An Introduction to Dorothy L. Sayers (1893–1957)* (Sevenoaks, 1975), p. 107.

53 Sayers, *Five Red Herrings*, p. 63.

54 D. L. Sayers, *Busman's Honeymoon* (1937, London, 2003), p. 132.

55 J. G. Cawelti, 'Artistic failures and successes: Christie and Sayers', in R. Winks (ed.), *Detective Fiction: A Collection of Critical Essays* (Englewood Cliffs, N. J., 1988), pp. 198–9.

56 D. L. Sayers, *The Nine Tailors* (1934, London, 1977), pp. 51, 54–5. Murder by a tramp is often suggested in Sayers and Ngaio Marsh: Sayers, *Busman's Honeymoon*, p. 238; D. L. Sayers, *Have His Carcase* (1932, London 1987), pp. 80, 96, 275; N. Marsh, *Scales of Justice* (1955, London, 1974), p. 114. The Revd W. Mahon commented that 'since the end of the war, the number [of tramps] had increased by leaps and bounds'. 'The problem of vagrancy', *The Times*, 28 Feb. 1924, p. 23; 'Vagrancy since the war', *The Times*, 31 Oct. 1924, p. 17. As for gypsies: 'They're a thieving lot.' Christie, *Endless Night*, p. 13.

57 Sayers, *Clouds of Witness* (1926, London, 1988), pp. 86–7.

58 Sayers, *Nine Tailors*, p. 89.

59 Sayers, *Clouds of Witness*, pp. 27–8, 37, 86–7, 179. Poachers are mentioned in Christie, *Murder at the Vicarage*, pp. 51–2.

60 Sayers, *Clouds of Witness*, pp. 87–94.

61 Reynolds, *Letters*, p. 215 (letter of 13 June 1924).

62 A. Conan Doyle, 'The adventure of the Mazarin stone', in *Case-Book of Sherlock Holmes* (1927, Harmondsworth, 1965), p. 63. Holmes had an 'aversion' to women. A. Conan Doyle, 'The Greek interpreter', in *The Memoirs of Sherlock Holmes* (1894, Harmondsworth, 1965), p. 179.

63 'Regal cinema: the methods of Sherlock Holmes', *The Times*, 20 July 1937, p. 14.

64 Porter, *Pursuit of Crime*, p. 137.

65 Sayers, *Busman's Honeymoon*, p. 365.

66 Sayers, *Unpleasantness*, p. 76.

67 J. Hitchman, 'Introduction' to Sayers, *Striding Folly*, p. 13.

68 Sayers, *Clouds of Witness*, p. 284.

69 Sayers, *Busman's Honeymoon*, p. 104.

70 Ibid., pp. 365, 431.

71 Sayers, *Unpleasantness*, p. 34. On use of French, notably about cars and *chauffeurs*, see M. Beard, *English Landed Society in the Twentieth Century* (London, 1989), pp. 59–60.

72 'The Wimsey chin', *The Times*, 4 Dec. 1937, p. 15, a letter signed 'Matthew Wimsey, *pp*. Dorothy L. Sayers'.

73 Sayers, *Clouds of Witness*, pp. 81–2.

74 Sayers, *Busman's Honeymoon*, pp. 74–5.

75 Sayers, *Nine Tailors*, p. 231.

76 Sayers, *Busman's Honeymoon*, p. 420. Compare another novel with an apparent murder, N. Mitford, *Pigeon Pie* (1940, Harmondsworth, 1961), p. 49: '"I fear my poor cousins must have fallen into Bolshevik hands. You know what that means in Russia – they were given over to their peasantry to do as they liked with". Olga gave a tremendous shudder. Sophia said there must be something wrong somewhere. If the Duchess of Devonshire, for instance, was handed over to the peasantry to do as they liked with, they would no doubt put her in the best bedroom and get her a cup of tea.'

77 Sayers, *Busman's Honeymoon*, pp. 174–5, 421.

78 L. Lee, *Cider with Rosie* (1959, Harmondsworth, 1962), p. 185.

79 G. Orwell, 'Boys' weeklies', in his *Inside the Whale and Other Essays* (1957, Harmondsworth, 1969), pp. 186, 198.

80 'Of course, *you* do investigate things, don't you, not just live on your estates in the country and shoot birds? So I suppose that makes a difference,' says Miss Tarrant to Wimsey in Sayers, *Clouds of Witness*, p. 133. I discuss here the literary figure, without disputing that Wimsey's 'type' was in reality still often looked upon as a source of advice, patronage and charity.

81 Sayers, *Unpleasantness*, p. 143. Ridicule of aristocrats was common in interwar fiction. See e.g. N. Mitford, *Highland Fling* (London, 1931) or her *Christmas Pudding* (London, 1931).

82 Hitchman, *Such a Strange Lady*, pp. 89–90, 98, 102–3, 113–14.

83 Sayers, *Busman's Honeymoon*, p. 105.

84 Christie, 'The affair at the bungalow', p. 222.

85 Christie, 'The four suspects', in *Thirteen Problems*, pp. 161, 164; Christie, 'The blue geranium', in ibid., pp. 104–5; Christie, 'Death by drowning', in ibid., p. 228.

86 Christie, 'The Tuesday night club', in *Thirteen Problems*, p. 9.

87 Christie, 'A Christmas tragedy', p. 170 (original italics).

88 Christie, *Murder at the Vicarage*, pp. 26, 279. One is reminded of the visual aids, the all-seeing eye behind a telescope, in Thomas Hardy, e.g. in *Two on a Tower* (1882).

89 Christie, 'Christmas tragedy', p. 67.

90 Ibid., p. 169 (original italics).

91 Christie, *Murder of Roger Ackroyd*, p. 17. On these issues, see M. Anderson, 'The social position of spinsters in mid-Victorian Britain', *Journal of Family History*, 9 (1984); M. Anderson, 'Highly restricted fertility: very small families in the British fertility decline', *Population Studies*, 52 (1998), pp. 195–6; V. Nicholson, *Singled Out: How Two Million Women Survived without Men after the First World War* (2007, London, 2008). Gender imbalance and related issues appear in much interwar fiction, e.g. E. H. Young, *Miss Mole* (1930, London, 1984); I. Compton-Burnett, *A House and its Head* (1935, London, 1951); A. G. Street, *Strawberry Roan* (1932, London, 1941), pp. 229–30.

92 D. L. Sayers, *The Documents in the Case* (1930, London, 1986), p. 10.

93 C. B. Ford, 'The village', in A. Bell et al., *The Legacy of England* (London, 1935), p. 95.

94 Marsh, *Overture to Death*, p. 87.

95 Ibid., p. 204.

96 Christie, 'The blue geranium', p. 105.

97 Christie, *Murder at the Vicarage*, p. 277.

98 Christie, 'A Christmas tragedy', p. 172; Christie, 'The blood-stained pavement', in *Thirteen Problems*, p. 68.

99 On gossip, M. Tebbutt, *Women's Talk?: A Social History of 'Gossip' in Working-Class Neighbourhoods, 1880–1960* (Aldershot, 1995); P. Crawford and S. H. Mendelson, *Women in Early Modern England, 1550–1720* (Oxford, 1998); B. S. Capp, *When Gossips Meet: Women, Family and Neighbourhood in Early Modern England* (Oxford, 2003); R. Sennett, *The Fall of Public Man* (1974, London, 2002), pp. 60–3.

100 Marsh, *Overture to Death*, pp. 18, 77.

101 Christie, *Mysterious Affair at Styles*, p. 133; Christie, *Murder at the Vicarage*, pp. 21, 25. On gossip binding people together, see R. Frankenberg, *Village on the Border* (London, 1957), pp. 20–2. Others, such as H. Batsford and C. Fry, *The English Cottage* (London, 1938), regarded gossip as 'the curse of village and country-town life. The hamlet is corroded with uncharitableness, the petty feuds and jealousy, paltry snobberies and trumpery vanities.' Quoted in E. Williams, 'Village life', letter to *The Times*, 15 Oct. 2009, from Cavendish, Suffolk.

102 Christie, *Murder at the Vicarage*, pp. 12, 109.

103 Ibid., pp. 36, 47, 50.

104 Christie, *Mirror Crack'd*, pp. 27, 206.

105 Christie, *Murder at the Vicarage*, p. 84.

106 Sayers, *Busman's Honeymoon*, p. 213.

107 Ibid., pp. 216–20; F. Thompson, *Lark Rise to Candleford* (1945, Harmondsworth, 1976), pp. 64–5.

108 Christie, *Murder of Roger Ackroyd*, p. 300.
109 Marsh, *Overture to Death*, pp. 19, 26, 29, 88, 202, 203.
110 Allingham, *Mystery Mile*, pp. 32, 46, 52, 58.
111 Christie, 'Tuesday night club', p. 10.
112 Sayers, *Have His Carcase*, p. 306.
113 Hitchman, *Such a Strange Lady*, pp. 47, 107.
114 D. L. Sayers, 'The human-not-quite-human', in her *Are Women Human?* (1971, Grand Rapids, MI, 2005), p. 53.
115 Sayers, *Busman's Honeymoon*, pp. 102, 107, 178, 265–6.
116 Sayers, *The Documents*, p. 49.
117 Christie, *Murder at the Vicarage*, pp. 9, 12.
118 *The Ringing World* is the Weekly Journal for Church Bell Ringers, since 1911.
119 L. K. Simmons, *Creed without Chaos: Exploring Theology in the Writings of Dorothy L. Sayers* (Grand Rapids, MI, 2005).
120 Sayers, *The Documents*, pp. 38, 109.
121 Sayers, *Busman's Honeymoon*, p. 189.
122 V. Bonham-Carter, *The English Village* (Harmondsworth, 1952), p. 234.
123 Sayers, *Busman's Honeymoon*, p. 254.
124 Sayers, *Have His Carcase*, p. 348.
125 Sayers, *Busman's Honeymoon*, p. 31.
126 Ibid., p. 53.
127 Ibid., pp. 346–7. See R. J. Moore-Colyer, 'Lighting the landscape: rural electrification in Wales', *Welsh History Review*, 23 (2007), on rural electrification and overlapping old and new technologies.
128 Sayers, *Busman's Honeymoon*, pp. 55, 337.
129 Sayers, *Have His Carcase*, pp. 14–18, 407.
130 D. L. Sayers, 'The necklace of pearls', in *Hangman's Holiday* (1933, Sevenoaks, 1982), pp. 79–80.
131 Christie, 'Death by drowning', p. 234.
132 P. Scott and C. Reid, '"The white slavery of the motor world": opportunism in the interwar road haulage industry', *Social History*, 25 (2000); H. J. Dyos and D. H. Aldcroft, *British Transport: An Economic Survey* (Leicester, 1969); S. O'Connell, *The Car in British Society: Class, Gender and Motoring, 1896–1939* (Manchester, 1998).
133 D. L. Sayers, 'The fantastic horror of the cat in the bag', in *Lord Peter Views the Body* (1928, London, 1989), p. 60.
134 Sayers, 'Murder in the morning', in *Hangman's Holiday*, pp. 122–3. On garages and roadside shackery, see D. N. Jeans, 'Planning and the myth of the English countryside in the interwar period', *Rural History*, 1 (1990); R. J. Moore-Colyer, 'From Great Wen to Toad Hall: aspects of the urban-rural divide in inter-war Britain', *Rural History*, 10 (1999).

135 'Mr Chesterton's life, philosophy and friendship', *The Times*, 5 Nov. 1936, p. 10; G. K. Chesterton, *Autobiography* (London, 1936), p. 330.
136 I. Kerr, *G. K. Chesterton: A Biography* (Oxford, 2011).
137 Chesterton, *Autobiography*, p. 37.
138 'Mr Chesterton's life, philosophy and friendship', p. 10.
139 G. K. Chesterton, 'The strange crime of John Boulnois', in *Father Brown: Selected Stories* (1992, Ware, 1993), p. 225.
140 Ibid., pp. 226–7.
141 Allingham, *Mystery Mile*, p. 46; Allingham, *The Crime at Black Dudley*, p. 7. Echoes of past faded life appear in other interwar novels. Elizabeth Bowen, *Look at all those Roses* (New York, 1941), or her *The Demon Lover and Other Stories* (London, 1945).
142 Chesterton, 'The strange crime', p. 228.
143 Chesterton, 'The dagger with wings', in *Father Brown: Selected Stories*, pp. 271–2.
144 Chesterton, 'The hammer of God', in *Father Brown: Selected Stories*, p. 113.
145 Ibid., pp. 116, 114.
146 Sayers, *Busman's Honeymoon*, pp. 111–12.
147 Ibid., p. 132. Ghosts from the past are a feature of some rural crime writing, e.g. Gladys Mitchell, *When Last I Died* (London, 1941).
148 Sayers, *Busman's Honeymoon*, p. 131.
149 A. Conan Doyle, 'The adventure of The Copper Beeches', in *Adventures of Sherlock Holmes* (1891, London, 1987), pp. 277–8. On 'the terrors of lonely houses', see S. Weyman, *Starvecrow Farm* (1911, London, 1922), p. 45.
150 'Silver Blaze', 'The yellow face', 'The naval treaty', in Conan Doyle, *Memoirs of Sherlock Holmes*; 'The adventure of the Three Gables', 'The adventure of the blanched soldier', 'The adventure of the Sussex vampire', 'The problem of Thor Bridge', 'The adventure of the lion's mane', in Conan Doyle, *Case-Book of Sherlock Holmes*; 'The adventure of the Boscombe Valley mystery', 'The adventure of the Copper Beeches', in Conan Doyle, *Adventures of Sherlock Holmes*; or Conan Doyle, *Hound of the Baskervilles*.
151 Christie, 'The blood-stained pavement', p. 70; Christie, 'The companion', in *Thirteen Problems*, p. 125.
152 Christie, 'The thumb mark of St. Peter', in *Thirteen Problems*, p. 87.
153 *Croxton Kerrial Parish Magazine* (April, 1899), Record Office for Leicestershire, Leicester and Rutland, DE 3136/18/4, p. 3.
154 Allingham, *Mystery Mile*, p. 159.
155 Allingham, *Crime at Black Dudley*, pp. 159–63.
156 M. Allingham, *The Oaken Heart: The Story of an English Village at War* (1941, Ingatestone, 1987).
157 M. Allingham, 'Billeting in villages', *The Times*, 13 Oct. 1938, p. 10.

158 'Crime stories as aid to virtue: Miss Dorothy Sayers on a moral art', *The Times*, 16 Feb. 1939, p. 11.

159 For other fictional use of the flood as a cleansing symbol, ending evil, see L. P. Hartley, *The Boat* (London, 1949).

160 Marsh, *Scales of Justice*, pp. 57, 181, 232.

161 A. E. Coppard, 'The Black Dog', in his *Dusky Ruth and Other Stories* (1923, Harmondsworth, 1975), pp. 74, 82.

162 Christie, *Murder at the Vicarage*, p. 103. On 'weeding' as an ordered 'garden culture' of modernity – eliminating the undesirable – see Z. Bauman, *Modernity and the Holocaust* (Cambridge, 1989); also A. Weiner (ed.), *Landscaping the Human Garden: Twentieth-Century Population Management in a Comparative Framework* (Stanford, 2003). Christie (in motive or reception) can be considered alongside such perspectives, although her 'weeding' lacks terminologies of social Darwinism or eugenics and probably derives from prior religious and moral views.

163 Allingham, *Mystery Mile*, p. 188.

164 Ibid., pp. 37, 54. On suspicion of outsiders, see K. D. M. Snell, *Parish and Belonging: Community, Identity and Welfare in England and Wales, 1700–1950* (Cambridge, 2006), ch. 2.

165 Allingham, *Mystery Mile*, p. 97.

166 Christie, *Murder of Roger Ackroyd*.

167 Allingham, *Mystery Mile*, pp. 78–9.

168 Light, *Forever England*, pp. 88–93.

169 N. Z. Davis, *The Return of Martin Guerre* (Cambridge, Mass., 1983).

170 The best example is Christie's *Nemesis* (London, 1971), although these themes are frequent in her earlier writing.

171 Burchardt, *Paradise Lost*, p. 197.

172 On 'core' families, see M. Strathern, *Kinship at the Core: An Anthropology of Elmdon, a Village in North-West Essex in the Nineteen-Sixties* (Cambridge, 1981).

173 Allingham, *Mystery Mile*, p. 95.

174 'The Wimsey chin', p. 15. Judging a person's character by their chin was common in this period.

175 Indeed, in A. G. Street, *The Gentleman of the Party* (London, 1936), the 'gentleman' turns out to be the trusty and respected dairyman, whose life witnesses a succession of farmers and gentry making a mess of the land.

176 J. Gardiner, *Wartime: Britain 1939–1945* (2004, London, 2005), p. 491.

177 Sayers, *Striding Folly*, p. 36.

178 Christie, *Endless Night*, p. 21.

179 Christie, *Mirror Crack'd*, p. 8.

180 Ibid., pp. 9, 11, 16, 31.

Chapter 7

1 D. Cannadine, *In Churchill's Shadow: Confronting the Past in Modern Britain* (2002, London 2003), p. xii.

2 J. Wentworth Day, *Wild Wings and some Footsteps* (London, 1948), p. 210.

3 W. Cobbett, *Rural Rides* (1830, Harmondsworth, 1975).

4 J. Wentworth Day, *Farming Adventure: A Thousand Miles through England on a Horse* (1943, London, 1949); and see the article about his departure in 'Tractors on the farm: study of new methods', *The Times*, 2 Sept. 1941, p. 2. On farming and East Anglia in this period: Viscount Astor and B. S. Rowntree, *British Agriculture: The Principles of Future Policy* (Harmondsworth, 1939); G. Walworth, *Feeding the Nation in Peace and War* (London, 1940); E. H. Whetham, *British Farming, 1939–49* (London, 1952); A. F. Cooper, *British Agricultural Policy, 1912–36: A Study in Conservative Politics* (Manchester, 1989); J. Martin, *The Development of Modern Agriculture: British Farming since 1931* (Basingstoke, 2000); P. Brassley, J. Burchardt and L. Thompson, *The English Countryside between the Wars: Regeneration or Decline?* (Woodbridge, 2006); B. Short, C. Watkins and J. Martin, *The Front Line of Freedom: British Farming in the Second World War* (Exeter, 2006); S. B. Ward, *War in the Countryside, 1939–45* (London, 1988); S. Wade Martins and T. Williamson, *The Countryside of East Anglia: Changing Landscapes, 1870–1950* (Woodbridge, 2008).

5 Wentworth Day, *Farming Adventure*, pp. 12–13, 120. A British Pathé newsreel film of Wentworth Day riding on Mersea Island during his 1941 tour is at http://www.britishpathe.com/video/two-horsemen-aka-wentworth-day-tour-issue-title.

6 'Mr James Wentworth Day', *The Times*, 6 Jan. 1983, p. 12.

7 Oral testimony, Dr Carl Hallam (21 July 2011). See also http://1914-1918.invisionzone.com/forums/index.php?showtopic=142933.

8 Oral testimony, Clare Hallam (21 July 2011).

9 J. Wentworth Day, *Lady Houston, D.B.E.: The Woman Who Won the War* (London, 1958); P. G. Zander, *Right Modern Technology, Nation, and Britain's Extreme Right in the Interwar Period, 1919–1940* (unpub. PhD thesis, Georgia Institute of Technology, 2009), pp. 119–26.

10 Wentworth Day's public interrogation of Harold Laski (the Socialist professor of political theory) is reported in J. Wentworth Day, *Harvest Adventure: On Farms and Sea Marshes, of Birds, Old Manors and Men* (London, 1946), pp. 330–4, and in the press during the subsequent libel action of 1946, which Laski lost: *The Times*, 27 Nov. 1946, p. 8; *The Times*, 28 Nov. 1946, p. 2; *The Times*, 29 Nov. 1946, pp. 4, 8; *The Times*, 30 Nov. 1946, p. 8; *The Times*, 3 Dec. 1946, p. 8; *Daily Express*, 27 Nov. 1946, pp. 1–2; *Daily Express*, 28 Nov. 1946, p. 3; *Daily Express*, 30 Nov. 1946, p. 3; *Daily Express*, 3 Dec. 1946, p. 2.

11 J. Wentworth Day, *The Queen Mother's Family Story* (1967, London, 1979).

12 Wentworth Day, *Wild Wings*, pp. 43–4. He fought a hard and unsuccessful battle against its drainage, burning and agricultural 'reclamation'.

13 Most notably, J. Wentworth Day, *The Modern Fowler* (London, 1934), his *Sporting Adventure* (London, 1937), his *Wild Wings*, and his *Marshland Adventure on Norfolk Broads and Rivers* (London, 1950). Many of his other books contain vivid wildfowling and nature writing, as do countless articles, e.g. his chapter on wildfowling in H. Benham (ed.), *Last Stronghold of Sail: The Story of the Essex Sailing-Smacks, Coasters and Barges* (London, 1948). That book is also a testimonial to the older coastal craft, then disappearing.

14 See e.g. J. Wentworth Day, *Rum Owd Boys: On Poachers, Wildfowlers, Longshore Pirates, Cut-Throat Islanders, Smugglers & 'Fen-tigers'* (Ipswich, 1974).

15 J. Wentworth Day, *Poison on the Land: The War on Wildlife, and Some Remedies* (London, 1957); J. Wentworth Day, 'The growing threat of Britain's poisoned rivers', *The Times*, 17 Aug. 1968, p. 7; R. Carson, *Silent Spring* (New York, 1962). These themes are resumed in C. M. Jameson, *Silent Spring Revisited* (London, 2012).

16 Wentworth Day, *Harvest Adventure*, ch. 16.

17 In older age he suffered from Alzheimer's disease and blindness through glaucoma, and some statements from later years should be discounted in assessments of him.

18 On these issues, J. Sheail, *Rural Conservation in Inter-War Britain* (Oxford, 1981); D. Evans, *History of Nature Conservation in Britain* (London, 1991); J. Martin, 'Wildfowling: its evolution as a sporting activity', in R. W. Hoyle (ed.), *Our Hunting Fathers: Field Sports in England after 1850* (Lancaster, 2007).

19 G. Markham, *Hungers Prevention: Or the Whole Art of Fowling by Water and Land* (London, 1621); P. Hawker, *Instructions to Young Sportsmen in All That Relates to Guns and Shooting* (London, 1826); M. Christy, *The Birds of Essex: A Contribution to the Natural History of the County* (Chelmsford, 1890), esp. pp. 47–71 on wildfowl decoying; N. Everitt, *Broadland Sport* (London, 1902); O. G. Ready, *Life and Sport on the Norfolk Broads* (London, 1910); S. Duncan and G. Thorne, *The Complete Wildfowler* (London, 1911); J. Whitaker, *British Duck Decoys of Today* (London, 1918); J. C. M. Nichols, *Birds of Marsh and Mere and How to Shoot Them* (London, 1926); J. C. M. Nichols, *Shooting Ways and Shooting Days* (London, 1945). A fine overview is Martin, 'Wildfowling'. On financial aspects of wildfowl and their importance for working families, see ibid., pp. 126–32, and Wentworth Day, *Wild Wings*, pp. 169–74.

20 D. Matless, 'Original theories: science and the currency of the local', *Cultural Geographies*, 10 (2003), p. 369; B. Short, 'The social impact of state control of agriculture in England, 1939–1955', in P. Brassley, Y. Segers and L. Van Molle (eds), *War, Agriculture, and Food: Rural Europe from the 1930s to the 1950s* (New York, 2012), p. 184; Martin, 'Wildfowling', pp. 127–30, 134–5. A relevant radio

programme was D. Matless, 'The Naturalists: Animals and Human Nature. A portrait of James Wentworth Day – The Prejudiced Naturalist', BBC Radio 3 (28 Jan. 2009). I am grateful to him for providing the script. Matless stresses Wentworth Day's bringing of political values into rural and nature writing.

21 He often took a cold bath 'to stiffen the back' or 'shake up the liver'; he regarded his gunroom as 'forever masculine'; his antlers and heads 'commonly drive females mad'; and he says little about women's lives in his tours and writing. Compare Cobbett's attacks on 'effeminacy': J. Sambrook, *William Cobbett* (London, 1973), pp. 60–1; Cobbett, *Rural Rides*, e.g. p. 78.

22 Photograph from Wentworth Day, *Coastal Adventure*, opposite title page.

23 Photograph courtesy of Clare Hallam.

24 'BB', *Dark Estuary* (1953, Woodbridge, 1984), p. 32.

25 Wentworth Day refers to many authors: Defoe, Gilbert White, Cobbett, Thomas Tusser, Robert Bloomfield, James Thomson, Arthur Young, Thomas Hood, Whyte Melville, Lord Ravensworth, Thomas Randolph, R. S. Surtees, Richard Jefferies, W. H. Ogilvie, Viscount Lymington, George Borrow, Arthur Morrison, Thoreau, Baring-Gould, Henry Williamson, Brett Young, W. S. Blunt, R. H. Mottram, C. J. Cornish, P. H. Emerson, Lord Northbourne, Alker Tripp, J. C. M. Nichols, Margery Allingham and S. L. Bensusan. It is easy to see how these cohere around his political views and interests in East Anglian rural life, farming, wildfowling and travel.

26 E. H. Whetham, 'The Agriculture Act (1920) and its repeal: "the great betrayal"', *Agricultural History Review*, 18 (1970); E. H. Whetham (ed.), *The Agrarian History of England and Wales, VIII, 1914–1939* (Cambridge, 1978), pp. 126, 139–43, 230–2; G. P. Marchildon, 'Wheat and trade policy in the Great Depression', *JSGS Working Paper Series*, 4 (July 2010), p. 5; T. J. Hatton and M. Thomas, 'Labour markets in the interwar period and economic recovery in the UK and the USA', *Oxford Review of Economic Policy*, 26 (2010), p. 466.

27 C. L. Mowat, *Britain between the Wars, 1918–1940* (1955, London, 1968), p. 491; Whetham, *Agrarian History*, p. 265; Viscount Astor and B. Seebohm Rowntree, *British Agriculture: The Principles of Future Policy* (London, 1938), p. 313; G. E. Fussell, *From Tolpuddle to T.U.C.: A Century of Farm Labourers' Politics* (Slough, 1948), p. 140. By 1950, farm wages were almost three times higher than they had been in 1938. P. Self and H. J. Storing, *The State and the Farmer* (1962, London, 1971), p. 167.

28 H. Barrett, *Early to Rise: A Suffolk Morning* (1967, Woodbridge, 1983), p. 99, and see pp. 100–4 on poor prices, farm deterioration, layoffs, agricultural debts and bankruptcies, suicides and auctions: 'what a nightmare time it was for everyone'.

29 Viscount Astor and B. S. Rowntree, *The Agricultural Dilemma* (London, 1935), pp. 65, 101; J. Wentworth Day, *The New Yeomen of England* (London, 1952), p. 22.

30 For example, A. G. Street, *The Gentleman of the Party* (1936, London, 1949), pp. 199, 206, 213, 215, 252.

31 R. J. Hammond, 'British food supplies, 1914–1939', *Economic History Review*, 16 (1946), pp. 6, 9.

32 J. Brown, *Farming in Lincolnshire, 1850–1945* (Lincoln, 2005), p. 260.

33 A. G. Street, *In His Own Country* (London, 1950), p. 251. The quote is from his *A Year of My Life* (London, 1939).

34 Street, *In His Own Country*, pp. 251–4; C. H. Warren, *The Land Is Yours* (1943, London, 1948), p. 58 on earlier village 'self-sufficiency'; or see Barrett, *Early to Rise*, pp. 83–4 on Suffolk village isolation. For debate about the idea of self-contained villages in the past, see C. Dyer (ed.), *The Self-Contained Village? The Social History of Rural Communities, 1250–1900* (Hatfield, 2007).

35 P. Thompson, *The Edwardians: The Remaking of British Society* (1975, London, 1984), p. 40.

36 Brassley, Burchardt and Thompson, *The English Countryside between the Wars*; K. Grieves, 'Common meeting places and the brightening of rural life: local debates on village halls in Sussex after the First World War', *Rural History*, 10 (1999); J. Burchardt, 'Reconstructing the rural community: village halls and the National Council of Social Service, 1919–1939', *Rural History*, 10 (1999).

37 Oral testimony, Clare Hallam (21 July 2011); J. Wentworth Day, *Broadland Adventure on Norfolk Broads and Rivers* (London, 1950), p. 143.

38 Wentworth Day, *Harvest Adventure*, p. 135. The atmosphere of the Essex saltmarshes is described in R. Macfarlane, *The Wild Places* (2007, London, 2008), pp. 271–98.

39 Wentworth Day, *Sporting Adventure*, p. 65.

40 W. Addison, *Essex Heyday* (London, 1949), p. 195.

41 J. Conrad, *Heart of Darkness* (1902, London, 1973), p. 6.

42 Wentworth Day, *Rum Owd Boys*, p. 140.

43 Wentworth Day, *Coastal Adventure*, p. 158.

44 Addison, *Essex Heyday*, p. 210; Wentworth Day, *Marshland Adventure*, p. 194.

45 S. Baring-Gould, *Mehalah* (1880, Pulborough, 1998), p. 17.

46 R. Platt, *Smuggling in the British Isles: A History* (Stroud, 2007); on such use of ghost stories, see E. S. Knights, *Essex Folk: Tales from Village, Farm and Marsh* (London, 1935), pp. 149–59. An example of this isolated coastal region's genre of ghost stories is M. R. James, *The Haunted Dolls' House and Other Stories* (London, 2008). Wentworth Day published on this subject: *Here Are Ghosts and Witches* (London, 1954); *A Ghost Hunter's Game Book* (London, 1958); *In Search of Ghosts* (London, 1969); *Essex Ghosts: The Haunted Towns and Villages of Essex* (Bourne End, 1973).

47 Knights, *Essex Folk*, ch. 1.

48 Ibid., p. 56; Wentworth Day, *Broadland Adventure*, p. 227.

49 Wentworth Day, *Farming Adventure*, p. 19.

50 H. Benham, *The Smugglers' Century: The Story of Smuggling on the Essex Coast, 1730–1830* (Chelmsford, 1986), pp. 165–8; Wentworth Day, *Harvest Adventure*, pp. 131–6.

51 Addison, *Essex Heyday*, p. 208; Wentworth Day, *Coastal Adventure*, pp. 100–1, 213; P. Hyde and D. Harrington, *Faversham Oyster Fishery through Eleven Centuries* (Folkestone, 2002); P. F. Anson, *Fishermen and Fishing Ways* (London, 1932), pp. 267–9; R. A. Beckett, *Romantic Essex: Pedestrian Impressions* (London, 1901), p. 75.

52 A. C. Edwards, *A History of Essex* (1958, London, 1978), p. 94.

53 J. C. Cox and C. H. Warren, *Essex* (1909, London, 1952), p. 12.

54 Wentworth Day, *Coastal Adventure*, pp. 117, 239. This contradiction (if it be such, for hunters need to preserve their game) should not avert us from the strong nature preservationist motives in Wentworth Day. See e.g. his outspoken statements against the 'butchery … appalling and devastating rate of slaughter' of whales, in *Coastal Adventure*, pp. 208–10.

55 Cox and Warren, *Essex*, p. 12.

56 *Benham's Guide to Clacton-on-Sea, Walton-on-Naze, Frinton-on-Sea, and Neighbourhood* (Colchester, 1901), p. 18.

57 J. Wentworth Day, 'The coast of enchanted wings', in R. Harman (ed.), *Countryside Character* (London, 1946).

58 Wentworth Day, *Harvest Adventure*, pp. 14–15, 80–1, 96–7, 160–1, or its dust-jacket of 'Young' George Stoker; Wentworth Day, *The Modern Fowler*, pp. 24–5, 30–1, 62–3, 138–9, 140–1, for examples of such photographs, often found in his publications, which are now of historical value in showing a past way of life.

59 G. Winter, *A Country Camera, 1844–1914* (1966, Harmondsworth, 1973); cf. the subjects of H. J. Massingham, *Untrodden Ways: Adventures of English Coasts, Heaths and Marshes* (London, 1923); H. J. Massingham, *Birds of the Seashore* (London, 1931); H. J. Massingham, *Country Relics* (1939, Cambridge, 2011); H. J. Massingham, *The English Countryman: A Study of the English Tradition* (1942); see also C. Ketteridge and S. Mays, *Five Miles from Bunkum: A Village and Its Crafts* (London, 1972), on an Essex market town.

60 Wentworth Day, *Harvest Adventure*, between pp. 160–1. These and other photographs were taken by a Norfolk professional photographer for Wentworth Day. Oral testimony, Clare Hallam (17 Sept. 2012).

61 Wentworth Day, *Farming Adventure*, between pp. 48–9; Wentworth Day, *Harvest Adventure*, between pp. 96–7.

62 J. Agee and W. Evans, *Let Us Now Praise Famous Men* (1941, New York, 1966).

63 See Massingham, *English Countryman*, photographs by pp. 1, 49, 54, 55, 63 (these are simply titled 'A Sussex shepherd', 'The kitchen of a Lakeland farm', 'A miller', 'Laying a hedge in Essex', 'A saddle-tree maker', 'A potter'; H. J. Massingham,

Remembrance: An Autobiography (London, n.d., *c.* 1941), by pp. 129, 140–1; A. G. Street, *Farming England* (London, 1937), pp. 8 ('An old hand'), 40–1, 58–9, 112–13 (cf. the middle-class man named and praised opposite p. 31); J. A. Scott Watson, *The Farming Year* (1938, London, 1939), where the photographs of working people again have labels like 'The shepherd and his dog', 'A north country shepherd'; J. W. Robertson Scott, *The Countryman Book* (London, 1948), opposite p. 84.

64 Photograph kindly supplied by Clare Hallam. This appears to have been published in the *Shooting Times*, and Wentworth Day's caption, instructions about print size, and request for return of the photograph to him at Ingatestone (Essex) are on its reverse side.

65 Wentworth Day, *Modern Fowler*, p. 61. Such persons are always in Wentworth Day's book indexes.

66 Wentworth Day, *Harvest Adventure*, p. 108.

67 Wentworth Day, *Sporting Adventure*, pp. 19–30; Wentworth Day, *Modern Fowler*, is full of such praise. On decoys, which he wanted to abolish, see ibid., p. 33.

68 Wentworth Day, *Harvest Adventure*, p. 104.

69 Wentworth Day, *Coastal Adventure*, p. 72.

70 H. Newby, *The Deferential Worker* (1977, Harmondsworth, 1979), a study of farm workers in Essex, analysing rural deference, and discussing the break-up of agricultural occupational communities, with many rural incomers unconnected to these.

71 Wentworth Day, *Harvest Adventure*, p. 96.

72 Ibid., pp. 95, 98.

73 Some of his nostalgic statements about Victorian labouring lives in East Anglia hardly accord with much sordid evidence to the contrary. See e.g. the mean little lives, ignorance, weak senses of community, and subjected predicaments described in M. E. Mann, *The Complete Tales of Dulditch* (Dereham, n.d., *c.* 2008), by an author born in 1848 who died in 1929. 'I am appalled [she wrote] at the bleakness, the dreariness of the prospect.' Ibid., p. 13.

74 Wentworth Day, *Coastal Adventure*, p. 192.

75 For an example, from an old man then living in a London basement, see ibid., pp. 198–200; or see his *Rum Owd Boys*.

76 Wentworth Day, *Marshland Adventure*, p. 214, a phrase used by others too, for example 'BB', *Dark Estuary*, p. x, on punt-gunners.

77 Wentworth Day, *Wild Wings*, p. 26.

78 Ibid., p. 18.

79 Wentworth Day, 'The coast of enchanted wings', pp. 109–11; on their kinship groups and seasonal work, see Martin, 'Wildfowling', p. 127.

80 Wentworth Day, *Harvest Adventure*, p. 244.

81 Wentworth Day, *Modern Fowler*, p. 23.

82 Wentworth Day, *Farming Adventure*, pp. 158, 179. 'I am a fenman born', *Harvest Adventure*, pp. 164, 182; or his *Rum Owd Boys*, p. 176; Wentworth Day, *Wild Wings*, pp. 39–41 attacks the National Trust for undermining the villagers' living from Wicken Fen. His brother Tom stayed living near Wicken. (Oral testimony, Clare Hallam, 21 July 2011). On this particular fen, see A. Bloom, *The Farm in the Fen* (London, 1944); E. A. R. Ennion, *Adventurers Fen* (London, 1942), a fen owned by Wentworth Day; for fenland farming and change in this period, see H. C. Darby, *The Draining of the Fens* (1940, Cambridge, 2011), pp. 252–62; J. Brown, *Farming in Lincolnshire, 1850–1945* (Lincoln, 2005).

83 Wentworth Day, *Farming Adventure*, pp. 171–2.

84 Wentworth Day, *Wild Wings*, pp. 50–1; on the interwar fens, see also E. Storey, *Fen Boy First* (London, 1992).

85 Wentworth Day, *Farming Adventure*, pp. 159–60.

86 Wentworth Day, *Sporting Adventure*, p. 64.

87 Wentworth Day, *Marshland Adventure*, p. 213.

88 Ibid., ch. 19, entitled '"Gun-running" on the Kent coast'.

89 Ibid., pp. 215–16. Many such people appear in his writing. See e.g. his vivid accounts of Ephraim in *Rum Owd Boys*, pp. 24–55, 72–8, 90–3, 105–9, 134–9, a figure who reminds one of H. E. Bates' Uncle Silas, discussed in my Chapter 9. (Wentworth Day and H. E. Bates were good friends. Oral testimony, Clare Hallam, 21 July 2011).

90 Wentworth Day, *Coastal Adventure*, p. 72; Wentworth Day, *Modern Fowler*, p. 22. Observations about the 'lonely' Essex coast were made by others, e.g. John Betjeman on the Blackwater and area around Bradwell-juxta-Mare. S. Games (ed.), *Betjeman's England* (London, 2010), p. 114 (the script for an ITV programme of 4 Nov. 1955).

91 Wentworth Day, *Coastal Adventure*, pp. 5, 24; Wentworth Day, *Wild Wings*, pp. 193–5.

92 Wentworth Day, *Marshland Adventure*, pp. 90, 133, 149, 182.

93 S. L. Bensusan, *Back of Beyond: A Countryman's Pre-war Commonplace Book* (London, *c.* 1945, written *c.* 1933), p. 222. He wrote from a village on the Essex-Suffolk border.

94 Wentworth Day, *Coastal Adventure*, p. 51.

95 Ibid., p. 162; Wentworth Day, *Modern Fowler*, p. 12. On such issues, see C. Williams-Ellis, *England and the Octopus* (London, 1929); D. N. Jeans, 'Planning and the myth of the English countryside in the interwar period', *Rural History*, 1 (1990). For similar points about an absence of 'close-knit community' in the new industrial areas elsewhere, 'which undermined the old sense of solidarity and community', see N. Branson and M. Heinemann, *Britain in the Nineteen Thirties* (1971, St Albans, 1973), pp. 83–4.

96 Wentworth Day, *Rum Owd Boys*, pp. 16, 19, 35, 67, 79, 91, 170, 180, 182; Wentworth Day, *Coastal Adventure*, p. 102.

97 A. Morrison, *Cunning Murrell* (1900, Ipswich, 1977), p. 29; Anon., *England's Green and Pleasant Land* (1925, London, 1931), p. 104; F. G. Thomas, *The Changing Village: An Essay on Rural Reconstruction* (1935, London, 1945), p. 21; H. Williamson, *The Phasian Bird* (1948, Woodbridge, 1984), pp. 103, 105, 108, 167, 173, 175, 176, 195; Bensusan, *Back of Beyond*, pp. 23–7, 59, 69, 102, 121–2, 136, 159; S. L. Bensusan, *Marshland Echoes* (London, 1937), pp. xi, 12, 22, 24, 27, 37, 128, 162, 165, 171–80, 247–8, 254, 266, 273, 279; J. Moore, *The Brensham Trilogy* (1946, Oxford, 1985), pp. 245, 260; M. F. Tilley, *Housing the Country Worker* (London, 1947), pp. 30, 45–6; K. D. M. Snell, *Parish and Belonging: Community, Identity and Welfare in England and Wales, 1700–1950* (Cambridge, 2006), pp. 42–4.

98 Wentworth Day, *Harvest Adventure*, p. 210; Wentworth Day, *Farming Adventure*, p. 108.

99 Wentworth Day, *Coastal Adventure*, p. 102; Wentworth Day, *Rum Owd Boys*, p. 176.

100 Wentworth Day, *Modern Fowler*, p. 69.

101 B. Vesey-Fitzgerald, *Rivermouth* (London, 1949), p. 37.

102 Wentworth Day, *Broadland Adventure*, p. 79.

103 Wentworth Day, *New Yeomen*, pp. 38, 49.

104 Wentworth Day, *Coastal Adventure*, p. 99.

105 Williamson, *Phasian Bird*, p. 241.

106 Oral testimony, Dr Carl Hallam (21 July 2011).

107 Wentworth Day, *Rum Owd Boys*, p. 10.

108 Wentworth Day, 'The coast of enchanted wings', pp. 106, 120; D. Hardy and C. Ward, *Arcadia for All: The Legacy of a Makeshift Landscape* (London, 1984).

109 Wentworth Day, *Coastal Adventure*, p. 27; Wentworth Day, *Broadland Adventure*, pp. 111, 121–2; Wentworth Day, *Harvest Adventure*, p. 155; Wentworth Day, 'The coast of enchanted wings', pp. 112–14, 120; J. Wentworth Day, *A Falcon on St. Paul's: Being a Book about the Birds, Beasts, Sports and Games of London* (London, n.d., *c.* 1935); J. Wentworth Day, 'How London got the finest park in the world', *Sunday Express*, 21 July 1929. Another East Anglian coastal writer referred to London as 'a black stain on the maps', Williamson, *Phasian Bird*, p. 241.

110 Wentworth Day, *Coastal Adventure*, pp. 86, 98; Wentworth Day, 'The coast of enchanted wings', pp. 117–18; Wentworth Day, *Sporting Adventure*, p. 31; Wentworth Day, *Wild Wings*, p. 131.

111 Wentworth Day, *Broadland Adventure*, p. 77; R. J. Moore-Colyer, 'From Great Wen to Toad Hall: aspects of the urban-rural divide in inter-war Britain', *Rural*

History, 10 (1999); Street, *In His Own Country*, p. 51, from his *Country Calendar* (1935, London, 1940), on the countryside being 'sacrificed to the towns'. Rural dislike of many wartime London evacuees further indicated such attitudes. For an Essex view, M. Allingham, *The Oaken Heart* (1941, Ingatestone, 1959), p. 51; or from Sussex, S. Kaye-Smith, *Kitchen Fugue* (London, 1945), p. 41 on evacuees: 'Rumour had prepared us for a vomit of squalor and unruliness, of ignorance and vermin – is not London famous in Sussex as the home of London bugs?' (the reality was much preferable to this fear).

112 'I. L. P. and political levy. Rural Conservatism', *The Times*, 16 Feb. 1925, p. 9, an account from the annual conference of the London and Southern Division of the Independent Labour Party.

113 Wentworth Day, *Marshland Adventure*, pp. 99–100, 123, 190, 208; Wentworth Day, *Harvest Adventure*, p. 280; cf. J. S. Collis, *The Worm Forgives the Plough* (1973, Harmondsworth, 1986), pp. 160–1, on the collapse of rural leadership, and on how 'You cannot farm from Whitehall'.

114 Wentworth Day, *Harvest Adventure*, p. 38. Such comment overlooked the fact that members of the 'War Ags' were not Whitehall bureaucrats, but farmers, land agents and landowners. And those on District Committees were local farmers, for the most part, who knew local conditions and their neighbours. B. Short, *The Battle of the Fields: Rural Community and Authority in Britain during the Second World War* (Woodbridge, 2014).

115 Wentworth Day, *Harvest Adventure*, p. 6. Threats to rural 'individualism' were often discussed at the time. See e.g. Street, *In His Own Country*, p. 324.

116 Wentworth Day, *Harvest Adventure*, pp. 5, 35, 67, 89, 162, 187–8; his *Wild Wings*, p. 46; see also A. G. Street, *Shameful Harvest* (London, 1952). For more favourable views of the County War Agricultural Executive Committees, stressing their reluctance to take over farms and their localism, see M. Wainwright (ed.), *Wartime Country Diaries* (London, 2007), pp. 99–100; Williamson, *Phasian Bird*, p. 253. Henry Williamson was politically to the right of Wentworth Day. The issues are assessed in Short, *The Battle of the Fields*; B. Short, 'War in the fields and villages: the County War Agricultural Committees in England, 1939–45', *Rural History*, 18 (2007); B. Short, 'Death of a farmer: fortunes of war and the strange case of Ray Walden', *Agricultural History Review*, 56 (2008); Short, 'The social impact of state control'; J. Brown, *Farming in Lincolnshire, 1850–1945* (Lincoln, 2005), pp. 238, 240–1, 260, 270.

117 Wentworth Day, *Harvest Adventure*, pp. 31, 191.

118 Wentworth Day, *Farming Adventure*, p. 110.

119 Wentworth Day, *Harvest Adventure*, p. 183. Barrett, *Early to Rise*, p. 57, wrote as a labouring man of the 'sheer pleasure of working and *belonging* to the estate' in the 1930s. (His italics).

120 Wentworth Day, *Harvest Adventure*, p. 194.

121 Ibid., p. 36. He often commented on house dilapidation, as did many others, e.g. S. Kaye-Smith, *The End of the House of Alard* (1923, London, 1946), p. 131; M. F. Tilley, *Housing the Country Worker* (London, 1947), pp. 39, 42, 69; C. Taylor, *Return to Akenfield: Portrait of an English Village in the Twenty-First Century* (London, 2006), p. 95; compare Cobbett, *Rural Rides*, e.g. pp. 66–7: 'the villages are regularly wasting away'.

122 Wentworth Day, *Harvest Adventure*, p. 36; J. Wentworth Day, 'A house with 365 rooms', *Sunday Express*, 30 Nov. 1930; Wentworth Day, *Coastal Adventure*, p. 227.

123 On these changes, see F. M. L. Thompson, *English Landed Society in the Nineteenth Century* (1963, London, 1980; M. Beard, *English Landed Society in the Twentieth Century* (London, 1989); H. Clemenson, *English Country Houses and Landed Estates* (Basingstoke, 1982); J. V. Beckett, *The Aristocracy in England, 1660–1914* (Oxford, 1986); F. M. L. Thompson, 'English landed society in the twentieth century: property: collapse and survival', *Trans. of the Royal Historical Society*, 40 (1990); B. Short, *Land and Society in Edwardian Britain* (Cambridge, 1997); D. Cannadine, *The Decline and Fall of the British Aristocracy* (1990, London, 2005).

124 Compare the diagnosis of the 'Tory interpretation of history' in J. Hart, 'Nineteenth-century social reform: a Tory interpretation of history', in M. W. Flinn and T. C. Smout (eds), *Essays in Social History* (Oxford, 1974), pp. 211–13, that things happen (in conservative interpretations) without key individual human agency. Wentworth Day, unquestionably Conservative, on the contrary tended to lay stress upon key historical personalities and their effects, whatever period he discussed. On features of high Toryism, see also D. Eastwood, 'Robert Southey and the intellectual origins of romantic Conservatism', *English Historical Review*, 104 (1989).

125 Wentworth Day, *Harvest Adventure*, pp. 298–9.

126 Ibid., p. 299.

127 Wentworth Day, *Queen Mother's Family Story*, p. 17.

128 Wentworth Day, *Harvest Adventure*, p. 298.

129 J. Betjeman, 'Slough', in *The Best of Betjeman* (Harmondsworth, 1978), p. 25.

130 Wentworth Day, *Queen Mother's Family Story*, p. 18; see also Wentworth Day, *New Yeomen*, pp. 11, 47.

131 Wentworth Day, *New Yeomen*, p. 13.

132 J. Stevenson, *British Society, 1914–45* (Harmondsworth, 1990), p. 333; Wentworth Day, *New Yeomen*, pp. 14, 22; for slightly different figures, see S. G. Sturmey, 'Owner-farming in England and Wales, 1900 to 1950', *The Manchester School*, 23 (1955), p. 245. Data on owner occupation may overstate the decline of the great estate, as after 1945 more great estates took their farms in hand and were thus classed as owner-farmers.

133 Wentworth Day, *New Yeomen*, p. 20.

134 See R. Kirk, *The Conservative Mind* (1953, Washington, 2001); Viscount Hailsham, *The Conservative Case* (Harmondsworth, 1959); R. Scruton, *Conservative Texts: An Anthology* (Basingstoke, 1991); R. Scruton, *The Meaning of Conservatism* (Harmondsworth, 1980); E. H. H. Green, *Ideologies of Conservatism: Conservative Political Ideas in the Twentieth Century* (Oxford, 2002); K. O'Hara, *Conservatism* (London, 2011).

135 S. Ball, *Portrait of a Party: The Conservative Party in Britain, 1918–1945* (Oxford, 2013), pp. 10–11, 'Conservatism: principles and temperament'. On agrarian questions and the Conservative Party, see S. Moore, 'The agrarian Conservative Party in Parliament, 1920–1929', *Parliamentary History*, 10 (1991).

136 Wentworth Day, *New Yeomen*, p. 32.

137 Wentworth Day, *Wild Wings*, p. 130.

138 Wentworth Day, *Modern Fowler*, p. 2.

139 'The rural vote. Grievance against the Party Machine', *The Times*, 7 Dec. 1918, p. 10. On the 'agricultural community', see also my next chapter on Adrian Bell.

140 Wentworth Day, *Farming Adventure*, p. 118.

141 Ibid., p. 141. On remuneration issues, see W. H. Pedley, *Labour on the Land: A Study of the Developments between the Two Great Wars* (London, 1942); R. Groves, *Sharpen the Sickle! The History of the Farm Workers' Union* (1949, London, 1981); A. Howkins, 'The Norfolk farm labourer, 1900–23', *Bulletin of the Society for the Study of Labour History*, 33 (1976); A. Howkins, *Poor Labouring Men: Rural Radicalism in Norfolk, 1870–1923* (London, 1985); S. Hussey, 'Low pay, underemployment and multiple occupations: men's work in the inter-war countryside', *Rural History*, 8 (1997); C. V. J. Griffiths, *Labour and the Countryside: The Politics of Rural Britain, 1918–1939* (Oxford, 2007).

142 Wentworth Day, *Harvest Adventure*, p. 286; compare Cobbett, *Rural Rides*, pp. 260–2, 265, on felons being better fed and clothed than 'honest labourers'.

143 Compare stereotypes of working-class behaviour often found among Conservatives in this period: R. McKibbin, *The Ideologies of Class: Social Relations in Britain, 1880–1950* (Oxford, 1991), p. 275.

144 Wentworth Day, *Wild Wings*, pp. 78–91.

145 Wentworth Day, *Farming Adventure*, p. 12.

146 *The Times*, 6 Nov. 1946, p. 3.

147 I. Dyck, *William Cobbett and Rural Popular Culture* (Cambridge, 1992), pp. 40–1. This excellent book is the best discussion of the cultural basis of Cobbett's thought.

148 *Harvest Adventure*, p. 325.

149 Newby, *Deferential Worker*, pp. 110, 137. On rural labour Conservatism in the interwar period, see N. Mansfield, *English Farmworkers and Local Patriotism,*

1900–1930 (Aldershot, 2001), pp. 189–90, 194–7; N. Mansfield, 'Farmworkers, local identity and conservatism, 1914–1930', in Brassley, Burchardt and Thompson (eds), *English Countryside between the Wars*.

150 Wentworth Day, *Harvest Adventure*, p. 199.

151 Wentworth Day, *Farming Adventure*, p. 144; Wentworth Day, *Coastal Adventure*, p. 64; cf. Cobbett, *Rural Rides*, for example, p. 227: 'as bare-faced upstart as any stock-jobber in the kingdom'. H. J. Massingham was another ruralist whose economic opinions were influenced by Cobbett. See R. J. Moore-Colyer, 'Back to basics: Rolf Gardiner, H. J. Massingham and "A Kinship in Husbandry"', *Rural History*, 12 (2001), pp. 94, 99.

152 Wentworth Day, *Coastal Adventure*, p. 95.

153 Wentworth Day, *Farming Adventure*, p. 178; see also R. Williams, *The Country and the City* (1973, London, 1985); Dyck, *William Cobbett*, pp. 47–8.

154 See M. J. Wiener, 'Conservatism, economic growth and English culture', *Parliamentary Affairs*, 34 (1981), p. 412; S. Baldwin, *On England, and Other Addresses* (1926, Harmondsworth, 1937), pp. 16, 133, 224, 228–9, and on individualism see pp. 14–15: 'We are a people of individuals, and a people of character.' Nevertheless, Wentworth Day disapproved of Baldwin. See J. Wentworth Day, 'The wolf in sheep's clothing. Mr. Baldwin, the dope-peddler of Conservatism', *Saturday Review*, 21 Oct. 1933, pp. 410–11, accusing Baldwin of 'disarmament of principle', unstable in his beliefs, preaching a doctrine of surrender, disarmament. 'And while he talked, Hitler the realist, was loading the torpedo that was to blow all this nonsense skyhigh.' Wentworth Day wrote this prediction in 1933.

155 Cobbett, *Rural Rides*, pp. 291–2; compare Scruton, *Conservative Texts*, p. 307.

156 Wentworth Day, *Harvest Adventure*, pp. 158, 208.

157 Ibid., p. 209, see pp. 228–30 on his Welsh ancestry, and p. 210 for his appreciation of Welsh co-operative practices at shearing-time.

158 Wentworth Day, *Marshland Adventure*, pp. 159–60; see *Harvest Adventure*, pp. 19, 155 for his praise for 'the real Norfolk Romany'. He complained about some US servicemen, ibid., pp. 140–2, 204, though he spoke of America's 'wide-open gift of goodwill' towards Britain and had high respect for Middle Westerners and Southerners. Compare his views (e.g. his fondness for gypsies) with the different ones outlined in R. Griffiths, *Fellow Travellers of the Right: British Enthusiasts for Nazi Germany, 1933–39* (London, 1980). Nor did he share the engagement with Germany of Rolf Gardiner, see M. Jefferies and M. Tyldesley (eds), *Rolf Gardiner: Folk, Nature and Culture in Interwar Britain* (Farnham, 2011); J. Field, 'An anti-urban education? Work camps and ideals of the land in interwar Britain', *Rural History*, 23 (2012), pp. 220–5. There is nothing in Wentworth Day akin to Gardiner's stress on re-made community, comradeship, mutual singing, folk

dance, body culture and organicist views. Needless to say, Wentworth Day was 'very patriotic' (oral testimony, Clare Hallam, 21 July 2011), was a devotee of Churchill, had huge fondness for the Royal Family, thought that Goering 'was a really indifferent shot' (this was severe criticism coming from Wentworth Day) who shared 'the oafish sentimentality peculiar to Germans', and was scathing against Hitler, whose 'deadly earnestness and malevolent intensity to "better" mankind' reminded him 'of a militant member of the London School of Economics'. *Harvest Adventure*, pp. 52–4.

159 Wentworth Day, *Harvest Adventure*, p. 12.

160 Wentworth Day, *Farming Adventure*, pp. 93, 219–23; Cobbett, *Rural Rides*, pp. 310, 337–8, 348–9, 396.

161 Oral testimony, Clare Hallam (21 July 2011).

162 Wentworth Day, *Rum Owd Boys*, pp. 40–1, 117–19, 136, 152–3, 180–1; or his *Marshland Adventure*, p. 194.

163 Wentworth Day, *Harvest Adventure*, p. 183.

164 Cobbett, *Rural Rides*, pp. 187–8, 366; W. Cobbett, *Cobbett's Legacy to Parsons* (1835, London, 1947), pp. 70–6, 82, 87, 102–3, 113, 117–18.

165 Cobbett, *Rural Rides*, p. 226.

166 Wentworth Day, *Farming Adventure*, pp. 57, 146; Wentworth Day, *Marshland Adventure*, p. 83; Wentworth Day, *Harvest Adventure*, pp. 177, 309.

167 Ibid., p. 132. In fact, this book contains a most affectionate dedication: 'To Marion, my wife, for whom "My heart no measure knows, nor other treasure".'

168 W. Cobbett, *Advice to Young Men, and (Incidentally) to Young Women* (1830, Oxford, 1980), e.g. pp. 108–17; Cobbett, *Rural Rides* for 2 Jan. 1822, http://www.gutenberg.org/files/34238/34238-h/34238-h.htm. Wentworth Day, *New Yeomen*, p. 22.

169 Cobbett, *Rural Rides*, pp. 317–18, 496; Wentworth Day, *Rum Owd Boys*, pp. 18, 173.

170 Cobbett, *Rural Rides*, p. 41.

171 Wentworth Day, *Wild Wings*, p. 42. Notice his use of 'who nest' for redshank, rather than 'that' or 'which'. This is common in his writing. His verdict on the twentieth century was not unique to him as a Conservative, but was shared (among others) by E. J. Hobsbawm, *Interesting Times: A Twentieth-Century Life* (2002, London, 2003), p. xii ('the most extraordinary and terrible century in human history').

172 Wentworth Day, *Sporting Adventure*, p. 176.

173 Wentworth Day, *Harvest Adventure*, p. 38.

174 Ibid., p. 44; compare C. S. Orwin, *Problems of the Countryside* (Cambridge, 1945), pp. 105–6, with his advocacy of 'good concrete roadways' and getting rid of 'dilapidated old barns'.

175 Wentworth Day, *Farming Adventure*, p. 152; Wentworth Day, *Queen Mother's Family Story*, p. 34; Wentworth Day, *New Yeomen*, p. 59; Cobbett, *Rural Rides*,

pp. 41, or 485 on the superior knowledge of a shepherd over any philosopher. Compare Baldwin, *On England*, pp. 28–9, extolling the high intelligence of an illiterate shepherd; or A. Bell, *The Cherry Tree* (1932, London, 1949), p. 117. Another famous East Anglian writer (Welsh in origin, but of very different political views to Wentworth Day) commented upon 'the exclusiveness, the class arrogance' of Cambridge at this time, perpetuating 'a cancer ... at the root of our class-infected society'. See G. E. Evans, *The Strength of the Hills: An Autobiography* (1983, London, 1985), p. 108. See also my discussion of *Jude the Obscure* in Chapter 5 above.

176 Wentworth Day, *Harvest Adventure*, p. 146. The ear-rings were worn to ward off the cold and to lengthen vision, Wentworth Day, *Wild Wings*, p. 185; Wentworth Day, *Coastal Adventure*, p. 27; Wentworth Day, *Rum Owd Boys*, p. 174.

177 Oral testimony, Clare Hallam (21 July 2011).

178 The wildfowling literature before the Protection of Birds Act (1954) is full of accounts of large 'bags', though Wentworth Day stressed the need to shoot edible, saleable birds, and not to overshoot, or shoot rare birds such as avocets, spoonbills, bitterns, marsh harriers, bearded tits, or Sandwich terns. See e.g. J. Wentworth Day, 'The story of Salthouse Broads', *The Field, the Country Newspaper*, 19 Sept. 1931, p. 435; J. Wentworth Day, 'Whiteslea – the enchanted marsh', *The Field, the Country Newspaper*, 22 Nov. 1930, p. 706. For his Broads quotations: D. Matless, *In the Nature of Landscape: Cultural Geography on the Norfolk Broads* (Oxford, 2014), pp. 73, 85.

179 Oral testimony, Clare Hallam (21 July 2011).

180 Wentworth Day, *Coastal Adventure*, p. 212.

181 Wentworth Day, *Wild Wings*, p. 74.

182 Ibid., p. 73.

Chapter 8

1 A. Bell, *The Cherry Tree* (1932, London, 1949), pp. 40–1.

2 R. Blythe, *Word from Wormingford: A Parish Year* (1997, London, 1998), p. 92, written with reference to George Mackay Brown, in Orkney.

3 R. Blythe, 'Prologue', in C. Taylor, *Return to Akenfield: Portrait of an English Village in the Twenty-First Century* (London, 2006), p. 4; or see R. Blythe, *The Time by the Sea: Aldeburgh, 1955–58* (London, 2013), p. 52.

4 Bell, *The Cherry Tree*, pp. 154–5.

5 He married Marjorie Gibson in 1931, and they had three children, Anthea (the eminent translator), Sylvia and Martin (the international news reporter and independent MP for Tatton from 1997). For a valuable biography of Adrian Bell, see A. Gander, *Adrian Bell: Voice of the Countryside* (Wenhaston, Suffolk, 2001).

6 The phrase is from G. Cavaliero, *The Rural Tradition in the English Novel, 1900–1939* (London, 1977), p. 116.
7 Personal correspondence (31 Mar. 2000).
8 C. Court, 'Adrian Bell', *Eastern Daily Press* (18 Feb. 1974).
9 F. R. Leavis rather condescendingly described Adrian Bell as having 'a light and pleasing talent'. M. Bell, 'My time in Cambridge', *Cam*, 46 (2005), p. 44.
10 Massingham dedicated his book *The Fall of the Year* (London, 1941) to Adrian Bell. Bell writes about reading him, and not living up to his ideals, in A. Bell, *The Black Donkey* (London, 1949), pp. 127–8.
11 Gander, *Adrian Bell*, p. 50.
12 See R. J. Moore-Colyer, 'Back to basics: Rolf Gardiner, H. J. Massingham and "A Kinship in Husbandry"', *Rural History*, 12 (2001), p. 97; R. J. Moore-Colyer, 'Rolf Gardiner, English patriot and the Council for the Church and Countryside', *Agricultural History Review*, 49 (2001); F. Trentmann, 'Civilization and its discontents: English neo-romanticism and the transformation of anti-modernism in twentieth-century western culture', *Journal of Contemporary History*, 29 (1994), pp. 604–11; P. Wright, *The Village That Died for England: The Strange Story of Tyneham* (1995, London, 1996); D. Matless, *Landscape and Englishness* (London, 1998); M. Jefferies and M. Tyldesley (eds), *Rolf Gardiner: Folk, Nature and Culture in Interwar Britain* (Farnham, 2011), p. 110; Gander, *Adrian Bell*, pp. 119–20, 139–42, 177. Gardiner praised Bell, summarizing the concerns in Bell's *By Road* as 'the contamination of mellowed spiritual by arbitrary economic makeshift', and arguing for the sustaining of skilled workers on the land. R. Gardiner, 'Labour for the land: science versus man', *The Times*, 12 July 1937, p. 18.
13 'Farmer-authors', *The Times*, 12 Feb. 1945, p. 5. Street started writing because of Adrian Bell's influence. A. G. Street, *Country Calendar* (1935, London, 1940), p. xi.
14 M. Bell, 'Introduction', to A. Bell, *Corduroy* (1930, Harmondsworth, 2000), pp. vi–vii.
15 Spencer wrote, 'the longer I stay in one place the nearer I get to life'. Arts Council, *Stanley Spencer, 1891–1959* (London, 1976), p. 23. See also the account of Spencer's sense of place in K. Hauser, *Stanley Spencer* (London, 2001), pp. 9–11, 21–45.
16 A. Bell, 'The Bible box', in his *A Countryman's Notebook: A Centenary Collection* (East Bergholt, 2001), p. 41; Gander, *Adrian Bell*, pp. 143–4. In East Anglia he is also affectionately remembered, not least by a very active Adrian Bell Society, for articles like this in the *Eastern Daily Press*.
17 A. Bell, 'To a poet', in Bell, *A Countryman's Notebook*, p. 72.
18 A. Bell, *Silver Ley* (1931, Oxford, 1983), p. 178. For a similar attitude towards the local, see the fine book by R. Macfarlane, *The Old Ways: A Journey on Foot* (London, 2012), pp. 78–9, discussing Martin Martin, Roger Deakin and Henry Thoreau.
19 For the interwar agricultural depression, see my discussion of James Wentworth Day, Chapter 7.

20 A. Bell, *The Flower and the Wheel* (London, 1949), p. 13.
21 A. Bell, *The Budding Morrow* (London, 1946), p. 35; Bell, *The Cherry Tree*, p. 41, 'for ultimately the earth is our only sustenance'.
22 Bell, 'The Bible box', p. 41. See also D. Howard, 'Adrian Bell', *Book and Magazine Collector*, 60 (Mar. 1989), p. 56: 'It is interesting to read Adrian Bell's books in chronological order, as they form an account of the astonishing social revolution in farming that occurred during his life.'
23 R. Blythe, *Borderland* (Norwich, 2005), pp. vii, 232; R. Blythe, *Out of the Valley: Another Year at Wormingford* (London, 2000), pp. 95–6, for his memories of Bell.
24 A. Bell, 'The family farm', in H. J. Massingham (ed.), *England and the Farmer* (London, 1941), p. 75.
25 A. Bell, *My Own Master* (London, 1961), p. 82.
26 The earwig survived. This remarkable Jain-like passage is in Bell, *My Own Master*, pp. 202–3.
27 Compare M. Castells, *The Information Age: Economy, Society and Culture. Vol. 2: The Power of Identity* (1997, Oxford, 2007), pp. 181–6.
28 Bell, *The Cherry Tree*, p. 11.
29 Ibid., p. 202.
30 A. Bell, *Sunrise to Sunset* (London, 1944).
31 Bell, *Corduroy*, p. 1.
32 Bell, *Silver Ley*, p. 88.
33 Bell, 'The family farm', pp. 74–5, 82.
34 Bell, *Silver Ley*, p. 68.
35 Bell, *My Own Master*, p. 83.
36 Ibid., p. 81; A. Bell, *A Suffolk Harvest* (London, 1956), p. 78.
37 A. Bell, *Apple Acre* (1942, London, 1943), p. 42.
38 Bell, *The Budding Morrow*, p. 76 (his italics).
39 J. Berger, *Pig Earth* (1979, London, 1985).
40 Bell, *My Own Master*, p. 82.
41 Bell, 'The family farm', p. 87. My aim is to outline his views, not to judge them as historical statements.
42 A. Bell, *The Open Air: An Anthology of English Country Life* (1936, London, 1943), pp. 11–13.
43 Bell, *Silver Ley*, p. 56. Compare the discussion of John Clare by J. Barrell, *The Idea of Landscape and the Sense of Place, 1730–1840: An Approach to the Poetry of John Clare* (Cambridge, 1972); and in relation to ideas about 'the parish state' see J. Clare, *The Parish: A Satire* (1820, London, 1986).
44 'Obituary: Adrian Bell', *Eastern Daily Press*, 8 Sept. 1980.
45 A. Bell, *By-Road* (1937, London, 1943), p. 206.
46 Bell, *The Budding Morrow*, p. 86. The term 'foreigner' was widely used in rural England, even for someone from another parish. For Essex, see S. L. Bensusan,

Marshland Echoes (London, 1937), pp. xi, 22, 24, 37, 165, 266, 273, 128; for a Worcestershire example, see F. Brett Young, *Portrait of a Village* (London, 1937), p. 45; or for Wiltshire, A. G. Street, 'The meddler and the drowner', in R. Tomalin (ed.), *Best Country Stories* (London, 1969), p. 117.

47 Bell, *By-Road*, p. 209. Much later, by comparison, Ronald Blythe despairingly commented: 'There are now people who … do not belong to anyone or anything', in his *Borderland*, p. 116.

48 Bell, *Silver Ley*, p. 64. On high endogamy in some East Anglian parishes, see K. D. M. Snell, *Parish and Belonging: Community, Identity and Welfare in England and Wales, 1700–1950* (Cambridge, 2006), pp. 186–201.

49 Bell, *Silver Ley*, p. 143.

50 A. Bell, *Men and the Fields* (London, 1939), p. 41.

51 Bell, *By-Road*, p. 206.

52 Ibid., p. 118.

53 Ibid., p. 240.

54 Bell, *Men and the Fields*, p. 10.

55 Ibid., p. 18.

56 Bell, *Silver Ley*, p. 265.

57 Bell, *Apple Acre*, pp. 119–20.

58 Ibid., p. 59. A more positive view of how the car expanded the radius of a farmer's social activities is in A. G. Street, *Farmer's Glory* (1932, London, 1956), p. 206.

59 Bell, *The Cherry Tree*, pp. 115–17.

60 G. E. Evans, *The Strength of the Hills: An Autobiography* (1983, London, 1985), p. 178.

61 Bell, *The Cherry Tree*, p. 115.

62 For this concept, see B. Anderson, *Imagined Communities: Reflections on the Origin and Spread of Nationalism* (1991, London, 2006). 'The agricultural community' is a term still used today, for example, in an eloquent speech by Henry Cator, Chairman of the Trustees of the Royal Agricultural Society of England, at Brooksby Melton College (25 Oct. 2012).

63 Bell, *Corduroy*, pp. 231–2.

64 M. E. Mann, *The Complete Tales of Dulditch* (Dereham, n.d., *c.* 2008), among her other books. Mann's dates were 1848–1929. Bell knew and admired Mann's work: see ibid., p. 14. On East Anglian regional fiction, see K. D. M. Snell, *The Bibliography of Regional Fiction in Britain and Ireland, 1800–2000* (Aldershot, 2002), pp. 18–20, 44–6, 91–3, 116–18. On the rural hardships of this region, see also L. M. Springall, *Labouring Life in Norfolk Villages, 1834–1914* (London, 1936).

65 Bell, *The Cherry Tree*, pp. 179–80.

66 A. G. Street, *The Endless Furrow* (1934, London, 1937), p. 26. It is possible that Street came closer to reality, as there was often a large social gulf between farmer and labourer. Disputes came to a head during Agricultural Wages Board

negotiations, and there were also Anglican and Nonconformist issues between the classes. Marriage patterns also reflected deep-seated social divides. See the extreme account of interwar Suffolk class conflict relayed in R. Blythe, *Akenfield* (1969, Harmondsworth, 1977), pp. 46–8 : 'So it was hate all around.'

67 Bell, *Men and the Fields*, p. 72.

68 Ibid., p. 74.

69 As, for example, later discussed in R. Frankenberg, *Communities in Britain: Social Life in Town and Country* (1966, Harmondsworth 1970); A. P. Cohen (ed.), *Belonging: Identity and Social Organisation in British Rural Cultures* (Manchester, 1982); A. P. Cohen (ed.), *Symbolising Boundaries: Identity and Diversity in British Cultures* (Manchester, 1986); G. Crow and G. Allan (eds), *Community Life: An Introduction to Local Social Relations* (London, 1994); G. Delanty, *Community* (London, 2003); G. Day, *Community and Everyday Life* (London, 2006).

70 Bell, *Corduroy*, pp. 64, 233, 236.

71 Bell, *The Black Donkey*, p. 89.

72 Bell, *The Cherry Tree*, p. 168.

73 Bell, *Corduroy*, pp. 154–6. Compare metropolitan relationships as depicted in E. Waugh, *Vile Bodies* (London, 1930).

74 Bell, *Corduroy*, p. 172.

75 A. G. Street referred to this as 'the combat of buying and selling' in his *Farmer's Glory*, p. 192; but also pointed out in *Country Calendar*, p. 75, that one has to live a long time with one's neighbours in rural areas, and so 'one crooked deal will crab future business for many years over a wide district … Country folk stay put, and therefore are forced to do business with each other continuously throughout their lives, and also to meet each other socially out of business hours. Consequently it does not pay to hurt one another.'

76 Bell, *Corduroy*, pp. 134–50, 178.

77 Ibid., p. 166.

78 Bell, *The Cherry Tree*, p. 222. Compare dances in T. Hardy, *Far from the Madding Crowd* (1874, London, 1971); T. Hardy, *The Return of the Native* (1878, London, 1971); or his 'The fiddler of the reels', in T. Hardy, *The Distracted Preacher and Other Tales* (Harmondsworth, 1979), pp. 286–304.

79 Bell, *Corduroy*, p. 84; Bell, *The Cherry Tree*, p. 232.

80 Ibid., pp. 231–3.

81 Adrian Bell receives passing praise in R. Williams, *The Country and the City* (1973, London, 1985), pp. 261–2, where, as 'more limited personal accounts', he is linked with 'some irreplaceable records' such as Flora Thompson, *Lark Rise to Candleford* (1939–43, Harmondsworth, 1977), or Ronald Blythe, *Akenfield*. Williams contrasts these works with H. J. Massingham, *The English Countryman* (London, 1943), or the journal *The Countryman*: forms of rural writing that Williams thinks are 'part-imagined, part-observed', quaint, middle-class, assuming a 'strange formation in

which observation, myth, record and half-history are so deeply entwined', 'in that conventionally strangled mummerset orthography: the natives overheard'. Williams extols rural writing based on 'real observation, the authentic feeling', as in the farm labourer Fred Kitchen's autobiographical *Brother to the Ox: The Autobiography of a Farm Labourer* (1942, London, 1945). The realism of Bell is also stressed in W. J. Keith, *The Rural Tradition* (Hassocks, Sussex, 1975), p. 256.

82 G. E. Evans, *Where Beards Wag All: the Relevance of the Oral Tradition* (1970, London, 1977), pp. 171–2. Evans and Bell knew at least one person in common in Suffolk, but it is not clear if they knew each other. See Evans, *The Strength of the Hills*, p. 171. A decline of shared interests by 1945 was also stressed by C. S. Orwin, *Problems of the Countryside* (Cambridge, 1945), pp. 61–2. Orwin wanted a break with the idea that the village community was 'a good thing in itself', socially or aesthetically, and a reassembly of the land in larger units. Ibid., pp. 98–9. On the loss of an economic basis for community existence, see R. Frankenberg, *Village on the Border* (London, 1957), pp. 19–20.

83 Compare Z. Bauman, *Community: Seeking Safety in an Insecure World* (2001, Cambridge, 2007). Bauman discusses the middle classes moving out of community, for 'they cannot see what staying *in and with* community could offer which they have not already secured for themselves or still hope to secure through their own exploits'. They wish to avoid 'messy intimacy' and 'the demands of communal solidarity'. 'The "secession of the successful" is, first and foremost, escape from community.' Ibid., pp. 48, 51–2, 57 (his italics). A. G. Street, rather like Bell, commented on the decline of communal festivities, such that 'in these days there are no great festivities at Christmas in rural districts, beyond the ordinary family ones'. Street, *Country Calendar*, p. 50.

84 Compare the accounts of borrowed implements and work reciprocity in A. D. Rees, *Life in a Welsh Countryside: A Social Study of Llanfihangel yng Ngwynfa* (1950, Cardiff, 1996), pp. 91–100 : 'the whole countryside is covered by a continuous network of reciprocities', affecting sheep-dipping, threshing, machine borrowing, hay and corn harvests and so on. This Suffolk–Montgomeryshire comparison seems to bear out Rees's contention that neighbourliness declines eastwards towards England (ibid., p. 91), whether for reasons relating to culture or relative farming wealth.

85 Bell, *Suffolk Harvest*, p. 162.

86 Bell, *The Cherry Tree*, p. 93.

87 Bell, *Silver Ley*, p. 71.

88 Bell, *Apple Acre*, p. 10; Bell, *Silver Ley*, pp. 225, 248, 272, 277, 285; Blythe, *Borderland*, p. 197: 'Empty cottages and tumbledown farms were part of the drama of my childhood. I would raise their latches with a beating heart, terrified of disturbing a tramp.'

89 Bell, *Silver Ley*, pp. 225, 254.

90 Bell, *The Cherry Tree*, pp. 139–42.

91 Ibid., p. 35.
92 The 1917 Corn Production Act guaranteed minimum prices for corn, with a minimum wage for farm workers, augmented as needed by new wages boards. The minimum price was adjusted by following legislation in 1918, 1919 and 1920. When market prices fell below such levels, deficiency payments to farmers made up the difference. Consumers still gained from the lower price. However, with the collapse of world cereal prices, the 1917 Act was repealed in 1921, ending price guarantees and minimum wage controls.
93 On this labour unrest, see A. Armstrong, *Farmworkers: A Social and Economic History, 1770–1980* (London, 1988), pp. 186–92; A. Howkins, *Reshaping Rural England: A Social History, 1850–1925* (London, 1991), pp. 283–5.
94 Bell, *Men and the Fields*, pp. 62–3.
95 Ibid., pp. 111–12.
96 Bell, *The Cherry Tree*, pp. 220–1; see also Bell, *Silver Ley*, p. 208, on farmer bankruptcies.
97 Ibid., pp. 179, 281.
98 Bell, *The Cherry Tree*, pp. 36–7.
99 Bell, *By-Road*, pp. 235, 238.
100 Bell, *Silver Ley*, p. 13. Isolation and solitude are also themes in his writing about his childhood – see *The Balcony* (1934, London, 1943), pp. 8, 13, 22, 42, 50, 57, 62, 132, 134, 139.
101 As one of Ronald Blythe's respondents put it, 'village people in Suffolk in my day were worked to death. It literally happened.' *Akenfield*, p. 41.
102 Bell, *Men and the Fields*, pp. 82–3; see also 'Mr Adrian Bell', *The Times*, 6 Sept. 1980, p. 14.
103 Bell, *My Own Master*, p. 11.
104 Bell, *The Budding Morrow*, p. 44.
105 S. L. Bensusan, *Back of Beyond* (1945, London, 1988), p. 131.
106 Bell, *The Cherry Tree*, p. 11; and for a similar view, H. J. Massingham, *An Englishman's Year* (London, 1948), p. 148.
107 Bell, *The Budding Morrow*, p. 45. However, some developments in countries like Denmark at that time, for example pig production methods, are rightly banned today.
108 Bell, *Men and the Fields*, p. 83.
109 Compare the modern Suffolk farmer Jonathan Pirkis, hoping that some children 'will see through all the glamour and the I.T. and the form filling and the computer screens and want something real. That's my big optimistic hope: that consumerism will seem so shallow that they'll want to get back to reality and get into producing something that we can touch and that we all need.' Taylor, *Return to Akenfield*, p. 155.
110 A similar concern is expressed in G. E. Evans, *Spoken History* (London, 1987), p. 193, discussing 'the manifest examples of the end of processes, tools and

customs – the whole apparatus of a material culture that is coming to an end almost before our eyes.' Such loss of rural craft skills was not universal. See E. J. T. Collins (ed.), *Crafts in the English Countryside: Towards a Future* (Wetherby, 2004).

111 Quotations in this paragraph are from A. Bell, 'Which England?', a review of D. Hartley, *Here's England*, in *Scrutiny* (Sept. 1934), pp. 206–7. It is interesting to compare Bell's views with R. Macfarlane, *The Wild Places* (2007, London, 2008), p. 203, an author unusual in his tactile senses, who writes of

> a turning away from a felt relationship with the natural world … this retreat from the real … there has been a prising away of life from place, an abstraction of experience into different kinds of touchlessness. We experience, as no historical period has before, disembodiment and dematerialisation. The almost infinite connectivity of the technological world, for all the benefits that it has brought, has exacted a toll in the coin of contact. We have in many ways forgotten what the world feels like. And so new maladies of the soul have emerged, unhappinesses which are complicated products of the distance we have set between ourselves and the world. We have come increasingly to forget that our minds are shaped by the bodily experience of being in the world – its spaces, textures, sounds, smells and habits … A constant and formidably defining exchange occurs between the physical forms of the world around us, and the cast of our inner world of imagination. The feel of a hot dry wind on the face, the smell of distant rain carried as a scent stream in the air, the touch of a bird's sharp foot on one's outstretched palm: such encounters shape our beings and our imagination in ways which are beyond analysis, but also beyond doubt.

Adrian Bell would have relished these finely expressed sentiments.

112 Gander, *Adrian Bell*, p. 204.

113 He regretted a lessening educational concern for natural history and local geology, in preference for more international education, which might make children 'forsake the fields around them and qualify for a desk in the town', in 'Lucy Andrews', a short story in Bell, *The Black Donkey*, p. 64.

114 Bell, *Apple Acre*, p. 115.

115 Bell, *The Budding Morrow*, p. 162.

116 Ibid., p. 124.

117 Bell, *Suffolk Harvest*, p. 217.

118 Ibid., p. 219.

119 Ibid., p. 211. Contrasts between father and son (the international reporter and UNICEF Ambassador Martin Bell) could hardly be more remarkable. See also Bell, *The Budding Morrow*, pp. 18, 80: 'Martin had been rather impatient the last hour or so … to do something different and be somewhere else, he didn't know what or where.'

120 Bell, *The Black Donkey*, p. 191.

121 See also the similar points in S. Neal, *Rural Identities: Ethnicity and Community in the Contemporary English Countryside* (Farnham, 2009), pp. 76, 80–1, 88–9, 109.

122 Bell, *Suffolk Harvest*, p. 190.

123 Bell, *Silver Ley*, p. 117.

124 Bell, *The Cherry Tree*, pp. 170–6; G. Sturt, *The Wheelwright's Shop* (1923, Cambridge, 2000). On craft decline, see also Bell, *Apple Acre*, pp. 52–3, 108–10.

125 Bell, *The Cherry Tree*, pp. 175–6.

126 Bell, *Men and the Fields*, pp. 116–17 (his italics).

127 Bell, *The Cherry Tree*, p. 202.

128 Ibid., pp. 203–4.

Chapter 9

1 H. E. Bates, *An Autobiography* (London, 2006), p. 514.

2 Ibid., p. 470.

3 H. E. Bates, 'The writer explains', in *Country Tales: Collected Short Stories* (London, 1938), p. 10.

4 Bates, *Autobiography*, p. 486, citing Elizabeth Bowen and the highly visual A. E. Coppard.

5 H. E. Bates, 'Concerning authors' cottages', in J. W. Robertson Scott (ed.), *The Countryman Book* (London, 1948). As he explained to Joe Braddock, who had hovered shyly around their garden wall: 'We are only ordinary folk & don't keep servants & aren't snooty, & we like people to come in … My wife was scared at you with your hand on your bike thinking you were a travelling communist come to pot.' Northamptonshire Central Library (hereafter NCL), letters of H. E. Bates (letter 2, to Joe Braddock, 29 Jan. 1935).

6 I will not discuss this 'eastern' writing as my interest is in Bates as a novelist of English community and rural life.

7 Archival material on H. E. Bates is very dispersed. I have mainly consulted the original papers, correspondence and other material in NCL. Among his children were Jonathan Bates, the film sound editor (who died in 2008), and Richard Bates, the television producer (who produced the TV serialization of *The Darling Buds of May* in 1991–93).

8 NCL, letters of H. E. Bates (letter 46, to Joe Braddock, 15 Jan. 1955).

9 NCL, letters of H. E. Bates (letter 21, to Joe Braddock, 21 Jan. 1940). He was active also in efforts to enhance sales and library proceeds to authors.

10 B. Baker, 'H. E. Bates, storyteller', *The New Criterion*, 6 (Mar. 1988), p. 72, reviewing H. E. Bates, *A Month by the Lake & Other Stories* (New York, 1987).

11 D. Head, 'Writing against the nostalgic grain: H. E. Bates in the 1950s', *Literature and History*, 19 (2010), pp. 5, 13.

12 D. R. Baldwin, 'Atmosphere in the stories of H. E. Bates', *Studies in Short Fiction*, 21 (1984), p. 215.

13 The key text is his autobiography, published as three volumes: *The Vanished World* (1969), *The Blossoming World* (1971) and *The World in Ripeness* (1972), superbly illustrated with drawings by John Ward; now published as Bates, *An Autobiography* (its drawings sadly unacknowledged there). See also D. Vannatta, *H. E. Bates* (Boston, 1983); D. R. Baldwin, *H. E. Bates: A Literary Life* (Ontario, 1987); P. Eads, *H. E. Bates: A Bibliographical Study* (London, 2007). An excellent guide to his works, the 'H. E. Bates Companion', is by P. Machlis at http://hebatescompanion.com/ (24 Aug. 2015). Critical discussion of Bates is limited, critics concentrating on the 'big name' authors, a point stressed by D. A. Hughes, 'The eclipsing of V. S. Pritchett and H. E. Bates: a representative case of critical myopia', *Studies in Short Fiction*, 19 (1982), pp. iii–v. W. Allen, *The Short Story in English* (Oxford, 1981), pp. 262–7, also considers Bates.

14 Bates, *Autobiography*, pp. 243, 277; see the critical comments on Hardy in H. E. Bates, 'Thomas Hardy and Joseph Conrad', in D. Verschoyle (ed.), *The English Novelists: A Survey of the Novel by Twenty Contemporary Novelists* (London, 1936).

15 Bates, *Autobiography*, pp. 394–5, 419.

16 W. DeAth, 'The quiet world of H. E. Bates', *Illustrated London News*, 6898 (26 May 1973).

17 Vannatta, *H. E. Bates*, pp. 130–1.

18 Bates, *Autobiography*, p. 514.

19 NCL, letters of H. E. Bates (letter 19, to Joe Braddock, 28 Oct. 1939).

20 Bates, 'The writer explains', p. 10.

21 NCL, letters of H. E. Bates (letter 16, to Joe Braddock, 10 June 1939). Bates refers here to three novellas of Katherine Anne Porter, *Pale Horse, Pale Rider* (New York, 1939).

22 Bates, 'The writer explains', p. 8.

23 R. Howe, 'A tribute to H. E. Bates', *Northamptonshire & Bedfordshire Life* (Mar. 1974).

24 'Obituary: Mr H. E. Bates, Novelist and Writer of Short Stories', *The Times*, 30 Jan. 1974, p. 16. The lyrical quality of his writing was often stressed by reviewers, e.g. by G. West, 'Mr H. E. Bates', *The Times Literary Supplement*, 24 Jan. 1935, p. 45, a review of *The Poacher*: 'He is … a primarily lyrical writer'.

25 NCL, letters of H. E. Bates (letter 17, to Joe Braddock, 10 July 1939).

26 H. E. Bates, *The Poacher* (1935, London, 1984).

27 H. E. Bates, 'The daffodil sky', in *The Daffodil Sky and Other Stories* (1955, Harmondsworth, 1959).

28 H. E. Bates, *The Sleepless Moon* (London, 1957), p. 241.

29 H. E. Bates, 'The ox', in *Seven by Five* (1963, Harmondsworth, 1977). Bates's women are often vulnerable, indeed they are victims of extreme violence in his novel set in India after Partition, *The Scarlet Sword* (1950, Harmondsworth, 1974).

30 See H. E. Bates, *Through the Woods: The English Woodland – April to April* (1936, London, 1995), pp. 104–7, for criticism of the hunt.

31 H. E. Bates, *Dulcima* (1953, Harmondsworth, 1977). (Dulcimer: sweet, soft, gentle; or the folk music instrument, with its elliptical body and usually three strings plucked with a goose quill.) Consider stories such as 'The park', in H. E. Bates, *Colonel Julian and Other Stories* (1951, Harmondsworth, 1955), its hollow empty house as a symbol of a marriage; 'The ox'; 'The flame', in *Seven by Five*; 'The wild cherry tree', in *The Wild Cherry Tree* (1968, Harmondsworth, 1973); 'The mill', or 'The house with the apricot', in *Country Tales.*

32 Bates, *Through the Woods*, p. 114.

33 His pleasure at different landscapes and people appears in correspondence, e.g. from Yugoslavia: 'You should certainly come here. A magnificent coast, with oranges & lemons, mimosa & irises now all going strong. But inland – entirely different. Barbaric, bitter hills, with Turkish-fezzed peasants getting a living off an ass, an ox, & two square yards of earth & subsisting on what looks like goat-flesh from some year B.C. A fascinating country. Very warm here now. Pitilessly hot, I think, in summer.' NCL, letters of H. E. Bates (letter 10, postcard to Joe Braddock, 7 Nov. 1938). Or consider this letter to Joe and Muriel Braddock: 'Madge & I are home after our long trip – West Indies, San Francisco (a living city, a sort of Pacific Paris), Honolulu (such girls as you never saw, on land or sea), Fiji (superb *men*, Muriel), Samoa (more & still superb men), Tahiti (girls again– easy come, easy go, Joe!)'. NCL, letters of H. E. Bates (letter 43, 29 Apr. 1954).

34 H. E. Bates, 'The snow line', in *Now Sleeps the Crimson Petal and Other Stories* (1961, Harmondsworth, 1962), p. 190.

35 Bates, *Autobiography*, p. 202. This trade was centred in Northamptonshire and Leicestershire: H. Rydberg, 'The location of the English shoe industry', *Geografiska Annaler. Series B, Human Geography*, 47 (1965); P. R. Mounfield, *The Footwear Industry of the East Midlands* (Nottingham, 1967); R. A. Church, 'Labour supply and innovation, 1800–1860: the boot and shoe industry', *Business History*, 12 (1970); R. L. Greenall, 'The history of boot and shoemaking at Long Buckby', *Northamptonshire Past and Present*, 5 (1977); D. Kirby, *Northampton Remembers Boot and Shoe* (Northampton, 1988); C. Brown, *Northampton, 1835–1985: Shoe Town, New Town* (Chichester, 1990); K. Morrison, *Built to Last: The Buildings of the Northamptonshire Boot and Shoe Industry* (London, 2004). On women's work in this industry, see E. Abbott, 'Women in industry: the manufacture of boots and shoes', *American Journal of Sociology*, 15 (1909); and on its street cultures, J. Seabrook, *The Unprivileged* (London, 1967).

36 J. C. H. Hurd, 'Science, technology and local industries', in N. Pye (ed.), *Leicester and Its Region* (Leicester, 1972), pp. 410–13; R. J. Clark, *Cost Control in the Boot and Shoe Industry* (London, 1950).

37 H. E. Bates, *The Feast of July* (1954, London, 2006), p. 16; H. E. Bates, *Charlotte's Row* (1931, Harmondsworth, 1987).

38 This was true of other putting-out industries, such as hosiery in the East Midlands. It is comparable to activities, rather than boundaries, creating senses of place and community, discussed in J. Gray, 'Community as place-making: ram auctions in the Scottish borderland', in V. Amit (ed.), *Realizing Community: Concepts, Social Relationships and Sentiments* (London, 2002), p. 41.

39 Bates, *Feast of July*, p. 48.

40 'Love in a wych-elm', in Bates, *Seven by Five*, p. 351; Bates, *Autobiography*, p. 202.

41 H. E. Bates, 'A Christmas song', in *Seven by Five*, p. 209.

42 Bates, *Feast of July*, p. 96.

43 Ibid., p. 58.

44 Bates, *Autobiography*, p. 203.

45 Bates, 'Love in a wych-elm', in *Seven by Five*, p. 358.

46 H. E. Bates, 'Let's play soldiers', in *Seven by Five*, pp. 364–6.

47 Bates, *Feast of July*, p. 24.

48 Bates 'The snow line', p. 191.

49 Bates, *Sleepless Moon*, pp. 164, 174; Bates, *Feast of July*, pp. 35.

50 Ibid., pp. 98, 100, 105.

51 Ibid., p. 104. Bates's father was a shoemaker and travelling boot and shoe salesman. DeAth, 'The quiet world of H. E. Bates'; G. Smith, 'Bates's rural idyll', *Chronicle and Echo*, 8 July 2006, p. 17, NCL, Local Studies Centre, Autobiographical Cutting File.

52 H. E. Bates, *The Poacher* (1935, London, 1989), p. 58; Bates, *Feast of July*, pp. 76–95; Bates, *Autobiography*, pp. 48–51.

53 Ibid., pp. 217, 305.

54 Bates, *Sleepless Moon*, pp. 172, 175, 265.

55 Bates, *Autobiography*, pp. 56–60; see also Bates, *Feast of July*, pp. 26–7, on repetitive Methodist services, and tramping between villages with 'Methodist rain-soaked fervour'. His accounts of Anglican clergy could be equally scathing: e.g. in his 'Oh! Sweeter than the Berry', in *The Song of the Wren* (1972, Harmondsworth, 1974), pp. 121–8, describing the Revd H. Sloane Arrowsmith: 'The old suet-head … typical parsonic twittery … like a pall-bearer suffering from acute dyspepsia … [his voice] grated, both on the nerves and on the teeth … [a] dark cadaverous figure … [with his] bloody silly language … [who has] "gone and mucked about with the Lord's Prayer … murdered the doxology … [with] that appalling modern version of the New Testament [which] reads like a batch of Urban Council Minutes from the backwoods somewhere"'. Or see his account of 'the Reverend Frog-face … as damned old humbug' in H. E. Bates, *Oh! To Be in England* (1963, Harmondsworth, 1966), p. 23.

56 Bates, *Feast of July*, p. 126.

57 Raphael Samuel, personal communication (2 Dec. 1991). On nostalgia in Bates, see Head, 'Writing against the nostalgic grain'.

58 Bates, *Feast of July*, pp. 97–8.

59 Ibid., p. 40.

60 C. Evans, *My People: Stories of the Peasantry of West Wales* (1915, London, 1919). This book was widely denounced, for it showed 'community' not as harmonious and mutually respectful *gwerin*, but as unequal, exploitative, sexually brutal and oppressively patriarchal in its domineering chapel elders or 'Fathers in Sion'. The hatred of Welsh community life and culture in Caradoc Evans seems to me to be more pronounced, and to render his work less historically informative, than that by Bates.

61 D. Thomas, *Under Milk Wood: A Play for Voices* (1954, London, 1986).

62 T. F. Powys, *Mr Weston's Good Wine* (1927, Harmondsworth, 1976), p. 130.

63 Ibid., pp. 40–1, 50–4.

64 NCL, letters of H. E. Bates (letter 39, to Joe Braddock, 31 Jan. 1948).

65 Powys, *Mr Weston's Good Wine*, p. 26.

66 Bates, *Autobiography*, pp. 302, 321, 380, 384, 392, 435, 486.

67 Bates, 'Daffodil sky', p. 36. Or consider the farm loneliness of Mrs Charlesworth in H. E. Bates, *The Triple Echo* (London, 1970); or of Angela Jefferson in 'The house with the apricot', in *Country Tales*, pp. 266, 271; or the 'grotesque desolation … a life utterly deprived of colour' affecting Mrs Boorman in 'The wild cherry tree', pp. 18–19; or the loneliness (in the countryside or in marriage) of some of the women in H. E. Bates, *The Four Beauties* (1968, Harmondsworth, 1976), pp. 9, 11, 16, 33–5.

68 Bates, 'The ox', in *Seven by Five*, pp. 133, 135, 145.

69 H. E. Bates, *The Fallow Land* (1932, London, 2006), p. 80.

70 S. J. Weyman, *Starvecrow Farm* (1911, London, 1922); M. E. Lambe, *Crag's Foot Farm: A Novel of Leicestershire* (London, 1931); C. Holme, *The Lonely Plough* (1914, Oxford, 1933); S. Kaye-Smith, *Joanna Godden* (London, 1921); H. W. Freeman, *Joseph and His Brethren* (1928, London, 1955); S. Gibbons, *Cold Comfort Farm* (London, 1932). On the isolation of women on farms, see A. G. Street, *Country Calendar* (1935, London, 1940), p. 40.

71 H. E. Bates, *Spella Ho* (London, 1938), pp. 412–14.

72 Bates, 'The man who loved squirrels', in *Song of the Wren*, p. 79; Bates, 'The mower', in *Seven by Five*, p. 23.

73 The best example is Bates, *Through the Woods*.

74 Ibid., p. 120.

75 Bates, *Poacher*, p. 203.

76 H. E. Bates, *The Face of England* (London, 1952), p. 42.

77 A. Bell, *Corduroy* (1930, London, 1946), p. 5.

78 H. E. Bates, 'Cloudburst', in *Country Tales*, p. 333.

79 Bates, *Fallow Land*, pp. 34, 37–8, 44.
80 Bates, *The Face of England*, p. 29.
81 Bates, *Fallow Land*, p. 69.
82 H. E. Bates, 'The grass God', in *The Nature of Love* (1953, Harmondsworth, 1984), pp. 76, 86. The 'dog eats dog' phrase is repeated later in the thoughts of Sir George Bluff-Gore, on his decaying mansion, in H. E. Bates, *The Darling Buds of May* (1958, London, 1970), p. 133. On the break-up of estates in interwar Kent, see A. Nicolson, *Sissinghurst: An Unfinished History* (London, 2008), 243–9, and pp. 26–7 on the mid-twentieth-century decline of mixed farms and hop-growing in that county; and C. Cordle, *Out of the Hay and into the Hops* (Hatfield, 2011), on Kentish hop cultivation.
83 H. E. Bates, 'A girl Called Peter', in *Colonel Julian and Other Stories* (1951, Harmondsworth, 1955).
84 H. E. Bates, 'The flag', in *Colonel Julian.*
85 H. E. Bates, 'Where the cloud breaks', in *Now Sleeps the Crimson Petal*, pp. 123–4.
86 H. E. Bates, 'The woman who had imagination', in *Country Tales*, p. 85.
87 H. E. Bates, 'The blue feather', in H. E. Bates, *Sugar for the Horse* (1957, London, 1959), pp. 37–42, 44.
88 H. E. Bates, *A Breath of French Air* (1959, Harmondsworth, 1962), p. 14; Bates, *Darling Buds*, pp. 132–4.
89 Bates, *Love for Lydia*, pp. 255–6.
90 Ibid., p. 285. Rushden, Bates's home town (just west of Wellingborough) is called Evensford in his writing.
91 H. E. Bates, 'Now sleeps the crimson petal', in *Now Sleeps the Crimson Petal.*
92 Bates, 'The grass God', p. 74.
93 Ibid., pp. 73–4.
94 Bates, *The Sleepless Moon*, p. 199.
95 Ibid., p. 308.
96 G. Sturt, *The Bettesworth Book* (1901, Firle, Sussex, 1978), a character whose conversations were 'practical, technical, racy with anecdotes and grim fun', p. 8; G. Bourne [G. Sturt], *Lucy Bettesworth* (1913, London, 1918).
97 Sturt, *Bettesworth Book*, p. 3.
98 Bates, *Through the Woods*, p. 24. Another influence may be Guy de Maupassant, 'My Uncle Jules', reprinted in G. de Maupassant, *Selected Short Stories* (Harmondsworth, 1972), a similarly named figure thought to be disreputable by his family. Bates included Maupassant among the authors 'at whose feet … I had long been religiously worshipping' (*Autobiography*, pp. 208, 473), partly for Maupassant's short-story or novella innovations, his verbal economy, and his countryside themes. He must also have appreciated his sexual candour, eye for hypocrisy and sympathy for ill-used women.

99 Bates, 'The blue feather', p. 41. Bates wrote with appreciation of 'an unconscious protest against the Puritanical poison in the English blood' in his 'Preface' to *My Uncle Silas* (1939, London, 2001), p. 10.

100 On Silas's mimicking play with his social superiors' attitudes, see 'Silas the good', in Bates, *My Uncle Silas*.

101 Bates, 'The foxes', in *Sugar for the Horse*, pp. 50–1, 58.

102 Bates, 'The grass God', p. 69.

103 H. E. Bates, 'Preface', in *My Uncle Silas* (1939, London, 2001), p. 11.

104 H. E. Bates, 'Queenie White', in *Sugar for the Horse* (1957, London, 1959), p. 34.

105 H. E. Bates, 'The return', in *My Uncle Silas*, p. 176.

106 Ibid., p. 181. Compare the account of the wholesale businessman's 'professional, orderly, impeccable, shorn and bloodless' garden and villa of 'correctest detail' in H. E. Bates, 'The world upside down', in *Wild Cherry Tree*, p. 77.

107 Bates, 'The return', pp. 189–90.

108 NCL, letters of H. E. Bates (letter 18, to Joe Braddock, 27 Sept. 1939).

109 NCL, letters of H. E. Bates (letter 23, to Joe and Muriel Braddock, 16 May 1940).

110 NCL, letters of H. E. Bates (letter 24, to Joe and Muriel Braddock, 5 Sept. 1940).

111 NCL, letters of H. E. Bates (letter 25, to Joe and Muriel Braddock, 30 Sept. 1940).

112 NCL, letters of H. E. Bates (letter 27, to Joe Braddock, 25 Nov. 1940).

113 Bates, *Autobiography*, p. 361.

114 Ibid., p. 384. In Sept. 1940, Oakington passed to No. 3 Group as the base for the first Stirling squadron, No. 7. There were 258 operational losses of bombers from this airfield: 113 Stirlings, 93 Lancasters, 36 Mosquitos and 16 Wellingtons. http://www.raf.mod.uk/history/ (24 Aug. 2015). Some Spitfires were also based there as part of the No. 3 Photographic Reconnaissance Unit. On this warfare, see C. Webster and N. Frankland, *The Strategic Air Offensive against Germany, 1939–1945*, 4 vols (London, 1961); A. J. Levine, *The Strategic Bombing of Germany, 1940–1945* (London, 1992); R. Overy, *Bomber Command, 1939–1945* (London, 1997); K. Wilson, *Men of Air: The Doomed Youth of Bomber Command* (London, 2007).

115 H. E. Bates, 'The Disinherited', in *The Stories of Flying Officer 'X'* (1952, London, 1965), pp. 92–3. Bates's RAF experience also went into his *A Moment in Time* (1964, Harmondsworth, 1969), and, most famously, *Fair Stood the Wind for France* (1944, London, 2005).

116 Bates, 'The disinherited', p. 93.

117 H. E. Bates, 'How sleep the brave', in *Stories of Flying Officer 'X'*, p. 83.

118 Bates, *Fair Stood the Wind*, p. 100.

119 H. E. Bates, 'Yours in the earth', in *Stories of Flying Officer 'X'*, p. 100.

120 Bates, *Fair Stood the Wind*, pp. 100, 119.

121 A 'Glossary of RAF slang' appears in H. E. Bates, *There's Something in the Air* (New York, 1943). Bates's private letters can share such language, as for example

to Joe Braddock: 'The odds are sure tough on you, buddy, but nuts! … Attaboy!' NCL, letters of H. E. Bates (letter 9, to Joe Braddock, 21 Jan. 1938). Compare the RAF/WAAF language of B. Rutter (ed.), *From Betty with Love: A Love Story of the Second World War* (Exeter, 1985), and its glossary of RAF terms, p. 144; see also the play by T. Rattigan, *Flare Path* (London, 1942).

122 Bates, 'The young man from Kalgoorlie', in *Stories of Flying Officer 'X'*, p. 24.

123 Ibid., p. 22.

124 Bates, 'The greatest people in the world', in *Stories of Flying Officer 'X'*, pp. 51, 55.

125 Bates, 'How sleep the brave', p. 79; Bates, *Fair Stood the Wind*, p. 7.

126 Ibid., p. 33.

127 Bates, *The Scarlet Sword*, pp. 42–3. Violence is a theme closer to home in H. E. Bates, *Dear Life* (London, 1950), set in postwar London, and certainly one of his bleakest novels.

128 H. E. Bates, 'There's something in the air', in *Stories of Flying Officer 'X'*, pp. 104, 107.

129 Ibid., pp. 104, 107.

130 H. E. Bates, 'The bell', in *Stories of Flying Officer 'X'*, p. 109; also published in *The Times Literary Supplement*, 3 Apr. 1943.

131 G. Eliot, *Silas Marner* (London, 1861).

132 A. Bell, *Corduroy* (1930, Harmondsworth, 2000), p. 133.

133 H. J. Massingham, *An Englishman's Year* (London, 1948), pp. 125–30. (Bates published alongside Massingham in H. E. Bates et al., *The English Countryside* (London, 1951), and shared many concerns with him). Slightly earlier, G. Sturt, *The Journals of George Sturt, 1890–1927* (Cambridge, 1967), vol. 1, p. 245, stressed villagers' 'true interest … in Work, especially in work on their gardens, in their crops, and in the management of their grounds'; Sturt, *The Bettesworth Book*, pp. 257–8.

134 Bates, 'Queenie White', in *Sugar for the Horse*, p. 35. Bates showed much candour on sexual matters and co-authored a letter to *The Times* attacking 'something like a police censorship of literature', in which authors write 'under the shadow of the Old Bailey'. 'Freedom of the pen. Authors' grave concern', *The Times*, 27 Oct. 1954, p. 7.

135 Vannatta, *H. E. Bates*, p. 129; DeAth, 'The quiet world of H. E. Bates', citing Angus Wilson.

136 Cited in Anthony Curtis's obituary, 'H. E. Bates', *The Financial Times*, 30 Jan. 1974.

137 Bates, *Autobiography*, p. 271.

138 Ibid., p. 514.

139 Bates adapted his writing in response to social change, yet seems not to have 'gone with the stream' politically in post-war Britain. His political views appear

sceptical of welfare legislation and 'the straitjacket of the State', and Pop Larkin's tax avoidance and declarations about 'the National Elf lark' seem to reflect Bates's own politics in his *Autobiography*, e.g. pp. 272, 274–5, 284, 512.

140 This stress upon the family is found in other modern rural novelists, e.g. Joanna Trollope, whose 'countryside' is largely family rather than community based. On 'growing individualism of the family' and 'the decline of community life', in this case affecting rural Ireland, see H. Brody, *Inishkillane: Change and Decline in the West of Ireland* (London, 1973), pp. 36–7.

141 Bates, *Autobiography*, p. 512.

142 Ibid., p. 514. His widow Madge said that much of her husband went into this character: R. Supple, 'Author Pop's the question', *Chronicle and Echo*, 25 Aug. 1995, NCL, Local Studies Centre, Autobiographical Cutting File. For H. E. Bates, 'Pop is not one person but 10, met or observed over a span of years and finally welded, purely by imagination, into a living credible whole.' R. Horner, 'Pop Larkin: the facts of fiction', *Daily Telegraph*, 8 Apr. 1991, p. 15.

143 J. Dalingpole, 'Pop's the tops for 18 million', *Daily Telegraph*, 11 May 1991, p. 7.

144 Ibid., p. 7; J. Gaskell, 'Business blooms for Darling Buds of May', *Sunday Telegraph*, 12 May 1991.

145 Bates, *Autobiography*, p. 514; Bates, *Oh! To Be in England*, pp. 136–7; H. E. Bates, *When the Green Woods Laugh* (London, 1960), p. 171, on scampi, asparagus and veal cutlets 'at the village shop nowadays. It was part of the rural revolution'.

146 H. E. Bates, 'An aspidistra in Babylon', in *The Grapes of Paradise: Eight Novellas* (1957, Harmondsworth, 1974), p. 165.

147 H. E. Bates, *A Little of What You Fancy* (1970, Harmondsworth 1973), pp. 32–3.

148 Ibid., p. 34.

149 Bates, *Darling Buds*, pp. 16, 43–4, 83.

150 Bates, *A Little of What You Fancy*, p. 176.

151 Small wonder also that the producer Richard Bates and Yorkshire Television held off serializing the fifth Larkin novel, in which this heart attack is the central theme. Bates's writing has emphases avoided in the serialization of his work. Given the popularity of this money-spinning television series, one can understand why Richard Bates said that 'It makes sense to hold off that final book for as long as possible.' Dalingpole, 'Pop's the tops', p. 7.

152 On these postwar consumption and affluence issues, see A. Offer, *The Challenge of Affluence: Self-Control and Well-Being in the United States and Britain since 1950* (Oxford, 2006), esp. ch. 13 on their effects on the family. Historiography on the post-1945 countryside is reticent on such matters, as are the rural community studies of the 1950s and 1960s. However, see N. Duckers and H. Davies, *A Place in the Country: Social Change in Rural England* (London, 1990).

153 J. Betjeman, review in the *Daily Telegraph*, cited in Dalingpole, 'Pop's the tops', p. 7.

154 Bates, *A Little of What You Fancy*, p. 35.

155 Ibid., pp. 38–9. ‘Mother’s little helpers’ were being discussed in many forms by this date.

156 Ibid., pp. 67, 151.

157 Bates, *Darling Buds*, pp. 130–1.

158 Ibid., p. 141.

159 On the rising control of families over their private affairs, and secrecy against neighbours, ‘community’ and the State, as compared with the interwar period or earlier, see D. Vincent, ‘Secrecy and the city, 1870–1939’, *Urban History*, 22 (1995).

160 Bates, *Darling Buds*, p. 134.

161 P. Connerton, *How Modernity Forgets* (Cambridge, 2009).

162 Bates, *A Little of What You Fancy*, p. 79. Of course, there was nothing ’new’ in a ‘passion for having a place in the country’, and this was a relatively prosperous time for farmers.

163 Bates, *Darling Buds*, p. 133.

164 Bates, *When the Green Woods Laugh*, pp. 41, 50.

165 Bates, *A Little of What You Fancy*, p. 29. Bates uses the term ‘foreigner’ here in the older rural sense, i.e. a person not from the locality or parish.

166 Ibid., pp. 29–32.

167 K. D. M. Snell, *Parish and Belonging: Community, Identity and Welfare in England and Wales, 1700–1950* (Cambridge, 2006), ch. 2.

168 Bates, *A Little of What You Fancy*, pp. 110–11.

169 R. Stivers, *Shades of Loneliness: Pathologies of a Technological Society* (Lanham, MD, 2004), pp. 23–4, 36.

170 NCL, letters of H. E. Bates (letter 69, to Joe Braddock, 22 May 1970).

Chapter 10

1 John Clare’s *The Parish: A Satire* (Harmondsworth, 1985); J. Skinner, *Journal of a Somerset Rector, 1803–1834* (1971, Oxford, 1985); M. K. Ashby, *Joseph Ashby of Tysoe, 1859–1919: A Study of English Village Life* (London, 1974); C. Evans, *My People* (1915, New York, 1995), *Capel Sion* (1916, Bridgend, 2002), *My Neighbours* (1919, New York, 1920), among other works.

2 On this issue, see K. D. M. Snell, *Parish and Belonging; Community, Identity and Welfare in England and Wales, 1700–1950* (Cambridge, 2006), ch. 2; E. J. Hobsbawm, ‘The making of the English working class, 1870–1914’, in his *Worlds of Labour* (London, 1984), ch. 11, and see also his ch. 10 – contrast the earlier chronologies in E. P. Thompson, *The Making of the English Working Class* (London, 1963).

Select Bibliography

Ambler, R. W., *Churches, Chapels and the Parish Communities of Lincolnshire, 1660–1900* (Lincoln, 2000).

Amit, V. (ed.), *Realizing Community: Concepts, Social Relationships and Sentiments* (London, 2002).

Amit. V. and Rapport, N., *The Trouble with Community: Anthropological Reflections on Movement, Identity and Collectivity* (London, 2002).

Anderson, B., *Imagined Communities: Reflections on the Origin and Spread of Nationalism* (1991, London, 2006).

Archbishops' Commission on Rural Areas (ACORA), *Faith in the Countryside* (Worthing, 1990).

Augé, M., *Non-Places: Introduction to an Anthropology of Supermodernity* (1995, London, 2000).

Ball, S., *Portrait of a Party: The Conservative Party in Britain, 1918–1945* (Oxford, 2013).

Bamford, S., *Early Days* (London, 1841).

Barrell, J., *The Dark Side of the Landscape: The Rural Poor in English Painting, 1730–1840* (Cambridge, 1980).

Barrell, J., *The Idea of Landscape and the Sense of Place, 1730–1840: An Approach to the Poetry of John Clare* (Cambridge, 1972).

Bate, J., *John Clare: A Biography* (London, 2003).

Bates, H. E., *A Little of What You Fancy* (1970, Harmondsworth 1973).

Bates, H. E., *An Autobiography* (London, 2006).

Bates, H. E., *Country Tales: Collected Short Stories* (London, 1938).

Bates, H. E., *My Uncle Silas* (1939, London, 2001).

Bates, H. E., *Now Sleeps the Crimson Petal and Other Stories* (1961, Harmondsworth, 1962).

Bates, H. E., *Oh! To Be in England* (1963, Harmondsworth, 1966).

Bates, H. E., *Seven by Five* (1963, Harmondsworth, 1977).

Bates, H. E., *The Daffodil Sky and Other Stories* (1955, Harmondsworth, 1959).

Bates, H. E., *The Darling Buds of May* (1958, London, 1970).

Bates, H. E., *The Fallow Land* (1932, London, 2006).

Bates, H. E., *The Feast of July* (1954, London, 2006).

Bates, H. E., *The Poacher* (1935, London, 1989).

Bates, H. E., *The Sleepless Moon* (London, 1957).

Bauman, Z., *Community: Seeking Safety in an Insecure World* (2001, Cambridge, 2007).

Bauman, Z., *Liquid Love: On the Frailty of Human Bonds* (Cambridge, 2003).
Beck, U., *Risk Society: Towards a New Modernity* (1986, London, 2007).
Bell, A., *A Suffolk Harvest* (London, 1956).
Bell, A., *Apple Acre* (1942, London, 1943).
Bell, A., *By-Road* (1937, London, 1943).
Bell, A., *Corduroy* (1930, Harmondsworth, 2000).
Bell, A., *Men and the Fields* (London, 1939).
Bell, A., *My Own Master* (London, 1961).
Bell, A., *Silver Ley* (1931, Oxford, 1983).
Bell, A., *Sunrise to Sunset* (London, 1944).
Bell, A., *The Budding Morrow* (London, 1946).
Bell, A., *The Cherry Tree* (1932, London, 1949).
Bell, C. and Newby, H., *Community Studies: An Introduction to the Sociology of the Local Community* (London, 1971).
Bermingham, A., *Landscape and Ideology: The English Rustic Tradition, 1740–1860* (1986, London, 1987).
Blythe, R., *A Year at Bottengoms Farm* (2006, Norwich, 2007).
Blythe, R., *Akenfield* (1969, Harmondsworth, 1977).
Blythe, R., *Borderland* (Norwich, 2005).
Blythe, R., *Out of the Valley: Another Year at Wormingford* (London, 2000).
Blythe, R., *The View in Winter* (1979, Harmondsworth, 1981).
Blythe, R., *Word from Wormingford: A Parish Year* (1997, London, 1998).
Bourdieu, P., *Outline of a Theory of Practice* (1972, Cambridge, 1977).
Boyes, G., *The Imagined Village: Culture, Ideology and the English Folk Revival* (Manchester, 1993).
Brassley, P., Burchardt, J. and Thompson, L., *The English Countryside between the Wars: Regeneration or Decline?* (Woodbridge, 2006).
Brody, H., *Inishkillane: Change and Decline in the West of Ireland* (London, 1973).
Burchardt, J., 'Reconstructing the rural community: village halls and the National Council of Social Service, 1919 to 1939', *Rural History*, 10 (1999).
Calhoun, C. J., 'Community: towards a variable conceptualization for comparative research', *Social History*, 5 (1980).
Castells, M., *The Information Age: Economy, Society and Culture. Volume 2: The Power of Identity* (1997, Oxford, 2007).
Cavaliero, G., *The Rural Tradition in the English Novel, 1900–1939* (London, 1977).
Christie, A., *Endless Night* (1967, London, 2007).
Christie, A., *The Mirror Crack'd from Side to Side* (Glasgow, 1962).
Christie, A., *The Murder at the Vicarage* (1930, London, 2005).
Christie, A., *The Murder of Roger Ackroyd* (1926, London, 2002).
Clare, J., *The Parish: A Satire* (1820, London, 1986).
Cobbett, W., *Rural Rides* (1830, Harmondsworth, 1975).

Cohen, A. P. (ed.), *Belonging: Identity and Social Organisation in British Rural Cultures* (Manchester, 1982).

Cohen, A. P. (ed.), *Symbolising Boundaries: Identity and Diversity in British Cultures* (Manchester, 1986).

Colls, R., *The Identity of England* (Oxford, 2002).

Colls, R., '"When we lived in communities": working-class culture and its critics', in R. Colls and R. Rodger (eds), *Cities of Ideas: Civil Society and Urban Governance in Britain, 1800–2000* (Aldershot, 2004).

Colls, R. and Dodd, P. (eds), *Englishness: Politics and Culture, 1880–1920* (London, 1986).

Conan Doyle, A., *The Hound of the Baskervilles* (1902, London, 2007).

Conan Doyle, A., *The Sign of Four* (1890, London, 2001).

Connerton, P., *How Modernity Forgets* (Cambridge, 2009).

Crow, G., 'Community studies: fifty years of theorization', *Sociological Research Online*, 7 (2002).

Crow, G. and Allan, G., *Community Life: An Introduction to Local Social Relations* (Hemel Hempstead, 1994).

Davies, E. and Rees, A. D. (eds), *Welsh Community Studies* (Cardiff, 1960).

Day, G., *Community and Everyday Life* (Abingdon, 2006).

Delanty, G., *Community* (London, 2003).

Dumm, T., *Loneliness as a Way of Life* (2008, Cambridge, Mass., 2010).

Dyck, I., *William Cobbett and Rural Popular Culture* (Cambridge, 1992).

Dyer, C., 'The English medieval village community and its decline', *Journal of British Studies*, 33 (1994).

Dyer, C. (ed.), *The Self-Contained Village? The Social History of Rural Communities, 1250–1900* (Hatfield, 2007).

Elias, N., *The Civilising Process: Sociogenetic and Psychogenetic Investigations* (Oxford, 2000).

Eliot, G., *Silas Marner* (London, 1861).

Englander, D., 'From the abyss: pauper petitions and correspondence in Victorian London', *London Journal*, 25 (2000).

Evans, G. E., *Spoken History* (London, 1987).

Evans, G. E., *The Strength of the Hills: An Autobiography* (1983, London, 1985).

Evans, G. E., *Where Beards Wag All: The Relevance of the Oral Tradition* (1970, London, 1977).

Field, J., *Social Capital* (London, 2003).

Frankenberg, R., *Communities in Britain: Social Life in Town and Country* (1966, Harmondsworth, 1970).

Frankenberg, R., *Village on the Border* (London, 1957).

Gander, A., *Adrian Bell: Voice of the Countryside* (Wenhaston, Suffolk, 2001).

Giddens, A., *Modernity and Self-Identity: Self and Society in the Late Modern Age* (Cambridge, 1991).

Giddens, A., *The Consequences of Modernity* (Cambridge, 1990).
Gilbert, A. D., *The Making of Post-Christian Britain: A History of the Secularization of Modern Society* (London, 1980).
Green, S. J. D., *Religion in the Age of Decline: Organisation and Experience in Industrial Yorkshire, 1870–1920* (Cambridge, 1996).
Hardy, D., *Utopian England: Community Experiments, 1900–1945* (London, 2000).
Hardy, F. M. [Hardy, T.], *The Life of Thomas Hardy, 1840–1928* (London, 1965).
Hardy, T., *Far From the Madding Crowd* (1874, London, 1971).
Hardy, T., *Jude the Obscure* (1895, London, 1974).
Hardy, T., *Selected Short Stories* (Ware, 1996).
Hardy, T., *Tess of the D'Urbervilles* (1891, London, 1970).
Hardy, T., *The Distracted Preacher and Other Tales* (Harmondsworth, 1979).
Hardy, T., 'The Dorsetshire labourer', *Longman's Magazine* (July 1883), in J. Moynahan (ed.), *The Portable Thomas Hardy* (London, 1977).
Hardy, T., *The Return of the Native* (1878, London, 1971).
Hardy, T., *The Well-Beloved* (1897, London, 1914).
Hardy, T., *The Woodlanders* (1887, Harmondsworth, 1985).
Hardy, T., *Under the Greenwood Tree* (1872, Harmondsworth 1985).
Hillery, G. A., 'Definitions of community: areas of agreement', *Rural Sociology*, 2 (1955).
Hillis Miller, J., 'Individual and community in *The Return of the Native*: a reappraisal', in K. Wilson (ed.), *Thomas Hardy Reappraised* (Toronto, 2006).
Hitchcock, T., *Down and Out in Eighteenth-Century London* (London, 2004).
Holderness, B. A., '"Open" and "close" parishes in England in the eighteenth and nineteenth centuries', *Agricultural History Review*, 20 (1972).
Hoskins, W. G., *The Midland Peasant: The Economic and Social History of a Leicestershire Village* (London, 1957).
Howkins, A., *Poor Labouring Men: Rural Radicalism in Norfolk, 1870–1923* (London, 1985).
Howkins. A., 'The discovery of rural England', in R. Colls and P. Dodd (eds), *Englishness: Politics and Culture, 1880–1920* (London, 1986).
Hutton, R., *The Rise and Fall of Merry England: The Ritual Year, 1400–1700* (1994, Oxford, 1996).
Jamieson, L. and Simpson, R., *Living Alone: Globalization, Identity and Belonging* (Basingstoke, 2013).
Joyce, P., *Visions of the People: Industrial England and the Question of Class, 1848–1914* (Cambridge, 1991).
Kaye-Smith, S., *The End of the House of Alard* (1923, London, 1946).
Keith, W. J., *The Rural Tradition* (Hassocks, Sussex, 1975).
King, P. (ed.), *Narratives of the Poor in Eighteenth-Century Britain. Volume 4: Institutional Responses: The Refuge for the Destitute* (London, 2006).

King, S., 'Friendship, kinship and belonging in the letters of urban paupers, 1800–1840', *Historical Social Research*, 33 (2008).
King, S., '"It is impossible for our vestry to judge his case into perfection from here": managing the distance dimensions of poor relief, 1800–40', *Rural History*, 16 (2005).
King, S., 'Pauper letters as a source', *Family and Community History*, 10 (2007).
King, S., *Poverty and Welfare in England, 1700–1850: A Regional Perspective* (Manchester, 2000).
King, S., Nutt, T. and Tomkins, A. (eds), *Narratives of the Poor in Eighteenth-Century Britain. Volume 1: Voices of the Poor: Poor Law Depositions and Letters* (London, 2006).
Klinenberg, E., *Going Solo: The Extraordinary Rise and Surprising Appeal of Living Alone* (2012, New York, 2013).
Laslett, P., *Family Life and Illicit Love in Earlier Generations* (Cambridge, 1977).
Levene, A. (ed.), *Narratives of the Poor in Eighteenth-Century Britain. Volume 3: Institutional Responses: The London Foundling Hospital* (London, 2006).
Lewis, G., 'Welsh rural community studies: retrospect and prospect', *Cambria*, 13 (1986).
Light, A., *Forever England: Femininity, Literature and Conservatism between the Wars* (London, 1991).
Macfarlane, A., 'History, anthropology and the study of communities', *Social History*, 2 (1977).
Macfarlane, A., *Reconstructing Historical Communities* (Cambridge, 1977).
Macfarlane, A., *The Culture of Capitalism* (Oxford, 1987).
Macfarlane, R., *The Wild Places* (2007, London, 2008).
Mandler, P., *The English National Character: The History of an Idea from Edmund Burke to Tony Blair* (New Haven, Conn., 2006).
Massingham, H. J., *An Englishman's Year* (London, 1948).
Massingham, H. J., *Remembrance: An Autobiography* (London, n.d., *c.* 1941).
Mental Health Foundation, *The Lonely Society?* (London, 2010).
Millgate, M., *Thomas Hardy: A Biography* (New York, 1982).
Mills, D., *Lord and Peasant in Nineteenth-Century Britain* (London, 1980).
Moore-Colyer, R. J., 'Back to basics: Rolf Gardiner, H. J. Massingham and "A Kinship in Husbandry"', *Rural History*, 12 (2001).
Moore-Colyer, R. J., 'From Great Wen to Toad Hall: aspects of the urban-rural divide in inter-war Britain', *Rural History*, 10 (1999).
Neal, S., *Rural Identities: Ethnicity and Community in the Contemporary English Countryside* (Farnham, 2009).
Neeson, J. M., *Commoners: Common Right, Enclosure and Social Change in England, 1700–1820* (Cambridge, 1993).
Newby, H., *The Deferential Worker* (1977, Harmondsworth, 1979).
Nicholson, V., *Singled Out: How Two Million Women Survived without Men after the First World War* (2007, London, 2008).

Obelkevich, J., *Religion and Rural Society: South Lindsey, 1825–1875* (Oxford, 1976).

Offer, A., *The Challenge of Affluence: Self-Control and Well-Being in the United States and Britain since 1950* (Oxford, 2006).

Pahl, R., *On Friendship* (Cambridge, 2000).

Pahl, R. E., *Divisions of Labour* (Oxford, 1984).

Parry-Jones, D., *My Own Folk* (Llandysul, 1972).

Perlman D. and Peplau, L. A., 'Loneliness research: a survey of empirical findings', in L. A. Peplau and S. Goldston (eds), *Preventing the Harmful Consequences of Severe and Persistent Loneliness* (Washington, 1984).

Poynter, J. R., *Society and Pauperism: English Ideas on Poor Relief, 1795–1834* (London, 1969).

Putnam, R., *Bowling Alone: The Collapse and Revival of American Community* (New York, 2001).

Rapport, N. and Davison, A. (eds), *Migrants of Identity: Perceptions of 'Home' in a World of Movement* (Oxford, 1998).

Redmonds, G., King, T. and Hey, D., *Surnames, DNA, and Family History* (Oxford, 2011).

Reed, M. and Wells, R. (eds), *Class, Conflict and Protest in the English Countryside, 1700–1880* (London, 1990).

Rees, A. D., *Life in a Welsh Countryside: A Social Study of Llanfihangel yng Ngwynfa* (1950, Cardiff, 1996).

Rokach A. and Brock, H., 'Loneliness: a multidimensional experience', *Psychology: A Journal of Human Behaviour*, 34 (1997).

Rosenthal, M., *British Landscape Painting* (Oxford, 1982).

Rutherford, J. (ed.), *Identity: Community, Culture, Difference* (London, 1990).

Sayers, D. L., *Busman's Honeymoon* (1937, London, 2003).

Sayers, D. L., *Clouds of Witness* (1926, London, 1988).

Sayers, D. L., *Five Red Herrings* (1931, London, 1982).

Sayers, D. L., *Have His Carcase* (1932, London 1987).

Sayers, D. L., *Striding Folly* (1972, Sevenoaks, 1987).

Sayers, D. L., *The Nine Tailors* (1934, London, 1977).

Scruton, R., *The Meaning of Conservatism* (Harmondsworth, 1980).

Short, B., *Land and Society in Edwardian Britain* (Cambridge, 1997).

Short, B., *The Battle of the Fields: Rural Community and Authority in Britain during the Second World War* (Woodbridge, 2014).

Simmel, G., 'The metropolis and mental life' (1903), in G. Bridge and S. Watson (eds), *The Blackwell City Reader* (Oxford, 2002).

Snell, K. D. M., 'Agendas for the historical study of loneliness and lone living', *The Open Psychology Journal*, 8 (2015).

Snell, K. D. M., *Annals of the Labouring Poor: Social Change and Agrarian England, 1660–1900* (Cambridge, 1985).

Snell, K. D. M., 'Churchyard closures, rural cemeteries and the village community in Leicestershire and Rutland, 1800–2010', *Journal of Ecclesiastical History*, 63 (2012).

Snell, K. D. M., *Parish and Belonging: Community, Identity and Welfare in England and Wales, 1700–1950* (Cambridge, 2006).

Snell, K. D. M. (ed.), *The Regional Novel in Britain and Ireland, 1800–1990* (1998, Cambridge, 2008).

Snell, K. D. M. and Ell, P. S., *Rival Jerusalems: The Geography of Victorian Religion* (Cambridge, 2000).

Sokoll, T. (ed.), *Essex Pauper Letters, 1731–1837* (Oxford, 2001).

Spencer, L. and Pahl, R. E., *Re-thinking Friendship: Hidden Solidarities Today* (Princeton, 2006).

Stein, M. R., *The Eclipse of Community: An Interpretation of American Studies* (Princeton, 1960).

Stivers, R., *Shades of Loneliness: Pathologies of a Technological Society* (Lanham, MD, 2004).

Strathern, M., *Kinship at the Core: An Anthropology of Elmdon, a Village in North-West Essex in the Nineteen-sixties* (Cambridge, 1981).

Street, A. G., *Country Calendar* (1935, London, 1940).

Street, A. G., *Farmer's Glory* (1932, London, 1956).

Street, A. G., *Shameful Harvest* (London, 1952).

Street, A. G., *The Gentleman of the Party* (1936, London, 1949).

Sturt, G., *Change in the Village* (1912, Harmondsworth, 1984).

Sturt, G., *The Bettesworth Book* (1901, Firle, Sussex, 1978).

Symonds, D. S. (ed.), *Narratives of the Poor in Eighteenth-Century Britain. Volume 2: Voices from the Street* (London, 2006).

Tadmor, N., *Family and Friends in Eighteenth-Century England: Household, Kinship, and Patronage* (Cambridge, 2001).

Taylor, C., *Return to Akenfield: Portrait of an English Village in the Twenty-First Century* (London, 2006).

Taylor, J. S., *Poverty, Migration, and Settlement in the Industrial Revolution: Sojourners' Narratives* (Palo Alto, Calif., 1989).

Tebbutt, M., *Women's Talk? A Social History of 'Gossip' in Working-Class Neighbourhoods, 1880–1960* (Aldershot, 1995).

Thomas, D., *Under Milk Wood: A Play for Voices* (1954, London, 1986).

Thompson, E. P., *Customs in Common* (1991, London, 1993).

Thompson, E. P., *The Making of the English Working Class* (1963, Harmondsworth, 1975).

Thompson, F., *Lark Rise to Candleford* (1939–43, Harmondsworth, 1977).

Tönnies, F., *Gemeinschaft und Gesellschaft* (Leipzig, 1887), trans. as *Community and Society* (Cambridge, 2001).

Vincent, D., 'Secrecy and the city, 1870–1939', *Urban History*, 22 (1995).

Weiss, R., *Loneliness: The Experience of Social and Emotional Loneliness* (Cambridge, Mass., 1973).

Wentworth Day, J., *Broadland Adventure on Norfolk Broads and Rivers* (London, 1950).

Wentworth Day, J., *Farming Adventure: A Thousand Miles through England on a Horse* (1943, London, 1949).

Wentworth Day, J., *Harvest Adventure: On Farms and Sea Marshes, of Birds, Old Manors and Men* (London, 1946).

Wentworth Day, J., *Marshland Adventure on Norfolk Broads and Rivers* (London, 1950).

Wentworth Day, J., *Rum Owd Boys: On Poachers, Wildfowlers, Longshore Pirates, Cut-Throat Islanders, Smugglers & 'Fen-tigers'* (Ipswich, 1974).

Wentworth Day, J., *Sporting Adventure* (London, 1937).

Wentworth Day, J., *The New Yeomen of England* (London, 1952).

Wiener, M. J., *English Culture and the Decline of the Industrial Spirit, 1850–1980* (1981, Cambridge, 1982).

Williams, R., *The Country and the City* (1973, London, 1985).

Williams, W. M., *The Sociology of an English Village: Gosforth* (London, 1964).

Wright, P., *On Living in an Old Country: The National Past in Contemporary Britain* (1985, Oxford, 2009).

Wright, P., *The Village That Died for England: The Strange Story of Tyneham* (1995, London, 1996).

Index

Note: page references with letter 'n' followed by locators denote note numbers

Lightning Source UK Ltd.
Milton Keynes UK
UKOW06f0645071217
314034UK00003B/298/P